9

WITHDRAWN

Language and Ontology

By Jack Kaminsky

SOUTHERN ILLINOIS UNIVERSITY PRESS

Carbondale and Edwardsville

FEFFER & SIMONS, INC.

London and Amsterdam

To Alice and Eric

Contents

Introduction

ONE of the important questions in contemporary philosophy is whether the advent of formalistic logical and linguistic techniques has eliminated all significant ontological presuppositions. According to certain philosophers, traditional philosophical speculation is permeated by linguistic ambiguities and by ignorance of important logical truisms, and as a result it has expounded various metaphysical beliefs which are no longer tenable in a modern analytic age. In this book I shall examine these issues.

To begin with I should like to make clear what I take an ontological commitment to be. An ontological commitment is any statement purporting either *1]* to express a language form which, like a traditional Kantian form, is a necessary part of any nonanalytic language or *2]* to designate a kind of nonconcrete, i.e., abstract entity, required as a value for a quantified variable or as a designatum for a descriptive term. Thus if it turns out that a necessary condition for any meaningful language is that it contain a language form consisting of individual and predicate terms, then this form is an ontological commitment in the language. In other words, a necessary condition for any communication dealing with an extralinguistic subject matter would be that it contain a particular linguistic form. But this means that if the form is one of individual and predicate terms, then the universe described by this language will be one of individuals and properties. And if our predicates must be polyadic as well as monadic, then our universe will contain not only ordinary properties of individuals but also relations between two or more individuals. Our ontology will be derived from the kind of language forms required if any communication is to occur.

Here then is an ontological commitment, only now we no longer speak of it in Kantian terms. That is, we no longer speak of the forms of experience or of the forms of the real. But we do speak of the forms of a language and the same questions of ontology arise here as they did in the prelinguistic ages of philosophy. If a language must have a given form, then we ought to be able to ask why this form is necessary and what its implications are for the realm of the extralinguistic.

Ontology also arises in terms of what is required in the explication of terms we are unwilling to reject from a language. Thus if we demand that such a sentential form as "X makes Y" as in "John makes a table" be significant in the language and if "makes" is definable only in terms of certain abstract entities or concepts called "intentions," then our language has an ontological commitment to intentions. We must admit intentions if we are going to retain "make" as a meaningful term. Similarly if "can" is significant in the language and its definition requires us to admit such abstractions as "potencies," "dispositions," "powers," or "forces"—although I shall argue against this requirement—then such abstractions must become part of the population described by the language. In brief, if a term is not rejectable in a language, if we require it as an important means for communication, then whatever kind of universe is needed to define this term is the universe to which we are committed. In a sense we are here recognizing in ordinary descriptive language what has been recognized—although begrudgingly—in mathematics for a long time. If we must have a universe of classes in order to explain the theory of sets, then this will be the kind of universe we shall have. If we require propositions in order to explain the sentential calculus, then our universe will consist of all the familiar concrete things with which we are acquainted as well as such unfamiliar things called propositions. Whatever extralinguistic phenomena are needed in order to make the language intelligible is precisely what is to be taken as the ontology of that language.

Those two criteria of ontology—namely, as presuppositions either of the kind of language forms or the kind of terms employed in the language—are of more intrinsic importance than the criterion specified by W. V. O. Quine. For Quine any expression can be employed in a language without involving any ontology so long as such expressions are not admitted as values for a quantified variable. I can say "John is moody" or "The chair is heavy" and not be committed to something called "moodiness" or "heaviness," so long as I do not take "moody" or "heavy" as values for a quantified predicate variable. But even if Quine is right, he is wrong in believing that here and only here, in the process of quantification, can we find our ontological commitments. Commitments of an ontological sort arise in the *kind* of language forms employed and in the *kind* of designata needed for certain descriptive terms. If "John is moody" is a significant sentence in a language and if "moody" is definable only by reference to a psychological entity, then this language is committed to an abstract entity regardless of whether the predicate is taken to be a value of a quantified predicate variable. Similarly, if a formal and a natural language must contain letters or place-holders as predicate and individual variables then, even prior to any discussion of any subject matter, we already know beforehand that every describable universe will consist of things, properties, re-lations, as well as the values of any other variables that might be required. Here we would have a commitment to an ontology even before we address ourselves to a particular inquiry.

In accordance with what I take ontology to be, I shall examine the views of several important philosophers who have either ad-mitted or denied that ontological commitments are necessary. I shall also deal with several linguistic expressions such as "can," "make," "is synonymous with," and "exists" which are important in our language and whose elimination would be damaging to the effective use of the language. I shall indicate certain curious questions that these expressions give rise to—questions usually reserved for the domain of ontological investigation.

I will attempt to show that the arguments of both defenders and detractors of ontology are defective. Neither Karl Popper nor P. F. Strawson, who seek to employ the best available techniques of logic and language analyses, have constructed a satisfactory view of ontology. Popper confuses well-formedness with truth and seems to think that because it is possible to construct a sentence about an omnipotent being in a formal language that, therefore, such a sen-tence must be true. Strawson does not do adequate justice to the influence of a language in creating the kind of universe to which one becomes committed.

On the other hand, neither Quine nor Carnap have given con-vincing arguments for eliminating ontological speculation. Quine himself explicitly acknowledges that his logic systems must finally admit the existence of such abstract entities as classes. Carnap with his insistence on intensions and extensions as dual designata of designative terms makes a strong commitment to an ontology of abstract concepts.

In a similar vein I will try to show that even though some language expressions seem but do not really have any implications for ontology, other expressions seem unable to avoid those implications. Thus I tend to agree that "exists" is ontologically neutral even though "exists" ought not to be identified solely with existential quantification. On the other hand, "make" as well as the syntactic particles are not easily explainable without the introduction of the kind of inquiry anti-ontologists would prefer to reject.

It should be clear that it is not my intention to become a defender of ontology and metaphysics in general. We can sympathize with those who are uneasy about populating the universe with a variety of concrete as well as abstract entities. But sympathy is not an argument. Issues of ontology arise even in those formal languages whose formulation at one time led Carnap and others of the positivist school to announce enthusiastically the death of metaphysics. But the issues remain and they cannot be ignored. In the final analysis, philosophers are like trouble shooters, questioning everything regardless of where it leads and arrogantly demanding answers even if they lead to the refutation of their own most cherished beliefs. The questions and views presented here in defense of ontological inquiry may yet be answered or reappraised without the need to resort to ontology. But it seems to me the answers and reappraisals have not as of now been provided in contemporary philosophical inquiry.

For special help in making this book possible I am indebted to the Research Foundation of the State University of New York for granting me two summer research fellowships as well as the Distinguished Research Fellowship for 1967; to Professor Raymond J. Nelson, to the *Journal of Philosophy,* and to *Philosophy and Phenomenological Research* for allowing me to republish several parts of articles that have already appeared in print. Finally I should like to thank my wife, Professor Alice R. Kaminsky, whose knowledge of how to write an English sentence shed considerable light where there might have been darkness.

Jack Kaminsky

Binghamton, N. Y.
June 1969

Language and Ontology

1
Language and Ontology

IN ALL pure calculi which are designed to form the structure of a formalized language serving scientific needs the assumption is made that some minimum number of marks will be used to signify "negation," "existential quantification," "class membership," "or," "if . . . then - - -," "and," and perhaps "is identical to." These expressions, or their synonyms, are taken to be appropriate substituends for the following respectively: $\sim$, $(\exists)$, ϵ, $\vee$, $\supset$, $\cdot$ and $=$.[1] There may be other kinds of formal languages in which the marks of the calculus are taken to signify in other ways. Thus "$\supset$" may be interpreted not as "if . . . then - - -" with its standard truth value analysis, but as some other expression with some other truth value analysis; or "$\sim u$" might be given the same meaning as "u," or the calculus might have four instead of two truth values, e.g. true, nearly true, nearly false, and false. In such a language "$\sim u$" might be true, or nearly true, or nearly false, or false according to whether "u" is false, nearly false, nearly true, or true;[2] or there might be other arrangements. But even though interpretations of this sort are possible they apparently would have little, if any, application in either scientific inquiries or even in ordinary discourse. If, for example, we were to change the standard truth-functional view of "$\supset$," drastic revisions would be required in both scientific as well as everyday uses of implication, equivalence, and other forms of inference. If "$p \supset q$" could not be taken as equivalent to "$\sim(p \sim q)$," then at least one usual and important scientific derivation could not be made. We might argue that perhaps the change need not be so radical. Perhaps we might take "$p \supset q$" to continue to be false when its antecedent is true and its consequent false. But we might also decide that it will remain false even when both the antecedent and the consequent are false. This change, however, is not as small and inconsequential as one might think. It would demand a wholesale revision of the truth-functional logic that we do normally employ. For "$p \supset q$" would then not be equivalent to "$\sim(p \sim q)$" but it would be equivalent to "$\sim(p \sim q)$ · $\sim(\sim p \sim q)$." And from this equivalence, if we then continue to use the remaining rules of the ordinary truth-functional calculus, we obtain that "$p \supset q$" is equivalent to "q." [3] Such an equivalence, we need hardly point out, would obliterate the distinction between a prediction and an assertion, and would make factual every hope that was stated in the form of a conditional. As attractive as all this may sound, it would, unfortunately, not serve any purpose in any scientific or everyday inquiry.

Furthermore, changes in an interpretation are, at least to some extent, governed by the language in which the interpretation is being presented. It would seem to be very difficult to revise or construct a language without relying at some point on some fundamental terms or expressions. In the very process of making linguistic revisions or reconstructions, we give directions and make stipulations on the basis of a prior language which itself incorporates some basic conceptions of negation, contradiction, existence, implication, and others. We might modify this prior language in order to avoid obvious ambiguities and incongruities, but we cannot modify the basic linguistic structures. These we require if we are to initiate the construction of a new and more precise kind of language. Thus to employ recursive rules effectively we must be able to understand what it means to say that one pattern of marks is allowable and another is not, that certain capital letters stand for predicates which designate or in some way indicate properties while certain small letters stand for subjects which designate or in some way indicate individuals. Even if we were to accept Quine's view [4] and speak only of schematic predicate and individual letters, thereby supposedly avoiding reference to properties and things, we would still need a prior language that tells us *this* letter is to be placed to the right and not to the left of that letter; or *this* letter is a predicate while that one is an individual term. Similarly, Tarski's and Wittgenstein's basic conception of concatenation requires that we have a predecessor language that has within it phrases such as "this immediately follows that" and "this is a successor of that." For this reason discussions about the primitives of a given system are misleading. Some primitive terms are indeed internal to a given system. But there are also primitives which may be regarded as external to the system. Thus "is a successor of" is a primitive expression, but its use contains the presumption that both sides of it will be filled in with "this," "that," "something," or other expressions which are permissible because of a language that has been accepted prior to a given interpretation. One has only to consider the applicability of "is the successor of" if the use of this phrase did not presuppose certain kinds of expressions on both sides to recognize the implicit acknowledgment we make to the sentential construction of a prior language.

The words that are substituted for the marks of the calculus are not actually parts of the calculus itself, but of the metalanguage which has these marks as its subject matter. But where do we obtain the words of the metalanguage? Words do not come from nothing and, indeed, the words of the metalanguage are themselves derived from a prior language that contains its own grammatical categories. We might now easily be led into an infinite regress of languages in which a logically prior language is always used to explain another language. But even though this is clearly possible, what would be the point? After a certain number of revisions and modifications, we would always be left with a language that would contain precisely those characteristics whose necessity or conventionality we are seeking to investigate. If, for example, we employed a language B in order to describe some of the essential syntactical structures of A, and another language C in order to describe some of the essential structures of B we would, sooner or later, find ourselves using a language with exactly the same syntactical structures of the language under investigation. Thus Wittgenstein was in a certain sense quite correct when he pointed out that any analysis of language assumes a language whose syntax can only be shown but never expressed.[5] Talking about the syntax of a language means that we are using a metalanguage whose syntax is being provided but not inspected. And when we investigate the metalanguage we are required to use a meta-metalanguage which, no matter how purified it may be, would still contain such basic components as "not" as well as the linguistic categories that would be filled either by individual or predicate terms. To this extent—that no matter how much we purify a language we are still left with an n-metalanguage that contains certain essential characteristics—Carnap's criticism of Wittgenstein is clearly wrong. Carnap believes that the fact that an uninspected language A is required to investigate another language B (which may or may not be a subspecies of A) does not mean that the syntax of B cannot be revised to allow for fewer ambiguities and to make contradiction less possible, nor does it mean that success in alterations in B cannot be used in turn to produce important alterations in A.[6] To revise a familiar metaphor, Carnap believes that we can pull ourselves up linguistically by our linguistic bootstraps. Or as Neurath and others have stated it, the task of the philosopher is like that of the sailor who must repair and perhaps even rebuild his ship while he is still on the open sea.[7] But the point is that the metaphor of the sailor is more favorable to Wittgenstein's rather than to Carnap's position. Even though a sailor can repair most things on his ship, there are some things which, if lost, destroy the ship's movement on the sea once and for all, e.g., the loss of fuel, or the loss of the rudder. Thus even though there can be an indefinite purification of a language, there will continue to be some expressions which are necessary if any language is to function. This is Wittgenstein's position even though he tries to minimize its ontological significance. We can and do make corrections in the language we use but some elements remain essential.

Thus we proceed to construct a formal language. But we ought to be aware that with all its arbitrariness and conventionality, a formal language presupposes a factor that is itself neither arbitrary nor conventional. We never escape the Göedelian paradox of assuming a predecessor language in the construction of every purely formal language, even though it is always possible to formalize what is, at any given stage, unformalized.

Besides such basic words as "if . . . then - - -" "and" and so forth that are substituted for the marks of the calculus, there are also various series of letters taken from different parts of the alphabet. These are called "variables" in the metalanguage and subdivided into various species labelled "individual," "propositional" and "predicate" variables if quantification is also permitted over the last two divisions.[8]

All these linguistic expressions—both those replacing the horseshoe, dot, vee, and quantifier signs as well as those indicating that a particular letter is a predicate or other variable—belong in the metalanguage and form a partial interpretation of the calculus. They serve as a partial interpretation because they only outline the general features of the language; they do not indicate any specific feature. In other words they tell us that the language must contain different sorts of terms serving different functions, but they do not tell us what specific term of any given sort must be included.[9] Thus, for example, they do not require that the specific term "red" be a member of the language or be substituted for the letter marked off in the metalanguage as a predicate variable. But what the partial interpretation does tell us is that the designative expressions introduced into the metalanguage must be substituends for the individual, propositional or predicate variables listed.

These admission requirements for a word that is intended to be included in the system are not restricted solely to the variables. The variables—by their dichotomy into individual, propositional and predicate—do certainly set up stringent qualifications. But similar qualifications are to be found in the use of "$(\exists x)$," "$\cdot$," "v" and "$\supset$" and the other logical particles. For we take $(\exists x)$ to be a quantifier of existence, or an existential quantifier, and we are, therefore, stating that even though no specific sentence of the form "There is such-and-such" or "There is something having such-and-such a property" need be included in the language, some sentences will either have this form or be translatable into this form. Of course there could be a formal language in which the quantifier is excluded or at least so modified that no sentence such as "There is something having such-and-such a property" is permitted. But such a language would make it impossible for us to formulate some of our most important mathematical and scientific concepts, especially those in set theory and in those parts of science that contain unrestricted general statements.[10] Furthermore, if we agree with Russell and Quine that all names are eliminable in favor of descriptions and if we then also accept Quine's claim that we discover what is extralinguistic only by finding out the values of our bound variable —if we accept these two views then certainly quantification cannot be eliminated. Descriptions and bound variables can be defined only in terms of quantifiers. Thus either we must reject the possibility of distinguishing languages which refer to the "real" from those which refer to the "unreal" or else we must accept quantification.

Similarly, the use of "·," "v" and "⊃" make further restrictions on what is allowable in a language since they are intended to signify for us, in their own fashion, under what conditions sentences can or cannot be asserted. At least according to Carnap, they tell us, for example, that the use of "·" between two sentences, $p \ q$, means that p and q are assertible only if both are taken to be true. It is sometimes argued that these restrictions are not really severe, that, indeed, they have very little significance since particles can always be eliminated in favor of other particles. Thus we know that "·" can be eliminated by means of "v" and "∽." Similar procedures can occur in relation to "⊃," "v" and "≡." But in this connection we must note two oddities.

First of all, we can substitute logical particles for logical particles but we cannot rid ourselves of logical particles. We simply cannot have a language which only contains variables or only contains constants. Or we might put it differently. Perhaps a language might contain only descriptive terms, but it surely would not be a linguistic system which could play any significant role in the sciences or in any subject matters where we wish to be able to assert other sentences on the basis of some given ones. We require some connective marks if our language is not to be a mere mechanical listing of sentences. Thus the capacity to eliminate logical particles ought not to be taken to mean that by some gradual process of reduction we will be able to show that no particles are needed. Perhaps not all that are normally included need be used, but it does not follow that, therefore, none need be used. Our interpretation is required to have some mark by which we can go from one sentence to another, even if it is merely from a set of atomic sentences to the same set regarded as a molecular sentence. This would seem to be an essential aspect of any language.

A second oddity that ought to be noted is that at least one

logical particle is sometimes taken to be never eliminable; or, if it is, then its function must reappear in some other logical particle. I am referring to the sign of negation. Unlike the other particles mentioned above, this sign has the curious characteristic that it cannot be eliminated in favor of any of them. In fact, it is essential if a move is to be made from "v" to "⊃" or from "⊃" to "·," etc. This does not mean that more than one single primitive particle is always required if a language is to be constructed. We know, for example, that the negation sign "N" in Lukasiewicz' system can be transformed by the use of "D." Thus "Np" would become "Dpp." [11] But it is not as if negation is no longer present since "Dpp" becomes interpreted as "Not both p and p" or "False both p and p." Similarly, Peirce, Sheffer, and Nicod were instrumental in showing that the propositional calculus can be formulated with only one primitive functor. [12] But the notion of negation was always either implicitly or explicitly given as part of the interpretation of the primitive sign. Thus Peirce takes "∼p" to be equivalent to "p⊃a" where a is taken to mean an "index of no matter what token." [13] Sheffer introduces "∧" as a sign of nondisjunction and Nicod uses the "Sheffer stroke function" as a sign of nonconjunction. Russell himself struggled to eliminate either implicitly or explicitly any commitment to negation in the primitive terms. But, as Church points out, [14] neither in the *Principles of Mathematics* nor in his papers of 1906 did he succeed. Russell was forced to take negation as "an additional primitive connective on the ground that it would otherwise be impossible to express the proposition that not everything is true— which he (Russell) holds is adequately expressed by ∼(p)p but not by (p)p ⊃ (s)s." [15] More specifically, Russell sought to eliminate the negative sentence by defining it in terms of the universal quantifier. Thus ∼p would be equal by definition to p ⊃ (s)s which would be expressing, in definitional form, the acknowledged truth-functional inference that only a false sentence implies all sentences. But the first objection to this is that the sense of negation is being adequately expressed only if (s)s is taken to refer to all sentences including false or contradictory ones. Otherwise (s)s could be taken as a list of true sentences and then it would simply be false to call a sentence negative because it implies a list of true sentences. Given that (s)s is false, then we can argue that it is inferred from a proposition that is itself false. But a true consequent can be inferred from either a true or false antecedent. Thus $(s)s$ must contain a false sentence within it: but in order to explain such a sentence we must have introduced negation. Similarly, if Russell had held onto this definition, then "Not everything is true" or $\sim(p)p$, becomes by substitution $(p)p \supset (s)s$ which states that everything implies everything else. Even if we could explicate "else" without the use of a negation sign, we would still not have the desired sense of "Not everything is true." Thus Russell was required to introduce negation as a primitive sign. A similar objection can be raised with regard to Church's attempt to use the Lukasiewicz-Tarski definition of negation as "$(s)s$." The definition would not yield the sense of negation required in ordinary and scientific usage where we hold "Not every proposition is true" to be a true proposition. On this analysis, "Not every proposition is true" or "There is a false proposition" would be defined as "Every proposition is true."

It should be mentioned that Wittgenstein also sought to eradicate this strange commitment to our use of the negation sign. In the *Tractatus* he argues that there is both an arbitrary and a nonarbitrary aspect to negation. The nonarbitrary aspect appears in the fact that once we decide to introduce a negation sign into a system, then certain specific rules must also be admitted, e.g., the rule of double negation.[16] Wittgenstein does not tell us why the concept of negation entails the kind of rules that it does. Presumably the notion of "not" has the rule of double negation as part of its definition although it is not altogether clear what kind of definition this is and why certain specific characteristics must prevail. Indeed, the intuitionist in mathematics has denied this. But the important point is that for Wittgenstein negation need not be included in any phase of interpretation of a system. If we have "not" then it must accord with certain rules. But we need not have "not." [17] In the *Philosophical Investigations* the point is made even more explicitly. We can assign values or make rules about the curl (or tilde) in any way we please. It is simply a matter of the kind of language game that is being played.[18]

Wittgenstein, however, does not tell us how a negationless language can be made to give us the statement Russell and others took to be true of any system purporting to deal with scientific data, namely, "Not everything is true." Thus in the terms of Wittgenstein's truth-functional language, this sentence cannot be expressed without a negation sign. Furthermore, if "not" is not permitted into a language then neither ought we to admit "false" nor any of the other substitutions that we make available. But then how are we to think of sentences that are falsifiable or false? What happens to a sentence when we decide to take away its label of being true? Does it then become nonsense? Clearly, at least in scientific inquiry, we do wish to speak of non-nonsensical sentences that simply turn out to be false. But how is this to be expressed if neither negation nor any of its synonyms are permitted in the language? Wittgenstein's view of negation is in accordance with what has been called the "traditional" view of negation, namely, that all negative sentences are derivative from positive ones. This view is endorsed by Kant,[19] Bergson,[20] Brentano,[21] W. H. Sheldon,[22] and C. J. Ducasse[23] to mention only a few. But how the proposed derivation is to be accomplished has not yet been adequately explained. As one writer has stated, "There do not happen to be any lizards, rocking chairs, or goldfish in my study, but need we suppose that these things are positively excluded by the things my study contains, or that their presence would be incompatible with something else that is there? If I believe that there is no elephant in my room, should we assume that some true positive proposition about my room renders necessary the absence of any elephant? Or that there is some feature about my room that could not coexist with an elephant? Again, I see no reason for thinking so."[24] If we accept the Humean analysis of knowledge then no fact can exclude the possibility of occurrence of another fact. Yet this would be required if we are to think of negative sentences as outcomes of positive ones.

Before we leave the problem of negative sentences it behooves us to examine briefly one recent attempt to make plausible Wittgenstein's negationless language. Max Black, in his commentary on Wittgenstein's *Tractatus*, has argued that negation can indeed be considered as something which is "grafted on" a language that is initially completely free of negative sentences.[25] Black presents us with an example of a child who is offered one picture at a time from a pack of cards "with the understanding that he scores a point in the game if the depicted object is on the mantelpiece, and loses a point otherwise."[26] The game is now modified by the introduction of some marker, say a red tab, which, when it is clipped onto a picture card converts a loss to a win and vice versa. Now if the attachment of two red tabs to any given card means that they cancel one another out, then, Black concludes, "we shall have a close analogue to the way in which the logical operator, '∼,' normally functions. We should be justified in saying that *negation* had been introduced into the game." [27] The difficulty in Black's analysis, however, relates primarily to the word "otherwise." Presumably we tell the child that he wins if the object depicted in the card is on the mantelpiece but he loses otherwise. But are we sure that we can explain "otherwise" to the child without using a negation mark? It is clearly possible for one not very well acquainted with the language to take "otherwise" to mean "if there are two objects on the mantelpiece" or "if the object is made of wood" or "if the object has different colors than that represented in the card" or "if the object is turned to the left," etc. In other words, to obtain the obvious intended meaning of "otherwise" we should be required to give the child some notion of negation at the very beginning of the game; otherwise the game could not even begin. We might think that "otherwise" is replaceable by "if the object is missing" and here no explicit form of negation is present. But it is implicit. If we do not want the child to take "missing" as some positive predicate indicating a given property, we would have to use some form of negation in explicating "missing." Of course, once the child has this basic notion then Black's further analysis can continue quite satisfactorily. But the main part of the argument—namely showing that negation can arbitrarily be introduced into an already functioning language game —is lost.

There are, therefore, some odd requirements that arise in the construction of any language and they should not be minimized. But it might be argued that these requirements are significant only to those who wish to construct ideal languages. Indeed, it might seem as if in discussing the various structures required in a language, we have been able to proceed without involving ourselves in any traditionally serious philosophical issues. At least we are apparently not committing ourselves to any claim that words designating essences, or natural laws, or specific qualities and properties are necessary in the primitive terminology of a language. We might require predicates, quantifiers, and negation expressions but this does not mean that we are making any claim that such-and-such is or that such-and-such is not. Nothing is being added to or subtracted from whatever is extralinguistic. At this stage the language would seem, so to speak, to be ontologically neutral. No necessary characteristics or abstract entities are being attributed to what is external to the language.

Of course as the language develops and as we do begin to specify what is to be the domain over which the variables are to range, we might suddenly find ourselves referring to entities such as forces or psyches or entelechies that may well be taken to have ontological significance. That is to say, the language might suddenly include terms referring to abstract entities. But it might be assumed that at least no philosophical issues of any consequence are present in the minimal amount of terminology that has so far been used in the interpretation of a calculus. However, this assumption would be a mistake. For even though we do not seem to be populating the world with abstract entities or involving ourselves in any obvious metaphysical speculations, the odd commitments we have indicated would seem to lend themselves quite easily to a discussion of a whole gamut of ontological problems. We have found, for example, that if our formal language is to function at all—or at least function for any scientific or ordinary discourse inquiry—it must have places for terms which will be substituends for individual variables and terms which will be substituends for predicate variables. In other words, even at this minimal stage of development in the language, even prior to the application of Quine's quantification principle as a criterion for ontology,[28] the commitment is already present that if, in the further development of the language, new expressions are introduced and they are to be used to replace variables, then we can be assured that these expressions will be suitable as predicate or individual expressions. Some way of identifying a word or phrase will be required by which one can legitimately say "This word (or phrase) is suitable for a predicate variable place and this other word (or phrase) is suitable for an individual variable place." How this identification is to be made has still to be determined, but it is important to recognize that the very need for the variable dichotomy in the basic framework of a formal language poses a major possibility for the introduction of an inquiry that has traditionally been called ontological. For after accepting this dichotomy in a formal language, we can, like Strawson, offer an appropriate explanation.[29] The need arises because there are things (substances?) and prop-

erties (attributes?) and just as ordinary language requires this
dichotomy so also does a formal language. Once this step has been
taken, all the traditional as well as contemporary issues of ontology
and metaphysics in general can begin to be raised. Of course, it
might be argued that the fact that an interpretation of a calculus
requires adjectives and names need not mean that the referents of
these linguistic expressions must be properties and/or classes and
things. Traditionally it has been argued that predicates, for example, need not refer to properties or to classes, but rather to specific characteristics of concrete objects. "X is F" means no more
than "This object is F, that object is F, etc." We need not speak of
some abstract entity called "F-ness" or "The class of F." But there
is this point to be made. To say "Something is both F and G" we
are required to bind the individual variable. That is, "Something is
both F and G" becomes "$(\exists x)(Fx \cdot Gx)$." Without such binding of
the variable we would be unable to say that a given object has both
F and G. Permitting "x" to be free would mean that perhaps one
object has F and another G. Similarly, if we wish to say "Two objects both have F" then we ought also to bind the predicate variable
since, otherwise, the sense of sameness of F would not be conveyed.
In other words, "Two objects both have the same F" would become
"$(\exists x)(\exists y)(\exists F)(Fx \cdot Fy)$." But the binding of a predicate variable
means we become committed to treating the referents of predicate
terms as existential entities in the same way we treat the referents
of individual terms. Thus in the very earliest stages of analyzing a
formal language, serious philosophical issues arise, and the way we
deal with these issues will decide whether the construction of formal
languages can indeed have any significant relevance for metaphysical inquiry.

Similarly, "$(\exists x)$" is merely a series of marks in a calculus; and
yet there would seem to be not only a need to have these marks or
some synonyms in the calculus but also a need to interpret them as
existential quantification. Quine has argued that the quantifier is
important because set theory and some conceptions of scientific law
require us to posit an infinite domain of objects.[30] But he implies
that if the problem of explicating infinity in mathematics could be
overcome without entailing an infinite number of numbers and if
we could finally find a way of making first-order scientific generalizations[31] without requiring a notion of an infinite number of enti-

ties, the quantifier could be eliminated. We could then simply recast all our existentially quantified sentences into a series of disjuncts and, therefore, eliminate the need for quantification. In other words, if it were not for the need to have infinite classes in mathematics, the issue of quantification would not arise. But I think that this view is mistaken. First of all, it does not account for at least one crucial sentence that must be stated in any description even about a finite class of objects, namely, "There are no more members." We can count each member or each individual class, but if we are to identify a finite group we must eventually be able to say, "This is the nth member. There are no more." Without the addition of this latter sentence we are not being told whether we are dealing with a finite set or with a part or a subclass of an infinite set. But the statement "There are no more" is translatable into $(\exists y)(x)$ $(x \epsilon y)$, and thus to explain a finite class requires the admission of a quantified sentence. Of course, we can remove this quantified sentence by reducing it to a series of conjuncts and disjuncts. But again we would require a final quantified sentence, "There are no more." Thus the price of exclusion of quantified sentences is an infinite regress.[32]

Secondly, there would seem to be a need in any language to make a distinction between what is and what is not. Even in the most formal language—assuming that we want to be dealing with scientific and everyday matters—we would clearly require some way of noting that a given sentence refers to what is actually the situation while another does not. A language could accommodate itself to the most intricate mathematical or purely scientific theory. But if it lacks an existential quantifier or some synonymous expression, all the proper names or descriptions of the system could refer to fictitious characters. Peirce once described Hegel's metaphysics as a model system with everything in it except one not so unimportant factor—it simply did not relate to what exists.[33] Similarly, the most imposing formal system would merely be another kind of Hegelian system unless it included some device for distinguishing the actual from the nonactual.[34]

Here, then is an important ontological commitment. We require, at the most basic level in the construction of a formal language, that some device be used for differentiating genuinely referring terms from those that only apparently refer. In other words, the traditional dichotomy of appearance and reality and their relations to one another becomes converted into the contemporary dichotomy of quantifiable and unquantifiable terms and their function in a formal system. Thus formal systems—even at their very beginnings —have elements that cannot be very easily accepted without a clear commitment to a serious ontological position. We would seem to be involved in the Kantian paradox of maintaining that even though no state-of-affairs need be described in any formal language, certain forms of language are needed if any state-of-affairs is to be described.[35] We do not have to be involved in the ontology of an Aristotle or Plato for we might not admit as values for our variables specific abstract entities. But there are other kinds of ontologies which can be just as significant. To argue, in a manner reminiscent of Kant, that some linguistic structures have a necessity devoid of conventional status is to create a strong suspicion that linguistic analysis has not yet downed the spectre of possible metaphysical inquiry.

2

The Ontology of Karl Popper

THE FACT that linguistic and logical analyses have become of primary philosophic importance in recent times does not mean that inquiries dealing with ontological questions are no longer of any philosophic worth. There are, indeed, those who still deal with ontology as if nothing of any philosophical consequence has been written since the Middle Ages.[1] But there are others who, so to speak, have entered into the contemporary intellectual crossfire and sought to show that ontology is not to be denied even in the most precise investigations of linguistic and logical analysts. In this chapter and the subsequent one, I should like to examine two such views, namely, those by Karl Popper and P. F. Strawson since they are representative of those philosophers trained in the best contemporary logical techniques and yet firmly committed to the view that ontology is a genuine and significant form of inquiry. I shall show that their notions of ontology are, indeed, connected with recent investigations into logic and language. But I shall also show that these connections are not satisfactorily explicated and cannot be used to sustain a fully developed and cogently reasoned system of ontology.

Popper's ontology arises primarily out of a criticism of Carnap's insistence on the need for a physicalistic language. According to Carnap, one of the advantages of a physicalistic language is not only that it can accommodate the statements of physics and the sciences in general, but that it makes impossible the inclusion of sentences traditionally called metaphysical.[2] The confirmation theory of meaning assumes that cognitive sentences which are not analytic are confirmable or disconfirmable. But only a physicalistic language can satisfy the confirmation criterion since only by reference to some series of observable objects can we speak of the confirmation or disconfirmation of a sentence. Therefore, any sentence that cannot be formulated in physical terms or cannot be shown to be connected, by either logical or correspondence rules, to sentences containing physical terms is simply not cognitive; and metaphysical sentences are of this sort.[3]

What Popper now sets out to do is to show that a physicalistic language is incapable of drawing the demarcation between metaphysical and scientific sentences.[4] To begin with, he reintroduces the arguments stated by Hempel and others, namely, that not all scientific terms can be accounted for by a strict physicalistic analysis. We cannot, for example, give a completely physicalistic definition of such expressions as "electricity" or "electronic gas" or "psyche." These expressions, like other theoretical terms, can only be partially defined by either physical or behavioral operations. In fact, Popper affirms Hempel's major position that one of the important aims in scientific inquiry is to be able to apply mathematical concepts to scientific subject matter. But we cannot do this and also claim we are relying strictly on observations. As Hempel puts it, "In view of the limits of discrimination in direct observation, there will be altogether only a finite, though large, number of observable characteristics; hence, the number of different complexes that can be formed out of them will be finite as well, whereas the number of theoretically permissive (mathematical) values is infinite."[5] Thus if we are to rely on measurement and mathematical analysis in science, we must sooner or later move out of the realm of observational testing. Similar criticisms have been voiced by both F. P. Ramsey and R. B. Braithwaite who have also argued that complete reliance on observation would ultimately lead to the denial of scientific inquiry since there would be no way of employing theoretical concepts with new data.[6] Theoretical terms are absolutely necessary in scientific inquiry, but their effectiveness rests on the fact that they "reach out" to data that has not yet been presented. They are supposed to give us some assurance of what the future will bring. But if the meaning of such terms were exhausted by the data already given, they would be inapplicable to any future occurrences.

Nor, Popper argues, can these difficulties be temporized by taking theoretical terms to be dispositional properties which can then be defined either by the use of subjunctive conditionals or by Carnap's reduction sentences. The problems concerning subjunctives are well known and no one has yet resolved them. We still do not know how to deal with false antecedents that make all conditionals true and, therefore, also make the dispositional terms they define applicable under all circumstances. Reduction sentences have served to overcome some of the shortcomings of the subjunctive conditional in that dispositional terms are not automatically applicable when the antecedent of the conditional is false. But their limitations are also quite severe since they make the dispositional term applicable only when specific test conditions have been met. They tell us nothing about whether an object does or does not have a given disposition prior to the actual testing of the object. Thus reduction sentences give us only a partial definition of dispositional expressions; the latter still retains a portion of meaning not displayed by the use of reduction sentences.[7] Furthermore, reduction sentences can be shown to be circular. What have we gained, Popper asks,[8] if we define "solubility" by the sentence "if x is put into water then x is soluble in water if and only if it dissolves?" We are still left with expressions that themselves can be understood only in terms of solubility. "We have still to reduce *'water'* and *'dissolves'*; and it is clear that, among the operational tests which characterize water we should have to include: 'if anything that is soluble in water is put into x, then if x is water, that thing dissolves.' In other words, not only are we forced, in introducing 'soluble' to fall back upon 'water' which is dispositional in perhaps even a higher degree, but in addition, we are forced into a circular mode of introducing 'soluble' with the help of a term ('water') which in its turn cannot be operationally introduced without 'soluble.' "[9]

These criticisms, according to Popper, show a major deficiency in the physicalistic analysis. Those theoretical terms that are most crucial to scientific inquiry cannot be accounted for by a strict physicalistic definition. From this Popper concludes that there can and must be expressions in a scientific language which receive their meaning—or at least part of their meaning—from something other than physicalistic criteria.

In effect, Popper's first remarks are directed towards exposing some fundamental weaknesses in those languages whose construction would seem to entail a rejection of any significant metaphysical sentence. Such languages, Popper holds, can never be so tightly woven that they do actually contain, as designating expressions, only observation terms. For this reason, even though metaphysical expressions are not definable by observation sentences, the observation criterion cannot be used to draw a line of demarcation between science and metaphysics "so as to exclude metaphysics as nonsensical from a meaningful language." [10]

Popper's remarks are, indeed, trenchant. Disposition and theoretical terms, as well as their subjunctive and reductionist analogues, have posed problems for Carnap, Goodman, and others of the formalist school. Some recent attempts have been made to solve these problems by conceiving of dispositional predicates as functioning in a formal language as hypotheses or suggestions for further possible knowledge.[11] But, the ambiguity in the notion of "possible" has detracted from the fruitfulness of these attempts. And, it seems to be glaringly circular to maintain that dispositional properties are now to be called hypotheses, or, more explicitly, hypothetical properties. A hypothetical property is no more clarifactory than the original dispositional one.[12]

Popper, therefore, makes a strong case. But two points must now be made. First, even though all of Popper's criticism may be perfectly acceptable, we need not agree with him that the defects in a formal or scientific system are reasons for subscribing to an ontology. It would be a primary example of the *argumentam ad ignorantiam* to make the claim that the problematical aspects of a scientific inquiry can be used to support an inference about something metaphysical. Thus, if Popper intends to show us how an analysis of a formal system requires us to support the belief in an ontology, then at least this first criticism of Carnap is not adequate. The shortcomings of Carnap's thesis of reducibility are not sufficient to warrant accepting an implicit ontology. The fact that we have not yet solved the difficulties in relativity theory does not mean that we are, therefore, supporting a return to a Newtonian or alternative theory. Secondly, as Carnap has shown us,[13] theoretical terms have one characteristic which metaphysical terms or constructs lack. Even though theoretical terms are not fully explicated by any given series of observation sentences they are taken to be nonreferential if the observational sentences turn out to be false. In other words, if I claim that there are atoms and this claim is taken to imply some series of observation reports, then the claim is rejectable if all or even most of the purported observation reports turn out to be false. Note that the reduction of theoretical terms to some finite series of observation predicates is not being affirmed. This is a difficulty of reductionism that empiricists have yet to solve. But at the same time we are maintaining that because of correspondence, or what Hempel calls "Bridge" Rules, there is a connection between theoretical terms and observation predicates, between sentences containing theoretical terms and pure observation sentences, a connection which has usually been rejected in metaphysical theories. Thus, for example, Hegel and others were able to state that their absolutes would exist even if no supporting evidence were forthcoming. That is to say, the metaphysician has frequently argued that empirical data is, or can be, implied by a metaphysical construct. To this extent metaphysical constructs are like theoretical terms. But the crucial difference between the two is that whereas the statement about theoretical or dispositional terms is falsified when the empirical data implied by it is false, this is not the case with a metaphysical construct. If x does not dissolve in water then x is not soluble. But this kind of falsification test has rarely been accepted with "There is Being" or "There is Nothing." Thus Popper has reasserted some well-known objections to any position of extreme reductionism. But none of these objections requires us to introduce ontology into scientific inquiry.

A more cogent attempt to show how a strict formalism can legitimately lead to metaphysical inquiry occurs when Popper constructs a purely physicalistic system and then shows how a metaphysical sentence can be derived from this system. More specifically Popper tries to prove the feasibility of constructing a language with primitive physicalistic predicates from which a strictly metaphysical sentence can be obtained. He begins by introducing the following four primitive physicalistic predicates.

1] "The thing *a* occupies a position *b*" or more precisely "*a* occupies a position of which the (point or) region *b* is part"; in symbols "*Pos (a, b)*."

2] "The thing (machine, or body, or person . . .) *a* can put the thing *b* into position *c*"; in symbols "*Put (a, b, c)*."

3] "*a* makes the utterance *b*"; in symbols "*Utt (a, b)*.

4] "*a* is asked (i.e., adequately stimulated by an utterance combined, say, with a truth drug) whether or not *b*"; in symbols "*Ask (a, b)*."

By explicit definition Popper then proceeds to introduce:

5] "*a* is omnipresent," or "*Opos (a)*" $= df$ "*(b) Pos (a, b)*."

6] "*a* is omnipotent," or "*Oput (a)*." $= df$ "*(b)(c) Put (a, b, c)*."

7] "*a* thinks *b*" or "*Th (a, b)*" $= df$ (using Carnap's reduction method) "*Ask (a, b)* $\supset$ *(Th (a, b) $\equiv$ Utt (a, b))*."[14]

Continuing in this way Popper proceeds to define several important psychological, epistemological and other sorts of predicates such as "thinking person," "personal spirit," "truthful," and "omniscient."[15]

Popper then formally derives an existential formula expressing what he calls the *arch-metaphysical assertion,* namely, "a thinking person *a* exists, positioned everywhere; able to put anything anywhere; thinking all and only what is in fact true; and with nobody else knowing all about *a*'s thinking."[16] This assertion, according to Popper, is a well-formed formula, constructed on the basis of a strict physicalistic language, without any subtle inclusions of terms that would be unacceptable to scientific inquirers or positivistic philosophers. Even the expression "thinks" has been given a formulation which omits any overt reference to something mental or closed to scientific scrutiny. Therefore, the *arch-metaphysical assertion* is perfectly meaningful and the fact that it can be derived without paradox or without the introduction of any *ad hoc* rules proves that not even a physicalistic language can prohibit the meaningful assertion of metaphysical statements.

This is a strong argument. It can be used to refute the views of those who, like Wittgenstein in the *Tractatus*,[17] maintain that a strict scientific language with every designative term carefully explicated and every syntactic one carefully defined can ultimately legislate metaphysics out of the realm of meaning and existence. Some questions, however, need to be raised about Popper's analysis.

Now I think that Popper argues effectively against those who have designated metaphysical statements as meaningless. Carnap in the *Aufbau* may have been influenced by Wittgenstein's *Tractatus* and accepted his position but even Popper admits that this view "was abandoned by Carnap long ago." [18] In his most recent statement Carnap has claimed that some statements with which metaphysicians have been concerned are perfectly proper both from a syntactic and semantic point of view.[19] Such statements are subject to all the rules of confirmation and disconfirmation and are, therefore, not rejectable. But there are also certain kinds of statements that are, as he puts it, "devoid of cognitive meaning." [20] These are neither magical nor astrological sorts of sentences but they are, on the contrary, statements in which one or more terms are so used that they are explicitly intended to lack empirical reference either directly or indirectly. Thus, Carnap argues: "The word 'God,' in its mythical use, has a clear, empirical meaning. In its metaphysical use, on the other hand, its old empirical meaning vanishes; since no new meaning is supplied, the term 'God' becomes meaningless." [21] In other words, for Carnap metaphysical statements are those which have empirically meaningless terms. To this extent, then, Popper's *arch-metaphysical assertion* would be perfectly acceptable to Carnap. The difference would be that Carnap would take Popper's statement to be empirical and, therefore, subject to all the rules of confirmation.

Of course, Popper might reply that Carnap is here arguing against a straw man since only the most esoteric metaphysicians give us statements in which terms are taken to lack all empirical reference. Thus both Plato and Aristotle took their notions of Form of the Good and Unmoved Mover as derivations from an analysis of experience. The Unmoved Mover, we are told, is that "to which experience points." [22] And more recently a commentator on Aquinas states "Any natural knowledge which we have of a being or beings transcending the visible world is attained by reflection on the data of experience. And it is this process of reflection, when carried through systematically, that constitutes the proofs of the proposition that God exists." [23] It is possible to think of metaphysics in the forms presented by a mystic such as Plotinus [24] or an existentialist such as Heidegger. But this would ignore the very branch of metaphysics that is concerned with the same kind of everyday experience utilized by empiricists and which is taken to entail metaphysical conclusions. It is clearly unsatisfactory to make the most extreme anti-empirical form of metaphysics an exemplar of ontological inquiry. And Popper might have maintained that Carnap has proceeded in this way. But Popper does not make this argument. And, as we have already seen, Carnap's argument is not directed against the use of terms that are only partially definable by observation predicates; rather it is directed against the use of terms whose meaning can never be impaired by either the affirmation or falsification of an observation sentence. Finally, even if Popper were correct in maintaining that Carnap was oversimplifying the metaphysician's argument, it would have little bearing on a second criticism we should now like to present.

Let us assume that Popper is right and that a metaphysical statement has been deduced from a set of physicalistic statements. What exactly has been accomplished? In one sense the derivation is trivial for we know that since the predicates in any given formal system must be independent of one another,[25] we cannot exclude such well-formed sentences as "Smith is fifteen feet tall" or "There is a man who is ¼ black, ¼ green, ¼ blue, and ¼ orange." These sentences are all well-formed and, therefore, meaningful. However, it so happens that they are false. Now similarly we can obtain a sentence such as "There is something which hears everything and sees everything but which nothing else sees or hears" (assuming that "see" and "hear" are legitimate predicates); the sentence is meaningful; but it is also false, or, following Carnap, highly disconfirmed. Thus the fact that Popper has deduced for us a sentence which we might accept as part of the traditional canon of metaphysical sentences does not mean that he has derived an ontology from a formal language. For the metaphysician it is no great accomplishment to show that a good metaphysical sentence can be produced in accordance with all the precise techniques of logic and semantics if the sentence can be shown to be false. There simply is no human being fifteen-feet tall nor is there a person who is ¼ black, ¼ green, ¼ blue, and ¼ orange. Popper has apparently overlooked the distinction to be made between truth and well-formedness. Many sentences are well-formed in that they consist of perfectly acceptable predicates. But there are also rules of truth and confirmation in a formal system and these ought not to be confused with the rules of formation.

However, there is another sense in which Popper might indicate to us that we have not considered one important conclusion that he has drawn. He wishes to insist that falsity is not applicable to the *arch-metaphysical assertion*. "Our purely existential arch-metaphysical formula cannot be submitted to any scientific test: there is no hope whatever of falsifying it—of finding out, if it is false, that it is false. For this reason I describe it as metaphysical—as falling outside the province of science." [26] Thus Popper denies that he has simply derived a well-formed statement that turns out to be false. What is significant is that the *arch-metaphysical assertion* is well-formed and therefore meaningful, but, unlike all the other sentences that can be formed, scientific tools are simply not applicable to it. And presumably when we encounter a sentence that is characterized in this way we are to regard it as a sentence of metaphysics. But the question that must be raised is this: why does Popper take the *arch-metaphysical statement* to be incapable of being falsified? Why is this statement any different from "There is a human being fifteen-feet tall"? We take the latter to be false. Why not the former? Why would it be impossible to frame the sentence, "There is an omnipotent person" and then infer that this sentence is false? Presumably Popper is constructing his system in terms of the usual truth-functional and quantificational rules. He is not subscribing to some nonnormal interpretation of predicates and variables. He is not presenting an argument that the *arch-metaphysical statement* is some deviant statement such as a subjunctive or an imperative or an interrogative. Nor is he presenting us with some intricate sentence whose combination of quantifiers makes it impossible to employ any known decision procedure. He is dealing with a standard formal system with the usual rules of formation and transformation. But in this kind of system we do claim to be able to ascribe truth or falsity to any complex sentence. Why then does Popper claim that his statement is unique and exempt from falsification?

One of the reasons that Popper gives for claiming such exemption appears to rest on an important logical paradox, namely, that existence sentences can never be falsified. We know that existentially quantified sentences are eliminable in favor of some series of disjuncts. But since we assume an infinite domain of objects—an assumption required both in scientific inquiry and in mathematics—this means we shall require an infinite amount of disjuncts and, therefore, the sole condition for falsification of existential sentences, namely, falsification of all disjuncts, can never be satisfied. Existential sentences can be shown to be true, but not false. Since the *arch-metaphysical assertion* is an existential statement, it cannot be falsified.

This is an important criticism of existential sentences and has been noted by most logicians. But Popper's use of this criticism is too general since it would serve automatically to convert all existential statements into metaphysical ones. If it is the existential characteristic that makes a sentence metaphysical, then the existential statements of science and mathematics are all to be taken as metaphysical. Furthermore, even positivists, empiricists, and linguist analysts must now become metaphysicians since they also make existential statements. In one fell swoop Popper has apparently converted all anti-metaphysicians into strong, albeit stubborn, metaphysicians. But the price, of course, is that the entire notion of metaphysics is now trivialized. Popper's attempt to characterize a metaphysical statement is so broad that it completely obliterates the crucial dictinctions made in scientific and philosophical inquiries. There is an important difference between the claim of "There are trees" and "There is an Absolute." In spite of the difficulties with the existential quantifier the latter, but not the former, commits us to a strong ontology. Existential statements are indeed paradoxical, but these paradoxes cannot be used to infer an ontology.

It would seem, therefore, that Popper gains very little when he argues for his untestable *arch-metaphysical assertion*. Certainly he has not succeeded in deriving a consequential ontology from a strict formal language. But before we leave Popper's analysis, we ought to ask whether he is correct in *1*] his analysis of existence sentences in general, and *2*] his analysis of the particular existence sentence that concerns him. Popper's comments here also are not without their difficulties.

In regard to existence sentences the logic is quite clear. Given an infinite series of disjuncts no falsification is possible. But the fact that a sentence cannot be falsified does not mean that it cannot be disconfirmed. As each disjunct turns out to be false, the sentence becomes increasingly disconfirmed. To this extent, then, Popper's use of the falsification criterion does not serve to make his *arch-metaphysical assertion* acceptable. What he has not shown is why we cannot speak in the way that both Carnap and C. I. Lewis do about the disconfirmation of existential sentences.[27] Clearly, the expression "disconfirmed to the degree n" can be introduced in the appropriate metalanguage to characterize sentences whose simplest disjunctive forms continually produce falsehoods. However, there is this point to be made in favor of Popper's position: existential sentences are peculiar. Perhaps it is fairly simple to speak of increasing disconfirmation with such sentences, but does it make sense to speak of increasing confirmation? We might argue that confirmation can be interpreted in a manner similar to disconfirmation. The more the number of true disjuncts the higher the degree of confirmation. But, first of all, an existential sentence is taken to have as part of its meaning its applicability to at least one given entity. Thus "There are trees" becomes "There is at least one thing that is a tree." But now it would seem to be incorrect to speak of an increasing confirmation once a given disjunct has turned out to be true. If I say "There is at least one thing that is a tree" then my indicating or my pointing to one tree should be all that is required to confirm the sentence. The observation of other trees would simply be irrelevant. I am not seeking evidence about whether there are many trees, but about whether there is merely one. Thus the notion of increasing confirmation seems to be inappropriate for existential sentences. Of course, it might be maintained that our error lies in speaking of true (or false) disjuncts. The disjuncts implied by an existential sentence are themselves either confirmable or disconfirmable to some specified degree and, therefore, the sentence itself can never be taken as completely confirmed. Thus insofar as the statement "That is a tree" is confirmable, it confirms "There are trees." But "That is a tree" is never completely confirmed. Still even Carnap grants that in a scientific language we will have some statements—namely, statements whose descriptive terms are solely the basic observation terms accepted in the language—which function strictly as evidence and are, therefore, not themselves open to confirmation or disconfirmation. In some sentences the notion of increasing confirmation will not be applicable. Therefore, at least one existentially quantified sentence, e.g., "Something is red," can be totally confirmed by one disjunct, but we are still unable to speak of complete disconfirmation. Hence Popper can argue that regardless of how we deal with disjuncts—either as true or confirmable—the existentially quantified sentence is neither falsifiable nor completely disconfirmable. However, even if Popper's *arch-metaphysical assertion* is neither falsifiable nor totally disconfirmable, we are not required to claim anything about its truth or confirmability. The fact that "There is an omnipotent Being" is not falsifiable does not mean that the sentence is now verifiable. To argue otherwise would again involve us in the *Argumentum ad ignorantiam*. Nonfalsifiability does not entail or in any other way imply verifiability. Thus even if Popper is right about the status of existential sentences, at most he can claim that his metaphysical statement cannot be made false. He cannot claim that it is true or that it is even confirmed.

A second peculiarity of existential sentences involves the entire relationship of truth to confirmation. Are there both true and confirmed sentences? Presumably evidential sentences produce confirmation (or disconfirmation) of some other given sentence. But then when if ever do evidential sentences lead to true sentences? Furthermore, if true sentences can lead to the confirmation of another sentence is the latter to be regarded as true or as merely confirmed? A question of order is at issue here. If the true disjunct came initially, then we might wish to argue in the way suggested in the previous paragraph. One true disjunct would be sufficient; all others would be irrelevant. On the other hand, if we began with a false disjunct and continued to have only false ones, would we take the sentence to be disconfirmed even if at some later date we found a true disjunct? Probably not. We would still want to claim that the existential sentence requires us to find one true disjunct—no matter where in the series of disjuncts it may happen to be—and that is sufficient to confirm the sentence. But confirmation now turns out to be an inappropriate word since one of the defining characteristics of confirmation is that both a decrease and an increase are possible.

These are important issues concerning existential sentences in general. And the answer I believe lies in the distinction both Tarski and Carnap sought to emphasize when they spoke of "truth" as a semantic concept,[28] applicable to linguistic segments and not to empirical data. Carnap, for example, makes it quite clear that the logical relation between an existential sentence and its disjunctive form is not the relation of confirmation and disconfirmation. To attach "true" to a sentence means that it can be inspected for possible inconsistency in relation to other sentences in the language.

But to attach "confirmed" means that we have inferred it—in some inductive sense—from some series of observation reports. Thus none of the disjuncts of an existential sentence is ever more than merely confirmable. But if we wished to investigate the logical relations between this sentence and others then we would be required to give the disjuncts a value of "true" or "false." This would not mean that either confirmation or disconfirmation has occurred, even though the former would normally take the value of "true" and the latter "false." [29] It would simply be a way of stating sentences so that the rules of logic would become applicable to them. How "true" and "false" operate in a formal language is not easily explicated without reference to the paradoxes and type theory. But here at least it is sufficient to point out that Popper is surely right in his recognition of the problems inherent in the existential sentence. But he is surely wrong in implying that the weaknesses of the existential statement necessarily entail an ontological commitment.

In an interesting footnote Popper attempts to give another reason for his belief that his arch-metaphysical formula can never be falsified. In his view a metaphysical sentence must be regarded as incapable of ever being disconfirmed because of how the observation predicate is employed in a formal language.

Now should anyone go so far as to commit himself to the admission that my arch-metaphysical formula is well-formed and therefore empirically true or false then I think he will encounter difficulties in extricating himself from this situation. For how could anybody defend the view that my arch-metaphysical formula is false, or disconfirmed? It is certainly unfalsifiable and non-disconfirmable. In fact it is expressible in the form

$$(\exists x)G(x)$$

—in words: "There exists something that has the properties of God." And on the assumption that "$G(x)$" is an empirical predicate, we can prove that its probability must equal 1. . . . I can prove, further, that this means that its probability cannot be diminished by any empirical information. . . . But this means that its degree of confirmation equals 1, and that it *cannot* be disconfirmed. . . .[30]

Popper's new argument is derived from Carnap's claim that given an hypothesis "$(\exists x)Px$" it will receive a degree of confirmation if an observer "makes the observation that b is P." [31] Or, less formally, Popper is maintaining that since the introduction of an empirical predicate into a formal language must mean that at least something has that property, an existential sentence having "Gx" as a function must have a probability of 1. Nothing can disconfirm the fact that something has the property of being G. But now what is interesting here is that Popper's "Gx" is curiously deceptive. "G" itself is not an observation predicate. It is an abbreviation for some series of observation predicates, e.g., "$Pos\ (a,\ b)$," "$Put\ (a,\ b,\ c)$," etc. But Popper apparently reasons that if a series of observation predicates each has a probability of 1, then their combination ought to have a probability of 1. In other words, Popper is arguing that if $(\exists x)Fx$ and $(\exists x)Gx$ each has a probability of 1 — and we know that they do on the basis of Carnap's formal argument and our own informal one — then $(\exists x)(Fx \cdot Gx)$ has a probability of 1. But logically a fusion of existential quantifiers cannot result from some series of conjoined existential sentences. Furthermore, even if the purely logical difficulty could be overcome, nothing in probability theory allows the kind of move that Popper has made. The probability that something is red may be 1 and the probability that something is round may be 1. But this does not at all mean that therefore the probability that something is both red and round is also 1. Popper has simply fallen into the fallacy of composition which is just as serious in probability theory as it is in ordinary deductive systems. The fact that each empirical predicate may have a probability of n does not mean that, therefore, the occurrence of the entire group of predicates also has a probability of n. Thus Popper's "Gx" may be a well-formed abbreviation for some series of empirical predicates, but it does not at all follow that it has the same probability as that of its components.

The conclusion to be drawn, then, from Popper's endeavor to derive an ontological commitment from a purely formal (physicalistic) language is that he has shown us that ontological statements can be constructed in a formal language. But since they are statements analogous to "There is a man who is $\frac{1}{4}$ black, $\frac{1}{4}$ green, $\frac{1}{4}$ blue, and $\frac{1}{4}$ orange" which, though meaningful, are easily disconfirmed, the ontology turns out to be trivial. Certainly this would not lead to the kind of metaphysics scientific inquirers and metaphysicians consider cogent.

3

The Ontology of P. F. Strawson

P. F. STRAWSON has been one of the few to elaborate an ontology which involves a serious existential commitment. In his *Individuals, an Essay in Descriptive Metaphysics,* he tells us at the very beginning that he will try to show that "there are categories and concepts which, in their most fundamental character, change not at all. . . . They are the commonplaces of the least refined thinking; and yet the indispensable core of the conceptual equipment of the most sophisticated human beings." [1] Metaphysics, in this sense, is concerned with absolute and permanent truths which, however, constantly need restatement in terms of the idioms of the times. As Strawson puts it, "though the central subject-matter of descriptive metaphysics does not change, the critical and analytical idiom of philosophy changes constantly. Permanent relationships are described in an impermanent idiom, which reflects both the age's climate of thought and the individual philosopher's personal style of thinking." [2]

Strawson's approach is quite clear. He begins by assuming that individuals do engage in discussion and then he raises the question concerning the extralinguistic conditions which must be present if we are to be assured that communication is actually occurring. The first and perhaps most important condition is that there be particulars to which the (nonsyntactic) words employed can refer. What these particulars are Strawson explicitly tells us. They are, among perhaps other items, historical occurrences, material objects, people, and their shadows. On the other hand, neither qualities, properties, numbers nor species are to be taken as particulars.[3]

It is important to be aware that Strawson's particulars are genuinely extralinguistic in the sense that a language is meant to reflect their existence; their existence is not dependent upon the language. We shall be returning to this point shortly.

Although Strawson suggests a number of possible entities that might serve as the most basic particular, he finally concludes that only material objects are suitable. There are two reasons for this choice. First of all, Strawson shows that for communication to occur at all some identification of and location of objects must be possible. We must be able to say, "Such-and-such is over there" and "Such-and-such is the same thing I saw a moment ago." Thus a spatio-temporal framework of four dimensions is required in which all our knowledge of particulars operates. From this Kantian position it follows that whatever our particulars are, they must be "three-dimensional objects with some endurance through time. They must also be accessible to such means of observation as we have; and, since those means are strictly limited in power, they must collectively have enough diversity, richness, stability and endurance to make possible and natural just that conception of a single unitary framework which we possess." [4] But the sole objects that can satisfy these demands are those "which are, or possess, material bodies." [5]

According to Strawson, a second reason for making material objects the most basic kind of particular is that they are the only means of avoiding solipsism. In a detailed and most ingenious argument Strawson considers the possibility of something else besides material objects as basic particulars, e.g., sounds.[6] He then shows us that if the category of material objects were eliminated there would be no way of distinguishing between oneself and one's own states, on the one hand, and something not oneself or one's own states on the other hand.[7] The distinction could not be made since all designata would, so to speak, be on the same ontological par. Both the chair in my dream and the chair I now observe would not be intelligibly differentiated; one could not be regarded as material and the other as nonmaterial. Similarly, since an important way in which I think of myself is that I have certain material characteristics in common with other material objects, the removal of "material" as an expression would mean the removal of perhaps the most cogent way of separating myself from what I experience.

Material objects, therefore, are primary in Strawson's ontology. However, we ought not to think that Strawson is here expounding the purely materialistic viewpoint sometimes attributed to him.[8] Strawson's key point is that particulars do not only consist of the class of material bodies but also of the class of entities that *possess* material bodies. And this modification, of course, makes a substantial difference in any strictly materialistic position. To maintain that some entities do possess material bodies is to present a position perfectly compatible with the most extreme forms of Platonism. In fact, Strawson goes on to contend that a pure individual consciousness ". . . might have a logically secondary existence."[9] That is to say, "each of us can quite intelligibly conceive of his or her individual survival of bodily death."[10] Strawson, however, acknowledges that there are distinct disadvantages to being disembodied: *1*] being invisible to everyone else, existence—or rather, logically secondary existence—would be rather lonely, and   *2*]   having no personal life of one's own, one would be required, like Sartre's characters in *No Exit,* to remain a kind of mute and invisible spectator of the passing scene. Disembodied survival, on such terms, Strawson agrees, "may well seem unattractive. No doubt it is for this reason that the orthodox have wisely insisted on the resurrection of the body."[11]

I shall not discuss the question of whether Strawson seriously wished to expound some notion of subsistence, or at least, some other form of existence than the one we normally might be taken to know. I am not at all sure that a notion of a logically secondary existence might not force us to deal with all the former issues that resulted in Meinong's theory of subsistent entities and Russell's refutation of them. In any event Strawson does little to explore all the delicate and subtle problems resulting from attributing to something a different form of existence. I will, therefore, not pursue this point further, but I would like to indicate why Strawson believes he must have two divisions of material objects—pure material objects and impure ones which he calls "persons."

The distinction between objects and persons is a familiar one

and most philosophers, both in the past and the present, have found
it to be inescapable. Other dualisms, e.g., particular and universal,
sense datum and reality, have been questioned and there are probably just as many monists as there are dualists in philosophical
circles. But it has been exceptionally difficult to reject the apparent
fact that there is an I which is quite distinct from what that I
experiences. We know that Hume, with his famous theory of a
bundle of perceptions, made a strong attempt to eliminate the I in
favor of some series of causally related perceptions. But his attempt,
as Hume himself recognized,[12] was simply not satisfactory.[13] Experiences by themselves are never sufficient to give the identity of their
owner. In more modern terms, given any set of observation sentences which exclude the I, there is no way of logically obtaining a
sentence which includes the I. Strawson simply affirms this difficulty
and posits persons as primitive entities such that we can only
maintain that they are those things to which both M-predicates,
predicates ascribing corporeal characteristics, and P-predicates,
predicates ascribing states of consciousness, are equally applicable.[14]
Thus persons exist because we all agree that there are P-predicates
and such predicates must be either directly or indirectly applicable
to something more than a pure material body. Strawson entertains
the possibility that P-predicates are perhaps merely more complex
M-predicates. The behaviorist might wish to make this claim. But
Strawson discounts such an objection by giving the usual criticisms
of attempts to explicate epistemic verbs, e.g., intend, expect, etc., by
purely physical and physiological expressions. The empirical data
attests to the fact that one can intend or expect or hope to do X even
if he never actually does it. Furthermore, psychologists also differentiate between correlations and definitions. A psychological predicate may be correlated with a series of behavioral and physicalistic
predicates. But it does not therefore follow that psychology is reducible to or definable in terms of physics and biology.

   The question arises as to how we distinguish two kinds of
predicates and how we know when to apply both to the same object.
Strawson explicitly rejects any answer that relies upon the use of
introspection and analogy. He does not want to give the Cartesian
reply that we somehow look into ourselves and by a process of doubt
and elimination recognize material and mental substances which
inhere in an ego. We do not introspect such information and there-

fore neither are we able by analogy to attribute consciousness to others on the basis of what we know about ourselves. Employing the criterion Wittgenstein stressed in the *Philosophical Investigations,* Strawson argues that a language is primarily public and that therefore the designative expressions included in it are, first and foremost, publicly applicable.[15] Only after further consideration do they become privately applicable by an individual to himself. Thus "consciousness," whatever this may be, is not something whose existence we intuit. On the contrary, it is because we first employ this expression as a way of accounting for behavior we observe in others that we then apply it to ourselves. As Strawson states: "There is no sense in the idea of ascribing states of consciousness to oneself, or at all, unless the ascriber already knows how to ascribe at least some states of consciousness to others."[16] Thus "consciousness" is an expression whose use we learn by the observation of things around us, and for this reason it is not intelligible to ask whether we can ever really know someone else's consciousness or whether he can ever really know ours. To know the consciousness of others is no more than to know that some entities are describable by terms that indicate phenomena explicable only by reference to some internal nonobservable state. If I say of someone that he is moody or pensive or thinking hard, then I am attributing to him certain behavioral characteristics which can be accounted for only by a reference to some nonobservable internal state. Then, by extension, I am able to apply the same predicate to myself as one who could or might act in ways that signify moodiness, etc., even though I might simply decide not to act in these ways. This double function of *P*-predicates by which we apply them to others on the basis of behavior and to ourselves regardless of behavior is, in the final analysis, essential for identifying those objects which we call "persons." A person is an object to which *P*-predicates apply. Without such predicates there would be no way of distinguishing persons from all those complex objects to which we normally attribute only *M*-predicates. In Strawson's words:

It is essential to the character of these predicates (*P*-predicates) that they have both first- and third-person ascriptive uses, that they are both self-ascribable otherwise than on the basis of observation of the behavior of the subject of them, and other-ascribable on the basis of behaviour criteria. To learn their use is to learn both aspects of their use. . . . If

there were no concepts answering to the characterization I have just given
. . . we should not have our concept of a person.[17]

Thus this is a world which requires description by both M and
P-predicates and we know when to apply P-predicates in the same
way that we know when to ascribe any predicate. We recognize that
certain objects are describable by ordinary predicates such as
"weighs ten stone" while others because of their behavior and activities take more complex predicates. And this very fact about the
nature of things leads us to regard entities with ordinary M-predi-
cates as pure material objects and entities with both M- and P-predi-
cates as impure material objects, namely, persons.

We now have the essential parts of Strawson's ontology—material objects and persons placed in a space-time framework. Once the
ontology has been presented, everything Strawson will go on to say
about language will follow. Proper names cannot be defined gram-
matically, but they can be defined by reference to material objects
—both pure and impure. Predicates refer to those properties or
universals that characterize these objects. Strawson makes a detailed analysis of the subject-predicate distinction with special attention given to the objections raised by Ramsey, Russell, and
Quine. I shall discuss this part of Strawson's ontology in another
chapter.[18] But here it suffices to point out that Strawson insists upon
the distinction between subject and predicate, and in his view the
sole way of making this distinction is by means of the material
object-universal criterion.

How shall we evaluate Strawson's ontology? I shall make two
kinds of criticism. First I shall make several internal criticisms—
namely, those that deal with the ontology *per se*. Secondly, I shall
show that even though Strawson's ontology is indeed a cogent one in
that it commits us to a very specific kind of reality, it does this at
the price of trivializing some important linguistic considerations and
of ignoring other possible linguistic structures which might yield
different ontological conclusions.

To begin with, one of the important reasons Strawson gives for
requiring material objects in his system of ontology is that they are
the only adequate candidates which can fulfill the needs of a space-
time framework. They alone, according to Strawson, have the important characteristics of being three dimensional, enduring in time,

stable, and open to observation. But, of course, Strawson is simply mistaken here. As other philosophers have pointed out, we can admit that the basic particulars required in an ontology must have the aforementioned characteristics without necessarily accepting the view that these particulars must be material objects. Kant, as well as many of the later idealists, were able to acknowledge particulars with all the characteristics we have just mentioned, but these did not entail objects which were material in the sense of being independent of mind. On the contrary, mind with its categorial structures imposed these characteristics on whatever was given to it.[19] Even such a staunch idealist as McTaggart who could maintain that nothing could possibly answer "to the definition of 'material thing,' "[20] had no difficulty accepting particulars which were, at least apparently, independent, enduring in time, etc.

In a similar vein it can be argued that even if it were true that an acceptance of material objects entails a denial of solipsism it does not at all follow that a denial of material objects entails an acceptance of solipsism. Both McTaggart and Bradley, for example, disclaimed any belief in material objects but they also rejected any accusation of solipsism. McTaggart's argument was quite plain, and follows some of Berkeley's own arguments.[21] I am only acquainted with what I perceive. But since it is quite obvious that at least some of my perceptions are not capable of being changed by me they must be under the control of someone else.[22] Ergo, there must be at least one other self to account for these unowned and uncontrolled perceptions.[23] I can, therefore, be an idealist, McTaggart argued, without being a solipsist. Bradley also denied the existence of material objects, but he also repudiated the solipsistic position. If solipsism means that only I and my perceptions are all that exist, Bradley maintained, then a denial of the existence of the ego would be sufficient to exclude solipsism. And, indeed, this is Bradley's view. If we rely on the word of professional psychologists we must reject the notion of an independent entity called an ego. There is only a mass of feelings, pleasures and pains distinguishable from other sorts of perceptual data. In Bradley's words, "The Ego that pretends to be anything either before or beyond its concrete psychical filling, is a gross fiction and mere monster, and for no purpose admissible."[24] Thus since we cannot countenance the existence of some particular thing called an ego, solipsism becomes untenable.

In brief, the view advanced by both McTaggart and Bradley was that material objects were not the sole means of denying solipsism. Just as the cinema presents us with seemingly real human beings, so also, it might be claimed, experience may present us with only seemingly material things. We might, more philosophically, define "material" in this context by referring to different kinds of perceptions and not by referring to something that is disengaged from perception. Thus we would say that we see a material body if we can touch it or if we see it much more vividly in comparison with dreams or memories or if it is one of those observed objects that we cannot very well wish away. In other words, the distinction between material and other kinds of entities is made by reference to different sorts of perceptual data rather than by an allusion to what is nonperceptual. Some things we see we cannot wish away, try as we may. But this doesn't mean that such things are in some way substances independent of perception. Fixations are psychological phenomena even though they cannot be made to disappear at will. Thus the whole notion of "material" as a way of escaping the solipsistic dilemma is gratuitous. If "material" is definable only in perceptual terms, then either *1*]   the reference to matter does not affect the issue of solipsism or else   *2*]   the issue must be settled by distinctions made in perceptual data themselves. It is [*2*]   as a possible alternative to the acceptance of material objects that Strawson has not adequately examined.

It is not my purpose to argue the effectiveness of McTaggart's or Bradley's arguments. The only point to be made is that Strawson has not dealt with all those views that reject both material objects and solipsism.

Furthermore Strawson's material objects are not to be regarded as the basic atomic particles in either the traditional atomist sense or in Wittgenstein's sense of atomic objects. Strawson takes a very common sense view relying upon the ordinary objects apparently implicit in our ordinary use of language.[25] Material objects are those obvious ones with which we are or can be acquainted—chairs, books, tables, John, etc. Thus proper names are easily explained. Unlike Wittgenstein who finally had to admit that his logically proper names named what was not capable of ever being found, Strawson gives his names very clear and obvious designata.[26] But in simplifying these matters Strawson has ignored all that led Wittgenstein and others to reject ordinary material objects as the basic particulars of an ontology.[27] Why can't we take "Socrates," for example, as a name designating a particular? Wittgenstein's answer was quite clear. If an expression refers to a basic particular then it is one that is used to define all other terms. We may be able to point to what the expression purports to denote. But we cannot define it. But "Socrates" is really an abbreviation for some series of definite descriptions which state certain essential characteristics about the thing being indicated. Thus Wittgenstein insisted that any name which can be reduced to some set of descriptions or predicates cannot have the status of being a basic particular. Wittgenstein is, of course, not presenting a new position here. The same dissatisfaction with taking ordinary objects as the designated values of the primitive terms of a formal system was expressed by the Greek atomists who regarded all experienced objects as being, in actuality, no more than clusters of atoms in motion. Similarly, Leibniz was not led to his theory of monads merely because he wished to posit some new ontological realm. Only by using the conception of some strange binding force, the monad, could Leibniz account for the existence of those very ordinary objects that appear before us. Thus both for the atomists and for Leibniz it became important to ask how ordinary objects are to be regarded. We do distinguish between living and nonliving things. But what does distinguish one from the other? We could differentiate between organic and complex wholes. But what makes an object organic? And if we label an entity as a complex then how do we relate the parts to one another? Are they necessary or contingent? Shall we describe them in terms of the theory of internal or external relations? None of these issues enters into Strawson's analysis. He has no problem accepting the material objects of naive realism. But at the same time he finds it unnecessary to analyze the kind of material bodies he finds acceptable. He tells us quite clearly that he will not accept pains and other emotions as particulars since they presuppose material bodies. We may well agree with this view. But what kind of material bodies does he mean? Atomic ones, complex ones, or contingent ones? On each determination of material bodies the metaphysical issues are profound and important. Yet this kind of analysis does not appear in Strawson's philosophy.[28]

Strawson might reply that he simply does not require involvement in such issues. Perhaps they belong to what he calls "revision-

ary" metaphysics, but he is not dealing with this kind of metaphysics. He might claim that material objects allude only to the fact that
there is something external and independent of sense perception.
But then the only way to avoid involvement in questions concerning
the nature of material objects would be to make such bodies noumena or things-in-themselves, or things-we-know-not-what. But the
traditional objections to these arguments are well known. Neither
noumena nor things-we-know-not-what can ever serve more than as
dei ex machina to escape an idealist position. Yet clearly for Strawson material objects play a much more vital role.

A final criticism of Strawson's ontology *per se* that I should like
to make concerns what I take to be a crucial principle basic to all of
Strawson's argument concerning persons. This is the principle that I
could not understand the ascription of consciousness to myself unless I could ascribe it to others. In fact, this view appears in diverse
forms throughout his book. It is used not only in reference to
consciousness but also in reference to identity. Thus to be able to
reidentify an object that I see now means that there must be objects
which can be reidentified even if I do not see them now.[29]

Now we might take Strawson to be defending this principle in
two possible ways. First of all, we might take it to be an inference
from a more general claim which asserts that given any concept or
linguistic expression its application to oneself or one's own perceptions presupposes its use with someone else or in relation to something exclusive of one's perceptions. This of course is a rather
enlarged version of Wittgenstein's belief that whoever tries to apply
expressions to his own private sensations must use expressions that
have functioned in public discourse.[30] Thus Strawson would apparently want to say that the very attempt to speak of our own
perceptions or sensations entails a commitment to a language or a
set of concepts that designate entities which are independent of our
perceptions. And specifically applying this reasoning to consciousness Strawson would maintain that attributing the concept or expression "consciousness" to oneself must presuppose attributing it
to others.

If we take this principle at its face value then it is most
assuredly false. I surely can apply to myself a description that is not
applicable to anyone else, e.g., having a certain set of fingerprints or
being the author of this book. To this extent, therefore, it is simply

false for anyone to assert that a language cannot be private. In fact, I can theoretically have a language that deals only with me so that any communication that goes on between myself and someone else always concerns some aspect of myself and nothing else. But of course we have oversimplified and we ought to see whether we can give the principle a more cogent justification. Perhaps the meaning intended is as follows: if I apply any concept or expression to myself then it must have originally functioned in some public discourse. But again this will not do. It may well be that every descriptive term must initially function in a public discourse, but that discourse may have been completely about me. Thus even though I might indeed be discussing consciousness with you it is always my consciousness we are discussing and never yours. Here then would be an instance where my expression or concept of consciousness does derive from a public discourse but it does not at all follow that I am therefore required to attribute a consciousness to you. This same objection, it would seem to me, would hold for all expressions. You and I might be speaking about pains and also about shapes but if the discourse is strictly about my shape and about my pain, the fact that we discuss these matters and use them entails nothing about whether you have either a pain or a shape. A counter argument might be relevant here, namely that two people cannot discuss pains or shapes unless each one knows what these concepts are. But knowledge here is rather amorphous. I may very well discuss your ailments without ever having had any of them. And even if I did have them it would not mean that anything in our discussion would necessarily lead you to believe that I have them. Thus again, even with the more closely formulated criterion presented, I need not become committed to the view that anyone else has a consciousness except myself.

We might try again by claiming that if I talk to you about my frustrations you must at least have something that enables you to understand what I am talking about even though you yourself may not be experiencing the frustrations. Thus our discourse may not commit me to attributing frustrations to you, but it certainly commits me to attributing to you a something that understands frustrations. Hence, if any psychological expressions enter a linguistic context, my applying them to myself and your understanding them means that you also must have a consciousness or at least some mental state which I am certain that I have. But here, of course, Wittgenstein's analysis is particularly apt.[31] In the particular situations in which we ask whether understanding occurs, reference to mental substances or processes do not arise. Or if they do arise they have no function. John understands if he goes on to do what we think he will do or if he uses a given expression in a certain way. To allude further to something hidden—his understanding—is to pose an unknowable that has no function in any communication.

We are trying to get hold of the mental process of understanding which seems to be hidden behind those coarser and therefore more readily visible accompaniments. But we do not succeed; or, rather, it does not get as far as a real attempt. For even supposing I had found something that happened in all those cases of understanding,—why should *it* be the understanding? And how can the process of understanding have been hidden, when I said "Now I understand" *because* I understood?! And if I say it is hidden—then how do I know what I have to look for? I am in a muddle.[32]

Thus any general rule concerning the public nature of language —or even of concepts—cannot be used to make a claim for the existence of another consciousness besides one's own. But perhaps with such a language the solipsistic dilemma is settled. Even if the existence of another consciousness has not been proved, certainly the existence of others besides myself must be presupposed. But some caution is advisable here. The existence of others need not mean the existence of other persons. I think Ayer is quite correct when he argues against Wittgenstein's view that someone alone on an island could construct his own language.[33] The solipsism issue would still not arise since at least some external objects would be presupposed.[34] But nothing need be said about another consciousness.

Strawson, however, does not rely solely on the language criterion to prove the existence of other persons. He presents another interesting and more cogent argument: Only if I understand what it means to say "the conscious states of others" can I understand what it means to speak of "my states of consciousness."[35] If I could not make this distinction then every conscious state would be indistinguishable—in terms of whether it is mine or not—from every other possible conscious state. The word "my" serves to point out that *these* conscious states belong together while others do not. In other words the use of "my" entails my knowing the meaning of what is not mine. Therefore it follows that I could not understand what it means to ascribe states of consciousness to myself unless I already understood as well how to ascribe it to others. But Strawson has confused meaning with existence. A very basic logical confusion often arises with existentially quantified sentences. To understand "Some trees are brown" it is probable that we must also understand "Some trees are not brown." But it would be false to claim that because "Some trees are brown" is true that, therefore, "Some trees are not brown" is also true. It may well be true that some trees are brown but it may also be true that all trees are brown or that there are no more trees than the ones I know and they are brown. Certainly I am not committing myself to the claim that some trees are also not brown. To syllogistic logicians, the obvious violation of a distribution rule would be immediately noted.

Now hasn't Strawson involved himself in a similar difficulty? He has claimed that to understand what it means to speak of my state of consciousness I must also understand what it means to speak of someone else's state. But it does not at all follow that someone else does indeed have a state of consciousness. I may speak of my state of consciousness with the fond hope that there are also other states of consciousness held by other persons. But just as from the fact that some trees are brown, it may follow that all of them are brown or that there are no other trees that are brown except the few that I have encountered, similarly, all states of consciousness may be mine or no other states of consciousness may exist except my own. I might be led to think of someone else who has states that belong to him rather than to me. But thinking in this way does not entail the existence of other states belonging to other persons. Strawson has simply tried to give us an ontological proof for the existence of the consciousness of other persons. But I think that the same arguments used against Anselm and Descartes can be used against Strawson.

The upshot then of this analysis is that Strawson's ontology has some key difficulties. Neither his notion of material objects nor his attempt to avoid the problems of other minds is acceptable. And if those arguments fail, then the cogency of his ontology fails as well.

I would now like to turn to my final criticism of Strawson, and, in an important sense, it is the only criticism relevant to the issues of this book. Strawson, along with many traditional philosophers, never questions that a language, in the final analysis, is the hand-maiden of that which it describes. In other words, Strawson quite clearly assumes that there is something extralinguistic and that language has the task of describing it adequately. Thus there are two subject matters that can be examined, related, and criticized.[36] They can influence each other but this does not mean that they cannot be investigated independently. Thus Strawson readily inves-tigates the nature of reality and explicitly tells us that his findings must be expressed in any language that purports to communicate information about the world, even though the particular linguistic expressions change. Subjects and predicates must be capable of being shown in a language since reality has within itself the dichot-omy of material objects and universals. The language may change —Anglo-Saxon may give way to Middle English—but no matter what changes occur linguistic expressions serve either as subjects or as predicates.

If we acquiesce in this assumption—that there is a language on the one hand and a reality on the other and that each one can be discussed independently of the other—then we are fully committed to the kind of game Strawson would have us play. We might disa-gree with his ontology, we might even quarrel with his insistence on the absoluteness of his arguments, but we would not question the legitimacy of his metaphysical inquiry. Once we permit a discussion of what is extralinguistic exclusive of its linguistic formulation, then metaphysical inquiry is as respectable as any other kind of inquiry. It may turn out to be too broad or perhaps not as pragmatically useful as other kinds of inquiries, but it cannot be relegated to the domain of pseudo studies.

However, an interesting parallel can be drawn between this dichotomy of language and reality and the Kantian dichotomy of phenomena and noumena. Kant's significant contribution was that he made a shambles of all traditional discussion of the so-called reality that exists independently of perception. In his famous paral-ogisms and antinomies he showed once and for all that all attempts to discuss reality without recognizing perception as the only avenue to reality are doomed to constant contradiction. Or, more explicitly, we cannot posit two domains—noumenal and phenomenal—and then claim that we are going to compare one with the other or that we are going to discuss noumena without mentioning phenomena. Nothing can be said about noumena unless it is filtered through an inquiry into phenomena. This analysis represents Kant's major contribution. But isn't Kant's doctrine also translatable into modern form and can it not be used as an argument against Strawson? Is it possible to speak of language on the one hand and reality on the other as if, somehow, they can be considered separately? Language is so all-pervasive that it is not possible to regard it as one object among many. There is certainly a type violation of the most elementary sort in any analysis that can speak of two domains—objects and linguistic signs—which can be examined in their own right. The very examination itself entails the use of linguistic signs and thus, like Kant's categories, the linguistic framework is not eliminable—at least not in any simple fashion.

If we grant the necessity that ties language to reality, then certain questions must be raised before anything can be said about what exists. How does language relate to what is extralinguistic? If a language form changes what would this mean for any ontological commitment? Would we still be committed to the category of material objects in a formal, more precise kind of language? These questions are not discussed by Strawson and yet the answers to them could very well decide whether Strawson's entire ontological system could survive.

We might now raise the question of how an ontology would be affected if a language were changed. And, of course, at its most elementary level we know that a more precise language does begin to eliminate ontological entities. In a language that has more explicitly formulated rules of confirmation and disconfirmation, the chances of wholesale introduction of abstract entities are minimized. And in a fairly precise language—such as the one using the signs of *Principia Mathematica* or of Quine's *ML* language—a commitment to abstract entities can be either totally eliminated or sharply restricted. We might ask whether there might still not be a need for the category of material objects in all languages. Carnap has argued that in a formal language sentences about material objects could be shown to be no more than sentences about linguistic rather than ontological categories, e.g., "There are material objects" becomes "There are thing-words conjoined to spatio-temporal expressions." [37] Goodman has argued that sense qualia are more adequate as the basic particulars of a formal system.[38] But more important is the contention that there are alternatives as to what is to be selected as a basic particular. Our selection is governed not by some a priori commitment to what exists, but rather by purely pragmatic consequences. The question we ask is not whether material objects are the genuinely real objects of existence, but whether by their use our inferences and predictions will be improved. We have a choice of ontologies depending upon what best satisfies our need to control what may occur.

Strawson's ontology, therefore, lacks one very significant ingredient: there is no discussion relating to the importance of a formal language for an ontology. The suspicion remains that Strawson has simply ignored the comparable lesson learned by Kant's successors —we must begin with phenomena in order to say anything—if anything can be said—about noumena. Similarly, we must begin with the language in order to say anything—if anything can be said —about what is extralinguistic. This is the translation of Kant's view into the idiom of contemporary philosophy.[39]

4

Quine on Ontological Commitment

IF NEITHER Popper nor Strawson offer convincing arguments for the admission of metaphysical inquiry, we ought not to suppose that, therefore, the palm automatically goes to the formalists, such as Quine and Carnap, who have in general been opposed to the inclusion of any ontological elements into logic and scientific theory. Both Quine and Carnap have acknowledged that even the most formal languages have elements which do seem to support the initiation of ontological inquiry. But they have claimed that these aspects can be shown to be trivial or they can be rigidly controlled. In this chapter I shall examine how Quine deals with ontological issues. In the two succeeding chapters I shall turn to the views expressed by Carnap.

Traditionally, the argument for the existence of properties, classes, and individuals—the three most significant categories of ontology—arose out of what seemed to be a clear picture of what a language is. There are two sorts of designative terms *1*] those which referred to individuals and *2*] those which referred to or designated or otherwise indicated a property or a class.[1] Certain modifications of this doctrine could be made without any serious loss of significance. For example, it could be readily granted that a formal language might more easily reveal which are the genuine subjects and which are not. Thus it may very well be that a natural language has too many subjects and perhaps too many predicates. In "A cat is on the mat" we ought not to take "a cat" as the subject but rather as part of the predicate and, to this extent, we reduce the number of subjects in a natural language. Similarly, in a highly formalized language observation predicates might be reduced to a minimum. But regardless of these possible modifications and emendations two facts remain certain. First, languages, especially those that have scientific applicability must contain categories of predicate and individual terms. Secondly, in order to label an expression either as a predicate or an individual term, i.e., a name, we apparently must know that the former indicates a property or a class while the latter indicates an individual. This is precisely how Carnap distinguishes predicates from individual terms.[2]

The difficulty, however, is that a crucial difference does exist between terms that designate objects and terms that designate classes (or properties). When we deal with objects we are aware that peculiarities attach to what is to count as an object and also to how objects are to be identified. That is to say, we are often undecided whether to include atoms, or electrons, or libidoes as objects to which terms can refer. And even when we do decide, questions still persist on how to identify such objects. John Dewey long ago showed us the problems that ensue when we employ pointing or some such indicative gesture in order to direct attention to objects. "It is impossible merely to point *at* something. For anything or everything in the line of vision or gesture may be equally pointed at." [3] But these problems about object-referring terms do not have the same philosophic import as those that accrue to terms which designate classes. We might decide that atoms and libidoes ought not to be treated as objects and thus refuse to countenance any names that purport to refer to them as objects. But no one really denies that individuals of some sort are the referents of individual terms. In the case of class terms, however, confusion exists as to what such terms designate in *any* context. It is not merely a matter of saying that we will accept these classes as referents, but not those. We are undecided about the whole issue of what it means to say that a class term designates something extralinguistic. Whatever classes are, they are not mere aggregates or clusters of objects since, first of all, classes in mathematics are frequently empty, and, secondly, even in ordinary contexts we distinguish between the collective and the distributive use of class terms. We are aware that characteristics can be attributed to classes that cannot be attributed to the members of such classes and vice-versa. Thus we are required, for logical purposes, to make sure that we know whether a given class term is an abbreviation for some set of terms referring to individuals or whether it has a reference of its own. It is this need for classes to be distinct from their members that has fascinated philosophers, logicians, and mathematicians. For what can this distinction consist in? One obvious answer is that if class terms do not designate objects in any sense understandable to us, then they must designate something uniquely different which we can reasonably call a "concept" or, simply, an abstract entity. And once this kind of answer is proposed we begin to see why all the arguments arise on how predicate terms refer and whether we are to be allowed to say that the referents of such terms exist in the same way as the referents of individual terms.[4] In an important sense one might argue that it is the attempt to understand how it is possible for a language to have predicates that leads to some of the most crucial issues in philosophy. For if certain expressions do not refer to objects in any usual way, then we must ask what makes them referring expressions and to what it is that they refer.

W. V. O. Quine is a philosopher who has sought to resist or at least to minimize the possible metaphysical inferences that might be drawn from questions on how terms refer to entities.[5] He is also an important logician who has brought to bear on philosophical issues some of the most precise tools of contemporary logic. We turn now to his analysis of terms and their referents.

Quine assumes that any investigation of philosophical matters must be in terms of a formal language in which the logical framework is clearly defined. In other words, linguistic designators are expressions that can serve as substituends for variables and constants in well-formed formulae that also employ quantification operators. This at least eliminates some of the problems previously mentioned since terms that might appear as subjects in ordinary language could become predicates in a formal language. Thus whereas in ordinary or natural language we might have to determine

how "a man" in "a man is walking down the street" can be a
subject, in a formal language this question would not appear. The
sentence would become "there is something which is a man and is
walking down the street." "A man" would become a substituend for
the predicate term.[6] But presumably the reduction could never be
complete. Some expressions would still serve as replacements for the
individual variable.

Given the structure of a formal language, Quine proposes to
give us a criterion by which we can identify precisely what entities
we are committed to in using the language. The criterion is fairly
simple. Quine argues that if we wish to know   *a*) whether a term
designates,[7] and   *b*) what sort of thing is being designated, then
we ought to ask whether existential quantification can be employed
with the term. Since existential generalization can operate with
variables of diverse sorts, e.g. predicate, individual and propositional, we can determine what is being designated by observing
whether the quantification that has occurred operates over individual, predicate, or some other variable. If, for example, we are given
a sentence "Socrates is wise" then we ask whether we can apply
quantification to it to obtain "$(\exists x)$ (x is wise)." And since it is
obvious that we can make this inference—if Socrates is wise then
something is surely wise—then "Socrates" is a designative term and,
at least in this instance, refers to a given individual since it is being
used as a substituend for the individual variable. On the other hand,
"Socrates" is not designative in " 'Socrates' has eight letters" since
the application of existential quantification to this sentence gives us
" 'Something' contains six letters" or "$(\exists x)$('x' contains six
letters)."[8] In the first instance the sentence is simply false if by
"contains six letters" we mean "exactly six letters." And in the
second instance the quantifier is irrelevant while " 'x' contains six
letters" is false. In a similar way Quine points out that by the
application of existential generalization we can now specifically
show that certain kinds of expressions that look like designators in
an oblique sentence are not really such at all. They are what Quine
calls "referentially opaque." He gives the example, "Philip is unaware that Tully denounced Catiline" which is to be taken as true
since, even though Philip knew that Cicero had denounced Catiline,
he did not know that Tully and Cicero were the same person. From
this sentence we cannot derive "There is someone (or something)

such that Philip is unaware that he (or it) denounced Catiline" for who can this "he (or it)" be that denounced Catiline without Philip being aware of it? Clearly, it must be the man, Cicero, and of this Philip is aware. Thus "Tully" is here referentially opaque and ought not to be construed as a designative term.

Quine, therefore, proposes a formal criterion for the discovery of the various kinds of referential terms. If existential quantification is applicable to the substituend of an individual variable then we have a name designating an individual; otherwise no designator is present. This criterion would seem at least to be able to take care of most of the difficulties concerning names without referents. Since expressions referring to fictitious entities cannot, according to Quine, be quantified, they should not be called names or, at least, they should not be confused with designators. We may, if we wish, replace them by descriptions which might more easily show their nonreferential use, or we may make a more liberal use of quotation marks and thereby indicate that we are dealing with the expressions for names rather than names themselves. But in any event we apparently have a means for indicating whether or not a given expression is to be taken as a designator, and, at the same time, a way of discovering what kind of ontology is presupposed in a given language.

How satisfactory is Quine's criterion? First of all, it ought to be noted that existential quantification is not a priori restricted to some given sort of entity. The criterion asserts that if such quantification holds with a given expression, then we can be assured that the expression designates, but it does not tell us that quantification can occur only with the individual variable. Thus even though Quine's examples are primarily with names that would designate individuals, we ought not to infer that, therefore, the use of existential quantification with other sorts of expressions will also only commit us to a domain of individuals. In fact, as we shall shortly see, Quine also permits quantification over predicates and then we seem to be allowing abstract entities as designata for expressions. More significantly even in the case of quantification with names, we ought not to think that if a name turns out to be a designator, then the designatum is automatically assumed to be an individual. This would be true only if names, as substituends of the individual variable, could only designate individuals. But we know that if we follow Frege,

Carnap, and Church, names have both a reference and a sense, an extension and an intension, and only if we assume that we are dealing with expressions as referents or extensions can we take it for granted that applying quantification to names means that the name refers solely to a concrete individual. Thus we should not mistakenly think that Quine has given us a tool that will lead to a strict nominalism. Quantification over individual variables can operate in intensional and modal logics as well as the logic of sense and synonymy proposed by Carnap,[9] and in each of these areas designata would probably not be concrete entities.

Secondly, we ought to recognize that Quine is here advancing a syntactical criterion. He wants to show how to discern designators by using the purely logical techniques that are to be found in a formal system. But in this connection a serious objection must be raised. For consider how Quine uses existential quantification. If we can apply it to an expression, then the expression is a designator; otherwise it is not. But now how are we to determine when quantification is applicable? Quine tells us that we can apply quantification over individuals to "Socrates is wise" but not "Pegasus is a winged horse." But why not? Taken simply as words, neither "Pegasus" nor "Socrates" tells us that one is really a term that is not referentially opaque while the other is. Nothing in either of these words points to a specific permissible quantification. What then does determine the decision? The answer quite clearly seems to be that we know beforehand that "Socrates" is a referring expression while "Pegasus" is not and that, therefore, the former and not the latter can take existential quantification. In brief, if we already know that a given expression is a genuine designator of a certain sort, then of course existential quantification is applicable to it. But it is not the mere fact of existential quantification that shows us that an expression is referential. This kind of reasoning would be the epitome of circularity.

Quine is apparently aware of these dangers for he acknowledges that the inference between a sentence with a singular term and existential generalization is not of the same logical sort as one in which only variables are involved. That is, I need only the syntactic rules of a system to tell me that from Fy I can move to $(\exists x)Fx$. Since "y" is a variable, applying existential generalization to it does not mean that we are inferring the existence of some specific entity.

But to judge whether a word, *W,* is a designator, Quine tells us, we must decide "whether existential generalization with respect to *W* is accepted as a valid form of inference." [10] But what are we to understand by *accepted* here? How are we to discover whether a certain sort of inference is or is not acceptable? The reply again would seem to be that we look to usage—either in natural or scientific contexts. But once we do this, we are, in effect, rejecting existential generalization as a genuine criterion for determining whether an expression is a designator of some sort. Even if existential generalization were found to be applicable always in relation to Socrates but not Pegasus, we would still want to know why this applicability occurs. History is filled with names to which existential generalization has been wrongly applied. Even in science names have been used, e.g. phlogiston, to which existence has been wrongly attributed. Furthermore, even though event$_1$ is always found with event$_2$, that is, existential generalization is always permitted with such-and-such a term, we still have no reason to believe that one is a means of showing that the other is a designator. Thus we might explain this constant conjunction not by taking existential quantification as a way of showing that the term with which it always occurs is a name, but rather by pointing out that it follows trivially from the acceptance of the name as having a referent. If we know that a term denotes something, then a basic part of its meaning is that there must be something for the term to denote. But first we would have to show that the term does denote.

What Quine does not tell us, therefore, is why one word permits existential generalization to be applied to it and another does not. Indeed, if I did not know beforehand that "a" was a particle playing a strictly syntactic role, or that "blue," "the," etc., had certain specific functions, there would be no reason for me to allow existential generalization with one expression but not with another. In short, prior to the use of quantification I must already be able to say, "This word refers to an object; that word does not. This word refers to a property; that word does not." Just as no purely syntactic or grammatical rule can be used to pick out subjects and predicates, so also no logical devices or techniques can be employed to make such discriminations.

Thus the statement "To be is to be the value of a variable" does not in and of itself give us a way of favoring one system of ontology as against some other. Nothing ontological is being ruled out. Even the most theological sort of proposition such as "God is wise" can fit the criterion since one who accepts "God" as a denoting term can obviously move to "Something is wise."

However, we would be doing Quine an extreme injustice if we did not analyze his criterion in conjunction with his other recommendations. Quine is aware that the test for quantification is primarily a way of discovering what ontology a theory might possess rather than what ontologies are allowable. In his own words, "to determine what entities a given theory presupposes is one thing, and to determine what entities a theory should be allowed to presuppose . . . is another." [11] The question, then, that must be raised concerns the status of the values that are to be regarded as values of variables. In other words, we must ask whether there is some way of showing that some terms are allowable while others are not.

Quine presents a theory which he believes has decided implications about what ontologies can be selected. He tells us that we must begin by thinking of designative terms not as we do in ordinary language but rather as we do when we are dealing with a strictly formal language. Under such circumstances we cannot simply introduce terms and call them either subjects or predicates. On the contrary they are introduced as members of a hierarchy of words which operates in accordance with rules similar to those in Russell's theory of types. Like prisoners they are given a certain number and placed at a given level; and only under certain very special conditions are they allowed to move either up or down in the hierarchy. Thus it is no longer possible to say "$(\exists x)$ (Pebbles have x)" but rather "$(\exists x_2^1)$ (Pebbles have x_2^1)," where the numbers serve to determine what level of expressions can properly be used as substituends for the variable. Quine does not completely subscribe to Russell's theory of types (either its simple or its ramified form) and he agrees with some of the criticism levelled against it. But he does not reject the view that some set of levels is required in order for the expressions to be introduced into a formal system. Thus, along with Russell, he acknowledges that there will be zero level expressions designating objects, then first level expressions designating properties or classes of objects, then second level expressions designating properties or classes of properties or classes of objects, etc.[12] Then once we accept this hierarchical ordering of terms Quine can claim that given this structure we need not worry about a commitment to abstract entities. Only quantification of the individual variable is permitted and the substituends for this variable are zero level terms —terms that are taken to refer directly to things or even to such basic empirical data as Carnap's "Elementary Experiences." [13] All other terms are part of the predicate. Thus we need not concern ourselves with whether we are committing ourselves to a belief in abstract entities since the expressions that might refer to such entities do not undergo quantification. A predicate expression is never in the position of designating some entity and is never identified exclusive of its being an aspect of an individual. In other words we need not think that by employing the sentence "Unpunctuality is reprehensible" we are referring to some strange abstract object. Quine would undoubtedly agree with Ryle that a sentence of this sort is better expressed as "Whoever is unpunctual deserves that other people should reprove him for being unpunctual." [14] Similarly, I cannot simply say "God is wise" and then use existential quantification with it unless I can place "God" on the appropriate linguistic level. Is it a zero level term and, does it, therefore, refer to a concrete object, or is it a predicator? Any term would have to be questioned in this way, and the result would be that all abstract terms, when they are translated into a more formal system, turn out to be predications of particular objects. They never stand alone. Our ontology, therefore, is still basically nominalistic since only of individual entities can we say that they are.

In terms of Quine's own view of what ontology is—namely the commitment to the entities designated by the quantified variable— this structure does indeed give us a safe ontology. But we ought to recognize that it does so only in so far as we agree that *1*] ontology depends upon what we decide to quantify and *2*] predicates are not allowed to be quantified. This latter condition is extremely important to Quine since permission to quantify over predicates means that predicates "acquire the status of a variable taking classes as values." [15] Under such circumstances we are suddenly forced to accept two kinds of entities *a*) individuals and *b*) abstract entities. Properties, like individuals, can then be considered as existent and as themselves having properties. But before we examine this crucial question of quantification over classes and properties let us consider the entire question concerning quantification. Is Quine right when he argues that our ontology arises only in terms of the values we attribute to our variables? Given a formal system, are we committed to an ontology only when we acknowledge which variables are to be bound by the existential quantifier? [16]

To begin with, we ought to note that quantifiers are not always taken to be essential in a formal system. Quine himself explicitly tells us that quantifiers are needed solely because we must deal with the infinite domains required in both mathematics and science.[17] The universal quantifier is necessary, for example, since it cannot be eliminated in favor of some finite number of conjuncts. But what this implies is that if we could do without infinite domains, then quantification would not be needed. We must ask, however, whether this would mean that a commitment to an ontology would also disappear. If we had a language without quantifiers would we, on Quine's analysis, have resolved all issues concerning the ontology of that language? I doubt this. Without quantification we might not be required to speak of infinite classes and this part of an ontology might be rejectible. But surely we would still want to know what expressions are to be taken as genuinely designative. We would still want to know how predicate terms are differentiated from names and whether a reference to properties and/or classes is required. In other words even with a language lacking quantifiers the question of ontology would arise.

Furthermore, Quine's criterion of quantification apparently depends upon a prior acceptance of some form of the theory of types, according to which only zero level terms are to be permitted to refer to entities and all predicate terms are definable by reference to these basic entities. But once he makes the claim that we must employ the theory of types, his whole criterion of how to uncover the ontology of a formal system becomes quite gratuitous. Why use the criterion of existential quantification to determine whether a given expression is a designator when we already know beforehand that in so far as the quantifier is used with names, the name must be a zero level term? The quantification test is simply redundant since the commitment to types tells us that any term to which quantification is applicable is either a designator of a concrete entity or reducible to such designators. Why look for the ontology of a given system when, even before the language is constructed, we have already been told what the ontology is to be? It is as if we were told to select any fruit, so long as it was a peach. It may well be that nominalism is the most preferable of ontologies but we ought not to come by it merely by postulation.[18] If we do this, there is simply no need for our elaborate techniques of existential quantification and variable substitution in order to find out what our ontological commitments are.

Finally, even if Quine were correct—that the substitutions for our variables show us what our ontological commitments are—it might still be wrong to claim that the language has no other ontological commitments until the variables are replaced by substituends. Quine tells us that the predicate letters, F and G, for example, can be taken as mere schemata which are replaceable by predicates when and if quantification is introduced. But so long as such introduction does not occur "there is nothing in the logic of truth functions of quantification to cause us to view statements or predicates as names of entities, or to cause us to view these schematic letters as variables taking any such entities as values. It is only the bound variable that demands values." [19] But it is interesting that Quine does not question the categorization of terms into predicates and individual variables. He accepts this dichotomy apparently without examining the possibility that this very necessity has an ontological import as significant as the values of the variable. It may be true that until we quantify no assertion is being made about what is extralinguistic. But that we take some letters of the alphabet to stand as dummies or schematic letters for predicates means that *if* the language becomes applicable—if quantification were to occur— then predicates would be required as appropriate substituends of the given letters of the alphabet. This kind of commitment is as *cogent* as the ontology which does occur with quantification. There seems to be little difference in terms of the *cogency* of the ontology between the two statements: *1*] If something exists then it must have such-and-such a property; *2*] something does exist and must have such-and-such a property. [*2*], of course, has the status of a categorical rather than a hypothetical imperative. But both have the same Kantian urgency. In Kantian terminology, it may well be that the categories are present only when I am experiencing. But this does not at all detract from the apodictic status of the categories. Similarly, I can, a lá Quine, talk without quantifiers in "an attitude of frivolity." [20] But this does not detract from the ontological commitment when the language is being used seriously.

There is, then, a sense in which ontology arises in a formal
system even before the system obtains an interpretation of its variables. The ontology becomes, so to speak, built into the system as
soon as we decide to differentiate one type of variable from another
for that already tells us what restrictions must be placed on all
possible interpretations. We know beforehand that whatever subject
matter is selected to be formalized, it will be categorized in certain
very specific ways. As we have seen, Quine does endeavor to counter
the seriousness of this sort of ontology by taking predicate letters to
be what he calls "schematic predicate letters," [21] i.e., letters which
serve merely as dummies for predicates that cannot be bound. Such
schematic letters do not name anything at all and, presumably, do
not commit us to anything at all. But the important point still
remains that even though the schematic letter does not name anything, it does serve to restrict interpretations to those which distinguish predicates from subjects, or adjectives from nouns. This primary commitment does not change. Quine's position in these matters can be compared to that of the artist who insists quite rightly
that his sketch of a painting must not be taken for the painting
itself. But even though the sketch does not show us as much as the
painting, it does show us the basic framework of the painting.
Similarly, a schematic predicate letter does not show us what would
be shown by predicates in a full blown interpretation, but it does
show us something, namely, that all forthcoming interpretations will
follow certain basic guidelines. This, I think, is a serious ontological
commitment. We are being told that in spite of the constant stress on
the conventionality in the construction of a formal language, some
patterns must be present if the language is to be constructed.

Now we ought to turn to Quine's second concern—how to avoid
the apparent Platonism that arises if quantification is permitted
over predicates. Quine is aware that even though we might restrict
quantification over predicates, we cannot eliminate it. He points to
many instances in which quantification over predicates can be
equated with quantification over individual variables. Thus the following predicate quantified sentences:

1] $(a)((x)(x\epsilon a) \supset (\exists x)(x\epsilon a))$ [22]
2] $(\exists a)((\exists x)(x\epsilon a) \cdot \sim(x)(x\epsilon a))$

can be equated with:

3] $(x)Fx \supset (\exists x)Fx$
4] $(\exists x)Fx \cdot \sim(x)Fx.$

If we were able to show that all quantified predicate sentences can be reduced to individual quantified ones our ontology would be fairly safe. All predicates supposedly designating entities called classes would be shown to be doing no more than indicating a characteristic of an individual. We could then, as Quine puts it, "regard our theory of classes merely as a picturesquely transcribed account of quantification theory; classes would not need to be acknowledged as seriously presupposed entities." [23] But, unfortunately, the postulation of classes is required for explicating certain mathematical problems as well as certain problems in philosophy and logic. For example, where we have a schema with the initial class quantifiers mixed, i.e., both universal and existential ones are used, no elimination of classes is possible. The following sentence is not expressible in terms of individual quantificational schemata:

5] $(x)(y)(\exists a)(\beta)(x \epsilon a \cdot \supset \cdot y \epsilon a : \supset : y \epsilon \beta \cdot \supset \cdot x \epsilon \beta).$[24]

Furthermore, certain expressions can be defined only by the use of predicate quantification. Thus x is defined as an ancestor of y if x belongs to *every* class which contains y and all parents of its own members.[25] Similarly, we can give a full definition of identity only by using class quantification. Whereas in the ordinary quantification theory, we must either add special rules for identity or disallow identity sentences altogether, by using class quantification we can define the identity of x and y as "$(F)(Fx \equiv Fy)$" or, using Quine's notations, "$(a)(x \epsilon a \cdot \equiv \cdot y \epsilon a)$." [26]

Quine, therefore, acknowledges that quantification over predicates is required if we are to deal adequately with important philosophical and logical notions. Nor could we justifiably prohibit such quantification without making some arbitrary *ad hoc* stipulation which prejudges the entire issue of whether or not there are classes. There is no way of logically moving from a calculus which starts with quantification over individuals to an inference that denies quantification over predicates. In fact, Church has shown us that only a minor change in the formation rules of his system makes possible inferences in which there is quantification over both individual and predicate variables.[27]

For Quine, then, at least some classes must be admitted as values for variables and, to this extent, he cannot support a nominalistic position.[28] It is a bad situation for Quine since the admission of classes apparently means that 1] abstract entities cannot be eliminated from formal systems and 2] quantification suddenly looms as a possibility over all descriptive terms in a system. If it is possible to quantify over predicates, then why not over sentences and even over expressions which are elements of a modal system? If we quantify over sentences, then we must take truth-values—both the True and the False—or propositions as values for the variable. And once this occurs it is difficult to see why Frege's Platonism was wrong.[29] Under these circumstances we ought to have either Trues and Falses populating the world or propositions. On either alternative we are faced with a Platonism that is as severe as it is undeniable. Similarly, if we can quantify in a modal language, then we must not only be willing to posit those intensional kinds of entities espoused by Carnap but also a whole domain of possible existences in which we can refer to predicates that have never been attached and perhaps never will be attached to individuals. In fact, recent studies on the analysis of the existential operator have already accepted the view that existence is to be attributed both to properties which are attached to individuals and those which may be *attachable*. Thus Nicholas Rescher has stated that "To qualify a property for . . . existence it surely suffices that it be *capable* of exemplification, and is not necessary that it be *actually* exemplified. . . . It appears, therefore, that the modal operator of logical possibility, $\lozenge$, is required adequately to formalize the concept of general existence."[30] Thus, curiously enough, Santayana's much maligned unenacted essences seem to reappear as ontological commitments in strictly formal systems.[31]

Quine is aware of this sudden resurgence of Platonistic and realistic positions in regard to the use of quantification and he attempts an interesting move to stem this torrent of abstract entities. He begins by reiterating his insistence that no expression can serve as a substituend for a variable unless it is a member of the kind of language hierarchy that Quine has himself constructed. As we have already noted, Quine's own theory of types is analogous to Russell's in that at least some stratification of some formulae must occur. Thus in the system of the *New Foundations* Quine requires that only ϕ must be stratified in the formula "$(\exists x)(y)((y\epsilon x \equiv \underline{\phi})$" and must not contain "$x$" since only in this way can Russell's paradox be avoided. With these restrictions we cannot infer "$(\exists x)((x\epsilon x) \equiv \sim(x\epsilon x)$" from "$(\exists x)(y)((y\epsilon x) \equiv \sim(y\epsilon y))$" since both "$\sim(y\epsilon y)$" and "$\sim(x\epsilon x)$" are unstratified and therefore a violation of the con-

ditions that have been set down.[32] This is Quine's simplest theory
of types. But with the need to recognize quantification over predicates Quine extends his theory so that all formulae become stratified.
In a later paper Quine posits language, L_o, which has as its first level
concrete objects. He then proceeds to construct classes "such that
membership in any of them is equivalent to some condition expressible in L_o."[33] L_o with its new extension becomes the new language, L_1. We then go on "to reify all further classes of such kind
that membership in any one of them is equivalent to some condition
expressible in L_1."[34] We continue with this procedure "concomi-
tantly admitting increasingly wide ranges of classes and relations
as values of our variables."[35] Once we have this scheme, it is Quine's
belief, we have done a great deal to ameliorate the threat of a sudden push into an extreme form of Platonism. Supposedly, we can at
least claim that if a predicate is quantified then it can only be a
predicate that is attached to a quantified individual variable; or, if
it is not attached to an individual variable, then it is attached to
another predicate variable which has been introduced by way of
combination with an individual variable. In other words we could
have a function such as "$(\exists F_2)(y_1)(F_2 y_1 \equiv G_2 y_1)$" and we could
also have the function $(\exists F_2)(F_3 F_2)$, where F_2 is understood to be
attachable to an individual variable. But we could not have a function "$(\exists F_n)(F_3 F_n)$" where F_n had not been introduced either directly
or indirectly by attachment to an individual variable. In this way
not only are the standard paradoxes avoided [36] but, at least according to Quine, the Platonism usually attendant in positing properties
and classes can be substantially reduced if not totally eliminated.
For, says Quine, the classes that arise in this kind of generation of
classes are "conceptual in nature and created by man."[37] Abstract
classes and properties are still acknowledged as existing because
they are taken as values for the variable of predicate quantification.
But the universe of classes which is being accepted here is really
posited by the user of the language; it is not found or discovered
by him. By a process of what Quine calls metaphorically "progressive creation"[38] the constructor of this language, or the "conceptualist" as Quine calls him, assumes "a universe of classes which
. . . is meagerer than the platonist's, and the principle by which he
limits it rests on a metaphor that has some intuitive worth."[39]

Two observations are relevant here. First of all, Quine never

clearly resolves an odd discrepancy. He tells us the new classes
conceptualized in accordance with "progressive creation" are such
that membership in them is equivalent to some condition expressible
in L_o. This way of speaking of the relation of L_o to all constructed
classes apparently means that given any class of classes we must
always be able to define such a class as a class of classes having
concrete objects. In other words we would be required to show that
all constructed classes really mean classes of classes of concrete
objects. In this way we never lose sight of the need to speak of
concrete objects whenever we are speaking of classes. But on this
analysis we presumably could not have any classes if there were no
concrete objects. Since the hierarchy of entities uses concrete objects
as its base, we must therefore acknowledge that classes which cannot
be shown to lead down to concrete objects simply do not exist. Now
this position would be perfectly compatible with a nominalistic
viewpoint and it would make quite clear what Quine means when
he claims that class membership must be expressible in the language
of L_o. But this position is not compatible with another position that
Quine takes, namely, that classes are not to be taken as mere
abbreviations for some series of individuals. The universals or
classes resulting from binding predicates, Quine declares, "are ir-
reducibly presupposed. The universals posited by binding the predicate letters have never been explained away in terms of any mere
convention of notational abbreviation." [40] In other words, we are
not to think of classes as somehow so dependent upon their members
that they disappear when the members disappear. But Quine cannot
have it both ways. He cannot give us a conventionalist approach to
classes and at the same time insist that classes are, in some way,
independent of their members. Yet Quine is apparently involved in
this anomaly when he proposes to give us a conceptualist analysis
of classes. There is an old adage that whatever man has made he
can most assuredly destroy, and from this it follows that if there is
something that man cannot destroy, then he has not made it.
Analogously, Quine may be right when he assures us that all classes
are "conceptualized" by man's "creativity." But he cannot then
also go on, as he does, to tell us that these classes are, therefore,
still to be regarded as independent of any members and hence not
expressible in terms of the concrete objects of L_o.

In this same connection we ought not to be misled by Quine's metaphor of "progressive creation" into thinking that classes rest upon individuals in the same way that the top layers of dominoes rest on the bottom layers. Nor ought we to think classes are in some way created conventionally by the mere bunching together of individuals—a view Quine himself is quick to reject. Classes are not mere aggregates of individuals; nor are they exhausted by any finite number of individuals. Quine's classes may be "conceptualized"— whatever that may mean—but it does not at all follow that their ontological status has been at all changed from what it was traditionally. If Quine is ready to posit classes not reducible to mere aggregates and he is also ready to admit quantification which takes such classes as values, then it would seem to me that no Platonist would quibble over use of the term "conceptualism." To the Platonist classes are not mere conventionalist stipulations eliminable by human means and this view seems to be attributable to Quine.

Furthermore even if we grant Quine his conceptualism and agree that classes could at one and the same time be, in some sense, both conventional as well as necessary, this would not preclude the possibility of constructing Platonistic sentences. According to a proof of Cantor's, once we permit quantification over predicates, there must be more classes than linguistic expressions that refer to them.[41] Since, according to Cantor, the subclass of a class A cannot be correlated with the members of A, and since a subclass of the class of predicates is the class of linguistic expressions, it follows that there will be more classes of predicates than linguistic expressions designating them. The ontological significance of this proof would be that not all classes are to be thought of as constructible; at least some of them must be present before any formulation about them has occurred. In other words, we cannot eliminate from a formal language containing quantification over predicates the statement, "There is a class which no linguistic expression designates" —a statement totally unpalatable to any nominalist.

In the same connection we ought to be able to say in any formal language that a certain property might *possibly* be attributable to an object even though it is not so attributable.[42] Thus we would want to be able to say a given property is possibly attributable to an object even if there is no such property. But this kind of information could only be formulated as "$(\exists F)\sim(\exists x)(Fx)$," i.e., there is a property that nothing has, or "$(\exists F)\sim(\exists x)(Fx) \cdot$

$\Diamond (\exists x) Fx,$" i.e., there is a property that nothing has but it is possible that something might have it. But if these statements can be formulated and taken to be true then we have before us some strong Platonistic commitments.

Quine's use of a formal system, therefore, has neither expelled nor minimized the puzzling issues of ontology. The use of formalistic techniques has perhaps made more explicit precisely where in a language we are to look for ontological commitments. Thus we must ask about the syntactical and quantificational commitments of a language if we are to uncover where the crucial ontology is to be found. To this extent Quine's analyses are significant and fruitful. But the traditional questions about abstract entities and unmembered classes still remain. Perhaps now we must think of the problem in other terms. Can predicates be quantified? Can we account for a sentence asserting a claim that there is something which we intuitively believe does not exist? The enigmas still remain. It still makes sense to ask whether some one is a nominalist, a realist, or perhaps even a conceptualist.

5

Carnap on Ontological Commitment

THING AND PROPERTY

ACCORDING TO Carnap, questions of ontology arise because we have not adequately analyzed three kinds of sentences: *1*] object sentences—those whose truth value is determined by some extralinguistic referent, *2*] syntactic sentences—those whose truth value is determined solely by the rules and conventions of the language, and *3*] pseudo-object sentences—those which look like object but are really syntactic sentences.[1] In his view, ontological issues can arise among any of these three categories. In the case of [*1*] we might come to believe something extralinguistic can completely confirm or verify an object sentence or that we can intuitively recognize its truth-value. Such sentences can then be taken to be necessarily true and used to support the view that synthetic a priori statements exist and, in some way, reflect or express some necessary structure of existence or experience. But Carnap rejects such an ontology for quite the same reasons it has been rejected traditionally. Intuition is not acceptable and total verification of an empirical sentence is no longer a defensible hypothesis. Thus even though the relation between evidential sentences and those for which they are evidence still requires explication Carnap is convinced that any ontological issue arising here is due to a fundamental misconception about the nature of verification. Undoubtedly, sooner or later, we must deal with unquestionable premises and, therefore, some empirical sentences must be taken as unfalsifiable. But Carnap denies that the need for unquestionable premises entails a commitment to sentences that can *never* be falsified. First of all, every sentence, except logical ones, can be placed in a context in which falsification can occur. Even "I see red" can be false if my memory is defective and I am employing the wrong word. Secondly, the basic sentences of any given language system are stipulated as true. They are not true in and of themselves. In brief, they are true as part of the internal structure of a language system and not because they are a priori unfalsifiable. In other words if we accept certain basic phenomenalistic or physicalistic sentences as ones which are not inferred, it is because these sentences with their references to phenomena or physical things do serve to support fruitful inferences.[2] What this would mean, then, is that it is by a *decision* that we make all sentences dependent either directly or indirectly on phenomenalistic or physicalistic sentences. And we would do this not because sense data and/or physical objects are to be regarded as the most fundamental aspects of knowledge, but rather because by accepting such basic designata we can make various fruitful inferences in scientific inquiry. If we "count on" using sentences with a given type of predicate as evidence, then our chances of success in some given venture are better than if we decide on some other criterion. No ontological commitment is involved in that we are not necessarily committing ourselves to sense data or to things. Rather we regard them as a scientist might if he said "I don't know at all whether there are such things as atoms, but if I assume there are such entities then I can make some significant predictions."[3] This is how Carnap deals with the notion of ontological commitment when it relates to so-called indubitable empirical sentences. We are free to make any commitment we want about what is extralinguistic just so long as we   *1*] do not assert that there are some entities which must be extralinguistic for all contexts and   *2*] are guided by the fruitfulness of our predictions. In point of fact, Carnap rejects a phenomenalistic language in favor of a physicalistic one. But his choice is not determined by some criterion of external reality which finally convinces him that physical things are somehow more substantial than sense phenomena, but by the fact that having predicates apply to things rather than to phenomena is more scientifically fruitful and avoids any involvement in extraneous psychological problems.[4]

Ontology can also arise when we are unaware that the truth or falsity of a statement can sometimes result from the kind of logical form it possesses. Thus Carnap is convinced that many traditional problems of philosophy arose because philosophers persisted in thinking that truth and falsity could only be decided by reference to some external state of affairs. The thesis then became plausible that those statements which are necessarily true must reflect something necessary in what is extralinguistic. With this view it became possible to attribute essences, forms, and other necessary characteristics to reality. But for Carnap the initial assertion that necessarily true sentences must reflect necessarily true states-of-affairs—is simply wrong. We can account for logical truth in a much simpler way by scrutinizing the linguistic forms implicit in ordinary language and explicit in formal ones. I shall not here deal with the detailed analysis Carnap has made in order to show how a language has both syntactical and semantical rules, and how the former contains rules determining why sentences of the form "p and not p," "if p implies q then it is false that p can be true and q false" are always true. It is sufficient for our purposes here merely to make the following observations. Carnap accepts Wittgenstein's analysis of logical truth as truth derivative solely from the rules or structure of the language. In any language there are a finite number of possible noncontradictory sets of sentences describing the world. Since each set or *state description*, as Wittgenstein calls it, is noncontradictory, then in every set either the statement p holds or $\sim p$, but not both. Thus "$p \vee \sim p$" holds for all possible sets of descriptions. And since "$p \vee \sim p$" holds also for that set of descriptions, whatever it may be, which is true of the actual world and not merely possibly true, "$p \vee \sim p$" is true. Thus logical truth turns out to be no more than a derivation from the fact that a language contains true and false sentences.

Carnap insists on the purely linguistic status inherent not only in logical rules but in those other curious sentences which have necessity attributed to them but are not logically true. Thus it is sometimes maintained that the sentences "all bachelors are unmarried" or "if A is larger than B then B is shorter than A" are necessarily true, but their truth cannot be attributed to their logical forms. Carnap's answer is that in ordinary language any expression can be stipulatively tied to any other expression. Thus nothing in a round piece of copper called a penny also makes it a form of currency. We have, for pragmatic reasons, decided to label something a penny which we have also arbitrarily defined as a form of currency. These are standard procedures we all follow. Similarly, even in a scientific language we might arbitrarily decide to make one word a synonym for another. Such arbitrary moves are by no means unusual. Nor should they be, since linguistic sounds are not divinely controlled nor guarded by police. Carnap himself speaks of the need to recognize that certain meaning postulates might take into account the fact that in a given inquiry it may be useful for the inquirers to have certain words always appear together.[5] Thus in some contexts it is taken as true by stipulation that "metals" is to be defined by means of "conductors." We attribute truth to the stipulation not because we think no other truth value can be assigned, but because it gives us a way of deriving certain other kinds of sentences. A sentence labelled true is analogous to an object with given mathematical dimensions. All our logical and mathematical techniques can begin to be employed. For Carnap necessity of this sort is not philosophically interesting except insofar as the conventional status of the necessity involved might be ignored and the necessity taken to entail some ontological factor. Thus Carnap is not concerned with explicating those true sentences which, on analysis, can be shown to be true merely by human decision, even though many of these sentences can have the bad pragmatic consequence of being taken to be absolutely unchangeable. Significant sentences for Carnap are those which have traditionally been taken to have more than mere conventional necessity and which have, therefore, led to the positing of various ontological entities. Very few philosophers have been able effectively to deny the necessity that characterizes logical truths. Logic, like mathematics, has been a primary subject matter refractory to purely conventionalist analysis. But by purporting to show that logical truths are no more than the rules derivative from the syntax of language Carnap claims to have explained away the demand for any serious ontological commitment.

Of course, Carnap's analysis of logical truths does not make him a conventionalist like Waismann [6] and others who not only speak of different kinds of logic but who also allude to contexts in which the rules of logic are not and ought not to be applicable, e.g., where the context is vague or ambiguous. Carnap agrees that logical systems are man-made games. But games are difficult to construct. Some games are not successful; the rules can lead to contradictions; they might not be adequate for expressing important scientific or mathematical statements. Thus we cannot simply set up some stipulations and then build a whole logical system. We do indeed create the games but it does not, therefore, follow that one game is as good as another. And, so far as those contexts are concerned in which no rules of any known logic are applicable, then we must either *1*] wait until someone does show us what the rules are or *2*] simply recognize we are dealing with aesthetic or ethical subject matters where logic, like mathematics, does not count.

The third and last category in which ontological commitment of a serious sort can result arises from those sentences which are true but apparently not because of any conventionalist ruling nor because they belong to the canon of logically true, or *L*-true, sentences. These are the pseudo-object sentences which often require elaborate work and analysis before their real status can be determined. Now we are aware that words play different roles in our language; we recognize that groups of words are usually taken to be subjects and other groups are taken to be predicates. We then assume that because these groups display, respectively, a given function, that is, they are names or predicators, therefore they must designate something in common. What is held in common is then given a particular name, say "thing" or "property" or "class" and before long we find ourselves talking about things in general as well as properties and classes unrelated to any individuals. But what we have done here is to hypostatize a grammatical category. It is as if we asked for a listing of the designata of some series of three letter words, and having obtained such a list, we proceeded to claim that the very fact that they are listed together must mean they have something in common which we call "treb." It then becomes plausible to make the statement "These designata have treb or 'trebhood' in common." But, of course, in actuality the only element these designata have in common is the fact that they are designated by three letter words. Everything else is pure hypostatization. Thus instead of saying "These designata have trebhood in common" we ought to say "These are the designata of three-lettered words." The word "treb," potentially a troublesome word from a philosophical point of view, is shown to be no more than an inappropriate way of referring to a particular linguistic category. In a similar way, Carnap argues that we have introduced words such as "thing," "property" and "class" as if they referred to specific furniture in the world in the same way as other referential expressions, and once we have done this it becomes quite easy to become involved in all the traditional discourse about things and properties and/or classes. We begin to ask what things are and what properties are and how they are related to one another. We begin to wonder whether things are no more than clusters of properties or whether there is some underlying substance to which properties are in some metaphysically peculiar way attached. But all these issues arise because of a mistaken analysis of language. We mistake a purely linguistic category for an ontological one. We believe that by calling an object a thing we are attributing something to it in the same way that we do when we call something a chair; or that by saying an object has a property we are simply adding or indicating another characteristic of the object. It would be as if some one for some reason had forgotten that he wore myopic contact lens and began to think that the world had certainly changed in dimension from a past time. Or it would be as if some one forgot about the die producing the castings and then began to wonder how such entities ever could have been produced by nature. Both Carnap and Wittgenstein note that we are frequently oblivious of the dielike effect language has on what we experience and as a result we confuse characteristics attributed to phenomena by the language with characteristics of the phenomena themselves. As Carnap puts it, if we say "the moon is a thing" we can easily be led to think that "being a thing" has the same predicate status as "being a man" or "being large." But what does it mean to attribute "being a thing" to something? In an important sense such attribution is tautological since it attributes to something that very something which it must have in order to be something. Or, more precisely, if in "Fx" the predicate "F" is taken to be "is a thing" and if only things can be substituends for the individual variable then we are simply saying "The thing which is a value for

'x' is a thing"—an obvious circularity. But more important is the fact, as Carnap points out,[7] that "being a thing" is one of those curious predicates—if we take it to be a predicate—which apparently applies to everything. But can there be such predicates without involving an immediate type error? Predicates can belong to level 1, or level 2 but are predicates applicable to all levels? This kind of application is not permitted either by Russell's theory of types or by Quine's modifications of it. But we can speak of the linguistic categories that all levels contain just as we can simply refer to the fact that all type levels have order functions, at least in the ramified theory of types. Thus when we do encounter predicates which seem to be applicable to everything, we must try to show either 1] such predicates are not really universally applicable or 2] they are predicates designating something syntactical rather than some property of individuals. According to Carnap, since "being a thing" is taken to be universally applicable, this predicate must really be a way of expressing something about the language rather than about what is extralinguistic. He maintains that "being a thing" refers to the syntactic status of a word and has no designative function as other predicates usually do. "The moon is a thing" ought really to be understood as " 'Moon' is a thing-word" where it becomes quite clear that we are mentioning but not using "moon." [8] Similarly, if we say "Five is not a thing but a number," unless we are careful, we might suddenly think that we are committed to a whole realm of abstract numbers. But this kind of statement is made metaphysically neutral when we change it into its proper form " 'Five' is not a thing-word but a number-word." [9]

Carnap's analysis now becomes applicable to all statements that have been traditionally part of the metaphysical canon. "A property is not a thing" becomes "An adjective (property-word) is not a thing-word." "A property cannot possess another property" becomes "There is no predicate of a level higher than the first." [10] "The world is the totality of facts, not of things" becomes "Science is a system of sentences, not of names." "God created the natural numbers (integers); fractions and real numbers, on the other hand, are the work of man," becomes "The natural-number symbols are primitive symbols; the fractional expressions and the real-number expressions are introduced by definition." [11] Even the thorny metaphysical issues dealing with internal and external relations can be shown to be no more than confusions concerning the relation of syntax to semantics. Carnap gives the following example which shows how the problems of internal and external relations might be removed if we become more aware of the distinctions to be made between designator and designata. A metaphysical theory could very easily use the sentence: "A property of an object c is called an *essential* (or: *internal*) property of c, if it is inconceivable that c should not possess it (or: if c necessarily possesses it); otherwise it is an *inessential* (or: *external*) property. (Correspondingly for a relation)." [12] Carnap then applies these definitions of internal and external relations to a concrete case. If on the basis of the definitions we thought of c as the father of Charles, then being related to Charles would be an essential property of c since it would be inconceivable that the father of Charles should not be related to Charles. On the other hand, being a landowner is not an essential property of the father of Charles since fatherhood does not entail being a landowner. However, being a landowner is an essential property of the owner of this piece of land since some one could not be the owner of this piece of land and not be a landowner. Charles' father is the owner of this piece of land. Therefore, on the basis of the definitions given it is both an essential and yet not an essential property of Charles' father to be a landowner. Thus, Carnap asserts, traditional terminology and analysis of internal and external relations leads to contradiction. But now let us change the above definition of essential and inessential properties into their corresponding syntactical forms: "F is called an analytic (or, if desired: essential or internal) predicate in relation to an object-designation c if Fc is analytic. Otherwise F is synthetic (or, if desired: inessential or external). (Correspondingly for a two- or more-termed predicate.)" [13] This definition does not lead to any of the traditional contradictions because, as Carnap puts it, " 'landowner' is an analytic predicate in relation to the object designation 'the owner of this piece of land,' but it is not an analytic predicate in relation to the object-designation 'the father of Charles.' Hence the fault of (the previous definition) lies in the fact that it is referred to the one *object* instead of the *object-designations,* which may be *different* even when the object is the same." [14] In other words, Carnap is telling us that if we distinguish predicate expressions from their designata then what would seem to be a contradiction in the external world turns out to be no more than a confusion about our use of descriptions. Two descriptions may apply to the same entity but it does not follow that what is analytic to one description will also be analytic to the other. X may be a general in the army and from this description it would follow that X is a general; X may also be a president of the United States but even though this description entails that X is a president it does not entail that X is a general. The puzzling feature that makes X appear to be both essentially and inessentially a general arises only if we overlook how descriptive words entail, either through synonymy or stipulation, other descriptions.[15]

Thus Carnap concludes that most metaphysical issues arise out of a confused view of how a language operates. This does not mean that all metaphysical issues are eliminated. Such questions as to whether there are certain kinds of abstract beings or even whether there is some omnipotent being are to be resolved just as other empirical questions are resolved. We look for the evidence that confirms or disconfirms them. But for the most part metaphysical problems do not permit the application of empirical techniques and these are the problems Carnap takes to originate in a linguistic confusion. If the traditional metaphysical sentences were changed into the syntactical forms they really ought to have, then "the situation in these commonly disputed cases becomes so unambiguous, and moreover so simple that no one can any longer be tempted to raise philosophical problems about it." [16]

Carnap's analysis has been very influential and, indeed, it would seem to be an enormous step to show that a proper understanding of sentences that have been traditionally labelled metaphysical occurs only when we show that such sentences are really derived from an improper use of syntax. However, two major arguments can be made against Carnap's general thesis concerning the elimination of words or sentences with ontological connotations. First, I shall argue that "thing" and "property" are not eliminable in favor of linguistic expressions and, therefore, any metaphysical problems accruing to the use of such expressions still remain. Secondly, I shall maintain that Carnap's own formalism requires him to introduce terminology which decidedly is not ontologically neutral and until he can resolve some of the perplexities resulting from this terminology, he has not formulated a language free of serious ontological commitment.

Carnap himself does not long forego the convenience of being able to speak of properties and things where these entities are not reducible to property and thing words. Thus even though he decries the hypostatizations of properties, Carnap does make it clear in later works that he will speak of properties as entities "in that sense in which (property) is used by scientists in statements of the following form: 'These two bodies have the same chemical properties, but there are certain physical properties in which they differ.' " [17] It is obvious that "property" as it is used here is not translatable into "property-word." It should also be noted that scientists speak of properties in various ways—as visual or perceptual phenomena, as abstract mathematical constructs,[18] and as "imageless dynamical patterns." [19] Such uses are clearly not ontologically neutral.[20] But the more serious objection to Carnap's view is that he places too much importance on the need to discern the dichotomy of word and object. Carnap is undoubtedly right when he warns us not to confuse designators with designata. But once we do this, it does not at all follow that we have in some way eliminated the intrusion of any metaphysical speculations. We should, of course, always be careful not to confuse the expression "class of men" with what it denotes. But we would not thereby automatically recognize the absurdity of admitting the existence of both men and classes of men. The commitment to troublesome ontological entities still persists. Perhaps some philosopher long ago mistook a purely syntactic or other nonreferential expression to be a semantic or referential expression, but the fact that philosophers today no longer make this mistake does not constitute a case against ontological commitments. Thus even though Carnap is correct when he shows us how we might confuse the analyticity that is attributable only to sentences with a necessity that is said to permeate nature, this kind of insight does not offer a telling blow against the metaphysician who permits himself to be enlightened and then points to those sentences in mathematics, logic, as well as epistemology that even the most toughminded empiricist has been unable to explain away. Classes, possibilities, meanings, propositions, and intentions are still required which cannot be defined behaviorally or by reference to concrete objects.

In a similar vein Carnap tells us that we should not be thinking of things, but of thing-words. And there is something plausible about his suggestion. We have seen how it would be a mistake to take "trebhood" as anything more than a reference to a linguistic category. Any ontological connotation is strictly accidental. And looking at the matter in a more familiar context, we would never say "there are nouns" and regard the statement to be on the same existential level as "there are trees" or "there are raindrops." We might not know why we would not group all these sentences together, but surely we would guess that at least one of these sentences deals only with grammar or with the language itself. In the same way we might come to believe that thing-words, like nouns, are apparently free of any implicit ontological issues. But are they? Are nouns, for that matter, definable only by reference to some conventions adopted in a given language? It is no easy matter to identify names and nouns without presupposing some major commitment to a domain of things and properties. The same dilemma arises in relation to thing and property words. How would we go about showing that a given linguistic mark or set of marks really is to be taken as a thing word rather than a property word? Carnap, like Quine, assumes that there is no difficulty in understanding what thing and property words are. But by labeling a word a thing word we are not noting some structural feature of the word. We are not, for example, saying that the word has five letters or that it is spelled in German. Nor are we referring to the positional status of a word. Thing and property words can occur anywhere in a sentence. Nor can we counter this by claiming that positional status is to be taken in terms of a formal language in which property words can occur in one and only one place and analogously for thing words. The kind of position a particular expression will take in a formal system is not a defining characteristic for its being a property or a thing word. The position is a result of a prior knowledge concerning what kind of word we have. Once we know that a term is of such and such a kind, i.e., that it is a property word, then we can use it as a substituend for the predicate variable. But the formula itself, the schema in the formal language, tells us nothing about whether a term is or is not an appropriate substituend.[21]

Applying our comments now specifically to Carnap's argument, we can claim that Carnap's notion of thing and property words involves a crucial circularity. Carnap tells us that when we say "The moon is a thing" we are really saying " 'Moon' is a thing word." But if thing-words themselves become intelligible only in so far as we

can say that such words refer to things, then we are in the peculiar
position of saying " 'Moon' is a thing-word. Thing-words refer to
things. Ergo, 'Moon' refers to a thing." This may be a better
formulation than "The moon is a thing," but nothing has been done
to take "things" out of the object language category and give the
expression a purely syntactic status. We have not yet been shown
that we cannot speak of things and properties in general, just as we
can speak of metallic objects and metals in general. Nothing has
been done to prove that those sentences which are normally taken to
be of a metaphysical sort are not discussible in the ways in which we
discuss other subject matters. In other areas of inquiry I can speak
of both the word as well as the designatum. In "This metal is a
conductor" I can, as a linguist, speak of the individual words and
perhaps even of the syntax of the sentence. But if I were a physicist
I would also be able to speak of metals and conductors themselves,
e.g., whether all metals are conductors. Similarly, it would seem to
me that if property words refer to properties and thing-words refer
to things, then I ought to be able to speak of the words as well as the
referents. And, therefore, questions about how things are related to
properties have not been ruled out by Carnap's analysis.

Carnap, however, is undoubtedly thinking of "thing" and
"property" in terms of Wittgenstein's analysis in which "things"
and (presumably "properties") cannot be included in a formal
language. Wittgenstein distinguishes between two uses of "thing,"
one proper and one improper. He says: ". . . the variable name 'x'
is the proper sign for the pseudo-concept *object*. Wherever the word
'object' ('thing,' etc.) is correctly used, it is expressed in conceptual
notation by a variable name. For example, in the proposition, 'There
are two objects which . . . ,' it is expressed by '($\exists x,y$) . . .' Wherever it is used in a different way, that is as a proper concept-word,
nonsensical pseudo-propositions are the result. So one cannot say,
for example, 'There are objects,' as one might say, 'There are
books.' " [22]

On this analysis "thing" operates strictly as a means of indicating the variable "x." Nothing ontological need be implied since the
variable itself has no referential status. But now let us consider the
question of variables. The textbooks tell us that variables are *place-
markers* or *place-holders*.[23] They operate as a means of indicating
that any one of a set of expressions can be allowably permitted in

the space where the variable appears. Thus in the propositional function *"Fx"* the *"x"* operates as a device for telling us that any one of a series of terms can replace *"x."* But we ought not to think that everything can be used to replace *"x."* Normally *"x"* in a propositional function is considered an *individual* variable by which we mean that if any expression replaces *"x"* it must be one that refers to an individual, or a thing. We do not intend to have the variable take properties or propositions or other propositional functions as values. But once we introduce these restrictions on *"x,"* we have made a rather interesting move. The neutrality of the variable has ceased to exist, for we are distinguishing at least two sets of expressions—those that are allowed for *"x"* and those that are not. *"x"* then serves to mark off those special expressions that are thing rather than property or propositional referring terms. In other words, our variable *"x"* has meaning in the usual formal calculus only in so far as it takes certain kinds of terms as substituends. But how do we identify these terms? They are those that refer to individuals as against those others which might replace the predicate variable and refer to properties. Both Wittgenstein and Carnap may have believed that they had eliminated a reference to things by the use of a variable. But once different kinds of variables are recognized, then it would seem that in order to show what this distinction is, the notion of things and properties must be introduced into the language. For this reason, those who speak of purely formal calculi and admit individual and predicate variables are unwittingly making the calculus quite impure. For the commitment to individual as distinct from predicate variables already presumes that all forthcoming interpretations will have a reference to things and properties. But if this is really what is implicit in such formal systems then why not clarify what we mean by variables—namely, those symbols which take terms which refer to things and those which take terms which refer to properties. This at least eliminates the curious self-deception sometimes practiced by those who believe that the use of symbolization in some way eliminates the old basic categories of thing and property.

Thus Carnap's reliance on variables to take care of the troublesome "thing" words is not sufficient. Still another attempt Carnap makes to give things and properties an appropriate ontological neutrality, deserves some attention. Carnap sometimes seems to be arguing that "thing" and "property" are to be understood contextually.[24] Just as Wittgenstein pointed out that it does not make sense to look for the common way in which "game" is used in discourse,[25] so also it does not make sense to look for some common use of "thing" and "property." These expressions play roles in specific discourses but this does not mean that they play a specific role in every discourse. Thus we cannot generalize about things and properties for not only does this show that we are not aware of how terms can change in meaning from inquiry to inquiry, but all such generalizations would be a violation of the theory of types. Things in general, like classes and properties in general, have no meaning unless we can specify the type of thing with which we are dealing. In this way Carnap reasons that in spite of our acceptance of thing and property, the important questions of metaphysical inquiry can still not be raised. We cannot speak about all properties and all things, and yet this is precisely what the metaphysician must be able to do if his inquiry is to be initiated.

Carnap's argument, however, is a two-edged one, for there are important objections to the theory of types and to all theories that do not permit generalizations about all subject matters. First of all, mathematicians who wish to be able to derive theorems that hold for *all* functions of numbers, and not just for some select level of numbers would object. The theory of types makes this kind of generalization impossible. Secondly, the mathematician insists that his principle of induction is applicable to all numbers. But the principle would have to be abandoned, if we could not legitimately state that a property of one number held for all numbers.[26]

We have also to deal with philosophical objections. It is worth noting that even in the theory of types, general statements can be made for the system as a whole. We can, for example, say attributing a property to a thing will mean the same at any given level as on any other level. In other words we might maintain that "$(\exists x)Fx$" must be replaced by a schema with the appropriate subscripts and superscripts. But no one denies that however x is numbered, it will be related to the numbered F that follows it as individual to property. We do not say that as we move to different levels we will suddenly be speaking of properties elsewhere in space and time which no longer "belong" to the x to which they are attached in the theory of types itself. Or to put the matter a little more clearly: No one questions that at every level of type theory we will find that expressions substitutable for the predicate variable are not substitutable for the individual variable. The property attribution remains invariant. It is as if we had an infinite regress of statements such as "*a* is the father of *b* who is the father of *c* who is the father of *d*, etc.*"* Any particular segment of this regress would give us different fathers and sons but the relation of fatherhood would be constant. In an analogous way the same dichotomy of individual and predicate variables persist at all levels of type theory. In fact, even where we quantify over predicates and obtain "$(^2F_1)(^1F_2{}^2F_1)$" it is with the explicit understanding that we are speaking of the *n*-order properties of some individual. In brief, the thing-property relationship is not disturbed by the introduction of a theory of types.

Carnap, then, has not been able to show that the kind of terminology that lends itself to ontological speculation is due to a confusion of syntax with semantics. It may well be such confusion does occur and some problems arising in this way may be simply pseudo-problems. But the major issues involving ontology have not been touched. Carnap has taught us to use more precise arguments; he has made us aware of how designators are embedded in a linguistic structure. Even a metaphysician can admire this. But nothing of consequence in ontology has been compromised.

6

Carnap on Ontological Commitment

INTENSIONS

IN THIS CHAPTER I should like to examine one explicit feature of Carnap's formalism—one that has been hailed as evidence of Carnap's final—albeit begrudging—rejection of his early nominalistic position. I am here referring to Carnap's attempt to deal with the various name antinomies and oblique paradoxes by employing a Fregean analysis.[1] We ought to recall that Frege's famous inquiry into logical equivalence led to his positing two ways of understanding an expression—through its nominatum or its sense.[2] The nominatum of an expression is the object or the state-of-affairs to which the expression refers; the sense consists of what we usually mean when we speak of the meaning of an expression. With this distinction, which is found in very similar form in J. S. Mill,[3] Frege was able to show why two such expressions as "evening star" and "morning star" are not mutually substitutable in all contexts even though both refer to the same object. The nominata are the same, but the senses are different. Presumably only identical expressions have the same nominata and senses; different words have at least different senses.

Frege applies the same reasoning to sentences for these also are referential in relating to an event or a state-of-affairs; and they also have meanings. But states-of-affairs can be spoken of as the true state-of-affairs referred to by a true sentence or the false state-of-affairs referred to by a false sentence. Thus truth and falsehood become for Frege the nominata of sentences, while propositions—which are generally taken as the meanings of sentences—are the sense.[4] Frege hypostatized "true" and "false" so that true sentences could be said to refer to the True while false ones referred to the False.[5] For this reason Church takes Frege to be a "thoroughgoing Platonic realist." [6]

Carnap accepts Frege's fundamental distinctions but he substitutes "extension" for "nominatum" and "intension" for "sense." Along with these substitutions he makes several important emendations. First of all, he claims he is avoiding any ontologizing of true and false by taking them to be semantical rather than extralinguistic entities. For Carnap the true and the false, although they are the extensions of sentences, are no more than expressions serving to distinguish one set of sentences from another. All true sentences except those L-true sentences which are true by virtue of the semantic rules are characterized by the fact that they apply, or that they are affirmed or asserted of some extralinguistic phenomenon. "True" simply marks such sentences. A similar analysis can be made for "false." All that is required for extensions is some characteristic that all F-true (or F-false), factually true (or factually false), sentences share in common. In fact, Carnap maintains that the extensions of sentences need not be truth-values at all. "There is nothing in the situation that compels us to take . . . truth and falsity as the extensions of sentences." [7] Anything will do so long as "the extension of all true sentences be the same entity and that the extension of all false sentences be the same entity but something different from the first." [8] Thus we find something that distinguishes the class of sentences called "true" from those called "false" and whatever this something is it serves as the extension of all true sentences. But now two questions arise. First of all, we ought to ask whether Carnap has really avoided Frege's Platonistic commitment to the true and the false.[9] Carnap seeks to show that all designators have, at least outside of oblique and modal contexts, both an extension and an intension. Even expressions that do not designate have a null entity as extension. Predicates have classes as extensions, properties as intensions. And thus for Carnap classes are extralinguistic entities. But now, analogously, one ought to argue that if sentences also have extensions, then whatever these may be, they also must be extralinguistic objective entities. "True" and "false" therefore, are objective entities in the same way that classes and null entities are objective. Carnap, of course, seeks to avoid any serious ontological commitment by taking classes, propositions, and any other apparently abstract entities as mere convenient devices devoid of traditional connotations. But only insofar as he can define such references strictly by the semantic rules of the language can he minimize their import. But this he cannot do. The intensions and extensions of L-true sentences are correctly defined in terms of the rules of language itself. But something more and different is required when we are dealing with F-true sentences.

A second question that must be raised concerns Carnap's view that there can be an alternative to truth-values as extensions. Carnap does consider the possibility recommended by C. I. Lewis that what all true sentences have in common is reference to "the actual world." [10] But even though this is a possible position, he rejects it since it would then mean that truth involves "in some sense the whole universe." [11] In other words we would be reverting to the traditional idealist position that all other sentences can be derived from a given true sentence which would make all knowledge analytic. It is at this point that Carnap suggests that if we are not happy with Lewis' proposal or with the use of truth-values as extensions, then we can have L-true propositions as the extensions of true sentences and L-false propositions as the extensions of false sentences. But this is indeed odd for how is all this to be squared with Carnap's strong insistence that all L-true and L-false sentences "are established on the basis of the semantical rules of the system S alone, without any reference to (extralinguistic) facts." [12] What now happens to the whole view that makes extensions the connectors to what is extralinguistic? If extensions can be logically true or logically false propositions, then we must look elsewhere for the transition from linguistic signs to that which is signified. We suddenly find ourselves taking extensions in the way we take intensions—as part of the meaning of expressions rather than their referents. If extensions can be L-true or L-false propositions, then we ought to be able to determine the extensions of propositions merely by investigating the rules and syntax of the language. Carnap tries to deny this. But even he acknowledges that a language can do without extensions but it cannot do without intensions.[13]

Carnap's first emendation of Frege is then not so clearly successful as he would wish it. A second emendation that Carnap proceeds to make in Frege's analysis concerns Frege's procedure in dealing with expressions in oblique contexts. Frege had tried to account for the loss of the usual nominatum when an expression is introduced into an oblique context. He does this by the expedient measure of ruling that in oblique contexts, that is, contexts in which "necessarily" or the words "X believes that . . ." precede the particular expression, the normal sense is to be taken as the nominatum. Thus in "Necessarily, the morning star is the evening star" the nominata of "morning star" and "evening star" are their normal senses or intensions and it is for this reason that we can accept this sentence as false even though "Necessarily the evening star is the evening star" is true.[14] "Morning star" does not have the same sense as "evening star." But Carnap points out that Frege's analysis on this issue leads to an infinite regress.[15] Frege takes all names to have senses and nominata. Thus if we have a name in an oblique context then it must have both a sense and nominatum. Since the nominatum in an oblique context is the usual sense then it must have another sense to correspond to the nominatum. But this new sense must also become a nominatum if it is to be used in oblique contexts and this, in turn, must lead to the positing of another sense, *ad infinitum*. Church sought to meet this objection by modifying Frege's view so that the same expression can be inserted in oblique contexts; but it would be used only with "some notational device," [16] e.g. quotation marks, that would distinguish oblique from normal usage. But Carnap argues that this would also lead to a certain kind of infinite regress.[17] We would need, for example, one notational device for "Scott is human" in "it is possible that Scott is human"; another notational device in "John believes that it is possible that Scott is human"; and still another in "it is not necessary that John believes that it is possible that Scott is human," etc. Carnap's point here is apparently well taken and his own use of intensions avoids this kind of infinite regress. In oblique contexts of any sort it is necessary to deal only with the intension of a term. There is no need to become involved in an infinite regress of names. Extensions require that there be intensions, but intensions do not require extensions. In this way no continual duplication of entities is needed.

This of course is an extremely brief review of Carnap's analysis and to do real justice to Carnap's position, I ought to show exactly how his notion of extensions and intensions becomes applicable to the various designators to be found in a language. But my aim here is not so much to examine whether intensions and extensions can be consistently applied to all designators. (I suspect that there are things to be said against Carnap's insistence that individual expressions have individual concepts as their intensions. How enlightening is it to say that individual expressions have individual concepts as their meanings!) But I do wish to examine the whole notion of "intension" as such since it is the introduction of this term that has led to the charge of Platonism against Carnap. Now what are intensions? Carnap explicitly tells us that when we speak of either extensions or intensions "we have to look for entities, or at least phrases apparently referring to entities." [18] This would seem to mean that whatever Carnap has called an intension is or can be exhibited as an entity. Under such circumstances propositions, individual concepts, and properties, along with classes and individuals would become concrete entities. Intensions would, so to speak, be on the same ontological par as extensions. In fact, Carnap apparently insists on this point by refusing to countenance propositions as mental entities or thoughts of some kind. Carnap explicitly describes propositions as nonlinguistic, nonmental, objective entities which "may or may not be exemplified in nature." [19] Propositions here almost have the same status as Santayana's essences. They may be enacted, but they are still to be taken as objective in some sense even if they do not happen to be exemplified in nature. In one fell swoop Carnap has not only adopted the moderate ontology that claims there are abstract entities which exist in the same sense as chairs, tables, etc. He has also taken the view that there are abstract entities even if they are never exemplified in the ways that chairs and tables are. This is a highly significant ontological commitment.

Carnap, however, is aware that his thesis concerning the existence of intensions is controversial and can lead to the charge—made by Quine and others [20]—that all the traditional ontological concepts have been reintroduced. He proceeds, therefore, to try to ameliorate

—if not completely obliterate [21]—the full-blown ontology that has suddenly reappeared. First of all, he claims that it is simply undeniable that sentences and words do have meanings which are distinct from their denotations. We can know the meaning of a sentence without looking to anything in experience. The meaning component of linguistic expressions, therefore, must simply be recognized as such and Carnap tells us that he "[will] not try to define this component." [22] But in spite of these remarks Carnap does present us with a way of explicating intensions that gives them a certain sort of relevance and plausibility. The explication appears in the example he uses in order to show how the intension of a term can be discovered empirically.[23] He asks how we would proceed to find out what the intension of the German expression "pferd" might be. The extension of the expression is quite easy to discover. We simply point to some selected group of entities. But now what would be required in order to uncover the intension? Carnap tells us that to obtain the intension we must "take into account not only the actual cases, but also possible cases." [24] And here, apparently, is revealed the true nature of intensions. They permit us to infer a set of possible cases from a set of actual ones. Thus if, for example, we are looking for the intension of a predicate term we ask ourselves what is required in order for us to be able to apply the same term to actual entities as well as entities that *could have been* members of the original extension.[25] We can then see why reference must be made to something which is shared by a number of entities for only in this way can we say that an entity, x, belongs with or is a member of the same class as another entity, y. "Properties" are precisely those shared and shareable elements that permit us to say that x is similar to y or, if all the properties are shared, that x is identical to y. Only of properties can we say that the same one appears or can appear in many objects. And in this way we are able to label future objects by the same name since the same property can reside in many objects. For similar reasons we can begin to understand why propositions are required as intensions for sentences. Sentences, like predicates, refer to actual as well as to possible cases. The actual case gives the sentence its status as either true, if there is such a case, or false, if there is no such case. Thus the extension of a sentence is the truth-value, true, if a given situation holds, and false, if a given situation does not hold. But in order to account for the possible cases where the sentence *may* become applicable, we must bring in the notion of a proposition. The proposition of a sentence permits us to make the sentence applicable to an event which had not been included in the original extension of the sentence. We might ask why sentences must be thought of in terms of applications to cases that have not yet been actualized or been included as part of the extension of the sentence. The reply, of course, is similar to that given for all designators. If an expression could be used only with some given specified designatum, no language could ever arise. We would, so to speak, be in the same dilemma in which Plato long ago placed Heraclitus when he asked whether language could be meaningful if expressions were applicable to one and only one given event at a given time.[26] Since events change from moment to moment an expression, *x*, at one time, could never again be used since the next time would require a different expression. Thus Carnap needs the distinction between intensions and extensions. Without it there would be a serious question as to whether a language could be constructed.

However, the point to be noted here is that to accept intensions as a necessity is also to affirm the need for a serious ontology. Carnap is making the claim that abstract entities cannot be eliminated. They are required if there is to be any language at all.

Now it might be argued that the foregoing criticism is weakened by the notion of "possible cases." It might be claimed that we have entered the realm of metaphysics because we have become involved in explicating the meaning of "possible." But if it can be shown that Carnap does not interpret "possible cases" as a subset of a more inclusive set, then we need not enter into the kind of metaphysical discourse that we have implied seems to be required. For if "possible cases" could be eliminated or could be shown to be a rather elliptical way of speaking of actual cases, then intensions would not become such a serious ontological commitment. But can Carnap modify the seriousness of speaking of "possible cases"? Carnap admits that the whole notion of the possible is ambiguous, but he asserts that there are two ways of treating possibility so that its seriousness can be minimized. First, he says that perhaps we can eliminate reference to possible cases by giving some series of descriptions of certain events known to have no actual occurrence. We might simply "describe . . . cases, which [are known] to be possible and leave it open whether there is anything satisfying these descriptions or not." [27] Thus, for example, if we want the intension of "pferd" we give a description of something which is known to be possible, but whose actuality is unknown. But of course we are still left here with the question of what it means to give a description of something known to be possible. What would the referent of such a description be? It is surely clear that such a description would not have the usual extension. A description of a possible situation has no extension. And if it is maintained that we are dealing solely with the intension of such a description, we are moving into a very obvious circle. To understand intensions we require the notion of the possible; to understand the possible we require the notion of an intension. Thus it does not help very much to be told that instead of using the expression "possible cases" we will use descriptions of a certain sort. An understanding of these descriptions requires that we have a prior understanding of what it means to speak of the possible or the impossible.

A second suggestion Carnap gives concerns changing the status of "possible" from an apparent adjectival status to a quantificational status. In other words, Carnap insists that if we use "possible" we ought to do to it what was finally done to "exists." At least for many philosophers it is no longer correct to speak of "existent objects" or "existent situations." On the contrary, the "existent" here must be converted into a form that does not have "existent" or any synonym as adjectival. Supposedly because of this change in the grammatical status of "exists," the ontological argument for the existence of God has been refuted.[28] Similarly, we ought no longer speak of "possible cases" but rather we must change this into a form such as "it is possible that x" where "it is possible that" has a role analogous to "there is an x such that." Whereas the latter uses the existential quantifier the former uses the modal operator. Under such circumstances we no longer can ask about possible entities since this would involve a glaring confusion of syntax with semantics. Quantifiers and operators simply do not designate. Thus Carnap can now say that when he refers to possibilities in his discussion of intensions, he is not intending to populate the world with a new class of abstract entities. Possibilities, like existences, are simply elliptical ways of speaking about purely syntactical matters. There are neither possibilities nor existences although there are symbols stating how certain linguistic structures function.

Now what shall we say to all this? First of all, it is not quite

clear how the "possibility" attributed to intensions relates to the
"possibility" of modality. Carnap specifically tells us that there are
intensional logics which take intensions for the values of their
variables. But it would be simply absurd to think that the values of
a variable are quantifiers—albeit modal ones—or some other syntactical phrase. The variables—either in extensional or intensional
systems—use modal or other quantifiers to bind them, but the operators themselves never become the values of a variable. Thus we
cannot easily eliminate the factor of possibility in intensions by
reducing them to strictly modal operators.[29]

Again, in defense of Carnap's position, it might be argued that
Carnap is not committing himself to giving possibilities a substan-
tive nature when he speaks of intensions. Possibilities enter into the
discussion only in so far as he is concerned with discovering what
the intension is. But the intension is what it is regardless of our
discovery of any cases that exhibit it. At one point Carnap equates
intensions with dispositional concepts [30] and this would lead us to
believe that Carnap does want us to think of intensions as primitive
meanings, like dispositional powers, that can be said to be present
even if no extension is ever forthcoming.[31] But this position would
lead us back into the very realm of abstract ontology that Carnap
has sought to avoid. Propositions, properties, and individual concepts would simply be accepted as the most basic aspects of any
theory of knowledge.

Carnap, however, presents one other approach to intensions
that ought not to be neglected. He tells us that it is possible to
accept intensions without involving ourselves in any discussions
about possibilities, dispositions, or any such abstractions. Like
Quine's virtual classes which can have the characteristics of classes
but yet not exist, so also intensions are to be taken as referring to
"neutral entities." [32] These entities are presumably to be regarded as
neither classes nor properties, neither individuals nor individual
concepts. They are simply designata that become one or the other in
accordance with the way a given expression functions. Carnap tries
to clarify this position in detail by showing how we can eliminate
such expressions as "property," "class," "individual," and "individual concept" from their appearance in a given metalanguage.[33] Instead of speaking of "the class Human" or "the property Human,"
we eliminate "class" and "property" and simply leave the designa-

tive word itself, namely, "human." The metalanguage, then, has no ontological significance. But in a metametalanguage we can introduce extensions and intensions. Thus in the metametalanguage, M_1, that discusses the metalanguage, M', we can say "The extension of 'Human' in M' is the class Human" and "The intension of 'Human' in M' is the property Human." [34] In this way, according to Carnap, such ontologically charged words as "class" and "property" do not appear in either the object language or its metalanguage. We can only use sentences such as "Scott is Human" or "Human is equivalent to featherless biped." Only in a metametalanguage do we become involved in the intension and extension of expressions. Thus, as Carnap says, when we are dealing with an object language and its metalanguage, no discourse need arise concerning whether our designators are referring to extensions or intensions. This concern arises only when we begin to talk *about* the metalanguage.

This is really an interesting attempt on the part of Carnap to show that perhaps a language can do everything expected of it and yet be devoid of any significant ontological expressions. But it seems difficult to see why moving ontologically charged words into a metametalanguage has in some way impaired the need to admit intensions and extensions. Even though the expressions "class" and "property" are not in a given metalanguage, they do appear again in a metametalanguage. And if we eliminate them in this latter language, then presumably we will require a further language in which they must appear. For Carnap never denies that a distinction is to be made between an expression operating in an intensional context and one operating in an extensional context. Nor does Carnap ever deny that logical equivalence is definable only by reference to the intensional rather than the extensional designata of terms. Carnap could have tried to show us that the various intensional expressions need not appear anywhere in a language—neither in the metalanguage nor in any n-metalanguage. But this, of course, Carnap can never do since intensions turn out to be more crucial for him than extensions. Only once we understand the intension of an expression can we ask about its extension.[35] Indeed, if we are to include modal logic in our language, only intensions of terms become significant; extensions are not relevant. Thus Carnap must accept Quine's law that intensions drive out extensions.[36]

Carnap, therefore, is left with all the abstract notions that arise when he admits intensions. He must simply accept the ontology. As far as his notion of "neutral objects" are concerned, we can only say that they apparently have the status of the smile of the famous Cheshire cat—they exist even if they cannot exist. This is what Carnap would like to say of all his commitments to entities that are not concrete. But he never really succeeds.

7

The Function of Language

NEITHER Quine's nor Carnap's formalism is sufficient to eliminate those inquiries that have been labelled metaphysical. A rigorous language can serve to define and regulate such inquiries more carefully, but it cannot prohibit them. There still persists, even in the construction of formal systems, a need to examine such concepts as meaning, class, existence, properties, and things.

I should now like, however, to turn to another view that also asserts that ontology need not arise if we understand language correctly. I shall call this the function analysis of language whose primary exponents have been Wittgenstein, Austin, Waismann, and others of the logical analyst school. On this view, if we think of the many uses to which a language can be put, then we will become aware that what is a commitment in one use of language is not a commitment in another. Thus what is necessary and uneliminable in one kind of discourse is unnecessary and eliminable in another kind. If this relativism is indeed legitimate, then all ontological issues would become specious.

In this chapter I shall examine some general issues that arise when we speak of the function of language. In the succeeding chapter I shall discuss what I take to be the primary function of a language—a function that will make more explicable certain kinds of logical issues. But, as we shall see, this view of language will not suffice to exclude the occurrence of certain odd metaphysical issues.

Various functions have been attributed to languages. Wittgenstein pointed out that languages are used to give orders, to report an event, to express emotions, initiate inquiries, etc. Still others have regarded language as primarily a kind of map whose function it is to give us a symbolic representation of all the important features of reality. This is the position that has been taken by Korzybzki,[1] Hayakawa,[2] and, more recently, Nelson Goodman who believes that the map function of a language is the major justification for the construction of formal languages.[3] Just as it is continually necessary to improve our road and other kinds of maps, so also is it necessary to keep improving our language maps.

These are important functions and it may well be that they are all performed by the use of language. But it ought to be recognized that such functions can also be accomplished in other—perhaps even better—ways. Models and pictures are frequently cited as better communicative tools than purely linguistic ones. Describing the physical characteristics of a criminal is not half as effective as being able to show a picture of him. In a similar vein scientists and philosophers have sometimes distinguished between language and mathematical systems, and they have claimed that at some future date all of science will be strictly mathematical. Carnap, for example, foresees the day when "red," "heat," and other such expressions will be replaced by their mathematical correlates.[4] Commands also can be given more effectively by arrows and other ideographic signs rather than by the use of a command in linguistic form. In fact, twisting someone's arm or scowling fiercely are probably much more effective ways of giving a command than any use of words. Artists and aestheticians, at least since the time of Hegel, have also persistently argued that meanings which allude primarily to emotions are more adequately transmitted by music, painting, or sculpture rather than by any medium employing words. Many philosophers have claimed that the arts give a "higher" knowledge than any which can be formulated in words. Croce's "intuition" exemplifies the attempt to show how art can produce knowledge quite distinct from and, at least according to Croce, more superior to anything which is statable in a language.[5]

Finally, if the analogy of language as a map is correct, then maps ought potentially to be as satisfactory as languages. Drawing a detailed map of China could convey much more information than simply describing it. Of course those who support the map theory of language think of a language as mapping much more than simply physical characteristics of land and people; emotions, attitudes, values, world-views, etc., are also to be mapped.[6] But it is rather vague to speak of a language as in some way mapping an emotion or a series of values. There may be a correspondence between "chair" and the actual chair, but clearly no such correspondence occurs between "fear" and some actual fear. We might argue that it is all a matter of degree. "Chair" designates the actual chair while "fear" designates certain kinds of behavior. We can map one as well as the other. But it is well known that "fear," like other psychological expressions, is not defined by behavior although the latter may be taken as evidence that fear is present. In fact, psychiatrists generally agree that a person can have fears without showing any of the usual symptoms. Thus there is an important sense in which language cannot map something, or, at most, can map something on the surface just as a camera can take a picture of a man but not of what he may be thinking or feeling. But still we might ask whether anything else except language can do the job any better. The kind of psychological state we seem to be examining is not really open to any kind of inspection and at least language, as it is used by such great writers as Proust, Joyce, and Freud, gives us the best possible means for gaining insight into the most private worlds of human beings. But the American poet Sidney Lanier maintained that the best conveyors of emotion are certain combinations of pure linguistic sounds regardless of whether the sounds happen to be words.[7] Perhaps expletives, curses, groans, and grunts which are not really part of a language might be more effective means of telling us about emotions and feelings. Surely the sound of a scream is a more incisive communicant of fear or pain than such possible linguistic alternates as "I am afraid" or "I am in pain." [8]

Thus many of the functions of a language can be taken over—albeit awkwardly—by other techniques. This does not mean that language, as an instrument for human survival, is being relegated to some subsidiary position. Even if every function of a language could be performed by some other nonlinguistic device, it would still be of incalculable importance that a language can incorporate into itself all the functions of so many diverse disciplines and methods.

We shall be arguing in the next chapter that every language has one essential function. But we should first like to comment on a view of language acccepted by many philosophers and linguists which might mistakenly be attributed to us as well. When we speak of the function of a language it might be thought that we are   *1*] calling attention to two separate subject matters—language and that which is extralinguistic and   *2*] examining the ways in which language serves to express or communicate information about this extralinguistic subject matter. Thus it might seem as if we were describing two distinct entities   *a*] a language and   *b*] that which the language is supposedly describing. But this kind of dichotomy makes for some interesting consequences. For it would then seem to be perfectly legitimate to make assertions about [*b*] and then to check whether [*a*] indeed has such assertions. It is as if we were to inspect two entities, a mirror and some object in front of it, and then to comment on how adequately the mirror reflects the object. Thus we might look to [*b*] and find, for example, that there are causes and then, after inspecting [*a*], argue that the language must contain the sentence "There are causes" just as in our analogy with the mirror we would certainly expect the object before the mirror to show all the essential characteristics of the reflection in the mirror. But at this point the analogy falls apart. For whereas it is perfectly legitimate to inspect separately a mirror and the object it reflects, it is not possible to make such an inspection of a language and its subject matter. In judging what [*b*] contains we are already using a language with its own peculiar rules and with a full complement of convcntionally or scientifically approved terms. We can judge of [*b*] that there are causes because we already have the term "causc" as a means of describing what is observed. The language, with all its rules and conventions, conditions every attempt at description. It might be argued that a statement about [*b*] is made in a language different from [*a*] and, therefore, even though a commitment to a language is still present, it is not the language of [*a*]. Hence [*a*] legitimately can be compared to [*b*]. In a third language [*c*] we can describe what is in [b] and then indicate whether such a descriptive statement appears in [a]. But, of course, even here prior linguistic commitments exist because of [c]. And this leads to the serious question of whether [a] must not be so constructed that it is translatable into the forms of [c]. In other words, the formation of [a] must have within it syntactic and semantic features which are isomorphic to those of [c]. Otherwise no translation of [a] would be possible. But, furthermore, I think it can be shown that positing a second language, [c], leads to the positing of an infinite number of languages. For consider if we argue that there are causes and this argument is given in terms of some language. It is not the language of [a] since the important question is whether [a] does contain the statements about [b]. Thus we are required to posit language [c] which has [b] as its subject matter. But now we must investigate language [c] for it might well be that the reason we are attributing causes to [b] is because [c] has "cause" as a legitimate term for describing phenomena. Therefore, we now posit language [d] which serves to check whether [b] really has what [c] attributes to it. But again with [d] another language [e] is required *ad infinitum*.

In a practical sense there is another reason for questioning the validity of separating a language from its subject matter. Those who think of language and its designata as two separate objects which can be discussed independently have found a self-defeating escape from all logical refutation. A sentence can be examined in the light of its connections to other sentences which are sometimes called "evidence" or "premises." It can also be scrutinized in terms of what its expressions designate. But to speak of truth or falsity exclusive of sentential formulation is to exclude the application of any logical or semantical rules. That there are causes can be taken to have truth-value even if the sentence "There are causes" is open to serious criticism both in its designative aspect and its possible logical symbolization. All kinds of claims about what is extralinguistic would then be perfectly justifiable even if their sentential formulation would either not be possible or would be open to serious objections. This, of course, is the important point made by the formalist philosophers, those who maintain that philosophical issues must be thought of in terms of a formal language. Their argument is that any discourse that purports to use such important expressions as "therefore," "is," "not," and "and" makes a claim that inference is occurring.[9] But inference-making is explicable only in terms of rules and conventions—those rules and conventions which are made explicit in a formal language. Thus if some one utters a sentence he is responsible for guaranteeing that it would be allowable in a formal language. Otherwise its use in the making of inferences is simply void. For this reason it is legitimate to ask whether metaphysical sentences or ordinary language can be formalized; metaphysicians and ordinary language philosophers do use sentences to draw inferences. And if such sentences are shown to be incapable of formalization then we might not reject them, but their use with logical particles would be suspect. This is the reply that I believe ought to be made to Paul Edwards' and A. N. Findlay's defense of ordinary language and ordinary analysis of everyday events.[10] Edwards argues that it is simply a fact that we do use sentences about the past to draw inferences about the future and we do give reasons for the procedure. Thus either the philosopher has (perhaps for the nth time) distorted the meaning of a perfectly good word "induction" to create philosophic perplexities or else the philosopher is simply wrong. But no one denies that inductions are made just as no one denies Findlay's assertion that in ordinary language we always speak of moving from one point to the next without ever involving ourselves in notions of infinites. But the fact that such occurrences and movements are indeed measured does not invalidate the philosophic issues posed by Zeno, Hume, and Russell. Zeno, and presumably Parmenides, were aware that motion occurred. They never had the fantastic impression that they were standing still. But the question revolved around how mathematical concepts could be applied to motion. They certainly wanted to use mathematics with movements, but the paradoxes that arose seemed to deny this possibility. Similarly, no one denies that inductions are made every day and that we try to substantiate them with the very best available reasons, but the question remains concerning how logical techniques can be used with such inferences. Edwards might have scored a major point if he had shown us that some ordinary language logic uses "if . . . then - - -," "and," "or" and the other logical particles in a way different from those defined in a formal system. He might have shown us that even though in inductive logic the move from "some" to "all" is extremely difficult, if it is at all possible, there is another ordinary language logic that makes this move perfectly comprehensible. But he does not deal with these issues, and we must rely on the available logic and continue to ask how it is possible to move logically from a certain kind of antecedent to a certain kind of consequent. The same criticism can also be directed against the views of Strawson, Austin, and others who have frequently pointed to the odd sentences which consistently elude formalization, or to the expressions which serve as designators or even as logical particles in formal systems that can be interpreted differently. Thus Austin has shown that many "if . . . then - - -" sentences are neither truth-functional nor counterfactual in any familiar sense.[11] Similarly, performative sentences cannot be included in any formal propositional calculus.[12] But we ought to note the reasons why these sentences become philosophically interesting. They pose dilemmas precisely because we do wish to consider them in relation to logical systems. The philosophical problem does not involve showing that these logically deviant sentences are over and above inclusion in any logical system, rather it does involve showing that their inclusion is possible. Carnap, in his reply to Strawson,[13] does not deny that the reconstruction of sentences is an important philosophical task. He simply denies that there is either some odd ordinary language logic that cannot be equated with the formal familiar logic or that there is some intuitive foundation that justifies the use of performatives or other logically odd sentences.

Thus the attempt to speak of language as an object among many other objects or to minimize the importance of the language in which knowledge is formulated is to overlook the pervasive way in which language affects knowledge. Even though we can make many divisions among objects and then discuss each one separately, this is not the case with language and something else called reality, or experience. Interestingly enough, Wittgenstein came to recognize this very fact. In the *Tractatus* Wittgenstein seemed quite convinced that things could be grasped in some pure sense even if the language is not entirely adequate. Thus originally Wittgenstein believed that there were simple objects even if they were never open to observation.[14] But in the *Philosophical Investigations* he completely reverses himself on this position and insists that reality can never be grasped outside the forms of language. "One thinks that one is tracing the outline of the thing's nature over and over again, and one

is merely tracing round the frame through which we look at it." [15]
The language—like a Kantian form—is with us as soon as we make
any dichotomy. We cannot simply say "There are causes" and then
either check whether such a sentence is in the language and, if it is
not, claim that the language is deficient. And the recognition of this
fact affects our ways of thinking about "true" and "false." We
confirm or disconfirm only states-of-affairs that have already been
shaped into forms provided by the linguistic tools at hand. Or we
might think of "true" and "false" as performing their most important function only in so far as they are attachable to sentences. This
does not mean that there are not other ways of using "true" and
"false," e.g., as in "true friend" or "false person." But in these latter
instances "true" and "false" are easily eliminable in favor of some
other expression, e.g., "sincere or faithful friend" or "hypocritical or
deceitful person." Nor does it mean that we are overlooking the
curious tie that is said to exist between sentences and those odd
entities sometimes called "propositions." Whether propositions exist
is a moot question to many philosophers. But regardless of what the
opinion may be about such entities it is clear that they must be
framed in sentences if they are to appear at all. Show me a proposition and you show me a sentence! For this reason we may speak of
true or false propositions, but when we are called upon to present
one we produce a sentence. Thus where "true" and "false" have
some key function for inquiry and prediction, they operate in
connection with sentences. Russell, Wittgenstein, and especially
Tarski, made a major contribution to the study of language when
they pointed out that only sentences can be true.[16] In one fell swoop
questions of truth or falsehood outside of precise linguistic formulation became meaningless or mystical. As Wittgenstein says, "What
we cannot speak about we must consign to silence." [17]

   The fact that language and its referents cannot be treated as
two distinct domains does not mean that we cannot indicate this
dichotomy. What it does mean is that we cannot consider a domain
to be free of linguistic commitments. Peter Caws has claimed that
there are domains of thought and perception, and that language
reflects the entities in these domains. But he also admits, without
recognizing the difficulty inherent in his main thesis, that "learning
a particular language may induce a characteristic way of dividing up
or 'segmenting' what presents itself in perception." [18] We can look to

our own experiences to test the truth or falsehood of some sentence but our own experiences are employable for such tests only in so far as they are modified and formed in accordance with prior linguistic conditioning. To ask for the confirmation of "There is a table in the next room" is to ask for a confrontation of something describable by a sentence such as "Here is the next room and here is the table" or "Jones says, 'There is a table in the next room.' " We may ask how evidential sentences are related to those for which they are evidence. But still whatever views we may have of "reality" or "experience" must be incorporated into sentences which alone can deal with such concepts. As D. F. Pears has put it: "Facts may be brute and propositions may be definite, but what exactly it is about them which is brute or definite can be specified only by reference to the sentences which were the unacknowledged starting points." [19] We can see this even more explicitly when we examine traditional ways of speaking of synthetic or empirical sentences. Such statements are said to refer to experience. But what, in any specific instance, is "experience"? To say "The chair is brown" refers to experience, can only mean that if some one observes he will encounter something describable, with the usual descriptive predicates, as "There is a chair (here) and it is brown" or he will encounter something describable as an evidential sentence for "The chair is brown." "Experience" becomes a significant expression if and only if it serves as a synonym for a specific descriptive sentence. If such a sentence could not be forthcoming, we would undoubtedly reject characterizing the original sentence as empirical.

We have been maintaining that whatever is extralinguistic is modified and conditioned by sentential formulation. In one sense this can be misleading. It is not as if we can first become acquainted with what is external to language and then note how it is changed by a linguistic description. The external element here plays the role of a Kantian noumenon. We can indicate something extralinguistic, but we cannot deal with it in any significant sense unless we can formulate it in a language. Whatever "pure" experience may be, whatever a world may be like without a description of it, we communicate it to others and learn of it from others only by a linguistic framework which requires us to examine this world in terms of certain specific linguistic categories.

Nor ought this to be very surprising, for both G. H. Mead and

Dewey, as well as various contemporary psychologists, have been arguing in a comparable way that there are no pure observational data.[20] The Ames experiments have afforded ample evidence of the fact that perception is always conditioned by prior perceptions and even expectations.[21] Thus whatever is taken as extralinguistic at any particular time is already conditioned by preceding social, psychological, and linguistic considerations. We might believe that prior to any linguistic account, things, properties, relationships, and perhaps classes are intuitively evident as the elements with which a language must deal. But there is no way of determining whether the acceptance of these elements is not the result of the very linguistic forms employed in every description. Thus the British anatomist, J. Z. Young, in describing the results of corneal transplantation that gives sight to patients blind from birth, tells us that the patient "reports only a spinning mass of lights and colors. . . . His brain has not been trained in the rules of seeing, does not know which features are significant and useful for naming objects and conducting life. We are not conscious that there are any such rules; we think that we see, as we say, 'naturally.' But we have in fact learned a whole set of rules during childhood." [22] There are no pure data, and, of course, this is Whorf's point when he asserts "no individual is free to describe nature with absolute impartiality but is constrained to certain modes of interpretation even while he thinks himself most free." [23] In the final analysis it may well be that this extralinguistic subject matter, whether it is experience or reality or something other than these, must be describable by the traditional onion metaphor. If we discarded the social, psychological, and linguistic components from observation, we would not be left with a pure neutral datum at all. We simply would have eliminated observation.

But exactly how stringent is our criticism to be. If what is extralinguistic cannot be discussed without a prior commitment, then are we not claiming that truth and falsehood are to be defined in terms of a given language and not by reference to something external to the language? By rejecting the correspondence theory of language are we not assuming some form of coherence theory? It would seem as if something radical is here being introduced, but the view is merely an attempt to describe what we actually do when we ask for the verification or confirmation of sentences. We simply produce more sentences. And if these latter sentences are to be confirmed, we produce still more sentences until we may finally reach one such as "This is it" or "That is what I meant." We may use gestures to help us, but finally we rely on sentences which, in some way, can be logically connected to other sentences. Goodman makes the same point in his criticisms of those who look for the original datum that is outside of linguistic formulation.

The search for the original given is sometimes envisaged as an interrogation in which I am first asked what I just saw. I reply "I saw the worst criminal alive today," but my questioner complains that I am making too many judgments about what I saw; he wants me to tell him exactly what I could see and nothing more. As he continues to press me, I reply successively: "I saw a man," "I saw a human-looking animal," "I saw a moving object," "I saw such-and-such a configuration of color patches." But if my questioner is consistent and persistent, none of these replies— or any other I can give him—will satisfy him; for all answers describe experience in words and so impose on it some organization or interpretation. What he is covertly demanding is that I describe what I saw without describing it. All my answers may be true descriptions of what I saw, but no description can be a satisfactory answer to the question what I *merely* saw; for the question is a bogus one.[24]

It might be argued that even though no data is ever presented without the influence of a linguistic framework, there is a sense in which the language itself does give us a clear and precise view of how things really are. Perhaps the language has places for names and predicates because there really are individuals with properties. Perhaps it is wrong to claim that trees or even human beings are to be found in the world, but that we discuss the world in terms of names and predicates ought to be sufficient evidence that individuals with properties exist regardless of whether any specific individual is designated. The reply to this, however, is that we are unable to move from a language to its referent without using the language. As we have already indicated, when we talk of what is extralinguistic we are required to use the structure of some language. Thus we cannot ask whether what is extralinguistic really has such and such characteristics for we cannot move to what is extralinguistic without a prior commitment to what is linguistic. As J. N. Findlay has said, the very process of postulating the existence of entities may very well be no more than "mere projections in another medium, of linguistic symbols and rules." [25] Furthermore, a verbalization of causality between a language and its referent cannot be given without circularity. In order to know that a datum causes the appearance of certain structural devices in a language, we would be required to know that the datum itself has a certain kind of division. For example, we would have to be able to say: "D (the datum) contains properties and things having these properties." But no sooner do we make this statement then we are already ascribing to D that which we are trying to prove it causes. Just as instruments interfere with attempts to give an adequate description of the submicroscopic level, so also language makes it impossible for us to discover whether its designata in some sense really has the divisions found in the language. A language may "work" for us in that its use leads to fruitful results in most if not all inquiries, but this does not mean that, therefore, sentences reflect or are caused by some similar extralinguistic subject matter.

We have been noting the pervasiveness of the linguistic framework in every attempt to convey information. But in an important sense this observation is not quite correct. What ought to be stressed is that it is *our* language that pervades all data and not some language or other. I mean by this that it is our language with all its structural rules and commitments and not some other possible language. When we communicate or receive information we implicitly use the categories of our language for otherwise nothing could become intelligible to us. We require all data to be formed into what we can recognize as sentences or as the linguistic segments formed by the rules that we constantly employ. All foreign languages, all esoteric documents, become intelligible to us once we have translated them into our specific language with its specific categories and language regulations. It is this fact that easily lends itself to an ontological interpretation of a language, for we can now proceed to use Kant's old epistemological categorical structures, translated into the rules and stipulations of a language system. We can speak in some theoretical sense, just as Kant did during his time, of other kinds of knowledge formulated in a language that is not translatable into our forms. But we would be required finally to say, as Kant also did of his realm of noumena, it is a realm which precludes understanding.

It could be argued that a language is like an historical occurrence. It could have developed in an indefinite number of ways and even the formal languages could have taken an indefinite number of different forms. The fact that ours is a language in which subjects and predicates as well as the various logical relationships seem to be essential is one of those curious facts that could have been otherwise. We have been taken in by custom. Thus both Entwistle [26] and Whorf [27] have told us of languages which are so completely different from our own that it makes no sense to speak of sentences or parts of sentences in such a language. Certainly there are no specific expressions that can be selected as subjects or predicates. Thus the Ewe language in Africa as well as the Malayan language appear to be uniquely different from our own. As one linguist puts it: "A European student . . . finds that words (in either the Ewe or Malayan languages) have a disconcerting habit of changing their 'grammatical' function without changing or modifying their appearance. No suffix, no internal change may indicate to you that the word you heard (or saw) a few moments before used as a preposition is now being used as a verb, or the verb as a preposition. The adverb . . . nouns and prepositions show the same chameleon quality, shifting functions as do verbs. . . ." [28]

However, the fact that a language changes or that there are different forms of language is not an argument against the view that certain kinds of structures seem to be necessary in all languages. The very fact that we can translate foreign languages into our own linguistic forms means that those languages must also have certain expressions which function in ways similar to those found in our own language. The expressions may be far different in length or they may occupy positions different from what they normally would in our own language. But there must still be something which is translatable into our words "or" or "therefore" or "and" and so forth. In other words, translation into our language forms must be permissible. Otherwise, if we encountered a series of marks as a language which could not be translated into our forms, we would simply have either to reject it or to look for the clue which would enable us to find corresponding forms in the foreign expressions. We would simply not take anything as a language unless it were potentially translatable into our forms. It does not matter if in different texts an expression changes from a preposition to a noun or to an adjective. What would be important is that in any context something has to be identifiable as a preposition or a noun or an adjective. Probably from the point of view of a language which, like the Egyptian art that Plato so admired,[29] did not change in a thousand years, our language would have a chameleon quality. We know quite well that English words change both in form and function.[30] Nor is this solely a temporal process since the same word at any given time is sometimes spelled in different ways and also used with a variety of meanings in different discourses, e.g., judg(e)ment. But in any given discourse we always presume that, if there is no equivocation or other type of ambiguity, the words have a specific grammatical function and meaning. We would presume that this same rule would also hold for the Ewe and the Malayan languages if they are translatable into English.

It might seem odd to argue that all languages must be decipherable into the linguistic forms which we employ. Some objections immediately come to mind. For example, imagine the discovery of some set of Martian parchments when the first spaceship lands on Mars. Presumably the marks discovered on them could very easily be thought of as evidence for a Martian language. Now if we had reasons to believe that the Martians were very scientifically advanced—much more so than we were—any difficulties in deciphering could be attributed to the superior status of the Martian language. These parchments could be taken to contain terminology so technical that no translation into our language would be possible. In such an instance it would seem to be perfectly proper to claim that there is a Martian language, only we are unable to understand it.

However, the more precise claim ought not to be that there is a Martian language but rather that there *may* be such a language. For, indeed, the marks on our hypothetical parchment could not be regarded as linguistic elements until some key were discovered which would distinguish at least one expression corresponding to an expression in our own language. Even if we found some consistent pattern of marks, we would not be able to call these marks parts of a linguistic system. They could be parts of some esoteric musical scale or of simple repetitious series of doodlings. (After all, Martians might also doodle.) Only once we uncovered correlations between an expression in our language and a mark or set of marks in the Martian document would the probability of a Martian language, as distinct from a mere possibility, begin to arise. As long as we were not able to make such correlations we could, of course, continue to speculate about whether we did have a sampling of Martian discourse, but we could not claim that we had found a new language. Only as we were able to introduce our linguistic rules and conventions, that is, only as we were able to identify with some degree of probability which marks were to be taken as subjects and predicates, would we begin to acknowledge the existence of a Martian language. But this would be no easy matter for we would first have to expand our own language on the basis of new observations in a new world before we could make transformations of one language into another.

The insistence on correlations between languages does not entail an analogous correlation of observations. Given any two or more individuals, those using either the same or different languages, if translation of one discourse into the other were possible and if the individuals concerned behaved and continued to discourse in ways normally associated with the use of the various languages, then what they actually perceive or otherwise experience would be unimportant. If I say, "The dog is running down the street" and if you say it in French or in some other standard foreign language, so long as we can both make the appropriate translations and can continue to discourse in ways which normally accompany the use of such a sentence, no appeal to what is happening in one's head is necessary. Of course, when we decipher dead languages, we do so without inquiring whether those who used the language experienced a world similar to our own. In the case of our hypothetical Martian language, we might never know whether our perception of an object on Mars was similar to the perception—if the term is allowable when applied to Martians—of a Martian on Mars. But this would not interfere with communication if their language could be converted into our linguistic forms.

8

The Function of Language

INFERENCE

IN THE PRECEDING chapter language is viewed as a kind of unique phenomenon. Our commitment to it is so inclusive that there is no way of disassociating it from what we take to be extralinguistic. At any stage of inquiry whatever is taken to be extralinguistic is already formed on the basis of prior linguistic considerations.

We ought now to raise the question again: what function does this all-inclusive tool have? I should now like to argue that, even though a language has many functions, it performs one function better than any other instrument. Only a language contains—at least implicitly—a set of rules or regulations by which new sentences can be derived from those already given. More specifically, a language has the means by which, given data formulated in sentences A and B, we can obtain further data formulated in another sentence, C. In other words a language has one remarkable feature. It is the only kind of instrument which has apparatus for distinguishing legitimate from nonlegitimate inferences. Once a subject matter has been converted into sentences or analogous expressions of different languages, derivations become possible that would be impossible under other conditions. No amount of study of a rat or a rabbit, for example, could produce any new data unless our observations could be put into sentential form. Once we have the *sentences* "This is a rat" and "That is a rabbit" or "This rabbit has reaction R_1 under circumstances C" and "That rat has reaction R_2 under circumstances C," then we can begin to formulate possible new inferences based upon the rules (implicit or explicit) which are part of the very structure of the language. For example, I can now state "if this is a rat and that is a rabbit then this is a rat," or the less trivial statement "if this is a rat and that is a rabbit implies (materially) that if that is not a rabbit then this is not a rat" or even the less obvious statement "if that is not a rabbit and this is not a rat then it is false that if that is not a rabbit then this is a rat." Or I can now make the very significant statement "if everytime this rabbit has reaction R_1 under circumstances C then that rat has reaction R_2 under circumstances C, then there is a probability, p, that given any rabbit and any rat if the rabbit has reaction R_1 under circumstances C then the rat will have reaction R_2 under circumstances C." The rules governing these sentences are not always clear and precise—especially where probable inferences are being derived—but in spite of all the deficiencies, these rules represent the only substantial ways we have of making inferences and then distinguishing the good ones from the bad ones.[1]

The fact that language has this feature—namely, that it is a primary means for making inferences—ought not to be surprising. We have been repeatedly told by John Dewey and scientists in general that the aim of knowledge is prediction and control. The entire instrumentalist viewpoint rests on the belief that all man-made objects, and this includes language, have the primary function of overcoming or countering some environmental problem.[2] Thus it might be feasible to think that the beginnings of language arose out of the need to be forewarned of impending dangers. By this means more time could be gained for preparation in meeting or escaping possible disasters. The creation by human beings of some means by which possible future occurrences could be examined in language before they actually occurred might have marked man's break with his animal forebears.

The question has sometimes been asked whether other means

of communication could not have arisen as an alternative to the use of symbols and sounds. And, indeed, it may well be by mere chance that symbolic systems arose. According to R. M. S. Heffner the vocal cords, for example, are improperly named. Their function is not to create sounds, but to help in some basic bodily activity. As Heffner puts it, the larynx "is essential to normal elimination from the alimentary canal and it plays an important part in normal childbirth. . . . If this mechanism did not exist, the nature and extent of our arm efforts would be drastically restricted. A great many of the muscular actions of our arms depend upon the creation of a partial vacuum beneath the vocal bands. Without these two valvular controls of the opening of the larynx the human animal would have very little power above the hips. He could not lift himself, or any object of size, with his arms." [3] In the vein of H. G. Wells we can conceive of societies in which a hand motion or some sort of physical object is the instrument of communication. But to be able to use a sound to indicate the presence of a dangerous animal is one of the most remarkable achievements in human history and certainly much more efficient than any known alternative. Sounds and written marks may, indeed, in a primitive stage have functioned aesthetically. As the centuries passed, marks written on stone may have served strictly to amuse or for religious ritual. But for a society whose survival was in constant jeopardy, the significance of language as a means for anticipating future perils must have completely overshadowed the aesthetic function. [4] Thus the most interesting feature of any language is that it can be used without any designata at all being present. The most esoteric subject matters can be discussed without an explicit appeal to designata. [5]

The most basic function of a language, therefore, is to be anticipatory. [6] It presents data in such a form that linguistic rules can be applied and inferences can be drawn. Information can be communicated in many ways and for all we know the artist may be right in judging his to be the best way. But only a language seems to give us information in such a form that further knowledge legitimately can be inferred from the knowledge we already have. This fact gives significance to a language, for it gives human beings a chance to avoid or to change possible natural occurrences before they actually occur. If a language were such that all inferential expressions were eliminated from it, it might still perhaps be called a language in that it might designate some extralinguistic state of affairs. But its most important function would be lacking. The user of such a language would be unable to anticipate new eventualities and the consequences of newly uncovered information. He would be like C. I. Lewis' passive spectator who, unable to act on the basis of observations, sees the world as "a stale cliché which could not be avoided or effected." [7]

It is important to recognize that emphasizing the function of language as an inference-producer does not mean that we are overlooking other functions. We can use language for aesthetic and persuasive purposes without any thought as to its role as inference-producer. But, perhaps we ought to distinguish use from function just as we do in relation to any instrument. A wrench, for example, has many uses and probably everyone has used it as a hammer at one time or another. But we would clearly distinguish the many ways in which the wrench can be employed from its proper functions. A parallel situation occurs in the employment of language. We employ it in many different ways. But not all of these ways exhibit its proper functions. My own view is that we determine the function of an object by observing the pragmatic purposes it can best accomplish. And what is more crucial to the very survival of human beings than to be able to have a way—as feeble as it may be—of anticipating and making inferences about some yet unactualized state of affairs. This is what language can, to some extent, accomplish and this is what determines the function of a language.

Thus those who call attention to the many different kinds of sentences incapable of being translated into any logical form are not really arguing against an investigation of the logical form exhibited by a language. No one ought to deny Austin's claim that performative sentences cannot, at least at first analysis, be regarded as substituends in a purely logical language.[8] But we ought not to take this as anything more than a challenge as to how such sentences are to be fitted into a logical system of sentences. Austin is undoubtedly correct when he shows us that the sentence "I do thee wed" said in the context of a wedding ceremony is not to be equated with the sentence "I am marrying you." The first gives us a ritualistic use of language while the second purports to describe a given state of affairs. Similarly, we ought not to equate the sentence "I name this ship Queen Elizabeth" said during a launching with the sentence "I am naming this ship Queen Elizabeth" said during the signing of ownership papers. But Austin himself tells us that performative sentences are odd only because *1*] they are part of the conditions needed before some given event can take place and *2*] we normally do not make verbal utterances one of the conditions for the occurrence of some event.[9] We tend to state that X can occur if conditions *a, b, c* . . . are present where we take *a, b, c* . . . as particular physical—or sometimes psychological—happenings. But there is no reason to disallow the possibility of *a, b,* or *c* as being no more than certain kinds of verbal utterance just as in many religious ceremonies there must be certain prayers said before the ceremony can be consummated. Once we decide what can be taken as a condition for the occurrence of an event, Austin's performative sentence then becomes utilizable in a formal logical schema. We would simply recognize that the sentences replacing schematic forms can just as easily refer to words as they can to objects. Austin would seem to have one strong objection to this procedure since normally the sentences that do replace schematic forms are either true or false, but performatives are apparently neither true nor false although they can be appropriate or inappropriate. Thus they could not be part of the usual formal systems. But Austin here confuses an expression with its designatum. When I specify the conditions for the occurrence of an event, I use the sentences describing these conditions. I do not, of course, bring forth the physical conditions themselves. Physical conditions are neither true nor false; only sentences are true or false. Similarly, when I speak of a verbal utterance as a condition, I give a sentence referring to the verbal utterance. I do not produce the utterance itself, which, in this kind of context, like other physical conditions, is neither true nor false. But sentences referring to the utterance, e.g., "He said, 'I do thee wed,' " are either true or false. Thus even though it is a little unusual to have utterances as the designata of sentences which are the conditions for a certain event or action, there is nothing inherently unformalizable in such sentences.

It might be mentioned here that Austin's insistence on the significance of performatives in a language has been recently strongly supported by W. P. Alston who has maintained that the analysis of Austin's perlocutionary, locutionary, and illocutionary sentences produces not only a genuine criticism of all purely formal approaches to language but also serves to explicate certain important difficulties in formalism.[10] Thus Alston tries to show that only by understanding the illocutionary potential of a sentence can we define synonymy, a concept that has eluded definition in a formalist system.[11] Given any two expressions, W_1 and W_2, we can take them to have the same meaning if "W_1 and W_2 can be substituted for each other in a wide range of sentences without altering the illocutionary act potentials of those sentences."[12] But now what is an illocutionary act? Alston defines this kind of act by referring to Austin's notion of a perlocutionary act. This latter kind of act is the function of those sentences which "involve the production of some effect."[13] Thus sentences designed to distract or to embarrass or to persuade someone are meant to have an effect on someone. On the other hand, illocutionary acts involve sentences which need not have any effect at all. Thus "I can be said to have reprimanded someone or to have made a certain announcement, prediction, or proposal no matter what effect I had on anyone, if, indeed, I had any effect at all."[14] Once we have made this distinction clear, Alston argues, we can begin to define such difficult expressions as "synonymy" and "sameness of meaning." We can look to the effect intended by sentences and, on this basis, determine whether the substitution of an expression, *A*, for another, *B*, would change the act potential of the sentence. Presumably we could show that "bachelor" is a synonym for "unmarried man" because its substitution in the majority of contexts does not change the locutionary, perlocutionary or illocutionary act potential of any sentence.

The difficulty here, however, is that the distinction between illocutionary and perlocutionary acts is not very precise. The same sentence might exhibit both types of acts. For example, if I say "Jones, you are a scoundrel" in some given context, how would we go about deciding what act potential is involved? It could be said to have perlocutionary act potential in that it is clearly meant to have an effect on Jones. But it may also be illocutionary in that I may know that Jones will simply not be affected at all. In fact, in the same context it is not an uncommon occurrence to have one individual take a sentence to have perlocutionary act potential while another takes it to have illocutionary act potential. If a father asks a child "Did you do your homework?" he may be asking an innocent question without any threatening implications. But to the child the question could well have such implications.

Furthermore, it is odd to speak of sentences that do not affect anyone. There is a sense in which it is correct to say that every sentence has an effect even if the effect is no more than some psychological state of enlightenment or confusion. Furthermore, if a sentence has no effect at all, we might agree with Wittgenstein, that it is not really a sentence at all but only a series of sounds since a sentence normally requires a public before it can be termed a sentence. But a private language can exist and a person can speak even if he is not speaking to anyone. However, it is highly questionable whether he could use a reprimanding sentence even if the one who is being reprimanded is not present or, if he is present, is not listening. Similarly, it would seem to involve a very deviant use of language to say that the sentence "You are a fool!" is a reprimand and "I propose to be the Captain here" is a proposal without 1] implying the presence of someone who is listening to these sentences and 2] using them to create a definite effect on someone's current or future behavior. In other words, it would seem to be quite difficult to believe in sentences which have no effect, and this would mean that we have still not determined the nature of an illocutionary potential sentence.

However, let us for the moment admit that with some careful consideration the illocutionary-perlocutionary dichotomy can be carefully drawn. How can this help us, as Alston claims it will, to solve or eliminate the issues of synonymy or analyticity that have baffled formalist philosophers? Returning now to Alston's former definition of synonymy—two expressions, W_1 and W_2 have the same meaning if "W_1 and W_2 can be substituted for each other in a wide range of sentences without altering the illocutionary act potentials of those sentences"—we must ask whether the legitimacy of the definition hinges solely on an explication of illocutionary act potential. I think we can see quite clearly that it does not. First of all, this definition has nothing at all to do with meaning since it does not tell us when two expressions can be substituted for one another. What is it that determines that W_1 is a legitimate substitute for W_2? Are we to say that it simply occurs in a language? Is "bachelor" equated with "unmarried man" because both expressions are mutually substitutable in the language? This will not do. There are many expressions which are mutually substitutable, e.g., "horse" and "mare," yet such substitution does not constitute a test for synonymity. We would have to inquire about the meaning of the terms in some more scientific sense, and then we would decide whether the terms have the same meaning. In other words, if Alston wants us to accept terms as synonymous because they replace one another in most contexts in a language, then he has confused effect with reason. If two terms are synonymous, or have the same meaning, they can replace one another in most contexts. This is the effect of synonymity. But the reason why terms are taken to be synonymous must be sought in a criterion other than mere language usage.

Secondly, presumably ordinary descriptive sentences can have the same illocutionary act potential in that both may have no effect at all. For example, I might simply want to tell someone, in a casual way, that a particular building, X, is on Chestnut Street and that another building, Y, is on Walnut Street. These sentences have the same act potential which would not change even if I had spoken of building Y on Chestnut Street and building X on Walnut Street. I might be wrong about these addresses, but this would not cause any deviations in the act potentials of the sentences. However, it would certainly be wrong to claim that since the potentials remain the same regardless of whether we have "building X" or "building Y" in the sentences that, therefore, "building X" is synonymous with "building Y." Of course, Alston might wish to claim that replacement of "building X" by "building Y" does create a different sentence with different illocutionary act potential. But it is difficult to see what this difference would be unless it dealt with the different meanings of the two expressions. But then nothing has been added to our understanding of a sentence by reference to illocutionary act potential. We must still continue the search for an adequate criterion.

Finally, it should be pointed out that nothing in Alston's analysis gives us a way of dealing with the synonymity that makes us distinguish "Sir Walter Scott" from "the author of Waverley." Since, in most contexts, these two expressions are mutually substitutable Alston would apparently have us believe that they are synonyms. But of course this view completely overlooks the crucial issue that arises in trying to determine why "Sir Walter Scott is Sir Walter Scott" is a trivial sentence while "Sir Walter Scott is the author of Waverley" is not. In other words, the notion of a sentence with illocutionary act potential may tell us something about the kind of use to which a sentence may be put, but it tells us very little about how a sentence operates when it is involved in an inference-producing discourse.

We have claimed then that the inference-producing function of a language is its most notable feature. There may be sentences which do not appear to have the forms that sentences of this category normally have, but if they are to be used for inference purposes we still try to give them familiar logical forms.

The view that the inference-producing devices in a language are of major philosophic interest is not new. Dewey in a less formal and Carnap in a more formal way have sought to emphasize this point. But what I believe has been overlooked are the implications of this view for the structure of a language generally. I shall maintain that the inferential process is so pervasive in a language that linguistic and logical forms themselves are designed to facilitate this process, that is to say, they are not reflections of some extralinguistic subject matter but are rather ways of making inferences possible in a language. Thus, for example, the subject-predicate form of sentence is not due to an Aristotelian commitment to the existence of substances and essences. The commitment is Kantian in the sense that without such categories a language could not perform its major function. In the history of philosophy good arguments have been produced to show that the world is a series of things or that it is a series of processes. It is doubtful that this dilemma can ever be satisfactorily resolved unless we recognize the kind of universe required if an inference-producing language is to become possible. If logical derivations are to occur then linguistic segments must have, either implicitly or explicitly, a certain form; and this form commits us to a belief in a universe classified and characterized in specific ways. But I should now like to make a more substantial defense of this claim.

Many sounds and many marks are not parts of any language. By some chance a wave on the shore might etch the marks "Go," but these marks are not part of a language. They become parts of a language when human beings take them to signify something or to be indicative of some further event. But why should anyone ever use marks in these ways? Why should the sounds made by a set of vocal cords become a mark quite distinct from the sounds made in cracking knuckles or whistling? And our answer has been that men use anything they can in order to gain some insight now into a possible tomorrow. Probably if men generally had the power to whistle in a variety of ways, whistling could have become a means of producing a language in the same way as that employed by the sounds of the vocal cords. But whatever means were used to form a language, certain characteristics could not have been avoided. There would necessarily have to be some marks that were designators and others that made it possible to infer one designator from another. It would not matter that the inference-producing techniques led to contradiction or to ambiguities; such consequences would not lead to an elimination of the basic division in the language but rather to a more adequate construction of it. In other words, if it is indeed the case that a language is to be equated with a pragmatic instrument that primarily serves to give human beings a way of anticipating difficulties, then the reason for being of a language requires it to be divided into logical particles and designators. This commitment permeates every language, both formal and otherwise. In a formal language we can eliminate many logical particles, but we cannot eliminate them all. As we have indicated earlier, even in the combinatorial logic of Curry and Schönfinkel, a mark for inference must be included. Thus every language, if it is to function at all for inferential purposes, requires some commitment to some rules which will allow certain combinations of expressions and disavow others.

The fact that a language has this inferential characteristic influences all the other characteristics of the language in the same way that a plus sign in mathematics requires numbers if the sign is to function. To be able to use "therefore" the linguistic elements coming before and after it must be formed in some way. There is no function to be attached to "therefore" in such linguistic combinations as "brown therefore or" or "John therefore yellow" or even "John therefore Smith." Whoever genuinely intends to have the logical connectives function for him is committed to use them with the appropriate syntactical equipment. For this reason, if he wishes to employ "if p then q" or "p or q," then he is required to have p and q formed and functioning in a certain way. But we ought now to ask what characteristics the substituends of p and q must have if they are to be adequate for use with "or" or "if . . . then - - -." And I think that the most significant characteristic—one we have been employing—is that the substituends be such that either "true" or "false" is applicable to them.[15] We might put it differently. In any language that purports to make inferences there must be some way of affirming or denying. Something must be correct and something else incorrect. The drawing of one inference must be legitimate while another must be illegitimate. The most primitive tribes have some way of agreeing or disagreeing. We might imagine a linguistic system in which no expression corresponding to "yes" or "no" could be found. But in such a language nothing could be inferred since there could be no affirmation or denial of an inference. To infer p from "if p then q, and q" would be just as legitimate as to infer q from "if p then q, and p." Not even the simplest calculus could be formulated unless there was a prior understanding of what "agreement" and "disagreement," "correct" and "incorrect" mean. The rule of inference may simply be a stipulation that given the well-formed formula "$p \supset q \cdot p$" then q can be asserted. But to understand the rule it is necessary to know that the assertion of q is correct while the assertion of p is not.

Thus, in order for "therefore," "and," and "if . . . then - - -" to function as inferential phrases, some expressions must be capable of being affirmed or denied. And this then seems to be the primary function of "true" and "false." Assuming that we are right and that languages arise because of a need to anticipate eventualities, i.e., to make inferences prior to the actual occurrence of events, then "true" and "false" are simply ways of marking certain linguistic patterns for inclusion in possible inference making. In an important sense "true" and "false," at this basic level, operate as parts of performative rather than indicative sentences.[16] When I say "it is true that it is raining" the phrase "it is true that" is indeed redundant unless I can show that something has been done to "it is raining" that would not have otherwise been done if "it is true that" had not been added. My claim is that in adding "it is true that" we are indicating that a given sentence, namely "it is raining," can be used in certain specific ways in the process of inference making. For example, alone all sentences imply it; combined by "and" to a sentence labelled "false" all sentences are inferred from it. As an antecedent in an "if . . . then - - -" construction containing a false consequent we can infer all sentences as well as the fact that a conditional with a true antecedent and false consequent cannot be affirmed. Thus "true" and "false" are ways of showing how a sentence is to function in some truth-value analysis. They indicate how the sentence is to be used when the language is performing its most important function. For this reason all questions about whether a sentence can be finally shown to be true or finally shown to be false are not meaningful. "True" and "false" are not achievement words, to use Ryle's expressions.[17] Nor are they expressions whose application depends upon an appeal to an extralinguistic subject matter. They can indeed be used with any sentences whose implications we wish to explore. In fact, even in the most ordinary discourse we frequently say, "Assume that p is true. What follows then?" p here could be either confirmed or disconfirmed; it could be of an impossible state of affairs. But when we use "true" with it we are asking what follows truth-functionally from it when it is combined with other true or false sentences.

I think of this analysis of "true" and "false" as revealing the primary function of these expressions. They perform a role without which the inference making processes of the language could not occur. But it would be a mistake to think that these are the only ways in which "true" and false" appear in a language. Those who have sought one all inclusive definition of "true" have always run afoul of the objection that there are recalcitrant examples. And the answer to such an objection has usually been a more intensified search for some definition of "true" which would be broad enough. In a natural language such a laudatory expression as "true"—laudatory in that it is so vitally involved in one of the most crucial tasks of the language—would undoubtedly come to be used in different contexts and for different purposes. There is an important view in linguistics which maintains that terms with favorable or highly significant connotations are applied to many more contexts than terms with more neutral connotations.[18] Thus we have only to open a dictionary to see how much use has been made of such expressions as "sweet," "nice," etc. In *Webster's Unabridged Dictionary* the word "sweet" requires almost four columns for explication while the word "sour," normally a pejorative term, takes only little more than one half of a column. This is not to imply that there is a general law about the expanded function of words when they are ameliorative. What does seem to be the case is that words, like "true" and "false," which have some highly important role in the language are very often employed in many other contexts as well. Thus we have "true" appearing in such sentences as:

1]   She is true to him.

2]   She is true blue.

3]   He is a true gentleman.

I do not believe that in any of these cases "true" is marking a sentence for inclusion in an inferential process. In the case of [*1*] "true" is easily replaceable by such terms as "faithful" or "trustworthy" where the problems of definition are certainly not as philosophically difficult as they would be if we took "true" at its face value. "True" is employed here not because we expect anyone to ask questions about what is true or false, but because it has the effectiveness of an ameliorative term. Imagine how much less effectual the probably synonymous sentence for [*1*] would be: "She is sitting home nights waiting for him." [19] [*2*] and [*3*] exemplify similar uses of "true." We can easily eliminate "true" in all of these sentences in favor of some phrase that completely avoids any distracting philosophical issues. [*2*], for example, could become "She is sincere," and [*3*] "He is a polite or kind man." But we might take a look at such a troublesome sentence as:

4]   He has a true belief.

"True" in [*4*] is possibly not so easily eliminable in favor of more neutral philosophic terminology. But I think there are many contexts in which it would be agreed that [*4*] means no more than "The sentence he asserts or has asserted is highly probable on the basis of certain sentences which are taken to be good evidence for it." Problems arise in relation to the terms "good evidence," "probable," "taken to be," and even "asserts." But they are not the same kind traditionally involved in the discussion of "true" in relation to metaphysical problems. There are contexts in which [*4*] is not intended as a mere statement about high probabilities and the relation of evidence to conclusion. "True" in [*4*] might be a means of indicating that a sentence states what is absolutely and undeniably so, and there is no longer a need to gather more evidence. But, first of all, if this is so then "true" in this context plays a rather minor role, if any role at all, since few sentences have ever been given the status of being undeniable; or if they have been held to be undeniable they have turned out to be no more than those syntactically true sentences of logic. Secondly, in those sentences which are not logical truths and yet seem to be undeniable, the application of "true" is simply redundant. We do not say "it is true that no two things can occupy the same place at the same time and in the same respect." Supposedly "it is true that" would be irrelevant. If a sentence is absolutely incapable of being wrong, its credentials ought to be immediately apparent. To add anything further would be analogous to saying "2 + 2 = 4. By the way, that is true." We would look askance at the addition of the second sentence. Of course, we might add "true" for purposes of insistence or emphasis as a child might when he says "I did go to the store! I did! It's true that I went!" But then "true" is no longer playing a significant cognitive role, just as "good" is no longer a significant cognitive word when it is taken to be no more than the verbal expression of an emotion. When then does "true" have an important role? My claim is that this occurs when the word is used to indicate a possible inference to be drawn, as in "Yes, it is true that such-and-such occurred, and for this reason we can expect the following event."

Thus "true" may be used in many ways, but not all these ways exemplify its most significant function. Just as with most words in the language we ought to distinguish essential from derivative operations. "True," when it is playing an essential part, is preparing a sentence for inclusion in an inference-making procedure and, in this kind of context, it cannot easily be replaced. The mark of affirmation is required if any inferences are to result.

In speaking of a true sentence, therefore, we ought not to look for the designation of the adjective "true" as we might look for the designation of the adjective "green" in "green apple." There might well be a green apple state-of-affairs. But there are no false nor true state-of-affairs. To look for something true or something false is to fall into the now familiar Rylean category mistake. Because "true" and "false" often appear in the grammatical space usually reserved for adjectives, we tend to think that their explication will be similar to that given to most adjectives. But the logical function of an expression is frequently far different from what its grammatical structure might suggest. "True" and "False," when they are genuinely functioning in an inquiry, are part of the logical equipment which is used to express data. They are the kind of signs which must be attachable to some linguistic expression if that expression is to be utilizable with logical connectives. Sentences may be labelled true or false for many different reasons. We may, for example, decide to call p true because there are many evidential sentences which confirm the assertion of *p,* or we call a sentence "true" or "false" when they hold strictly because of the semantical rules of the language. But to label *p* true is not to make a claim that some final answer has been given or that some "really" true statement has been made. Using "true" and "false" with sentences means that we wish to see what further data can be drawn from these sentences if they are made part of a logical system of inferences and derivations. It is as if we decide to call a board three feet in length in spite of the fact that more refined measurements give us measurements that are more or less than three feet. By applying a specific number to the board, we begin to utilize a whole system of numerical relationships. "True" and "False" have a similar use.

Even though we have all along been assuming the answer to this question, we ought still to ask about the sort of expression or expressions to which true and false are applicable. For it is clear that not everything in a language can be called true or false, e.g., "Go!" or "Good morning." Just as logical connectives, when they are being utilized for communicative purposes, require truth-values so also truth-values require certain kinds of linguistic structures. We ought, therefore, to ask to what "true" and "false" are applicable when these expressions are functioning in a logical system. Or perhaps we might put it differently. Are there some general charac- teristics that accrue to a linguistic segment, *p,* when it occurs in the context "It is true that *p*"? I think there are several important characteristics. First of all *p* must consist of several smaller linguis- tic segments since affirming something to be true means that we are agreeing to a given combination of language marks. We are claiming that it is legitimate for certain language parts to be combined to make up "*p.*" Thus if I agree that John loves Mary I am claiming that it is legitimate for the parts "John," "loves" and "Mary" to be united to form "John loves Mary." This is how agreement operates in a linguistic context. If I agree with you I am claiming that a given combination of sounds uttered by you is correct or legitimate. I am approving of *this* combination rather than of one of which I might disapprove. We cannot agree or disagree about a single linguistic mark. Only with the combinations of such marks can we employ agreement. I might think that I am agreeing with something that is not linguistic or, at least, not directly linguistic as, for example, if I say "I agree with his policy" or "I agree with what you plan to do."

But these are only abbreviated ways of saying "I agree with what he has said" or "I agree with what you told me you plan to do." In brief, agreement applies to combinations of expressions. When we disagree we are simply denying that a given combination is permissible. Thus "*p*" must be characterized by some set of more basic linguistic segments. But there is a second characteristic of "*p*" also. It is not merely the combination making up *p* that I agree to or affirm when I say "It is true that *p*" but rather the combination *in a given order*. If I say "It is true that John loves Mary" I am claiming the legitimacy of the combination "John," "loves" and "Mary" *in that order* since it might very well be false that Mary loves John. In other words *p* must also be characterized by linguistic segments that are ordinally arranged. If *p* consists of *a, b,* and *c* then it is of importance that *b* and *c* are added or connected to *a* rather than that *a* and *c* are added to or connected to *b*.

We begin to observe here the interesting phenomenon of a commitment to linguistic categories arising because of the need to make inference possible. Later [20] we shall have more to say about these sentential parts that turn out to be what we call "subjects" and "predicates." But I wish to point out that the commitment to sentences—and for that matter to subjects and predicates—is not due to some intuited knowledge of atomic facts or atomic entities which atomic sentences and names in a language are taken to reflect. Atomic sentences arise because of a need to infer and to agree and to disagree. The nature of agreement, when it is used with linguistic segments, is such that the language must become divided into certain specific categories. This is the Kantian commitment on the level of language. It determines the general characteristics that we attribute to what we call a universe.

9

Logic and Ontology

THE DEMAND that whatever we call a language must have basic linguistic structures is readily discernible when we allude to certain basic rules that seem to be absolutely essential to the construction of any language. I am referring to the logical truths in a language, especially the laws of contradiction, excluded middle, and identity. As Von Wright puts it, these are principles that must be accepted even before any language can be constructed.[1] But certain questions still continually arise: how serious is this commitment? Is it possible to have a language in which some or all of these laws have been discarded? In normal language systems—that is, those which contain regular declarative sentences that can be asserted as true or false—the need would seem to be absolute since a denial of the law of contradiction, for example, would make all sentences inferable and, therefore, render the whole inference-producing procedure useless. Thus if we wish to be able to draw conclusions from data—and this certainly seems to be one of the most desirable features of any language—the law is required. In Quine's words, if one "were to accept contradiction, he would so readjust his logical laws as to insure distinctions of some sort; for the classical laws yield all sentences as consequences of any contradiction. But then he would proceed to reconstrue his heroically novel logic as a noncontradictory logic, perhaps even as familiar logic, in perverse notation." [2] Similarly, if we were unable to say that two expressions in different discourses were identical, no communication of any consequence could ever occur since we could never talk about the same subject more than once. These basic laws of logic, therefore, seem to be a necessity in any series of marks taken to be symbols of a language. It is for this reason that the Syadvada logic of Jainism, which makes a proposition capable of being both true and false at one and the same time and in the same context, is unintelligible to us. [3] We reject it either as a mistaken analysis of how a language is actually being used or as a form of indefinable mysticism.

The need for laws of logic in any language was pointed out long ago by Aristotle. [4] He also made the point that they cannot be refuted without at the same time being endorsed. That is to say, if we deny these laws and we are doing this in the language that we normally use, then we are in the curious position of using these laws in order to deny them. This is the charge that can be made against Hegel, [5] Korzybski, [6] and many contemporary formalist mathematicians [7] who believed that they could construct a language which would contain a denial of these laws. But the difficulty with their analysis is that they never explicitly explain their use of the term "denial." More recently Alonzo Church has given us a "nonstandard" interpretation of a formal system in which "not" has different rules attached to it than what is normally ascribed. [8] And under such circumstances, where denial is defined differently, the law of contradiction could be shown to be nullified, for then $\sim p \vee p$ would not be interpretable as not-p or p. But, first of all, it is difficult to see how negation can be redefined and still remain applicable to scientific and ordinary language inquiries. Secondly, those who deny the law of contradiction do not present us with a new way of employing negation, and, therefore, we must assume that they wish both to deny the law and still hold on to the normal use of denial. But normally when we employ a denial we affirm other kinds of sentences. For example, if I deny "x is identical to x" then I affirm "it is false that x is identical to x." If we agree to this, then of course we are agreeing [a] to a rule and interpretation for using "not," and [b], unless shown otherwise, to the very same rules and meanings that we normally use. But the rules and meanings that we normally employ in either an ordinary or a more formal language are such that from them it is possible to prove that anyone who denies the law of identity, for example, is also committed to it. For a denial of identity is equivalent to "$\sim(F)(Fx \equiv Fx)$" which in turn reduces to "$Fx \sim Fx$." But from a contradiction everything follows and, therefore we can derive "$(F)(Fx \equiv Fx)$," the law of identity. Thus from a statement denying the law of identity we can derive the law of identity. Similarly, of course, if we deny $pv \smile p$ we obtain a contradiction and from this we can infer $pv \sim p$.

The point is sometimes made that in an ordinary, as distinct from a formal, language logical and other syntactical rules are constantly violated. How then can we argue for their necessity? Thus Alston has maintained that ordinary language is filled with so much vagueness that as a result we must make "some sort of qualification in the supposedly self-evident 'Law of Excluded Middle,' that every statement is either true or false. For . . . where we have a borderline application of a vague term, it is, in principle, impossible to pronounce the statement either true or false."[9] But of course a language, like any other tool, can be manipulated for numerous different purposes. Even mathematical symbols can be explored as decorative designs for the modern bedroom, and hammers might be part of an Indian war dance. But no one confuses such uses with the serious application for which language, mathematics, and hammers were intended. We can play with linguistic symbols and we might refuse to take seriously the rules and conventions that are implicit in our introduction of such expressions as "add," "multiply," "and," "if," "this," "or," etc. Thus if someone asks me whether I am going to the theater I might reply, "Well, yes and no." Or in a moment of reverie I might say that something was both good and bad. But Alston also gives a number of examples of the "theoretical advantages of vagueness."[10] Thus when we are engaged in international diplomacy we are probably better off if we keep our words vague rather than precise. If government A states that it will strongly oppose the policies of government B the word "strongly" may be much more effective if it is vague than if its meaning were clearly spelled out. Furthermore, in some sociological studies if we try to be too determinate about some of the terms, e.g., "city," "culture," it becomes exceedingly difficult to make any general statements. Alston's defense of vagueness and its implicit denial of the law of excluded middle is similar to Waismann's views that even in science vagueness persists.[11] Thus Waismann, in indicating the "open texture" of words, shows that in a scientific context the application of terms is never so carefully prescribed that error is impossible. Since testing can go on indefinitely it is always possible that what was formerly taken to be gold, for example, was not gold at all—in fact, the dispositional terms of science are deliberately left "open" so that their definitions can be extended as new tests result in new applications.

However, no one will deny that it might be advantageous to keep words vague. Wittgenstein was convinced that for certain purposes vagueness was not only adequate but also preferable to clarity.[12] Alston is probably right when he claims that vague words can produce success in diplomacy and other such contexts. But why would any of this imply a denial of any of the basic logical laws? After all, we know that the demagogues of the world have been highly effective in their own way without requiring any logical acumen and they have usually appealed to the most illogical sorts of arguments. In fact, linguists, aestheticians, and rhetoricians have shown us conclusively that the very phonemes and morphemes of a language, combined in certain ways, can by themselves cause severe political and sociological repercussions. We do not need Alice in Wonderland to tell us that *Jabberwocky* can be very pretty even if it is meaningless. But what do these matters have to do with language when it is being used to make reasoned predictions and inferences about some yet unknown state of affairs? In its most crucial aspect a language is a means of gaining some insight into possible future occurrences. It is for this reason that its techniques for inference-making have been the source of intensive study by philosophers and those concerned with the methodology of the sciences. But one of the conditions for using these tools adequately is that we are able to say of terms and sentences that they have *this* rather than *that* meaning. How valueless a syllogistic piece of reasoning would be if we were always suspicious that the middle term in the major premise means something different from the middle term in the minor one! Inference-making would simply lose all of its effectiveness. Thus Alston may be correct when he shows us the various ways in which language can be used successfully for various pragmatic ends.

But this has no relevance to the use of language in so far as it is concerned with giving us reasoned inferences. The law of excluded middle, like any other law of logic, can always be violated when the language is being employed rhetorically or for some emotive effect. But the important question is whether it can be violated when we are using the language for purposes of knowledge, inference, and prediction.

In the same vein we can very well agree that in a science as in other areas of inquiry, words frequently involve us in borderline disputes so that we cannot tell whether a given word is genuinely applicable. Examples of this kind abound, and practically every logic book, in its section on definitions, gives some sampling. But such disputes do not mean that inquiry stops or that we reject our logical canons. We do not blithely accept the fact that some sentences are both true and false or are neither true nor false. We arbitrarily stipulate on the basis of the best available knowledge that a given statement is true or false; probable or not probable. If this were not possible, all the logical and scientific tools would become unavailable to us. Neither probability nor axiomatic theories could be employed. In brief, bothersome sentences are not allowed to remain bothersome. We keep accumulating data until we believe little risk is involved in giving a sentence a truth-value or a particular probability number. Thus, in so far as a language is being used to draw logical inferences and make predictions about an unknown future, sentences and expressions that make the application of logical techniques and the formulation of inferences and predictions more rather than less difficult should be avoided.

It should be noted that the insistence that a sentence be either true or false but not both relates to a language that takes a two-valued logic as part of its fundamental structure. Alston does not deny that the ordinary formal true-false calculi indicate the ways in which logical particles are to be interpreted and used in both ordinary and formal languages. He does not reject the law of excluded middle because it might not hold in many-valued or intuitionist logics. If these different logics were his grounds for rejecting or modifying what we have called the basic rules of logic, then he would indeed be presenting a serious challenge. But he wishes to accept a language incorporating a two-valued logic and yet to deny that all sentences in the language can be regarded as true or false.

But the previous argument is applicable again in that such sentences, in a sense, have nowhere to go. They cannot be used for the crucial purposes of inference and prediction.

However, do intuitionist and many-valued logics reject the law of excluded middle? There are numerous and intricate difficulties involving the relation of two-valued to other kinds of logics and at least one commentator has claimed that "The day of the unlimited and unconcerned application of the law of excluded middle . . . seems to have passed." [13] It would lead us far afield to see how the various laws of logic fare in the light of more recent developments in metamathematics and metalogic. But perhaps a few comments ought to be made.

There is little question that the intuitionist logic and mathematics of Brouwer, Heyting, and Weyl lead to the rejection of the law of excluded middle.[14] The primary reason for rejecting the law rests on the fact that whereas the law is applicable to finite sets or classes, it is not applicable to infinite sets or classes. Given any infinite set, it is impossible, by the very fact of the infinity of the set, to discover whether every member of the set either has or has not some given property. It is not possible to construct a test to prove that every member will definitely have a given property. We simply cannot run through an infinite number of objects. On this analysis, Fermat's "last theorem," for example, is simply neither true nor false since we cannot prove the thesis that the equation, $x^n + y^n = z^n$ has no solution in positive integers when n is more than 2.[15] We are unable to move through all the positive integers. In a similar vein, any general statement that applies to an infinite domain must be listed as neither true nor false since it is impossible to construct some actual test for every n so that "There exists an n such that n has the property, p" is always true. In classical mathematics and logic, indirect proofs can be introduced so that from the assumption that it is false that there exists an n which is Pn, a contradiction can be derived. But the intuitionist rejects this kind of reasoning. Since the assumption itself can never be validated, that is, it can never be discovered whether it is false that there exists an n which is Pn, we cannot use it to prove the existence of anything.

The intuitionist thesis, however, is hardly accepted as basic mathematical knowledge. Both mathematicians and logicians have found it to be generally unsatisfactory. First of all, there is the question of how a proof is to be understood. Intuitionists demand that all theorems and logical truths be demonstrated by the actual construction of a proof that is clearly inspectable. Thus we must be able actually to observe the particular steps that are taken in the derivation of theorems. If we cannot do this, then we have no right to claim that a given formula is either a theorem or some other logical truth. On this analysis, we can see why the intuitionist refuses to countenance notions that refer to infinity. There is no way of showing how we can derive a statement about infinity from statements that deal exclusively with what is finite. But, unfortunately, the intuitionist thesis cannot rest merely on the actual observation of a derivation since some logical truths cannot be given the usual derivation and yet clearly they are logical truths. Consider, for example, "A square circle cannot exist." Both Brouwer and Heyting must admit this statement as a theorem. But no proof of it can be given either in some formal or empirical fashion. It is something we recognize in some intuitive fashion, and Brouwer explicitly admits this intuition. Brouwer bases the notion of construction primarily on what is called "urintuition"—basic intuition. This kind of knowledge is "fundamental and irreducible" [16] in his philosophy. It consists in the occurrence of some mental act by which the supposition that a given formula is not a logical truth is immediately shown to be incorrect. Thus Brouwer states that the way we can recognize that "A square circle cannot exist" is by first supposing that we have constructed a square which is at the same time a circle, and then deriving a contradiction from the supposition. [17] Similarly, the intuitionist is able to deny that $\sim \sim p$ implies p since there is no clear and self-evident way of showing that a supposition of a double denial will lead to their mutual cancellation. However, this will not do. First of all, the intuitionist rejects the use of this kind of indirect proof to validate any of the usual theorems. We cannot conclude that an object with property P exists by showing that its denial involves a contradiction. But more important, the whole notion of what Körner calls an "unrealizable supposition" makes Brouwer's basic intuition suspect. [18] If we can suppose a square circle and even a doubly negated proposition, then we ought also to be able to suppose infinite sets, unending series of numbers and all the other concepts that intuitionists seek to reject. At least if I accept a basic intuition of a square circle, then surely someone else's claim of having other odd intuitions is just as feasible. Thus the very fundamental premise which relies on a type of Cartesian self-evidency is a very shaky and uncertain foundation.

A second criticism concerns the consequences for mathematics proper that follow from the intuitionist position. An important axiom in mathematics is Zermelo's multiplicative axiom, or Axiom of Choice, which states "Given any class of mutually exclusive classes, of which none is null, there is at least one class which has exactly one term in common with each of the given classes." [19] In other words, given any set of classes we can always select at least one object from each class and in this way construct a new class. This axiom is not only required in analysis and in set theory but also in the derivation of mathematical propositions from Peano's axioms.[20] Now if only a finite number of classes were involved, it would be at least theoretically possible to form a new class by selecting one object from all the available classes. But as soon as we begin to deal with an infinite number of classes, this procedure becomes impossible. Since we can never, either actually or theoretically, go through an infinite number of classes selecting an object from each, it becomes impossible to fulfill Zermelo's axiom. Therefore, since the axiom deals with unconstructible classes the intuitionist must reject it.[21]

Similarly, an important axiom in analysis is that given an arbitrary non-empty set of real numbers having an upper bound, then the set also has a least upper bound. The intuitionist is forced to reject this axiom because it utilizes an impredicative definition, that is, a definition which must mention the set to which the object being defined belongs. Thus in order to define the real number that is the least upper bound, we must refer to the set in which the number is already a member. The intuitionist rejects the use of impredicative definitions since they require us to assume the existence of a set whose members have not yet been constructed. In other words, to prove the existence of the real number that is the least upper bound, we must assume the existence of the class that is constituted by the membership of this number.[22]

Thus the intuitionist thesis with its implicit exclusion of the law of excluded middle is by no means a fully accepted part of mathematical knowledge. As Barker has put it, "Is the philosophy behind intuitionism attractive enough to make this price (the rejection of the law of excluded middle as well as some basic concepts of classical mathematics) seem worth while? Surely not. The whole doctrine that numbers and sets are brought into being by pure intuition . . . is an exceedingly wooly and objectionable doctrine, if taken at all literally." [23]

The notion of many-valued logics has also often been taken to entail a rejection of the law of excluded middle. Since such logics have more values than simply true or false, it is apparently false to claim that every sentence must be either true or false. We are faced with an obvious violation of the law. But here is an excellent example of how we can be misled by an informal use of expressions. The law of excluded middle is sometimes interpreted as "A sentence, S, must be either true or false, and not both." But this sentence can be taken to mean "A sentence, S, must be either true or false only, and not both." The use of "only" has the force of making the law applicable only to a two-valued logic. But this is a mistake. The law is of course applicable to a two-valued logic but this is not its only application. It can also be stated for three or more valued logics. Thus if we have "possible" as a third value then the rule becomes "A sentence, S, if it is true or not-true (false), must be either true or not-true (false), and not both; a sentence, S, if it is possible or not-possible (impossible), must be either possible or not-possible (impossible), not both." A similar procedure would be followed if our third value were n or ?. We would simply substitute n or ? for *possible*. Thus the necessity of the law of logic is not that of claiming that a sentence can have only certain kinds of truth values; the necessity comes into play once we have signified some set of truth values.[24] In this way we need not defend the law of excluded middle, in the way that Russell does, for example, by showing that verifiable and possible sentences are in some way connected to true and false ones.[25] The law is a form applicable to any logical system that attributes values to its sentences or propositional functions. If "verifiable" and "unverifiable" can be used in the same way as "true" and "false," then the law tells us "A sentence, S, if it is verifiable or not-verifiable, must be either verifiable or not-verifiable, but not both."

We find, then, that even in formal systems such fundamental laws as that of excluded middle are difficult to eliminate. Furthermore, if we think of formal systems as systems which can, at least potentially, take empirical terms as parts of their interpretation, then there must be symbols for individual and predicate expressions. A well-formed formula would then consist of a predicate—either monadic or polyadic—conjoined to one or more individual variables. The implication of this would be that, regardless of the truth, falsity, or ? of the formula, we would still be required to claim that, in any given context, a term cannot be both a predicate and not a predicate, or both an individual term and not an individual term. In other words, even if we were to deny the law of excluded middle at any given level of interpretation, it would still appear as a law at some other, more fundamental, level.

Certain basic rules, therefore, remain a requirement in any series of marks taken to be symbols of a language. Undoubtedly this curious fact has led many philosophers, from Aristotle to many contemporary philosophers, to posit an ontological basis for the truths of logic. Thus the early Wittgenstein was prone to say that philosophy "consists of logic and metaphysics, the former its basis." [26] And more recently Veatch has insisted that "mathematical logic is not really about logical forms at all, but rather about real forms and relations." [27] Similarly, Dufrenne states: "Logical rules are justified by logical laws that constitute a formal ontology and grasps the formal aspects of the world." [28] If a language must contain certain specific logical forms, so the argument is made, then we have here the reflection of an underlying ontology.

Numerous attempts, of course, have been made to counter the charge of ontology. An important one consists of the argument that generalization has been confused with necessity. This has been the position of Mill and Russell [29] who claimed that the rules of logic are simply more general generalizations. But, if this were true, then it would mean that we could have a logic and a language which could violate the laws of contradiction and excluded middle. Theoretically it might be possible to have a language even if its logical rules require everything to be inferred. But we have already shown that in any scientific language this condition would be intolerable. Furthemore, few empiricists are willing to grant this empirical character of logic. [30] If the laws of logic were no more than empirical generalizations, then they must be taken to be in some sense referential just as the laws of science are taken to have both extensions and intensions. But to speak of the laws of logic as having some external reference is to become involved in the most peculiar difficulties, for these laws are said to apply regardless of what reference is present. Normally when an expression refers, it does so in the sense that it can also not refer. That is, it does not refer under all and any conditions. It is quite easy to think of a context in which a normally designative term would not denote. I say, for example, "There is a dog in the street" under circumstances in which there is no dog. But if the laws of logic are referential, they are referential no matter what occurs in the extralinguistic subject matter; and, for this reason, there is no way of indicating what they denote. It is as if we were to say the expression, F, has an extension even though no possible extension can ever be the extension of F. If F were a predicate, we would simply reject it as meaningless. It would be a modal contradiction to affirm an extension for F and yet to deny the possibility of such an extension. If F were a sentence, the same criterion of rejection would apply unless we omitted the phrase "has an extension," for then there could be sentences which had no possible extensions. Indeed when logicians speak of logical truths they mean truths that have no possible extension or, in Carnap's terms, have truth-values which depend upon something other than what is extralinguistic.[31] But of course this would be a complete denial of the position taken by those who connect logic with reality.

One might counter by maintaining that these basic logical truths do denote but in a uniquely different fashion from other kinds of expressions. Thus one might say, as Wittgenstein did, that logical sentences "show" but do not signify something extralinguistic.[32] But how can a sentence be said to "show" something and yet not itself be signifying anything? If we employ Wittgenstein's mirror metaphor, then perhaps we might argue that a logical form is an image. But we must also add, as Wittgenstein would want us to add, that it is an image of something. And then our logic both shows and signifies and it becomes appropriate to ask exactly what is being signified. Black regards the entire use of "showing" as confusing and takes it to mean that the truth of a logical sentence is established by the meaning solely of the symbols themselves.[33] But this only further deepens the problem since we must then inquire as to how the meaning of one symbol is connected to the meaning of another. This connection itself must be examined in terms of the necessity present, whether it is conventional or some other kind. We would have to ask again how it is possible to have a form of necessity that is neither stipulative nor conventional. In this same connection it ought to be noted that to explain logical truths strictly in terms of some series of symbols is unsatisfactory. It does not seem to be much of an argument to attribute necessity to one set of symbols or one form of symbolization without knowing why the necessity is attributed. This is Barker's point when he criticizes works in logic for claiming that the validity of a piece of reasoning is due to its form. What we want to know is why one form produces validity and not another.[34]

Finally, comment ought to be made about one other attempt to give fundamental rules an empirical referent. Sometimes it has been claimed that these rules denote the conditions or the limits or perhaps the presuppositions of what is extralinguistic. But how are we to explicate what it means for an expression to denote a condition or limit or presupposition in this sort of context? None of these referents are capable of being denoted in any of the usually known and reliable procedures. A limit cannot be pointed to or thought of as a theoretical construct. Limits are not even good imaginary concepts—exclusive of whether such concepts have any existential content—for what does it mean to imagine a limitation to what is extralinguistic? The Heisenberg Principle has sometimes been used as a scientific exemplification of what philosophers might mean when they speak of a limitation of human knowledge. But even if we agreed that the need for light in order to see is a limitation on our seeing powers, we surely do not mean limitation in this sense when we speak of a logical rule. The rules of logic do not limit us in the sense of telling us that inquiry can go so far and no more. These rules operate regardless of where our inquiry proceeds. Nor are they presuppositions in some scientific sense which assumes their existence without actually involving them in the inquiry. For example, scientific inquirers might acknowledge a belief in a law of causality, or simply causes, and yet they would concede that all known scientific laws are probably no more than statistical correlations. But a rule of logic is not accepted in this fashion. Perhaps it is presupposed, but it is also required in the very process of forming and inferring statements.

Language seems, therefore, not only to be an all pervasive factor in obtaining knowledge, but some of its features seem to be absolutely necessary. The acceptance of the view of apparent linguistic necessity has led to the reappearance of the notion of ontology in contemporary discussions of logic and language. If we are unable to account for the necessity which characterizes certain linguistic features by any appeal to empirical data, then the field remains open for speculation of another sort. It suddenly becomes apparent why logicians and philosophers of the past were usually led to discuss precisely those concepts, e.g., intuition, innate reasoning, associated with the domain of metaphysics. These concepts offered ways of dealing with issues which known empirical techniques did not seem capable of resolving. Perhaps metaphysical speculation cannot be avoided and those who argue, like Nagel, that logical laws are "implicit definitions" [35] have not dealt with the critical question of why certain rules of a logical system are not changeable in the way that implicit definitions are. But before we simply admit that the necessity of logical truths seems to entail an ontology, we ought to inspect the position put forth by Wittgenstein, and to some extent by Carnap, that logical truths can be accounted for on truth table analysis. This analysis, it is maintained, finally eliminates any need to account for logical necessity by means of an ontological commitment.

10

The
Truth-Functional Analysis of Logic

LOGIC has traditionally been a primary source for ontological speculation, especially in relation to logical truths which have a necessity
about them that empirical truths do not have. It is easy to see how
the curious necessity accruing to logical statements can lead us to
infer similar necessities in nature or in reality. After all, we do speak
of the designata of sentences, and we might maintain that logical
sentences designate logical elements in what is extralinguistic just
as empirical sentences designate empirical elements. As we noted in
the last chapter, Mill and other empiricists sought to defend this
view and at the same time to deny any ontology by viewing logical
truths as more general scientific laws. In this way logical truths
could still be taken as designative, but they would have no ontological status. Logical truths, like scientific ones, could be changed—
only the chances of such change were considered to be quite slim.
Mill's arguments, however, have long since been refuted. Even those
who are opposed to the admission of ontology into logic maintain
that logical truths cannot be regarded as simply another species of
scientific truth.[1] Some other accounting must be made.

In the contemporary period Wittgenstein, Russell, Carnap,

Nagel, and Quine have made the most significant contributions in trying to present an analysis of logical truths that neither makes logic empirical nor entails an ontological commitment.[2] But Wittgenstein is probably the seminal mind in these endeavors. Although there is a great deal of metaphysics in the *Tractatus*, Wittgenstein's notion of a truth-table interpretation of the basic logical particles has been most influential in minimizing the import of ontology in logic and this notion is worth examining. For if Wittgenstein is right, then logical truths are no more than mere resultants of certain arbitrary decisions concerning the interpretation of logical systems.[3] It is this view involving truth tables and logic that I should like to examine.

To understand Wittgenstein in a more modern context, let us construct a simple logical calculus and then observe how logical necessity arises within it.[4] We shall begin by imagining the construction of a calculus which will have the following as its basic marks: two variables, p and q; left and right hand parentheses; and finally the logical particles, $\supset$, $\cdot$, and $\sim$. We shall also have recursive formation rules about these marks. They will be the standard ones that will make $p \supset q$ allowable, but not $\supset pq$; $p \cdot q$, but not $\cdot pq$, etc. We shall then introduce into the appropriate metalanguage the expressions "true" and "false" and stipulate that these expressions are applicable, but not at the same time, to p and to q, and to all formulae made up out of p and q and the logical particles. We find then that four permutations of true and false can be applied to p and q:

p	q
T	T
T	F
F	T
F	F

In terms of these four permutations, we can obtain sixteen possible combinations. Each of these ways is given in the following truth tables:

1			2			3			4			5			6			7			8		
p	q		p	q		p	q		p	q		p	q		p	q		p	q		p	q	
T	T	T	T	T	T	T	T	T	T	T	T	T	T	T	T	T	T	T	T	T	T	T	T
T	F	T	T	F	T	T	F	T	T	F	T	T	F	F	T	F	F	T	F	F	T	F	F
F	T	T	F	T	T	F	T	F	F	T	F	F	T	T	F	T	T	F	T	F	F	T	F
F	F	T	F	F	F	F	F	T	F	F	F	F	F	T	F	F	F	F	F	T	F	F	F

	9			10			11			12			13			14			15			16	
p	*q*		*p*	*q*		*p*	*q*		*p*	*q*		*p*	*q*		*p*	*q*		*p*	*q*		*p*	*q*	
T	T	F	T	T	F	T	T	F	T	T	F	T	T	F	T	T	F	T	T	F	T	T	F
T	F	T	T	F	T	T	F	T	T	F	T	T	F	F	T	F	F	T	F	F	T	F	F
F	T	T	F	T	T	F	T	F	F	T	T	F	T	T	F	T	T	F	T	F	F	T	F
F	F	T	F	F	F	F	F	T	F	F	F	F	F	T	F	F	F	F	F	T	F	F	F

These sixteen tables give us all the possible ways in which the variables *p* (or ∼*p*) or *q* (or ∼*q*) conjoined by ⊃ or · can be interpreted. For example, we might decide to use table 2 as an interpretation of *p* ⊃ *q*. This would mean that *p* ⊃ *q* is to be taken as false only when both *p* and *q* are both false. Similarly, we might decide to use table 15 as an interpretation of *p* · *q*. This would mean that *p* · *q* is to be taken as true only when both *p* and *q* are false. Of course if we want · to be interpreted as "and" and to function in a way similar to its functioning in our ordinary language, we would probably employ table 8; or if we wanted ⊃ to be used in the everyday sense of "if . . . then - - -" which is considered equivalent to "it is false that . . . and not - - -," then we would select table 5.

Now the important point is that once we have selected a given truth table as the definition for ⊃ or · , certain interesting consequences follow. Consider if we decided to use table 10 as an interpretation of ⊃. Then by using the following mechanical truth table analysis, we can show that (*p* ⊃ *q*) ⊃ (*p* ⊃ ∼*q*) is logically true:

$$
\begin{array}{ccccccc}
(p & \supset & q) & \supset & (p & \supset & \sim q) \\
T & F & T & T & T & T & F \\
T & T & F & T & T & F & T \\
F & T & T & T & F & F & F \\
F & F & F & T & F & T & T
\end{array}
$$

Similarly, consider if we decided to use table 3 as an interpretation of ⊃ and table 8 as an interpretation of ·. Then again employing a strictly mechanical truth table analysis we can show that (*p* ⊃ *q*) ⊃ (*p* · *q*) is logically true:

$$
\begin{array}{ccccccc}
(p & \supset & q) & \supset & (p & \cdot & q) \\
T & T & T & T & T & T & T \\
T & T & F & T & T & F & F \\
F & F & T & T & F & F & T \\
F & T & F & T & F & F & F
\end{array}
$$

Now what is interesting in all this is that we have been able to show how logically necessary truths arise simply by virtue of the kind of interpretation we decide to give our logical particles. In our language—both formal and informal—such logical truths as $(p \supset q) \supset (\sim q \supset \sim p)$ are not due to some a priori demand made by reality. Logical truths arise in the very process of giving one interpretation rather than some other to the connective particles used in the language. Once we have decided that our meaning of "if . . . then - - -" is best expressed by table 5 and that "and" is best expressed by table 8 then numerous logical truths are suddenly imposed upon us by our very stipulations. There is no need to look to reality or to some external subject matter. Logical truths become built into the system.

The problem, however, that must arise is this: we can derive necessary truths from the interpretation we give to the logical particles, but what about these basic interpretations? Why is it that "if . . . then - - -" and "and," for example, are best expressed by tables 5 and 8 respectively? Why do these tables rather than others give us the appropriate interpretations? It is not surprising that certain things follow, once we stipulate a given interpretation, but why is this interpretation required? Church has shown us that there are many nonnormal interpretations.[5] But why are these called nonnormal? Are we not here involved in an implicit ontological commitment? We are required to use tables 5 and 8 simply because they, unlike the other tables, do express what is, in some sense, necessary. If, for example, we did try to use table 10 as an interpretation of "if . . . then - - -" we would at some point be required to reject this since it would then make $(p \supset q) \supset (p \supset \sim q)$ logically true,[6] and this would not be tolerable in our language.

This limitation on truth-table interpretations of the logical particles could have very serious ontological implications. It would mean that there are many possible truth table arrangements but not all of them are permissible. We would in a sense have here a modernized version of Leibniz's view that only the compossible worlds of all possible ones can really be enacted.[7] All arrangements of truth tables are possible but only specific ones can be used in a language.

However, before we accept the commitment to an ontology, we ought to inquire more closely into the relation of truth tables to particles. We have stated that there are specific logical expressions

in a language, e.g., "if . . . then - - -," and then we proceeded to give
these particles a truth-table analysis. But this way of stating the
entire matter makes it seem as if truth tables are apparently governed by a prior meaning of the logical particles. If a given table
does not reflect the meaning, then the table is to be rejected as an
interpretation. By this formulation we permit someone to attribute
to the particles an ontological power that determines how truth-values are to be represented in the language. But we need not formulate
the relation of truth tables to logical particles in this way. We can
think of particles as being no more than abbreviations for some set
of arrangements of truth values. For example, we can well imagine a
language such as the simple one we outlined above in which p and q
operate in the following manner: given p true and q true then the
combination pq is true, given p true and q false then the combination pq is true, given that p false and q true then the combination pq
is false, and finally given p false and q false then the combination pq
is false. We have of course simply stated table 4. The entire truth
table analysis could be given in this language whenever pq is used.
That is to say, if we wanted to distinguish pq operating in accordance with table 4 from pq operating in accordance with some other
table, we could simply always give the entire table. But languages
operate no differently from other instruments. We want them to
operate with a maximum of efficiency and a minimum of effort. Thus
there would be nothing strange if we decided that instead of giving
whole truth tables we simply gave some stipulated marks that stood
for the truth tables. We might, for example, use the expression $p \# q$
as a way of alluding to table 4; and in a similar way use $p \supset q$ as a
way of alluding to table 5. In this way we can account for the
function and origin of logical particles. They arise as abbreviations
for specific truth tables. No ontology of any serious sort is needed.
If we are required to interpret $p \supset q$ by table 5 it is not because the
sign $\supset$ makes some mystic demand. Table 5 is a frequently used one
and "if . . . then - - -" or $\supset$ is the abbreviatory form. When we
reject another interpretation for $\supset$, we are simply questioning the
wisdom and practicality of making "if . . . then - - -" and $\supset$ serve
as signs for tables that are not the familiar ones normally used.
This, and not some ontological demand, is our reason for holding on
to table 5 as our interpretation of $\supset$. Why change what has been
accepted for so long?

Thus we have shown how logical particles receive their interpretation. They are merely arbitrarily selected signs taken to stand for one of the possible arrangements among sentences having truth values. If I want to say that the combination of p and q is to be true only when p is false or q is true then I assert "$p \supset q$." If I want to say that the combination of p and q is to be true only when p and q are both true then I assert "$p \cdot q$." A logical truth is simply a mechanical result of following these basic arbitrary stipulations. Thus if I substitute p for q in "$p \supset q$" I obtain "$p \supset p$" which is always true if I follow the rules that have been laid down for "$p \supset q$." Tautologies, or logical truths, are now seen to be fairly innocuous and without any serious ontological implications. If this analysis is correct then Von Wright is correct when he chides Wittgenstein for speaking of logical truths as holding in "all possible situations." [8] "Possible situations" is easily confused with "possible worlds" which would again lead us into traditional metaphysical issues. What Wittgenstein ought to have said and undoubtedly meant was that the rules of logic hold in "all possible linguistic situations," for logic consists of rules about true and false sentences and not of laws about the universe.[9]

However, two criticisms of this truth-functional explication of logic and logical truths are relevant here. The first criticism relates to the adequacy of this view for any logical calculus higher than the ordinary propositional one. The second criticism is more fundamental in that it challenges the entire enterprise of defining logical particles by truth-table analysis.

It has been pointed out that Wittgenstein's truth-functional analysis of sentences has one serious limitation. It cannot deal adequately with logics beyond the propositional level. Wittgenstein assumed that all quantificational logics could be reduced to the basic forms of the propositional calculus. Then of course there would be a specific decision procedure for determining which sentences of quantificational logic were logically true. But it has been proved that no general decision procedure is possible for testing the logical truth or falsehood of all quantified formulae.[10] Logical truth can be tested in the instances of quantified formulae with only monadic predicate variables, or prenex normal forms with only either universal or existential quantifiers.[11] But it has been shown that, for example, where our formulae contain one or more dyadic predicates or have three or more existential quantifiers preceding a universal quantifier, no general way of determining logical truth is available.[12]

Furthermore, the use of truth tables is limited only to cases which do not involve even the possibility of an infinite domain. For if the domain is infinite, no exhaustive set of truth tables is possible. And if the domain is taken to be finite, but an infinite domain is possible, then the same formula can have the odd characteristic of being both logically true and false. For consider the following formula:

$$((x)\sim Fxx \cdot (x)(y)(z)((Fxy \cdot Fyz) \supset Rxz) \cdot (x)(\exists y)Fyx)\ ^{13}$$

If we interpret the variables as the natural numbers and "F" as "is greater than" then, in a finite domain, this conjunction is logically false since the last conjunct is false. In a finite domain there would be at least one number for which no other was greater. On the other hand, in an infinite domain the conjunction is logically true. Thus only in the rare instances where clearly no infinite domain is involved are truth tables applicable.

I think that this objection to Wittgenstein is unanswerable and, according to Moore, Wittgenstein himself later admitted his error in believing that quantified sentences were all reducible to elementary truth-functional propositions.[14] But we ought to be aware that this deficiency in the truth-functional analysis of sentences and of logical truths in general is no small matter. It is not as if we have some simple mechanical breakdown we can repair, as we might repair a Turing machine, and then proceed to grind out all the logical truths of the higher calculi. Church's theorem tells us that it is in principle impossible to devise a mechanical procedure by which all well-formed formulae of the higher calculi can be tested for logical truth. What this means, then, is that some sentences, if they are true, will be true in spite of the fact that they are not reducible to basic true or false atomic sentences. But what further truth can they have? It is not my intent to become involved here in answering this question. But it is important to point out that a pure truth-functional analysis of sentences—such as that presented by Wittgenstein—is limited not only in accounting for the statements of logic, but also in trying to eliminate possible ontological inquiry. Once we admit sentences whose truth is not dependent on the truth of their truth-functional atomic components, then many traditional theories and inquiries become permissive just as the admission of null classes and classes whose properties are different from those of its members has made permissive various inquiries concerning the ontological status of such classes. What is this sentence that is not truth-functional? In formal scientific languages, truth-functional sentences are constructed out of atomic parts that are interpreted in terms of phenomenal or physical objects. In this way we obtain either a phenomenalistic or a physicalistic language. But if a sentence is admissible into such languages and is not constructible out of the basic phenomenalistic or physicalistic parts, then how are we to regard it? In a certain sense the traditional vitalist argument concerning parts and wholes finds its analogue here on the language level. If we take a sentence, S, to be meaningful but this meaningfulness cannot be attributed solely to its component parts, then we must be able to speak of meanings that attach to wholes which are distinct from the meanings of the parts. In other words, if I make the claim that "All X is Y" is not reducible to some specific series of conjuncts then I must be attributing a more inclusive meaning to this sentence. This, of course, was why Wittgenstein was so concerned about finding out what "etc." means. "All X is Y" is sometimes taken to be definable as "X_1 is conjoined to X_1, X_2 is conjoined to Y_2, etc." But how are we to think of "etc."? It is not a simple matter of saying "etc." is the same as saying "and continue in this way" or "keep going on" since neither of these latter phrases can be understood without reference to some rule or concept that tells us how to continue. But a rule or a concept is uniquely different from that which it governs or guides. Thus to maintain that a sentence is not truth-functional is to become directly involved in the very kind of ontological problems that we have tried to avoid. Suddenly we find ourselves trying to explain what concepts and rules are since they are obviously different from the concrete entities which are controlled by concepts and rules. In so far, then as we cannot account for all true sentences by a truth-functional analysis, we have left the door open to other accounts that do admit abstract concepts.

As far as the second criticism is concerned, I think this is of far more serious consequence since it would even trivialize the cogency of Wittgenstein's reasoning about logical truths on the propositional level. The criticism can be stated in the following way: [15] Wittgenstein wished to define the logical particles strictly by reference to the truth tables. But in the very reading of the tables he is required to introduce those very particles he is seeking to define. Thus table 5 for example would read: pq true if p is true and q is true or p is false and q is true or p is false and q is false. The logical particles "or" and "and" as well as "if . . . then - - -" (if we take the *if* to be an abbreviatory form for "if . . . then - - -") are presumably understood before the truth table can be read. Otherwise there would be no reason to read it in this way rather than in an indefinite number of other ways, e.g., p is to the left of q, below p is T, below T is another T, etc.[16] Thus to explain the logical particles by the truth tables, a prior knowledge of the particles is required. We may speak of interpreting "or" in terms of this or that truth table, but of what significance can this be if we already require the use of "or" in order to explain the truth table? It would be as if we suddenly found ourselves with two "ors"—one defined by the truth table and one that explains it. How, without involving ourselves in an infinite regress, are we to define the latter? And since this latter "or" operates in such a way that the formula "p or $\sim p$" is tautological, then little has really been done to explain the notion of logical truth. The formula is a logical truth before its inclusion in a truth table. In a sense we are involved in the same difficulty Aristotle long ago noted when he asked how it was possible for someone to question the truth of the law of contradiction.[17] In the very act of questioning the law, we must be using the law if our words are to continue to remain meaningful. Wittgenstein faces the same dilemma. In explaining the particles and logical truth he already presupposes their meaningfulness exclusive of truth table analysis. In Black's words, "By his theory of tautologies Wittgenstein showed only how to convert some a priori truths into the standard disjunctive normal form. . . . When the imagery is discarded, what remains is the truism that a priori propositions are—a priori. Wittgenstein's 'solution' merely brought him back to his starting point."[18]

If we accept this criticism then we are led to make a very serious ontological claim. We find ourselves committed to a new sort of Kantianism in which certain kinds of logical relations are required to be present in any description of a world and that truth tables merely express them. Indeed this was the position taken by Russell in his earlier work where he speaks of logical words as standing for "universals" whose apprehension is as "ultimate as sensations."[19] And more recently we find Price arguing in a similar vein that "not," for example, is not a syntactic expression that has arisen because men have developed languages. Negation arises because experience itself contains moods, attitudes, and feelings which language reflects just as it does any other extralinguistic subject matter. "Disappointed expectation is what brings NOT into our lives." [20] Similarly, Price continues, existential quantification and the "if . . . then - - -" construction are not simple syntactical structures that are peculiar to and useful only in a language. On the contrary such patterns come into being because they reflect certain experiential conditions. Quantification is the linguistic component indicating actuality as against illusoriness; "if . . . then - - -" indicates the constant conjunction of certain events, e.g., lightning is in fact usually followed by thunder.[21]

A more radical consequence of the belief that logical particles are not mere abbreviations for truth tables is that drawn by the French philosopher, Mikel Dufrenne. Dufrenne accepts the view that logical particles are necessary parts of any language and then uses it to justify a teleological ontology. The purpose of a language, he argues, is not only to describe the world but also to describe the working of the logical process in the world.[22] In other words, if we think of a logical system as consisting of axioms and derived theorems then, on Dufrenne's view, this kind of system ought to be showing us what is fundamental in experience or in reality. Hegel's ontology has indeed been justified.

We see, then, that serious ontological consequences can ensue if the charge of circularity against the truth-functional definition of logical particles is upheld. And, at least to this point, the argument against Wittgenstein appears to be conclusive. To explain one logical particle, a truth table or some technique similar to a truth table is required. To explain the truth table I need the same or some other logical particle whose explanation, in turn, must eventually rest upon our using the original particle. The circularity appears to be unavoidable. But now let us ask whether Wittgenstein could have escaped this dilemma.

To begin with, it ought to be noted that even if the criticism were correct, it would not necessarily mean that an ontological theory must now be proposed. Circularity could be accepted in the same way that Hume accepted an infinite regress as being just as intelligible as the concept of an Unmoved Mover.[23] It might very well be that we need an "or_2" in order to define "or_1" and an "or_3" in order to define an "or_2", etc. But this might be perfectly acceptable without any presupposition of something more ultimate. If an infinite regress can be taken as intelligible without recourse to some final metaphysical principle, then the same reasoning ought to be applicable here as well.

However, infinite regresses—in no matter what subject matter—are not satisfying. Not only is the whole notion of an infinite suspect but the fact that some given expression can be conceived as continuously entailing a prior use whenever it is being used seems to give a uniquely odd characteristic to the relation. Furthermore, we ought not to confuse infinite regresses with circular definitions. For example, having given an appropriate definition of "cause," we can go on to show that when this relation is attributed to a series of objects, it leads to an infinite regress. The infinite regress occurs when we attempt to apply the concept of "cause." On the other hand, the definition of a logical particle requires that the definiens contains within it a reference to a logical particle. This kind of necessity occurs within the concept itself of logical connectedness. We can speak without circularity of what it means for something to be a cause of something else. But we cannot speak this way when we endeavor to define a logical connector. Thus even if infinite regresses were allowable, they would not make Wittgenstein's analysis any more satisfactory.

Wittgenstein might now reply that we have too easily accepted the supposed circularity of definition. Is it really the case that the logical particles cannot be defined unless logical particles are used? Of course any particular particle (except perhaps the negation sign), can be eliminated in favor of some other. That is to say, if I describe the truth table in forms of "or" I can also describe it in terms of "and." But then the criticism would remain intact. "And" is also a logical particle. However, there is still another possible way of describing a truth table.

The important logical feature about the ordinary truth table is the fact that the final column gives the value of the combination of values of the other columns. For example, given p as true and q as true on the same horizontal line, then the value on the same line in the last column is the value for the combination of p and q. If all this information could be given without using any particles, then the truth tables could be explained with a series of expressions without logical particles. Then abbreviatory symbols such as ⊃, v, etc. could be introduced to characterize different tables. However, can we give a particle free description of the tables?

To begin with, we can give an explicit set of directions concerning how the truth table is to be read, e.g., *1*] "Read each line of symbols downwards from left to right." *2*] "State each symbol consecutively by using 'followed immediately by.'" *3*] "The truth value of the final column is to be taken as the value of the combination of the two values given previously." Thus table 5 is now taken to read: "First line, left parenthesis followed immediately by T followed immediately by T followed immediately by right parenthesis followed immediately by T, second line, left parenthesis followed immediately by T followed immediately by F followed immediately by right parenthesis followed immediately by F, third line, left parenthesis followed immediately by F followed immediately by T followed immediately by right parenthesis followed immediately by T, fourth line, left parenthesis followed immediately by F followed immediately by F followed immediately by right parenthesis followed immediately by T."

Some features ought to be noted in both our directions and our example. First of all, parentheses are introduced in order to give a symbol for the combination of p and q, required in direction 3. The directions could mention that parentheses would be used. Secondly, it is important to indicate when a line begins and when it ends. Otherwise we would mistakenly read all the lines as one long sentence conjoined by conjunctions. Thirdly, there are still technical deficiences in the directions, e.g., it ought to be explicitly stated that the T's and F's are those of p and q and no other variables. But we shall assume that if we desire we can give a set of directions that would make explicit exactly how we propose to read a truth table.[24]

These directions are analogous to Wittgenstein's command language [25] which is devoid of any logical particles. They simply stipulate for us how we are to read a given set of symbols or marks. Even the phrase "followed immediately by" is logically neutral in the same way that it would be mathematically neutral if we said "2 followed immediately by 3" since no inference could be drawn as to whether we mean to add or subtract or divide or multiply 2 by 3. We would not even be able to infer that we mean to be ordering 2 and 3 so that we could then go on to 4, etc. At most we might attribute a sense to "followed immediately by" such as "being as close to without touching" or "being as close to without having a part in common." But this would be quite distinct from any notion of a logical function.

If our analysis is correct, then we have been able to show that there could be a language—albeit as primitive as Wittgenstein believed it to be—[26] which could be used to show us how to regard some set of marks called a truth table and which never employs the kind of symbols defined by the truth table. Not only is it interesting that Black's charge against Wittgenstein can be refuted but what is perhaps even more interesting is the fact that it is apparently quite possible to generate a truth-functional logic out of a language which is made up solely of commands or directions.

However, this attempt to give an explanation of truth tables without logical particles is not satisfactory. First of all, certain terms in the explanation are synonyms for logical particles. Thus we explain left and right parentheses as ways of showing that the variables between them are combined and the variables outside are to be excluded. But are we not here simply being evasive? Does not "combine" mean the same as "conjoin" or "put together by conjunction"? I must at least be able to say that p and q are together. But all such expressions as "combine" or "being together" are elusive ways of saying that given p and q it is proper to say "p and q." The relation of "and" cannot be avoided. And if we were asked to define "and" we would find that it abides by all the same rules of the "and" explicitly defined by the truth table. In fact, if we were not aware of what was meant by "parenthesis" we would have to be told that it was a way of keeping certain groups together and excluding others.

Similarly, we can argue that logical particles are implicit in the syntactic structure of the very sentences used to give directions. In other words the very use of such expressions as "each," "the," and "is" commits us implicitly to a whole logical terminology just as the meaningful assertion of "$2 + 2 = 4$" commits us to all the rules of addition, subtraction, etc. We might be able to reconstruct our sentences so that these commitments cease to exist. But as we have argued in the initial chapter of this book, we cannot construct a metalanguage that eliminates all notions of logical connectedness. We can purify language$_1$ by rules we set down in language$_2$ and then we can purify language$_2$ by rules we set down in language$_3$. But we soon reach a point where no further modification can occur. Some basic rules of inference must still be present; some basic linguistic structures must remain ineliminable.

Thus we find that Wittgenstein has clarified for us much of what is meant when we use logical particles. But he has not succeeded in eliminating the ontological commitment that the use of such particles can be taken to imply. That commitment remains as well as the one implicit in the failure to show that all logical calculi are truth-functional.

11

Subject and Predicate

WE HAVE been arguing that the basic rules of logic are implicit in any language intended to communicate information. But apparently other patterns or categories seem to be required if a language is to make sense. This is the view of some linguists who deny that everything in a language is transitory. Modern English is not Anglo-Saxon or Middle English; and yet we can show the changes that have transformed Middle into Modern English. But it is claimed that despite all these changes, some devices have always existed to distinguish different parts of a sentence. The device might be one of inflection or position in a given sentence or in some larger group of sentences. But apparently there has always been a means of indicating a subject and a predicate. The most complicated Anglo-Saxon sentence can be translated into a sentence with a subject and predicate. In fact, some linguists and philosophers have maintained that there could not be a language—at least one communicating information about an empirical subject matter—unless these basic linguistic categories, as well as many others, were present. Thus Sapir has stated: "What, then, are the absolutely essential concepts in speech (and written language), the concepts that must be expressed if language is to be a satisfactory means of communication? Clearly, we must have, first of all, a large stock of basic or radical concepts, the concrete wherewithal of speech. We must have objects, actions, qualities to talk about, and these must have their corresponding symbols in independent words or in radical elements." [1] And Chomsky has also viewed language in a Platonistic fashion that presupposes certain essential linguistic categories. [2] Nor are linguists the sole exponents of this view. Even Ryle who has argued strongly that there are no ontological commitments, linguistic or otherwise, has admitted that "it is not easy to accept . . . that it is just by convention that a given grammatical form is especially dedicated to facts of a given logical form . . . and, moreover, it is hard to explain how in the genesis of languages our presumably non-philosophical forbears could have decided on or happened on the dedication of a given grammatical form to facts of a given logical form." [3]

This does not mean that different kinds of sentential and other linguistic forms do not exist. Even in a single language, sentences are and can be expressed in the most perverse fashion. As some linguists have stated: "All grammars leak." [4] Obviously, all general rules of grammar have exceptions. "To the parlor I will go" may seem to be an awkward and probably not very commonplace sort of utterance; there may be some confusion about what the subject is. But the minimal requirement in this sentence, as in any other one, is that some expression finally be identifiable as a subject.

Since both linguists and grammarians accept the subject-predicate distinction, subjects and predicates ought to be clearly and distinctly definable. But curiously enough, one of the major problems for contemporary philosophers has been to determine not only how a differentiation is to be made between subjects and predicates, but also whether there really is such a distinction at all.

The average grammar book has very little analysis of either subject or predicate. Thus one standard grammar speaks of the subject of a sentence as that which "names the starting point of the statement; the (predicate) advances the statement." [5] These remarks might be useful if it were made clear—although it is not— what the starting point of a statement is and how an expression makes a statement advance. Is the "starting point" the first or second word of the sentence? Is it the first descriptive term? And when a sentence is advanced what is taking place? It might also be helpful to know whether we are to identify a statement with a sentence for it might well be that if a statement is to be distinguished from a sentence, then the starting point for one need not be the starting point for the other. Another text employs the traditional definition that the subject is "what we are thinking about and propose to talk about. The (predicate) tells something about the subject; that is, it asserts, postulates, or declares about the subject." [6] These definitions are much too broad. I might be thinking about or proposing to talk about X where X is really part of the predicate as in "Y loves X." Furthermore, in terms of the definition of a predicate "Y loves" can easily be taken as the predicate of "Y loves X" since it certainly does tell us something about X, namely, that Y loves X.

We cannot, therefore, turn to ordinary grammar books in order to find an adequate definition of subject and predicate. Now it might be thought that the entire matter of subject and predicate is strictly syntactical. It might be argued that subjects are merely expressions which, for the most part, appear in certain parts of a sentence. Everything else in the sentence is then taken to be a predicate, or part of a predicate. Thus, using some of the techniques proposed by Ziff, we might begin by making certain kinds of distinctions in a language.[7] Sentences would be classified as either semantically regular or semantically deviant. Then "the tree is brown" would be taken as a semantically regular sentence in that the sentence not only appears in the language in this form, but is also a member of a standard pattern of sentences having this form, e.g., "The chair is white," "The table is red," etc. On the other hand, "Brown is the tree" is semantically deviant in that it rarely appears in the language in this form and is not a member of any standard pattern of sentences having this form. On the basis of this distinction, various parts of sentences can be differentiated which continually appear in the semantically regular pattern of sentences. Thus given "The tree is brown" and "The chair is white" we can correlate similar parts and then use a general name to label any word appearing in a given position. "The tree" would then be taken as a subject because we have arbitrarily decided to label any complex of words "subject" if these words appear at a given position in our canon of sentences. The same procedure could be used in explicating "predicate."

This is, indeed, a possible way of indicating subjects and predicates even though in ordinary language subjects and predicates can appear anywhere in a sentence. Sentences can be transformed into semantically regular sentences and analyzed in the way Ziff suggests. However, an explanation of this sort has little relation to the kind of issue which the use of subject and predicate is intended to explicate. In any sentence each word can be given a number in accordance with its position in the sentence. Thus in "The tree is brown" the word "the" can be numbered "1"; "tree" numbered "2," etc. And we can then go on to call "2" words or "1" combined with "2" words as "subjects." But what is still to be answered is how a specific expression serves to give us the meaning of the sentence as a whole. Given any linguistic segment we presumably can attach a number to it. But this does not tell us what the role of this numbered segment is in advancing the meaning of the sentence. Yet this is what the subject-predicate distinction, in its traditional role, is meant to explicate. It tells us what the role or function of an expression is in a sentence. For example, if a linguistic segment is listed as a subject, then we are not simply being told that it ought normally to be at a certain position in a sentence, but also that it designates or in some way refers to the primary object of the meaning of the sentence. We are being informed that the designatum of a given term is one that the other designata modify or in some way condition. Thus the words of a sentence can be numbered or placed in some special position, but the important problem is how these words function to produce the meaning of the sentence. Not every word is a designator; or, if there are only designators, we assume that they designate in different ways. Thus in a sentence such as "John runs" both words designate, but surely not in the same way. At the very least "John" would seem to be designative simply by itself while "runs" is designative only in so far as it is connected to other expressions. Or we might note the distinction made by Geach that some designative expressions lend themselves as answers to the question "Who or what did such-and-such?" while others do not.[8] In order to account for these different functions of words in a sentence the expressions "subject" and "predicate" become important. To call some word a subject means that it is a certain kind of designator to be differentiated from other possible ones in the sentence. For example, it designates that on which attention must be focused or around which the action described by the sentence revolves. I am not saying that these ways of discussing the function of the subject are by any means satisfactory. But I wish to indicate that something other than syntactic position is being alluded to when an expression is labelled "subject" or "predicate."

One final remark concerning the purely syntactical analysis of expressions is relevant: if we pursue the syntactical approach in some detail, we would find it necessary to introduce terms that would play roles very similar to the traditional roles of subject and predicate. Thus we would have to acknowledge that some combinations of numbers would not lead to meaningful discourse, e.g., a sentence consisting solely of number 1 words. But then it would be a perfectly proper question to ask why some combinations are meaningful and others are not. In this way only certain combinations of numbers would be taken as significant and we would want to know why this is so. At this point we would have to make reference to the functions of these numbered words. We might have to say that a particular combination is satisfactory because the first word refers to the object whose property is indicated by the second word. Then we would generalize by asserting that usually when expressions are arranged in a certain way and also refer in a certain way, then meaningful arrangements are obtained. In other words, the mere numbering would have to be supplemented by some statement indicating the role of words in the sentence. The same traditional acknowledgment that some words tell us what the sentence is about would need to be made.[9]

However, before I continue our analysis of the subject-predicate distinction, I should like to examine one familiar kind of criticism of the distinction even before any real inquiry can proceed. The point is often made that even if the English and romance languages in general do have a subject-predicate type of structure, this is surely at most an accident of history, for there is no difficulty constructing a language in which the distinction does not occur. This argument has been presented most forcefully by Max Black.

Black has argued that we need not go through the trouble of speculating about whether there can be a language which does not have a subject-predicate form or which is not reducible to such a form. There is a specific language which surely does not employ the subject-predicate form.[10] A chess move can be described as "The

King's pawn moved to the King's fourth square." This sentence can easily be analyzed in terms of subject and predicate. But there are alternative ways of expressing this chess move. English speaking chess players commonly use the notation, "*P-K4*," and in the so-called "Continental notation" the same move is described by "*e2-e4*." Surely, Black argues, such formulations are distinct from any subject-predicate analysis. These letters are certainly far removed from any subject and predicate notions. Black admits that with a bit of effort some of these notations can be treated as subject-predicate form. For example, "*e2*" might be taken as a subject specifying the chess piece moved. But Black maintains, "it becomes progressively harder to perceive the subject-predicate form in every conceivable chess notation as alternative notations are imagined. . . . Absurd loyalty to a preconception about logical form would be needed in order to view a line drawn on a chessboard as having a subject and a predicate. Long before this point was reached, most of us would prefer to abandon the dogma of the omnipresence of subject-predicate form." [11]

Of course Black need not have gone solely to chess in order to show apparent alternative notations for subject-predicate forms of sentences. He could also have referred to the entire scientific enterprise which stresses the use of mathematical descriptions rather than the usual descriptive predicates of both ordinary and scientific languages. Thus such physicists as Hertz, Minkowski, and Dirac, to mention only a few, have minimized reliance on a language relating to observations or even models based on observations. They believe that all the essentials of physical theory can be translated into strict mathematical formulae or into symbols signifying pointer readings. Black might have pointed to Carnap's belief that as a scientific language develops its semantic terms will become convertible into mathematical form.[12] Color words, e.g., "red," will be replaced by the number of their wave-lengths.

However, in all these instances it is important to note that, as Toulmin has put it, "the mathematical theory may be an excellent way of expressing the relations we study, but to understand them— to 'see the connection' between sun-height and shadow-depth, say— one must have also some clearly intelligible way of conceiving the physical systems we study." [13] In other words, the fact that we utilize mathematics in physics does not mean that we have either replaced all observation terms by mathematical ones or that where such replacement does occur, we can dispense with the usual scientific commitments. The mathematical formula by itself tells us nothing unless there are distinctions for employing these formulae with elements capable of being described by the empirical language of science. Thus Poincaré states that pointer readings by themselves are simply meaningless until someone can use them in conjunction with a sort of language that contains observation predicates and the categorial features that make up the language of science. "The crude fact is this: I see the spot displace itself on the scale (of the galvanometer), and the scientific fact is this: a current passes in the circuit. . . . If I ask an ignorant visitor: Is the current passing? He looks at the wire to try to see something pass; but if I put the same question to my assistant who understands my language, he will know I mean: Does the spot move: And he will look at the scale." [14] A mathematical language can be constructed but its application, its use with some empirical subject matter, requires the introduction of additional statements which are given in a language with the structure of the language normally employed in both scientific and everyday contexts.

Thus the answer to Black is that our understanding of the various symbolic chess notations which he introduces rests upon our being able to explain them in terms of sentences that do or can have a formal structure in which a subject term is conjoined with a predicate term. What could "$e2$-$e4$" possibly mean to anyone unless he could ask the following questions and obtain a reply in the normal language of subjects and predicates: "What do these letters and numbers mean? Could you describe what can or will occur when this pattern of letters and numbers is asserted?" The fact that such questions are rarely asked does not mean that the user of such symbolic notations is, therefore, not dealing with a normal subject-predicate language. It is certainly possible to work up an enigmatic cipher employing only numbers, but the intelligibility of the cipher would depend upon a language having a subject-predicate commitment. Thus we must be told what the various numbers and letters stand for or mean; and such an explanation can be given either in an ordinary or more formalized language. But in either case the need for subjects and predicates remains. Even in the most complicated games involving highly complex symbols, a metalanguage must be employed which states how these symbols are to be manipulated. This is especially true when we are dealing with other than purely logical or mathematical subject matters. The chemical formula, $NaOH$, plays no role at all in an inquiry unless directions are offered to explain how these symbols are to be used and what their referents are. But such directions are given either in ordinary or more formal language—both of which need spaces for predicate and individual variables if the directions are to be meaningful. Thus a sentence can be given in mathematical form just as a Göedel number can be given for a linguistic expression. But in both instances we can understand what the mathematical statement and the Göedel number mean only in so far as we are given some explanation in a language which utilizes the subject-predicate distinction. Even in the construction of pure logistic systems the symbols do not combine by themselves. Well-formed formulae are not intuited as such. Recursive definitions are needed.[15] But these definitions are not given in symbolic form, but in the linguistic forms with which we are familiar. All systems which are constructed and all games which are played require explanations in terms of languages that do employ ordinary subject-predicate forms.

There is, however, an objection that can be raised here. Obviously languages change, and Modern English is not the English of *Beowulf* or of Chaucer. Now what if Modern English were to change so that it employed only mathematical concepts. Thus let us assume for the moment that in this hypothetical language of the far future, color terms were replaced by mathematical symbols and even proper names were changed into numerals. All designative expressions would henceforth be given in terms of some set of numerals. Under such conditions would it not be rather foolish to still insist upon some sort of distinction between subjects and predicates? Numbers are numbers and no number is somehow more of a number than some other. Instead of saying "John is bright" I might be saying, in this language of the future, "12958-I.Q.160." This would indeed be a language with basic categorial commitments far different from our own! We would, so to speak, be spouting numbers instead of words and, therefore, the very structure of the language would be different from our own.

Such a language could plausibly evolve, but, first of all, it should be noted that numbers are neutral in terms of their applications. That is, "12958" in and of itself is no more than a series of numbers. Unless there were some prior understanding in the language—that, for example, numbers of five digits referred to human beings rather than to horses—there would be no reason to believe that "12958" was applicable to a human being. Prior information would have to be offered about what these marks represented. In brief, the language would require the inclusion of some designative expressions that were not mathematical even if they were simply words such as "this" or "that." [16] In case of error or ambiguity we would at least be required to say "12958" refers to "this" or to "that." And for "I.Q.160" we would need to be able to say "I.Q." stands for "intelligence quotient" or for "adjustment level," etc. In fact, some prior understanding would be implicit that *someone* labelled "12958" *has* the intelligence quotient stated as "I.Q.160." Some notion of the having of some predicate by something would be needed as a crucial concept in the language. Thus even in this highly mathematical language, some descriptive terms would be required which would describe something having some property and this would be equivalent to a subject-predicate commitment.

Black's arguments, therefore, show us that we can construct a language without any apparent subjects or predicates. But if such a language is to be applicable to what is of some human concern, then a subject-predicate distinction seems to be needed as an explanatory dictionary for such a language.

Assuming, therefore, that it is no easy matter to construct a language free of the ordinary subject-predicate dichotomy, we can now scrutinize this odd commitment more closely. Perhaps the best approach is to discuss the various ways in which the dichotomy has been defined and defended by several important philosophers. We turn, therefore, to the positions taken by Frege, Geach, and Strawson since they have been most active in this connection.

Frege was one of those rare philosopher-mathematicians who felt no compunctions about accepting the existence of abstract entities. Thus he was able to explain the subject-predicate distinction in a fairly simple way. Frege divides what is extralinguistic into two domains, objects and concepts.[17] A subject term is then defined as that expression in a sentence which refers to the object; the predicate term is that expression which refers to the concept. Objects and concepts are mutually exclusive so that an expression referring to a concept, in so far as it keeps its reference, can never be the subject of a sentence. Concepts are always predicative and, similarly, "a name of an object, a proper name, is quite incapable of being used as a grammatical predicate." [18] Frege recognizes that in such sentences as "The morning star is Venus" and "He is Alexander the Great" the name is taken to be predicative. But this is a confusion of the two senses of "is"; one for identity and the other for predication. Frege analyzes identity sentences as consisting of two subjects referring to the same object, and this analysis leads Frege into acknowledging the differences between the senses and nominata of terms. But if we are not dealing with identity sentences then we can, according to Frege, easily find the subject and the predicate. We look for that expression in the sentence which designates an object and this is the subject; the rest of the sentence is the predicate. In Frege's words, "A concept is the reference of a predicate; an object is . . . the reference of a subject." [19]

One of Frege's fundamental difficulties—one that was even pointed out during his own lifetime [20]—concerns the ambiguity of "concept." Frege is aware that concepts have sometimes been referred to as psychological, logical, and "perhaps a confused mixture of both." [21] But he tells us that he intends to "keep strictly to a logical use." [22] This would be satisfactory if we knew what it meant to speak of a concept in its logical use. It is not as if we have a logic of concepts that will give us rules and information about how concepts are to be used. Frege recognizes the difficulty and maintains that concepts are like other primitive terms. We cannot define them; we can only attempt to clarify them "by means of hints." [23] Frege gives us one of these hints when he states that it is a mark of a concept-referring term if it is accompanied by or, presumably, can be accompanied by "the indefinite article." [24] Frege seems to be thinking here of ordinary language contexts in which the terms we acknowledge as predicates either have "a" or "an" before them or can be translated into a form in which these articles can appear, e.g., "The house is white" becomes "The house is a white house" where "white" is seen to be a predicate because of its easy transition to "a white house." But, first of all, "a" and "an" sometimes play the role of universal operators as in "A dog is a man's best friend." Secondly, these particles are sometimes attached to words that Frege might very well want to call subjects, as when we speak of "A

Napoleon of finance" or "A new Genghis Khan." There are probably ways of showing that in these examples both "Napoleon" and
"Genghis Khan" are not operating as names at all. But the point is
that in order to discern predicates we cannot merely rely on how the
particles "a" and "an" operate. Such tests would not be very reliable. In the final analysis we must look to concepts and objects
themselves and ask whether a given expression refers to one or the
other. But then the question arises again as to how concepts are to
be identified. There is no way of pointing to a concept or showing it
to someone as one might point to or show someone the referent of a
subject. There is a further complication in that concepts are taken
to be "had" or "possessed by" or "connected to" or "contained in" a
given object. And in this connection all the standard objections
raised against the use of such metaphorical terms in explaining the
relation of predicate to subject seem to be relevant.[25] Concepts are
not parts of objects in the way the parts of a pie are parts. Nor are
they contained in an object in the way water is contained in a
container. Nor are concepts connected to objects in the way one
object may be linked to another. Perhaps it is more appropriate to
say an object is an instance of a concept, but it is certainly not an
instance in the way that something may be an instance produced
from a die or a cast. Dies or casts are themselves objects used to
construct other objects. But concepts are not of this sort. They
themselves are taken to be totally excluded from the domain of
objects. In an important sense Parmenides' old argument against
Socrates holds here as well. Parmenides argued that even if we posit
the Platonic forms, it is difficult to see how the forms come into
contact with objects.[26] Similarly, even if Frege's concepts are accepted it is by no means clear how such entities relate to objects.
Frege suggests the possibility of a new relationship between concepts and objects by referring to concepts as "unsaturated" while
objects are "saturated."[27] That is to say, concepts are incomplete
entities; they require something more and for this reason the expressions referring to them have a dependent position in the sentence. These expressions we call predicates. On the other hand, since
objects are saturated, i.e., complete in themselves, the terms referring to them are of such a sort that they can stand alone exclusive of
their membership in a sentence.[28] These expressions are subjects.
But both Wittgenstein and Ramsey criticized this whole notion on

the grounds that "saturation" is a metaphor that does not help to
clarify how an object is to be distinguished from a concept and,
furthermore, "incompleteness" is a characteristic any expression
can attain. "There is a sense in which any object is incomplete;
namely that it can only occur in a fact by connection with an object
or objects of suitable type; just as any name is incomplete, because
to form a proposition we have to join to it certain other names of
suitable type." [29] Thus if there is difficulty in understanding what it
means to call something complete or incomplete, then Frege's notion
of "saturation" is not very enlightening.

Frege sometimes seems to be thinking of concepts in a purely
psychological sense when he refers to them as "thoughts." But,
paradoxically, he specifically warns against taking thoughts to be
"the subjective performance of thinking." [30] They are supposedly of
such a sort that many persons can be said to have the same thoughts
or, perhaps, to be sharing in the same thoughts. But again we face
the question of determining what it means to say that many persons
can have the same thought or that they are sharing in such thoughts.
The old arguments of Parmenides arise here as well. How can
diverse minds contain the same thought? Or how do they share in
such thoughts? Does one mind take one part and another mind take
a different part? Furthermore, how are we to think of these
thoughts? Can we think about them in the same way we think about
chairs and tables? These questions serve to show us that neither
thoughts nor concepts are adequate designata. Thus Frege's defense
of the subject-predicate form rests on an ambiguous metaphysical
position. And until this ambiguity is eliminated he cannot be cred-
ited with giving us a way of substantiating the need for the subject-
predicate form of sentence as the basic form of a language.

P. T. Geach also attempts to show that a language must have
the basic subject-predicate distinction if we are going to communicate any information at all. He begins by making the distinction
between predicate and subject on the one hand and their referents
on the other.[31] Now even if we cannot say very much about the
referents directly, the language itself tells us that there must be
some basic object-property distinction. In any sentence, according
to Geach, we find that we are attributing something or other to
something else. This, on Geach's analysis, is the basic form of all
meaning. Something is being referred to; something is being attrib-

uted or predicated of something else. He then gives us the following definition of subject and predicate: "A *predicate* is an expression that gives us an assertion about something if we attach it to another expression that stands for what we are making the assertion about. A *subject* of a sentence S is an expression standing for something that S is about, S itself being formed by attaching a predicate to that expression." [32] Now, as Strawson points out, [33] the significance of these definitions rests on an understanding of two key expressions, "about" and "stand(ing) for." We can supposedly recognize the subject of a sentence because it stands for something while the predicate tells us about something, namely, the thing the subject stands for. But unless we are told exactly how "standing for" is to be distinguished from "being about" the definitions are not sufficient to indicate what word is a subject or a predicate. Thus consider the sentence "John loves Mary." What is the subject? "John" of course satisfies the definition. But so does "Mary" since "Mary" can be said to stand for something that the sentence is about and if we attach "John loves" to "Mary" (in the proper way) then "John loves" becomes the predicate. In fact, it is possible to claim that "loves" is the subject since, if we accept relational expressions, we could take "loves" to stand for the relation of loving, and both "John" and "Mary," when they are appropriately attached to "loves," become the predicate. Thus Geach, like Peirce before him who thought that "stands for" was a perfectly clear expression for indicating the relation of a word to its designatum, [34] is hampered by the essential ambiguity of his basic linking expression.

Geach attempts to overcome some of these problems by supplying another criterion for the definition of a subject. He says that we can tell whether an expression within a proposition is being used as a subject if we can also use it alone simply to name something outside of the context of a proposition. [35] Geach recognizes that both Frege, at least in his early work, and Wittgenstein deny that names can be used outside of a propositional context. [36] But he takes this to be "clearly wrong. A name may be used outside the context of a sentence simply to name something—to acknowledge the presence of the thing named." [37] Examples of such independent use are "Poison" placed on medicine bottles and "Wolf!" and "Fire!" said at the appropriate occasions. Presumably then if we wish to find the subject of a sentence, we look for the expression that can have this independent use. But, first of all, in any sentence containing many names each name might be able to stand alone but this would not at all tell us which name was the subject. In "John loves Mary" both "John" and "Mary" can stand alone, as in a surprise meeting one might say, "John!" or "Mary!" Secondly, I am not at all sure that even a relational word could not be held to be capable of use outside the context of a sentence. I might see a man and woman embracing and simply say—perhaps aesthetically—"ah, love!" and here I might be naming something, namely, the fact that there is love. Or I might imagine someone simply saying "Trouble!" instead of "Such-and-such is troubling so-and-so." Or instead of saying "X is fighting Y" I might shout, "Fight! Fight!" It might be countered that even though we might stretch some relational words to make them capable of independent use this is clearly deviant from the usual practice. I might say, "John!" but I would not say "is running" or "runs." These latter expressions simply cannot stand alone. But the question to be answered is whether or not this is merely a matter of custom. In other words it might be that an independent use of words arises only when the word has some very special significance. Thus "Fire!" and "Poison" have immediate emotive connotations. When these expressions are employed, it is usually the case that a significant event is taking place. But a situation might arise in which a word normally not used with any emotional connotations suddenly obtains such connotations and then it is not surprising when the word begins to be used independently. For example, consider a situation in which placing one's ear to the ground and hearing someone running in the distance might mean danger of some sort. Under these circumstances someone would simply exclaim, "Running!" just as, in television Westerns, it is standard practice for the hero to cock his ear and then say, "Hoofbeats!" During the last war it was not uncommon for a soldier to cry, "Shelling!" instead of "The enemy is shelling us." The significance of the relational word gradually led to its separate use.

Thus it may well be that Geach is right when he points out that some expressions can stand alone.[38] But the reason for this may not be of any great philosophical consequence at all. It may simply be that some expressions are or can be employed in relation to significant events and this may lead to their independent use. It is no longer necessary to say, "Someone has been murdered!" The exclamation, "Murder!" is all that is required.

I should now like to direct another criticism against both Frege and Geach although it is also applicable to Russell and Ramsey. Very frequently the entire discussion of subjects and predicates is viewed primarily as an attempt to define proper names. Russell explicitly states that once we have found the proper names in a sentence we have found the subject or subjects.[39] (For Russell a sentence can have more than one subject.) Geach moves from a discussion concerning subjects into a discussion involving proper names as if there was no distinction to be made between the two.[40] Now even though it has been difficult to formulate a definition of a proper name, we can take it to be exemplified by the following sort of expressions: "Caesar," "Socrates," "John," and "Mary." But then it does not follow at all that once we have found the proper names of a sentence, or once we have defined what a proper name is, that at the same time we have found or defined the subject of a sentence. In the example, "John loves Mary" we might be able to identify what the proper names are but this would not help us identify the subject. Only once we know the subject of the sentence can we begin to be assured that in such a sentence as "John loves Mary" the subject is "John" and not "Mary." Both names are proper names, but they are not both subjects, and to extract the proper meaning of the sentence, we would have to identify the name which is the subject. Thus the search for proper names should not be confused with the search for subjects. Every subject may be a proper name (or a description) but it does not follow that the converse is true. Russell exhibits the same confusion about this matter when he argues that sentences are capable of having many subjects. For example, relational sentences have two or more subjects as in "A gives B to C." [41] But to call A, B, and C subjects is to ignore the fact that, in some sense, A is more of a subject than either B or C. In saying "A gives B to C" we are saying something quite different from "B gives A to C" or "B gives C to A." But if all these letters are taken to be subjects in the same sense, then we cannot distinguish one sentence from the other. Russell and Ramsey did not want the definition of subject to lead to the acceptance of some permanent kind of substance. They did not want to support the view that sentences reflect the Aristotelian conception of some permanent unchanging entity possessing properties. But be this as it may, it does not help matters to try to reduce subjects down to proper names. Furthermore, to say that sentences must have subjects is not to invest the world with permanent, eternal substances. The fact that every sentence requires a subject expression does not mean that such an expression retains its status in every sentence in which it appears. In *"A gives B to C"* we might mark *A* as the subject of the sentence. But *A* might not be the subject in *"B gives A to C."* A name becomes a subject in so far as it is performing a certain kind of function; there is nothing in a name that automatically makes it a subject. Geach, it seems to me, is clearly wrong when he states that "a name can occur in a proposition only as a logical subject." [42] And Frege is mistaken as well when he insists that proper names cannot be predicated. They can be and are predicates in relational sentences and, as Quine has shown us, in a strictly formal language we can place "is Socrates" as a substituend for the predicate variable.[43]

Neither Frege nor Geach, therefore, has given us a sufficiently clear way of distinguishing subjects from predicates. But P. F. Strawson has also made the claim that the distinction can be maintained and we ought, therefore, to consider his views on this matter.

There is, Strawson believes, a way of sharpening the distinction to avoid confusion and ambiguity. He begins by introducing Frege's notion of complete (*saturated*) and incomplete (*unsaturated*) objects. But Strawson now proceeds to defend the division by pointing out that some expressions can be completed "into *any* kind of remark, not necessarily a proposition (while other expressions) . . . demand a certain kind of completion, namely completion into a proposition or propositional clause." [44] For example, "Socrates" might be completed into a question "Where is Socrates?" or into an hypothesis "If Socrates is wise then he is truthful" or a command "Socrates will drink the hemlock!" On the other hand, "is wise" would seem to be completable only into a proposition or propositional clause. But now it is difficult to see why Strawson thinks "Socrates" has such versatility while "is wise" does not. I can, of course, use "is wise" to complete a question as in "Who is wise?" or a command as in "Socrates is wise!" and also an hypothesis as in "If Socrates is wise then he is truthful." What exactly is it that can be done with "Socrates" but not with "is wise"? I can construct all kinds of sentences with "is wise," declarative sentences, conjunctions, disjunctions, etc., just as I can with "Socrates." Of course, in some remarks "Socrates" is more of a completing agent than "is wise" as in a greeting. I can say "Hello, Socrates," but not "Hello, is wise." But then some remarks can be made complete by "is wise" which cannot be made complete by "Socrates," or any other name, as in "It is wise to be silent." Perhaps Strawson recognizes that certain examples could violate his criterion of completion and incompletion, for he concludes at one point that a mere inspection of the terms should show us which are complete and which incomplete. "The latter expression ('is wise') looks fragmentary just because it suggests a particular kind of completion; the former expression ('Socrates') looks non-fragmentary just because it carries no such suggestion." [45] But I don't think any expression "looks" more fragmentary than another or carries with it some "suggestion" of completion or incompletion. This sort of psychologism cannot be utilized to distinguish subjects from predicates.

Strawson also offers a different definition by introducing an ontology of things, properties, and their conjunction into "facts." Then he is able to state that a subject-expression is one which "presents a fact in its own right and is to that extent complete. A predicate-expression is one which in no sense presents a fact in its own right and is to that extent incomplete." [46] "Facts" are, however, quite problematic, and Strawson compounds the difficulty by speaking of facts as entities which are gradually "unfolded" by particulars. [47] But even if we allow this intrusion of Hegelianism, the key expressions "present" and "complete" have the same equivocal status as "about" and "stand for." Strawson sometimes substitutes "introduce" for "present," but it still remains obscure why a subject presents or introduces a fact while a predicate does not. The objections that Strawson directs against Geach can also be directed against him.

It would seem, therefore, that it is not possible to make an absolute distinction between subject terms on the one hand, and predicate terms on the other. With a bit of manipulation a subject in one sentence can be shown to be a predicate in another or a definition of a subject is also shown to be applicable to the predicate. In fact, if Quine and Russell are right, then names can be totally eliminated in favor of descriptions which, in turn, become a series of predicates. [48] We can even simplify matters more by converting every subject into a predicate form without using the standard equipment of existential quantification that Russell supplies in his theory of descriptions. We can, following Quine, change the name into some predicate form, no matter how odd it may appear. Thus "Pegasus flies" becomes "x pegasizes and flies"; "John is happy" becomes "x is johnlike and is happy." [49] And we can claim that these are predicates because they characterize in their particular way just as other predicates characterize. If something can be described as "moody" or "frustrated" or "nervous" or "impulsive" then why can it not also be described as "johnlike" and "pegasizing." And if these latter terms apparently are applicable in only one instance, then we simply answer that such predicates need not be so unusual. A painting might contain a color which has never been duplicated and perhaps may never be duplicated. The expression designating this color would have the same kind of application power as "pegasizing" and "johnlike."

No expressions, therefore, have some inherent claim to be either subjects or predicates. But then what argument are we presenting? What does it mean to say, as we have been saying, that the subject-predicate form of sentence seems to be a kind of necessary construction if a language is to communicate information of an empirical subject matter? First of all, it should be clear that even though we have been arguing that no designative expressions are inherently subjects or predicates, it does not follow that sentences need not have a subject and a predicate. Even though no specific term need be either a subject or a predicate in any given context, it may still be true that in all contexts some terms must function as subject and other terms as predicate.

Secondly, we ought to differentiate between syntactic and semantic necessity. Before a formal language can be initiated, rules for the well-formedness of expressions must be given. These rules must be present even before we can introduce rules of inference and transformation. Thus, for example, we must be able to show that $(x)Fx$ is well-formed, but not $Fx(x)$. Rules of this sort would be a minimum requirement for any language even if we lacked knowledge as to which expressions could actually be used to fill in the formula. In the usual languages constructed by Carnap, Quine, Church, Martin, and others, a firm commitment is made to predicate and individual variables as the fundamental elements of a well-formed formula. Yet further interpretation would be required before we could determine which expressions will really serve as replacements for predicate or individual variables. In other words, a distinction ought to be made between a possible subject-predicate commitment on the syntactic level and one on the semantic or interpretative level.[50] What is required in order to identify a specific expression as a subject or a predicate may be an important issue filled with its own obscurities. But if the linguistic structure itself demands the inclusion of such expressions for its interpretation, then we are indeed committed to a subject-predicate form even if there is no decision forthcoming as to whether any terms fulfill this need. In a sense we are simply modernizing the traditional argument presented by Kant that form and content are to be sharply differentiated. Kant, in attempting to answer Hume and other strict empiricists, claimed that the commitment to causality is an a priori rule needed in every act of thought even if no specific cause can actually be identified. The category of causality permeates thinking but to determine whether a given phenomenon is the cause of some other is to be left to science.[51] I do not wish to argue the merits of Kant's position, but it serves to exemplify the general position offered here, namely that it is not illogical to uphold the theory of subject and predicate even though its application in any particular context poses problems.

The discussion of subjects and predicates in formal languages leads to two important questions: *1*] Why are at least two sorts of substituends needed for variables in a formal language? That is, why must well-formed expressions consist of at least predicate and individual variables? *2*] What are the conditions an expression must satisfy if it is to be termed suitable as a predicate or individual substituend? In other words, we must analyze subjects and predicates in terms of kinds of expressions needed to interpret formal calculi. If certain linguistic constructions are needed in a language and if the language demands that there be some places for subjects and others for predicates, we must ask for the rationale for this demand. In this way we may finally be able to obtain adequate definitions for "subject" and "predicate."

The analysis of subject and predicate in terms of a formal language also enables us to reply to Russell, Ramsey, and Black who point to sentences which do not have subject-predicate form. I think their objections are directed towards those who do not think of language in terms of formal structures. Thus Ramsey could ask where the subject is in such a sentence as "Either Socrates is wise or Plato is foolish." [52] The subject here is not "Socrates and Plato" nor is the predicate "is wise and foolish." But of course this is an example primarily directed to those who look to natural languages to discover subjects and predicates. Symbolized into a formal language the sentence becomes converted into two atomic sentences each of which has substituends for individual and predicate variables. Then it seems to be quite clear that some terms in the example will be used for replacing the individual variable and, indeed, these are the terms "Socrates" and "Plato." If we wished we could call both names the subject of the entire sentence or simply list each one as subject for the respective atomic sentence. The important point is that we automatically assume that if a sentence is to be well-formed and usable, then it will fall into the standard pattern found in a formal language. Even those sentences with indexical terms, e.g., as in "This is red" and "You are tall," which Russell claims do not have subject-predicate form,[53] do take on subject-predicate form when we symbolize them in what Bar-Hillel has called "the pragmatic context of the production of the indexical sentence-tokens." [54] That is, when we symbolize indexical terms with the recognition that such terms are abbreviations for names given either implicitly or explicitly in the linguistic discourse, their translation into subject-predicate form becomes quite apparent.

The fact that many problematic terms, e.g., indexical ones, have been shown to be translatable into the standard forms of the standard logical calculus does not, however, mean that all sentences in a natural language can be accommodated in this way. Other sentences, such as "it is raining" where the "it" is obviously not an indexical term, may not be very adaptable to translation. But what should be noted is that sentences which are not usable in a calculus having individual and predicate variables are not simply left alone. We insist on finding some paraphrase which will make them formalizable for only in this way can they be used to bring precision to scientific and other empirical discourses. Thus "it is raining" is often translated into "rain is falling."

Criticism of the subject-predicate distinction in a natural language, therefore, can be fairly cogent. Not only is there the constant problem of finding some set of definitions that will be adequate, but there is also the problem of untangling sentences whose subjects are not readily discernible. German sentences, for example, are noto-rious for irregularly placed subjects. But once we begin to deal with formal languages, many of these issues disappear. Given the formal structure of the language, we know that some expression must be a replacement for a given variable. Otherwise we do not have a sentence. Thus regardless of what set of expressions we encounter, they must be rearranged to fit the calculus of the language. This commitment is basic.

This Kantian commitment is important in a language. But there is one phase of our inquiry into subjects and predicates that must now be discussed. We have to ask why a given expression becomes a substituend for a given variable. Why do we take a given word and substitute it in one place rather than another? The reply can be the standard one that certain words refer to individuals and others to properties. But then we would be claiming that the ontol-ogy of individuals, classes, and properties is not caused by linguistic forms; there are also specific individuals, classes, and properties in the extralinguistic subject matter itself and, to this extent, we are making a strong ontological commitment. But is there some way of avoiding this kind of platonistic commitment? Can we deny or at least substantially argue this ontological claim without at the same time making major revisions in our consideration of the kind of values to be attributed to sentential, individual, and predicate varia-bles in formal systems? We would not want to make such drastic revisions in the meanings and referents of words so that we would no longer be able to speak of the truth-value of sentences or of the class analysis of predicates. But what are the things that are named in a language? If we try to answer this question, we discover some interesting features of both ordinary and formal languages. First of all, as we have already indicated, states of affairs named in one discourse might remain unnamed or might be referred to by a predicate in another discourse. "Napoleon" in one discourse can be "a Napoleon" in another; "Pegasus" in one discourse can be "pega-sizes" in another. Secondly, we would find that whenever the lan-guage is operating in a scientific or problem-solving context, then all expressions are manipulated so as to make possible the best kind of explanatory or predictive inferences. Now if we think of a language in these terms—i.e., as an instrument designed for inquiry—then we can ask about what kind of entities can take on names in such a language. In other words, what must entities be like if they are to be named by the names in the language? Whatever they are like, they must be such that when they are taken to be individuals in the language and then named, all our logical rules can be used with them. This is a prime criterion. But what is the condition for something to be an individual for any scientific language? The reply is that whatever it is, it must have some degree of permanency for only the naming of such things can give us the kind of names to be used in scientific discourse. Anything selected with little or unnoticeable changeability can become eligible for namehood for only such named entities can give us the desired kind of inferences. Thus in scientific discourses we are governed by the need to make predictions and inferences, and these are the factors that determine what we will decide to name. We look for the something that, when it is named, will have the degree of permanency that will make inference possible. Thus there is no a priori commitment to some set of objects or properties or classes. On the contrary, something attains namehood only as it is found to satisfy the needs of inquiry and for similar reasons something can lose its namehood. We look to name that which will enable us to make even more successful inquiries than ever before. Individuals, per se, outside the scope of an operating language cannot even be pointed at or referred to.

It is namehood in the sense mentioned above that Carnap referred to when he spoke of commitments internal to a given language. There is no a priori command from the extralinguistic that certain objects be named in a language. Whatever is named in a language is what leads to important consequences in the language. The vast amount of extralinguistic data remains unnamed and undescribed. Only when something attains a relative degree of permanency do we find the terms that can serve as substituends for the individual variable. It is not as if we look to the raw material of experience or reality and then ask how the language can be fitted to accommodate what we find there. On the contrary, we start with the language and then we look for what can be used to make the language a more effective instrument. Names indeed refer to individuals and predicates refer to properties or classes. But what individuals are to be given names and what properties or classes are to be labelled as predicates is decided by how we want the language to function. The language requires all subject matters to be formulated by means of individual-naming terms and predicates modifying such terms. This is the Kantian commitment on the level of language. But it does not follow that there are or must be certain specific individual-naming terms or predicates present in every subject matter.

12

Descriptive Sentences

IN THE FOLLOWING chapters I should like to examine several words and concepts which, I consider to be of major importance in both ordinary and formal languages: *1*] descriptive sentences, *2*] "Exists," *3*] "Synonymity," *4*] "Make" and *5*] "Can." I take these to be interesting philosophically because the attempt to give them some formal analysis leads to curious complexities and each one has implications for certain traditional ontological issues. I shall argue that in some instances the ontological issues arise only because of an improper analysis of some of the ways in which a language operates. But in other instances the commitment to some basic ontology still remains.

It is now fairly well-established that there are two sorts of sentences, those which describe or refer to or designate some extra-linguistic subject matter—synthetic sentences—and those which do not describe such subject matter—analytic sentences. At times philosophers such as Quine and White have challenged this dichotomy.[1] But they deny that there are any sentences which function as analytic (or synthetic) in *all* contexts. What they do not deny is that in all contexts—except perhaps for those which deal exclusively with mathematics or logic—some sentences function as analytic ones and some as synthetic ones. Austin has also criticized this distinction.[2] But again he does not wish to deny that both kinds of sentences exist, but rather to insist that there is at least one other category of sentences, namely, the performative, which is just as important as other kinds of sentences but which requires a different kind of analysis.

Now a great deal of work has been expended on the analytic sentence. And probably the effort was required since the necessity attributed to analytic sentences seemed to imply a serious ontological commitment. But too often it has been assumed either that synthetic sentences are fairly easy to explain or that they can be defined by giving the definition of an analytic one. Thus Carnap explains an analytic sentence as one whose truth-value is obtained strictly by virtue of its syntax. Then he goes on to tell us that a synthetic sentence is simply one whose truth-value is not obtained in this way.[3] But aside from the very obvious objection to giving a negative definition of a term, more important reasons can be given for rejecting Carnap's view. First of all, there are some statements whose truth-value is not syntactically determined and yet there is serious question whether they ought to be regarded as synthetic, e.g., "A thing cannot be both green and blue at the same time and in the same respect," or "if A is the son of B then B is the parent of A," or "all bachelors are unmarried men," or "No event precedes itself." As Quine and others have shown, all attempts to demonstrate that the truth-values of such statements are determined by their syntax have failed.[4] There simply is no logical form that can be extracted which would at once show us that the sentences are mere substitution instances of tautologies or other sorts of formal truths. Not even the use of synonymy to show that two different expressions are really identical is effective since synonymy itself has been shown to depend upon some prior notion of analyticity.[5] Secondly, the sort of negative definition given by Carnap does not tell us how a truth-value is obtained for a synthetic sentence. What we want to know is, if the truth of a so-called synthetic sentence is not decided by its syntax, then what exactly does determine the decision. And here also traditional explanations such as, "The predicate is not contained in the subject" or "The denial of the sentence is not itself self-contradictory" are not satisfactory. Such possible explanations depend upon a prior understanding of what is meant by "containment" and "self-contradictoriness." But neither one of these expressions has yet been adequately explicated. The ambiguity in "containment" is fairly obvious while "self-contradictoriness" as it supposedly appears in "all bachelors are not unmarried men" relies upon the still unclear notion of synonymy.[6] What is needed, therefore, is not a glib statement that whatever is not self-contradictory is synthetic, but some further analysis that does more than simply state a syntactic criterion for syntheticity.

The criticism raised here might be regarded as trivial for it would seem to be almost obvious how a synthetic sentence obtains its truth value. As Carnap himself finally tells us, a synthetic sentence "says something as to what facts exist. (They) are the *genuine statements about reality.*"[7] In other words, a sentence is synthetic in so far as it is taken to describe or indicate or otherwise designate some extralinguistic state-of-affairs. Whereas "all men are men" is analytic simply because of its form, "all men are rational" is synthetic because it purports to describe some extralinguistic phenomena. And it is this descriptive claim of a sentence that would seem to make it synthetic in a given context, even though the elimination of such a claim in another context could make it analytic. In short, synthetic sentences are those which claim to be descriptive; analytic ones do not incorporate such a claim.

To say that a sentence can be descriptive would seem, I should think, to be a truism of the most obvious kind. If there is one widely accepted belief about language it is that some sentences are designed to describe some extralinguistic subject matter. In fact, in order for a set of marks to be called a language and to be applicable in the contexts in which men act and interact, it is supposed to perform the function of describing some state-of-affairs. However, even though everyone seems to be quite certain of the existence of descriptive sentences, the various attempts to make a language more precise and less ambiguous have produced curious difficulties in the analysis of descriptive sentences. We shall show that sentences normally taken to be descriptive, even in a formal language, are simply abbreviations for other sentences which are taken to be "really" descriptive and these latter, in turn, are abbreviations for still other sentences which are "really" really descriptive. I will not maintain that we are led into an infinite regress, but neither will I deny this. I will simply claim that the attempt to discover genuinely descriptive sentences is no easy matter. In fact, I will hardly be able to find any at all.

The examination of descriptive sentences will begin with a type of sentence usually classified as descriptive. I shall show that they are not descriptive, and, finally, I shall examine a class of sentences almost unanimously held to be descriptive and show that the descriptive status of these sentences is not at all clear and distinct.

Sentences which have quantifiers—either universal or particular—as their initial expressions, e.g., "all metals are conductors" or "some metals are conductors," have frequently been taken to be assertions about "reality" or "nature" or perhaps "experience." Scientists, as well as philosophers, are prone to claim that univeral sentences, for example, which are not trivial indicate laws of nature or causal relationships or even essences. In fact, traditionally such sentences were used as evidence to support a belief in some minimum type of ontology. As Geach points out, at one time the quantifier was regarded as part of the subject term.[8] Therefore the view was fostered that just as "a dog" in "a dog ran down the street" refers to a specific object so also "some dog" or "all dogs" as in "some dogs are friendly" and "all dogs are friendly" refers to specific abstract entities designated by "some dogs" and "all dogs" respectively. But with the construction of formal languages, such views of quantified sentences have been shown to be archaic.

One reason for trying to formalize a natural language sentence is that we can then more effectively apply logical techniques to it. But another reason is that formalization explicitly reveals the syntactic, as distinct from the semantic, elements of a language. Thus when we convert the natural language sentence "all metals are conductors" into $(x)(Mx \supset Cx)$ we become aware of what parts of the sentence belong to the syntax of the language and what parts to the semantics. We recognize that quantifier terms such as "some" and "all" are really not referential at all since, on symbolization, they are seen to be purely syntactic terms. Furthermore, by formalizing a universal sentence as $(x)(Mx \supset Cx)$, we can use all the logical equipment available and thus discern that we do not have here a descriptive sentence but rather an abbreviation for a series of possible descriptive sentences.[9] When truth or falsity is attributed to $(x)(Mx \supset Cx)$ it is done so on the basis that each instance of

$Mx \supset Cx$ is true. In other words universal sentences reduce down to the truth or falsity of a conjunction of instances in which specific substituends replace the individual variable. $(x)(Mx \supset Cx)$ is true if and only if $Ma \supset Ca \cdot Mb \supset Cb \cdot Mc \supset Cc \ldots Mn \supset Cn$ is true where $a, b, c \ldots n$ are constants indicating specific entities. Universal sentences are not in themselves descriptive. Rather they operate in the same way as stipulated definitions in mathematics. 8^n is not itself a new number. Rather it must be understood as an abbreviation for $8 \times 8 \times 8 \times \ldots 8$ (for n factors). Thus universal sentences are abbreviations of what supposedly are the genuinely descriptive sentences, namely, those which result from eliminating the quantifier and replacing the variables by constants. But we still have to determine whether these resultant sentences are the truly descriptive ones.

Similarly, sentences of the form $(\exists x)(Fx \cdot Gx)$ are taken to be descriptive of particular states-of-affairs. But the analysis applicable to universal sentences is relevant in this connection. When truth or falsity is attributed to $(\exists x)(Fx \cdot Gx)$ it is done so on the basis that at least one instance of an alternate series of instances is true. In other words $(\exists x)(Fx \cdot Gx)$ is true if and only if $Fa \cdot Ga \cdot v \cdot Fb \cdot Gb \cdot v \cdot Fc \cdot Gc \cdot v \ldots Fn \cdot Gn$ is true where $a, b, c \ldots n$ are constants indicating specific entities.[10]

The search for the genuinely descriptive sentence, therefore, has led us to universal and existential instantiation. But before we examine instantiated sentences, we ought to be aware of certain important problems that arise when we attempt to eliminate quantifiers. We might mistakenly be led to believe that conjunctive or disjunctive sentences—those that occur with instantiation—are indeed the descriptive sentences we have been looking for. But we must inquire further into the way our reduction from quantification to specific sentences has occurred. We shall find that at least two kinds of sentences are inferable. Also we must ask some questions about the instances themselves for, using the available logical techniques, we will discover that these instantiated sentences are either not descriptive at all, or, if some of them are taken to be descriptive, they lead to some odd issues with interesting ontological implications.

Let us consider then how instantiation occurs. We begin with an ordinary quantified sentence and then, with the rule of universal or existential instantiation, we reduce it to some series of conjuncts (or disjuncts). Now we should note that nothing here tells us whether this series of conjuncts is to be finite or infinite. Nor are we told whether reductionism of this sort is also applicable to the universal statements of scientific discourse. It is possible to state, without dogmatism, that in both science and mathematics infinite domains are assumed and that by a universally quantified sentence more is meant than a mere abbreviation for some enumerable set of conjuncts. For example, if we say "all metals are conductors," we do not merely mean that we have inspected a given number of objects called metals and have found them to be conductors. We also mean that if we were to encounter some other still uninspected object which we could call a metal, then it also could be called a conductor.[11] Our universal quantification, then, would reduce to two kinds of sentences, ordinary truth-functional sentences and subjunctives.

If a subjunctive conditional sentence is required in order to explicate quantification, then we ought to recognize that if this sentence is to be taken as descriptive, we are very close to making an important ontological commitment. Subjunctive conditionals are often taken to describe dispositional properties such as tendencies, powers, inclinations, and potentialities—all of which are part of the significant terminology of traditional ontological discourse. Thus if this kind of conditional is part of the process of instantiation, then we might indeed have a descriptive sentence, but all empiricists ought to be concerned about what it describes.

Of course, at least one major attempt has been made to translate the subjunctive into a form that permits us to use the available logical techniques, namely, the introduction of reduction sentences by both Carnap and Hempel. Reduction sentences eliminate the need to be concerned about whether a dispositional term is applicable every time the antecedent of the conditional is false. False antecedents simply leave undecided the question of whether a given dispositional term is applicable. But the reduction sentence has not been satisfactory for this very reason. It represents no improvement in formulating a general law to replace the use of subjunctive conditionals with a statement to the effect that if the antecedent is false the dispositional term may or may not be applicable. What we do claim to be saying is that something is disposed in a certain way even if we are not at present investigating it or submitting it to test conditions. This meaning, and not the one discovered in a reduction sentence, is to be attributed to the general laws of science.

Thus if quantified sentences do contain subjunctive conditionals as part of their meaning and these are not transformable into reduction sentences, then there is at least one aspect of a quantified sentence that lends itself to possible ontological inquiry. The difficulty inherent in analyzing the subjunctive sentence suggests that a possible solution rests with the admission of such abstract terms as "disposition" and "potentiality," terms whose descriptive status is at least highly controversial.

But more is involved than the subjunctive conditional in seeking to determine what is the genuinely descriptive sentence. Perhaps if we could show that quantified sentences were really no more than abbreviations for some finite series of conjuncts, or disjuncts, this would show us where the descriptive sentence is. It would be the specific truth-functional conjunct or disjunct obtained from instantiation. But even if the subjunctive were not an issue, we would still have to deal with the problems of finding a descriptive sentence among ordinary truth-functional components. Let us ask whether the sentences we seek are the substitution instances of the components of quantified sentences. Are the instantiations, $Fa \supset Ga$, $Fb \supset Gb, Fc \supset Gc \ldots Fn \supset Gn$ as well as $Fa \cdot Ga \cdot v \cdot Fb \cdot Gb \cdot vFc \cdot Gc \ldots v \cdot Fn \cdot Gn$ the real descriptive sentences of a language?

It is quite clear that molecular sentences are never descriptive. Rather they are made up of two or more component sentences whose truth or falsity determine the truth or falsity of the sentence as a whole. On this analysis a molecular sentence such as "$Fa \supset Ga$" or "$Fa \cdot Ga$" is a device for indicating the conditions under which certain so-called atomic sentences Fa, Ga, Fb, etc. can function. Thus, for example, placing the horseshoe sign, $\supset$, between Fa and Ga, as in $Fa \supset Ga$, indicates that in a given context the truth of Fa is incompatible with the denial of Ga. Similarly, when the v sign appears between Fa and Ga we are being told that in a given context the denial of Fa is incompatible with the denial of Ga.[12] In general, connective signs such as "or," "if . . . then - - -," and "and" do not add a descriptive element to sentences. For this reason Carnap calls them logical as distinct from *descriptive* signs and they serve "chiefly for connecting descriptive signs in the construction of sentences but do not themselves designate things, properties of things, etc."[13]

Are we then to say that descriptive sentences can be identified as those elementary sentences which appear immediately following and preceding logical signs operating without a quantifier? It might seem to be so. But would it make a difference if the logical connectives were dealing with intensions rather than extensions? If the logical connectives are combined with terms whose extensions can be stated as true or false, then it does follow that molecular sentences are ways of stipulating conditions for asserting atomic sentences. But if we are dealing with an intensional logic, one treating the so-called logical modalities i.e., such expressions as "necessity," "possibility," etc., then we could not simply speak of true or false sentences and the rules for combining them. For in an intensional logic, unlike an extensional one, we cannot substitute any true (or false) sentence for any other true (or false) sentence. Consider, for example, what occurs if it is not raining here now.[14] Then the sentence "it is raining" is false, and so has the same extension (or truth-value) as the logically false sentence "It is raining and it is not raining." Now let us make this last sentence a part of a larger modal sentence; when "it is raining and it is not raining" is replaced by "it is raining" the truth-value of the whole modal sentence does not always remain the same. For example, the modal sentence "it is impossible that it is raining and it is not raining" is true, while the sentence "it is impossible that it is raining" is false since even though it may not be raining here now, it is nevertheless possible.

We shall treat some of the problems of "possible" in another chapter.[15] But here it is sufficient to point out that if the values of the variables are intensions rather than extensions then the atomic sentences resulting from instantiation commit us to populating the universe with curiously abstract but obviously ontological entities such as "individual concepts" or "meanings."[16] And this makes the problem of explicating a descriptive sentence exceedingly difficult.[17] In the ordinary interpreted calculus, instantiated schema can be said to describe or to refer or to indicate some state-of-affairs. We shall shortly see that descriptive sentences are not really clearly understood in this connection either. But with an intensional logic, reference to a descriptive sentence is apparently out of place.[18] Quantification can supposedly be used in intensional logics, but what would remain when instantiation is used is by no means clear. In fact, in quantifying are we committed to postulating a realm of possible entities or of subsistent entities in the old Hegelian sense? Thus if we are to speak of a descriptive sentence with some degree of familiarity it must be in terms of an extensional rather than an intensional context.

We seem, then, to be left with what are really the genuinely descriptive sentences in a language—namely, those basic atomic sentences used as substituends for the open schemata of propositional or first order functional calculi. These seem to be our descriptive sentences. But are they?

To begin with we ought to clarify what an atomic sentence is. Russell speaks of an atomic sentence as one which contains no logical words and no subordinate sentence. More specifically, the atomic sentence "must not contain 'or,' 'not,' 'all,' 'some,' or any equivalent; nor must it be such as 'I think it will rain,' because this contains the subordinate sentence 'it will rain.' " [19] But Russell's explanation does not make atomic sentences easily recognizable. There are many sentences which would seem to satisfy Russell's conditions but which are not atomic, e.g., "a tree is brown," "a dog barked." Only when these sentences are symbolized does the fact that they are not atomic become apparent. "A tree is brown" becomes "$(\exists x)Tx \cdot Bx$"; "a dog barked" becomes "$(\exists x)Dx \cdot Bx$." [20] Similarly, even such obviously nonmolecular sentences as "there are dogs" or "there are men" are not atomic because they also are symbolizable into the quantified schemata "$(\exists x)Dx$" and "$(\exists x)Mx$" respectively. A sentence cannot be considered atomic if it is implicitly molecular or quantifiable.

Whatever an atomic sentence is, then, it must not be reducible to a sentence which is quantifiable or which contains some other logical connective. Therefore there would seem to be little question that the following set of sentences are atomic and hence are the sort of descriptive sentences we have been searching for:

a]   Socrates is a man.

b]   That is a chair.

c]   I see a dog.

d]   I see Rover.

a] seems to be clearly an atomic sentence. Church and others have asserted that at least one class of substituends of the individual variable consists of proper names. [21] And since "Socrates" is a proper name, its use in a schema ought to produce the instantiating sentence we have been seeking. "Socrates is a man" would seem to be a perfectly good instance of the schema "$(\exists x)Fx$." However, several curious difficulties now arise.

Both Russell and Quine have maintained that proper names are not really needed in a language.[22] They are mere alternative ways of giving definite descriptions. Thus "Sir Walter Scott" is replaceable by "the author of Waverley," "Pegasus" is replaceable by "the winged horse that was captured by Bellerophon" or simply "the thing that pegasizes," and "Socrates" is replaceable by "the father of (Western) Philosophy." But when proper names are replaced by singular descriptions, then [a] is no longer an atomic sentence. Rather it now reads as: "Something is a father of (Western) Philosophy and is a man and nothing else is a father of (Western) Philosophy." Quantifiers and logical connectives have blossomed into abundance. If Russell and Quine are correct then [a] cannot be regarded as atomic and, by the same token, cannot be regarded as descriptive. But are proper names no more than descriptions?

Strawson, Church, and Carnap have argued that proper names cannot be so easily dismissed.[23] First of all, if a proper name is a mere abbreviation for a description, then one ought always to be replaceable by the other. But this is obviously not the case in such famous examples as "Sir Walter Scott is the author of Waverley." Whatever else I may be stating in this sentence, it is clear that I am not simply saying "Sir Walter Scott is Sir Walter Scott" nor "The author of Waverley is the author of Waverley." Thus the argument is made that names cannot be identified with descriptions since one cannot replace the other in all contexts. But the obvious reply to this is that once the language does have names then, of course, names are different from descriptions. We can know the name but not the description of an individual or vice-versa. In a language already committed to names as entrants, the relation between the name and the description is synthetic, just as in a language with both names and nicknames, we might only know nicknames. What must be asked is whether, in a formal language, anything would be compromised if names were not permitted. Would there be something that could not be referred to? We might agree with Mill that names are needed because they refer specifically to individuals rather than to their characteristics. But descriptions can do this just as well. I could speak of "the author of Waverley" as referring to one and only one individual just as "Scott" presumably does. Sometimes descriptions are only partially, while names are totally, applicable to the entire lifetime of an individual. Thus "Lyndon Baynes Johnson" was always applicable to him and always will be while "The recent President of the United States" is only applicable for a short period. But, of course, names change also; in fact, in some societies the child is given one name which is then replaced by another when he reaches a certain age. Furthermore, different kinds of descriptions hold for different lengths of time. "The recent President of the United States" holds for a short period of time, but "the person born in 1908 near Stonewall, Texas, and educated at Southwest State Teachers College and the Georgetown University Law School" is a description that will always hold. Strawson has claimed that descriptions apply to particulars which are themselves nameable. His point is that we can ask of any description "To whom does it apply?" and then give another description or a name. But if we give another description, then we can ask of it to whom it applies. Thus we are either led into an infinite regress or we must finally reach a point when we give a proper name. But why should a proper name stop the infinite regress? We could always ask to whom the name applies. Giving a name as a reply to a question can be as unsatisfactory (or satisfactory) as a description. It might be argued that when I give a description of someone I am attaching it to some person who is always more than any sum of descriptions. Thus when I speak of the recent President of the United States I am referring to one aspect of a person who is also characterized by many more aspects. He is also, for example, the man who was Vice-President under the assassinated President John F. Kennedy. A name, it could be claimed, refers to the person who is implicit or is only partially revealed by any finite number of descriptions. But a name then attains the status of a term that has some sort of thing-in-itself as a designatum since we never observe the person who is implicit or who is revealed in this way. In an important sense this was Locke's and Hume's argument against substance. If we think of a man as consisting of a substance having properties then we can never discover this substance. We only find properties. For this reason Hume insisted that personal identity consisted of a cluster of ideas and impressions and nothing more. Names, therefore, that allude to something more besides characteristics are simply alluding to what is indefinable and unknowable.

Perhaps the major reason for trying to argue for the admission of names as distinct from descriptions is that a formal language seems to require them. Formal languages are committed to distinguishing individual from predicate variables. But what are the substituends for individual variables? If they are descriptions, and descriptions are symbolized in the way suggested by Russell, then we find ourselves in an infinite regress of descriptions. To avoid this, something other than a description must replace the variable that appears in the description. What can be more appropriate than the admission of names. Indeed, in examples given in textbooks proper names are taken to be adequate exemplifications of instantiation from quantification. From "$(\exists x)$ tall x" it is proper to go to "John is tall" or "Robert is tall" or "William is tall," etc., where "John," "Robert," and "William" are proper names.

We are caught then in a curious dilemma. To obtain a descriptive sentence, we must accept proper names. But proper names, we are told, are reducible to descriptions; and since descriptions contain variables we no longer have descriptive sentences. That is to say, the introduction of descriptions drives out descriptive sentences.

Now I think that it is not sufficient to hold onto names simply because they can or have been used as replacements for the individual variable. After all, names are not the only expressions that can be substituted for the variable. Carnap has given us formal languages in which the replacements are certain positions. Thus a proper instantiation of $(\exists x)Fx$ would be "Position, O', is blue." It is also possible to imagine a language whose expressions are divided into types but whose lowest level does not consist of terms designating concrete entities but rather properties as in "Blueness is bright" or "Blue is mellow." Such a language might involve us in the issues of nominalism and realism. But it is surely plausible to think of a formal language whose individual variables take something other than the usual proper names as substituends.

However, even though other linguistic elements besides names might be substituends, these other linguistic substitutes do not seem to give us a descriptive sentence. If we say "Blueness is bright" or "Blue is mellow" these sentences begin to have descriptive force only insofar as they are translatable into a sentence such as "Any color of the sort appearing on this object is blue and bright (or mellow)." In other words, the identification of "blueness" depends upon the possibility of indicating an object in which blueness is displayed. Thus even though many linguistic terms might be substitutable for the individual variable, the occurrence of a descriptive sentence requires a replacement that has reference to a specific object. But are there terms without the difficulties that beset names?

We might try using demonstrative terms such as "this" or "that" and thus we are led to sentences of the type [b] "This is a chair." [b] would appear to have all the earmarks of a descriptive sentence. It contains an immediate designation of an extralinguistic subject matter, an immediate reference to something characterized by the property of being a chair. It would seem, therefore, that "this" is the kind of substituend whose insertion for the individual variable can make the schema descriptive.

Russell, however, has argued otherwise. In his view "this" is neither a proper name nor a description.[24] "This" is not a proper name since proper names are arbitrary conventions. Smith could have been given another name. "But it is not an arbitrary convention that leads us to call a thing 'this' when we do so call it, or cease to call it 'this' on subsequent occasions when we have to mention it."[25] Nor is "this" a description since then it ought to apply to one and only one individual when actually it applies to all individuals no matter how diverse. Russell concludes that expressions such as "this," "that," and "I-now" (as in "I now notice a cat") are "not needed in any part of the description of the world, whether physical or psychological."[26]

Thus if [b] is descriptive, then it must be descriptive because it conceals some other kind of sentence that really makes it descriptive. But what that other kind of sentence is, and how it would be symbolized as an instance of a quantified sentence, Russell does not tell us.

Thus far the following have been eliminated as possible candidates for descriptive sentences: quantified sentences and all instantiated sentences having either descriptions, proper names, or demonstratives as substituends for the individual variable. For the same reasons also both [c] and [d]—the observation sentences which have frequently been taken to be the most indubitably descriptive— are also rejected. Symbolizing "I see a dog" and "I see Rover" is difficult in itself since "seeing" like "making" is a singularly peculiar relation. The symbolization of "I run to the store" is

$("\exists x)(Sx \cdot Rix")$ using obvious symbolism. If I run to the store then there must be a store to which I run if "running to the store" is to be a meaningful phrase. But if I see a dog, it does not at all mean that there must be a dog for me to see. I could very well insist that I see a dog even though I know that there is no dog present. Thus it would be a mistake to symbolize a sentence whose verb is "see" (or any other psychological verb) as an ordinary polyadic relational sentence employing an existential quantifier. But exclusive of this difficulty the important one for us here is that both "I" and "Rover" become converted into descriptions containing a variable and this eliminates both [c] and [d] as descriptive sentences.

We have then eliminated all candidates for atomic sentences. And we seem to be in the odd situation of comparing the basic forms of our formal language to Wittgenstein's elementary propositions which, as Black tells us, we can never produce and "would not recognize them if we had them." [27] Unless we can escape from this difficulty there seems to be no way of ever starting the construction of a formal language. Wittgenstein did indeed claim that all of truth-functional logic is derived from our elementary atomic propositions. But what does it mean to say that an entire language can be constructed even though its elementary or primitive sentences are unknowable? [28]

This constant elusiveness of the substituend for the individual variable should by this time be raising in us a dawning suspicion. Perhaps nothing can replace the individual variable! Or, to put it differently, perhaps the only descriptive sentences are those which simply leave the variable uninstantiated. But what a variable which is not permitted any instantiation can possibly stand for is quite puzzling. We are in the odd position of arguing that in spite of the fact that logicians generally speak of the individual variables as ranging over "a certain domain of objects," [29] no name of one of these substituends can be used as a substituend for the variable; not even such a comparatively innocuous term as "this." In fact, at one point Quine himself appears to recognize how peculiar it is to have singular terms regarded as substituends for the variable. He tells us, "Mistaken critical remarks keep one reminded that there are those who fancy the mathematical phrase 'value of the variables' to mean 'singular terms substitutable for the variables.' It is rather the object designated by such a term that counts as a value of the variable; and the objects stay on as values of the variables though the singular terms be swept away." [30] Thus, on Quine's view, the genuine substituends for the variable are the objects themselves and not the expressions designating such objects. But I must confess that I do not know what it would mean to substitute the object itself for the variable. Quine surely does not want us to believe that, like Swift's famous linguist philosopher, we are required to carry with us what we discourse about. Nor can I understand what it means to say that an object is still a value even if singular terms be swept away. Cantor proved that there are more objects than names for them. But this does not mean that in a discourse about such objects we need not concern ourselves with naming them. There would seem to be a fundamental error here for Quine is assuming that there is a way of speaking about objects without requiring a language. But, as we have already shown, it is not meaningful to dichotomize language and its referents and then to insist that we can discuss objects in their own right. If we swept away the designative terms of a language we would not be left with a world of objects but rather with a world of Kantian noumena, for how could we discuss a world if there was no language with which to discuss it? Finally, if singular terms are not at all necessary, then what does it mean to speak of the instantiation of a quantified sentence? We assume that in instantiating we produce the genuinely descriptive sentence. But the exhibition of an object with the accompanying utterance of a verb or some other predicate form is not a sentence. As Copi points out, in instantiating, individual constants, e.g., Aristotle, Boston, are substituted for the individual variable.[31] We substitute the names, not the objects.

We are left, therefore, with the curious difficulty of having a variable for which no substituends are permissible. But let us now think of the substituend for the variable in another way. To begin with we shall assume that our problem is with the individual variable and not with the predicate term. I mean by this that the question is whether we can identify expressions that can replace the individual variable and not the predicate term. Thus if predicates are identifiable, then we ought to ask what kind of expressions can be appropriately joined to a predicate so that the combination would make sense to anyone using the language. Or, to put it differently, how ought an expression to be functioning if it can be used with another expression functioning in the way that predicates normally do, namely, to indicate a property or a relation. When we think of the values of the individual variable in this way, then we can begin to notice some of the characteristics that an expression must have if it is to be a legitimate substituend, for we know that certain word combinations are not permissible.

The first characteristic that any term must have if it is to be suitable as a substituend is one we have mentioned in the preceding chapter. It must be taken to designate something with some degree of permanency. That is to say, it must be indicating something that is unaffected by temporal and spatial changes, even if it loses some of the various properties attributed to it. For example, if I say "John is bright" and it should turn out that John is not bright I can still talk about John. I can still use "John" even if certain predicates normally accompanying it are discarded or certain new predicates are added. However, permanency here is not to be equated with the substantival permanency that metaphysicians sometimes insist upon. If it should turn out that the majority of predicates normally conjoined to "John" are no longer suitable, then we would begin to question whether anything at all is designated by "John." Thus permanence is relative not only in the sense that what may be taken as permanent in one discourse may not be permanent in another, but also in the sense that whatever is permanent may simply become impermanent. But when we do employ a predicate, we intend it to function with a term designating something with some degree of permanence.

It might be asked how we would deal with such a sentence as "Blue is cheerful." "Blue" could be taken as a term designating some permanent entity which would be identifiable even if the properties changed. I could identify what is meant by "blue" even if it were incorrect to label it "cheerful." But if "blue" can also be an appropriate substituend for the variable, then there is no demarcation to be made between predicates and subjects. "Blue" can be as legitimate a subject as "John Smith." But even though, as we shall shortly see, predicates of a certain sort can be converted into subjects for the individual variable, in this instance, "Blue" cannot be a subject since it violates a second characteristic of possible substituends for the variable.

A second characteristic expected of any term filling the posi-

tion of the individual variable is that its designatum be locatable. I
mean by this that in attributing a predicate to something we are
committing ourselves to claiming that *this* predicate and not some
other is to be attributed. But such a selection can only occur if the
designatum of the variable replacing term is capable of being given
some location. Thus if we say "Jones is six feet tall" we assume that
the predicate is selected, that we have chosen one predicate over
many others. But our selection presupposes that there is some way
of indicating that the subject does indeed have the predicate and not
some other. But this can only be shown if the designatum of the
subject is locatable; we can find out whether this predicate and not
some other is the correct one. Thus whatever term fits the slot of the
variable it must designate something permanent and also something
discoverable. But now we can see why "Blue" in "Blue is cheerful"
is not an appropriate subject and why we really mean "Something
(other than blue) is blue and is cheerful." If I say "Blue is cheerful" I ought to be able to locate "Blue" just as I would be able to
locate "Jones" in "Jones is six feet tall." But note what occurs here.
The locating of Jones means that I will be able to say "Jones, at a
given place and time, is six feet tall." In this way we "find" Jones
and discover whether the appropriate predicate has been assigned.
But if there is no Jones then no predicate is applicable. In other
words, if there is no Jones then it follows that nothing at that place
and time can be six feet tall unless someone else from some other
place and time has replaced Jones. But if I say "Blue at this place
and time is cheerful" and there is no blue at the given place and time
something can still be termed cheerful without the introduction of
something from some other place and time. In brief, "cheerful" can
still be applicable even if "blue" is not present, but this cannot occur
with "Jones." In the language of the scholastics, "Jones" or whatever we finally decide is an appropriate substituend for the individual variable designates a primary substance while "blue" does not.
If we eliminate "Jones" the sentence, so to speak, ceases to exist.
But if we eliminate "blue" we can still infer a sentence without the
introduction of any new entities.

Reference to spatial and temporal predicates can locate the
designatum of a subject term. But such predicates are not necessary
conditions for locatability. Some designata are locatable in space
and time. But if I say "Hamlet was a neurotic" I cannot find

Hamlet in a space-time continuum. We know that Hamlet never existed—at least Shakespeare's Hamlet never existed. But it is still true that Hamlet can be located. If I am asked a question about Hamlet I can refer to one of Shakespeare's plays and then explain that Hamlet is a character described by Shakespeare but he never lived. I can ascribe to "Hamlet" the predicates ascribed to him by Shakespeare but I need never say that Hamlet lived. Thus I have located Hamlet, but he is not amenable to space-time coordinates. In fact, the introduction of locatability without dependence on space and time gives us a way of dealing with all those expressions taken to be meaningful which cannot be designated in space and time, e.g. elves, unicorns, etc. There certainly are unicorns in the sense that we can speak about them in either true or false sentences. But we must be able to give such entities a location, in this case in various books on mythology in which unicorns are mentioned and described but in which no evidence is ever presented that they lived. There is nothing philosophically unsound about speaking of Pegasus or Hamlet or of Sir Walter Scott so long as we are aware of the different ways they are located. There is evidence that there was a space-time entity called "Sir Walter Scott" and when we refer to such an entity we do mean it to be locatable in space and time. But this, of course, is not the way we find Hamlet and Pegasus, who are locatable, but neither spatially nor temporally. In fact, this modification of the existential quantifier to signify only location serves to eliminate a certain paradox in Russell's theory of descriptions. Russell had argued that when we deal with a proper name that does not have a referent, then we ought to treat it as a description. But then "Hamlet was a neurotic" becomes "There was one and only one moody Danish prince and he was neurotic"; and since there never was such a moody Danish prince all statements attributing properties to him turn out to be false. Yet, in some sense, it is legitimate to ask whether or not Hamlet was a neurotic or was vengeful or really loved his mother. On our analysis "There was one and only one moody Danish prince, and he was neurotic" turns out to be true since the quantifier requires us only to locate the moody Dane, but not necessarily to locate him in space and time. In other words, we can accept Russell's definition without thereby changing seemingly true sentences into false ones.

Thus permanence and locatability are the key characteristics a

term must exemplify if it is to be taken as a substituend for the
individual variable. This is not some a priori demand; if the predicate is to function in the language then it can do so only with a
subject that also functions in a certain way. We require locatable
objects if we are to obtain terms with which we can use predicate
expressions.

On the basis of our analysis we ought now to ask again what
familiar terms can become appropriate substituends for the individual variable. We have already apparently eliminated all the standard terms. Names become descriptions which lead us into an infinite
regress; "this" and "that" are too general. What kind of term, then,
can be used which will still not involve us in the difficulties mentioned? The answer would seem to lie in one and only one area,
namely, the area of predicates since predicates are all that remain as
descriptive elements once we have eliminated names. Names are
reduced to descriptions which, if we follow Russell, consist solely of
logical particles, quantifiers, variables, and predicate terms. Predicates, therefore, are the only descriptive items that remain intact.
But can we use predicates in some way to obtain an appropriate
substitution term for the variable? I think before we can answer this
we must make some general observations about predicates.

First of all, we ought to recognize differences among predicates.
Some predicates are all-inclusive in the sense that they apply to
almost everything with which we are familiar. Practically everything is extended or has some gravitational pull or is colored. But
now note such predicates as "blue," "large," "small," and "heavy."
These predicates apply to a much smaller class of objects even
though we may still not be able to count them all. Other kinds of
predicates such as "having an I.Q. of 120" or "being heroic" or
"having an I.Q. of 120 and being heroic" characterize still smaller
groups. Finally we have such predicates as "being an author, having
written Waverley, and being identical to anyone else who wrote
Waverley." These predicates are employed with one and only one
individual.

This hierarchy of predicates which moves from one inclusive to
less inclusive utilization is by no means an unfamiliar one. Its
analogue appears in the traditional hierarchy of predicates whose
extensions (and intensions) can be shown to vary as we add or
subtract predicates. But what is interesting is that predicates with

the largest extension, that is, which characterize the largest groups, are less identificatory than those with the smallest extension. If I say "Something is blue" an indefinite number of objects can satisfy this statement; a lesser number can satisfy the sentence "Something is heavy and has an I.Q. of 120"; finally, one and only one object can satisfy "Something is an author, wrote Waverley, and is identical with anyone else who wrote Waverley." This latter complex predicate I shall call an *identifying predicate*. Unlike "blue" and "having an I.Q. of 120" an identifying predicate may be used with one and only one entity. It serves to identify the uniqueness of an entity rather than that which it has in common with other things. This, then, is the first observation to be made about predicates. They can have larger, smaller, and singular employment.

A second observation is that predicates can be divided into those which have been applied and those which are applicable. Thus if I speak of "The boy in the house across the street" the chances are that I have met this boy or seen him or I am in some way acquainted with him. I not only can speak about him but I also know him or I can locate him for you. But speaking about this boy is quite different from speaking about "The Emperor of Japan." I may speak more about the Emperor of Japan than I do about the boy across the street, but the chances are that I have never met the Emperor of Japan and probably never will. In this case I use the description "The Emperor of Japan" but I do not and never will apply it. On the other hand, "The boy in the house across the street" is both used and applied by me. In other words we must distinguish between applied discourse and discourse which may be or could be but still never has been applied. Most discourse probably consists of the latter. We talk of many things concerning the earth, the planets, stars, etc. But much of this discourse has not been actually applied. We can speak of the planet, Mars. But few of us have ever gone to the trouble of actually looking through a telescope and seeing that planet. Thus we ought to recognize that at any particular moment only a very small part of our discourse has ever been applied.

With these two observations concerning the identification and application functions of predicates, we can now present our argument for what we take to be the possible substituends for the individual variable. What we shall argue is that the only expression capable of becoming a proper substituend for the individual variable is a definite description containing an identifying predicate that has been applied. Of all the descriptive elements in a language, this is the sole one that satisfies the criterion of indicating a locatable permanent entity. Furthermore, if proper names are not allowed then the definite description is the next best candidate as the subject term of a sentence. Both in formal and informal languages, definite descriptions have frequently been listed as suitable substituends for the individual variable. But can we accept this without at once becoming involved in all the objections raised previously about accepting a description as a possible substituend? Descriptions involve variables. Therefore, why do they not involve the infinite regresses formerly rejected?

The reply to this question rests on the further contention that the description that can serve as a substituend for the variable must also be an applied description. It must be one that is not only used but also applied. An example might make this point clearer. Consider the following discourse:

A.   Someone is the author of Ivanhoe.
B.   Who is the author of Ivanhoe?
A.   The author of Waverley is the author of Ivanhoe.

Note the different kinds of descriptions being employed here. "The author of Ivanhoe" is a description in use, but it has not been applied for otherwise the question would be pointless. I would not ask who someone was if I had some knowledge about him or if I could identify him in some way. My asking means that I am looking for some description with which I am already familiar and with which I can now associate the given description. This is the role of "The author of Waverley." If this is a satisfactory answer, it gives us a "familiar" description, one whose designatum has been given a location either through history or literature books or other documents attesting to the life and career of someone who was the author of Waverley. The answer, of course, would not be satisfactory if there were not this familiarity. We would then go on to ask "Who is the author of Waverley?" Only when we receive a description that has been applied in the sense indicated here, can we be sure that we have an appropriate substituend for the individual variable. We ought to note, incidentally, that this distinction between use and application also shows us quite clearly why it is not paradoxical to say "The author of Waverley" is not synonymous with "The author of Ivanhoe." Two expressions are synonyms when their use and applications are the same. But, as we have seen, they may have similar uses but only one may have been applied.

However, we apparently have still not shown how to avoid the infinite regress paradox. No matter what we do, we are still permitting a description to replace the variable. But the distinction of the various functions of an expression now leads to a solution. The way we would symbolize an expression performing in one manner need not be the way it would be symbolized when the same expression is performing in another manner. For example, we now know enough to use quotation marks around a word when we are mentioning but not using the word itself. In this way we indicate that the rules which govern unquoted terms are not to be employed with quoted terms. Similarly, we know that the rules governing an expression which is part of an oblique or modal context will not necessarily be governed by the same rules when it is outside that context. In an analogous fashion we can argue that the way we symbolize "the author of Waverley" as a definite description is not necessarily the way we would symbolize it as a substituend for the individual variable, or rather when it is functioning as both a used and applied term. When the same expressions function differently in different contexts we can construct rules to show the difference. We can state that where a description is being used as a substituend for the variable, then we are to omit quantification in the description. We are to treat it as a whole unity operating in the way that proper names are traditionally taken to function. We symbolize an ordinary definite description by means of the Russellian notation, but the other can be symbolized by some arbitrary procedure; an alphabetical letter, an asterisk attached to the description or some other mark that explicitly tells us the description is to be governed by different rules than when these marks are missing. In other words, we can select an expression that normally operates as a definite description and make it a substituend for the individual variable without thereby becoming involved in an infinite regress. Thus in our sentence above, "The author of Waverley is the author of Ivanhoe," we do not employ both descriptions with quantifiers. Only "The author of Ivanhoe" is given the usual Russellian notation; "The author of Waverley" becomes incorporated as "$A*$" or some other suitable symbol. Definite descriptions with identifying predicates become the only names available in the language.

Thus we now have, after a rather arduous exploration, what

would seem to be the genuinely descriptive sentences of a language. They are the basic atomic sentences which contain definite descriptions with identifying predicates in place of the individual variable. If the analysis is correct, then at least on this one point the ontology has been lessened. There is still the subjunctive to account for and we are still committed to a distinction between predicates and subjects. But neither substances nor things-we-know-not-what need become the subjects of predicates. In any discourse the subject of an atomic sentence is that which has been identified in another discourse and has also been applied. There are no ultimate subjects but only those relative to a given context of inquiry.

13
"Exists"

THE ATTEMPT to define "exists" has been one of the major traditional problems in philosophy. Applying this expression to an object
or to some state-of-affairs has seemed, at least to some philosophers,
to be applying an expression uniquely unlike such words as "red" or
"large" or "chair" or "Socrates." Questions dealing with what these
differences are have preoccupied philosophers for many years. But
in recent times a supposedly definitive explication of "exists" has
been discovered. Finally, it has been maintained, all those complex
issues growing out of the use of "exists" have been dissipated
because it can now be shown that all uses of "exist" are explicable in
one of two possible ways.

First of all, "exists" in many of its uses is really devoid of any
serious philosophical involvement. Thus if I say "He exists for
himself alone" I simply mean "He is a great egotist" or perhaps "He
is very selfish." The word "exists" in this context is eliminable in
favor of some expression whose substitution in the original sentence
does not significantly change the meaning of the sentence but serves
to free the sentence of any serious philosophical difficulties. Of
course, some interesting questions may be raised about such terms

as "egotist" or "selfish," but these clearly would not be as perplexing as those which have normally been attributed to "exists." Similarly, in many other sentences such as "With this drug he can continue to exist" or "He just exists from day to day" we can easily find ways of replacing "exist(s)" by some phrase or expression which does not violate the original meaning of the sentence but which, at the same time, minimizes the need for any genuine philosophical scrutiny. For example, "With this drug he can continue to exist" could become "With this drug he can continue to live" and "He just exists from day to day" could be changed into "He just barely manages from day to day." These translations are not necessarily synonyms for the original sentences. But unquestionably they would be satisfactory except in the most unusual contexts. And even in those instances where one might quibble about the synonymity of expressions, I doubt whether an expression could not be found which could adequately and justifiably be substituted for "exists."

Of course, numerous different sorts of sentences do use "exist" and dictionaries offer quite a number of definitions of this term.[1] But the important point to remember is that in the majority of these uses of the word no real philosophic issue is involved. In our ordinary employment of language a word may be philosophically troublesome, but this does not mean that the term is really troublesome. We can speak of the substance of an issue or the substance of the experiment and yet not be involved in the whole metaphysical issue of substance. Things happen in the functioning of a language and we ought not to mistake philosophically insignificant uses of terms with philosophically significant ones. "Exists," in most contexts, is not a very difficult word with which to deal.

However, even though there is a sense of "exists" which can be quite adequately managed, there is another sense that really produces—or at least has produced—some of the major questions with which philosophers concern themselves. Granted that "exists" is often not very consequential, there are contexts in which its use is very interesting. In these instances "exists" is not a simple designative expression which can be cancelled out by the substitution of some other designative expression. Rather "exists" here operates as a means of distinguishing fact from fiction, reality from both illusion and hallucination. Thus we may say "Dogs exist" not only when we want to say that dogs have been perceived or that someone is able to verify that he has seen dogs, but also that there really are dogs present regardless of our perceptions. Or again we might think of the sense of "exist" as signifying Kant's old distinction between the real thaler and the imagined one. We can psychologically conjure up a vivid and very forceful picture of a coin—perhaps even give it an appropriate dent—but surely listing all the properties pictured does not entail its existence. Similarly, it is well known that we can actually claim to be seeing the most vivid scene and yet, of course, it would simply be false to say the scene exists; or at least we would say that it does not exist in the same way we think that most of the objects around us exist. Or again we might think of the sentence "Unicorns exist" as false not because all unicorns are dead or have never been observed, but simply because there are no unicorns at all. If I may be pardoned an inordinate looseness of language, the "exists" whose contradictory is nonexistence is here being discussed and, at least until recently, it has been argued that "exists" in such a sense cannot be simply and easily eliminated in favor of some familiar designative expression. We cannot, it has been claimed, find some familiar philosophically neutral phrase that will convey the same meaning of "exist" in "Dogs exist."

"Exists" in this second sense has produced some of the most serious philosophical questions and it is this sense which supposedly many contemporary logicians and philosophical linguists have claimed they have finally explicated. If we wish to know how to treat "exists" we find its role in a formal language. And in a formal language "exists" is clearly seen to be expressed by means of the existential quantifier. Thus "exists" is no more than a synonym for existential quantification. When we recognize this, so the argument goes, the whole gamut of ontological problems usually accompanying this word cease to exist. For, as is well known, quantifiers do not play designative roles in a language. They are part and parcel of the syntactic equipment of the language and as such we cannot ask about them what they refer to—reality or what not—just as we cannot ask what the logical particles "and" "or" and so forth refer to. Thus even though many questions still revolve around syntax, these questions, it is maintained, are not to be confused with the old ontological problems taken to be part of the difficulty with "exists." Existence is really a matter of quantification and once we recognize this, then asking certain questions simply becomes illegitimate.

This then is the way we finally resolve all questions of existence. And it is, therefore, quite understandable for Quine to state that " 'exists' has perhaps no independent business in our vocabulary when '($\exists x$)' is at our disposal,"[2] and for Alonzo Church to criticize those who look for some further meaning in "exists" than that given by the quantifier.[3] To exist is indeed to be quantified by an existential quantifier. And if this explication of "exists" is correct then something very important has occurred, for it is then certainly the case that philosophers, as Kneale explicitly states, have confused a grammatical with a logical category.[4] They have mistakenly believed that because "exists" is usually predicated of a noun in ordinary language that, therefore, it is a designative expression. But this is wrong . . . at least this is what we have been told.

Now I believe that this translation of "exists," in its most philosophically significant sense, is not the simple matter that it would appear to be. I shall try to show that there is a sense in which the meaning we expect of "exists" is not to be found in existential quantification. Then I shall argue that even if it were the case that all philosophically significant uses of "exists" could be given a quantification translation we ought not, therefore, to think that [1] we have made "exists" into a purely syntactic phrase or that [2] all serious philosophical questions concerning "exists" have been eliminated.

Let us begin the criticism by making quite certain what the argument for existential quantification is. The argument can be stated in the following way: All such sentences as "Trees exist," "Men exist," or "Unicorns exist" are perfectly proper. The mistake occurs, however, in believing that "exists" is a predicate of some sort because it occupies an adjectival place. Thus we come to believe that "exists," like other predicate words, is a semantic expression with the same designative characteristic as other semantic expressions. But actually "exists" is not adjectival at all. It is a piece of syntactic equipment which could be readily identified if our language were a little more precise and a little better formulated logically. Thus we would find that just as "a man" in the ordinary language sentence "A man walked down the street" is transformed into a predicate when the sentence is formalized, so also "exists" in "Dogs exist" would be transformed from a semantic into a syntactic phrase.

Furthermore, consider the consequences of permitting "exists" to be a predicate. Then it would be perfectly proper to say "Some animals do not exist." But if the quantifier is treated in the usual manner, then this sentence is translatable into "There exists an animal that does not exist," or "There is an animal that is not," or "Some animal has being but it does not exist." The self-contradictoriness of all these translations is quite apparent. I shall shortly have something more to say about the way we believe quantifiers ought to be interpreted. But if we assume the usual interpretations, then it does seem to be quite clear why "exists" cannot be treated as a predicate.

These, then, are the arguments for the substitution of "There is something such that" for "exists." Nor is the translation vitiated by the fact that proper names as well as general ones are used with "exists" as in "Socrates exists." For, as Quine has shown us, we can translate such sentences as "Socrates exists" into "$(\exists x)$ $(x = \text{Socrates})$" or even "$(\exists x)(Sx)$" where "Socrates" plays the same role as any adjective.[5] Or, finally, we can simply decide to eliminate all proper names in favor of descriptions and here the quantifier can be employed without much awkwardness.

How satisfactory is the translation? If I were a metaphysician or someone who at least had formerly believed that the definition of "exists" comprises one of the major problems of philosophy, I would find it odd. In spite of all the apparent advantages that seem to accrue to treating "exists" as a quantification expression, it offers a curious sense of illusion, as if somehow the understanding of "there is something such that" was quite obviously clear in comparison with the complex and ambiguous expression "exists." It is as if by eliminating sense data in favor of appearance sentences, we believe we have also eliminated traditional epistemological problems, as if to speak of the appearance of an object is perfectly clear while to speak of the sense datum of an object is not. Or it is as if the substitution of "intensional object" for "meaning" suddenly makes the whole problem of meaning clear and easily explicable. But, of course, none of these substitutions has done any more than simply shift the issues to other linguistic levels in which the same traditional issues reappear.[6]

We have then an initial suspicion. But suspicions are not reasons. Are there any legitimate reasons for rejecting the equivalence of "exists" with existential quantification? First of all, we know that the existential quantifier can be eliminated in certain limited languages. Thus $(\exists x)Fx$ is reducible to $FavFbv \ldots Fn$. There is a problem about this reduction if we assume an infinite domain of objects. But this does not affect the elimination of existential quantification by instantiation. Moreover, we can always raise the question of whether the whole notion of infinites is intelligible. We can point out the logical dilemmas involved in positing an infinite series of disjuncts which in relation to at least one important criterion of verification, makes all existential sentences empirically meaningless. As Hempel has put it, "The sentences to be qualified as cognitively meaningful are precisely those which can be significantly said to be either true or false." [7] But how is an infinite series of disjuncts ever to be judged false? Hempel does propose a means of avoiding this dilemma by introducing an artificial empiricist language which precludes the possibility of forming certain troublesome kinds of sentences.[8] But the point here is that no attempt is made to deny that the quantifier is to be regarded, at least in theory if not in practice, as reducible either to a finite or an infinite series of disjuncts. A language, therefore, can be constructed which is technical and yet does not have an existential operator.

The construction of such a language, however, would not necessarily mean that we have also eliminated the kind of problem traditionally engendered by the use of "exists." For as Carnap tells us, even in a propositional language, that is, one having only propositions without quantifiers we do want to speak of some of these propositions as having objective reference while others do not. In Carnap's words, a proposition is used to designate "something objective that may or may not be exemplified in nature. . . . (By) the proposition that this table is black we mean something that actually is the case with the table, something that is exemplified by the fact of the table's being as it is." [9] The insertion of such phrases as "exemplifies," "objective," and "actually is the case" does not at all conceal the implicit commitment to the view that something either exists or does not exist. In other words, the elimination of the existential quantifier does not mean we no longer need distinguish "objective" from "subjective," "is actually the case" from "is actually not the case,"—the very distinctions which are the core of all the problems involving "exists."

Furthermore, if the existential quantifier is equivalent to some disjunctive series of propositions, then the preanalytic meaning of "exists" ought to be exhausted in this disjunction. Specifically if I say "Dogs exist," then this should mean the same as "Rover is a dog or Pluto is a dog . . . or Fido is a dog." But let us now question this identity. Would it be improper to deny every disjunct and to claim that this does not entail that dogs do not exist? Now, of course, there are many contexts in which the disjuncts could be denied and yet this would not mean that dogs do not exist. For example, I might be shown some object named "Rover" but it is not a dog; similarly for both Pluto and Fido. Thus here I would be perfectly justified in saying "Rover is not a dog nor is Pluto a dog nor is Fido a dog." But it would simply be wrong for me to deny that there are any dogs. Now, of course, the immediate objection is that the names I substitute for the constants of the disjunction must belong to the proper range. I must use as substituends names which are usually taken to be names of dogs. But if the only names allowable are those which are known to be names of dogs, then how is it ever possible to falsify the obviously falsifiable sentence "Dogs exist"? It must be true, by definition, that Rover, Pluto, and Fido are dogs and, therefore, dogs must exist. But obviously we do intend our existential sentences to be falsifiable. Thus we must be able to falsify—at least theoretically —every disjunct. And under such circumstances we could have a situation such as we have indicated in which every disjunct would be false but it would still not entail a denial of the fact that dogs exist.

Nor does it necessarily follow that if we affirm that Rover, Pluto, and Fido are dogs that, therefore, dogs exist. Rover, Pluto, and Fido could be Disneyan dogs just as we know there as Disneyan dinosaurs which do not exist. Again we might try to restrict the application of names only to those objects which are not Disneyan nor imaginary in some other way. But then the traditional problems raised by "exists" reappear. For what we should like to know is how to distinguish the imaginary from the nonimaginary, the actual from the nonactual. In brief, translating "exists" into quantification terms seems to lead to an inevitable circle. Quantification is reducible to a disjunction of propositions, but the resultant propositions cannot be adequately understood unless there is a prior recognition of what it means to say something does or does not exist.

The equivalence itself, therefore, is suspect. But perhaps it might be possible to make the restrictions more precise. What if the possibility of including Disneyan among actual dogs could be curbed! What exactly has been accomplished when we can show that "exists" is reducible to existential quantification? A possible answer is that we can now discern that "exists" is not a predicate since quantifiers are not predicates. But what is a quantifier, especially the existential quantifier? Again the answer is that it is part of the syntactic equipment of the language. But if it is a syntactic element, it is far different from any of the other syntactic elements. The function of "or," for example, is considered to be fairly clear and uncomplicated. It simply signifies for us which sentences are allowed to be combined, e.g., given p and q combined by "or" we are being told that it cannot be the case that both are false. The functions of conjunction, implication, and equivalence can be similarly expressed.[10] But what does the quantifier do? If its function is strictly abbreviatory, doing no more than abbreviating a disjunctive series, then what does this have to do with "exists"? If I say "Men exist" I am saying more than merely "a is a man or b is a man or . . . n is a man." I want it understood, even if I do not explicitly express it, that a is a man and is not Disneyan but actual, or b is a man and is not Disneyan but actual, or c is a man and is not Disneyan but actual. So the existential quantifier might very well be used in the way it is normally used, but why confuse this with the traditional problem of existence? We might argue that "is actual" is redundant since the use of "is" in the disjunct already incorporates the meaning of actuality.[11] But "is" does not entail "exists." Neither in formal nor in ordinary languages is "is" always the "is" of existence. Everything really is, but not everything exists. I do say "Dinosaurs are large animals" or "Unicorns are not real" or "God is great" and so on for all possible names. But the "is" in the sense of the actual is quite another matter and, therefore, the mere use of "is" in the disjuncts does not account for the meaning we wish to attach to "exists."

What then are we to do with "exists"? We obviously cannot reject it as a nonsense term to be placed in the same category as those old-fashioned expressions, "essence," "thing-in-itself," and "forces"? In rejecting "exists" we would simply be required to find some other word to mark the distinction between the two senses of "is." Thus we cannot arbitrarily reject "exists."

Another alternative is to re-examine the rejected hypothesis that makes "exists" out to be a predicate. Can we account for the various logical and other difficulties that beset the attempts to view "exists" as a predicate without eliminating its status as a predicate? Kant, of course, has given the classic criticism of taking existence as a predicate.[12] And his observations have been buttressed by the recent remarks of Moore,[13] Kneale,[14] Malcolm,[15] and others.[16] Certainly we cannot think of "exists" as having the same logical status as "green," "is larger than," and other predicates of this sort. Furthermore, if quantification is permitted over predicates, then we can anticipate quantification over "exists" and it would seem to be highly irregular—even for the most metaphysically inclined philosophers—to say that the property of existence also exists. But what does suggest itself here is that perhaps some very obvious fact about predicates has been overlooked, namely, that technically we have no right to speak of predicates unless we have some way of categorizing these predicates. That is to say, following Russell, we must indicate the level and degree of each predicate being used.[17] Otherwise we are faced with the traditional paradoxes Russell and Whitehead sought to overcome. Thus even though on some level of predicates "exists" cannot be a predicate we have not shown that "exists" cannot be a predicate at some other level. In brief, we are constantly thinking of predicates in the sense of "green," "is larger than," etc., and neglecting the fact that there can be and are different types of predicates. I refer to such predicates as "useful" as in "The object is useful"; or "manufactured" as in "This automobile was manufactured by U.S. Steel"; or "non-empty" as in "I want a non-empty box"; or "packaged" as in "The chocolates are packaged."[18] To say an object is useful or manufactured or non-empty or packaged is not to add some further properties to the properties it already has. It is to say something about the entire cluster of properties. In a similar way logicians distinguish distributive from collective predicates. If I say lions are numerous I do not mean that each lion has the property of being numerous. But if I say that lions are carnivorous, then I do mean this to apply to each individual lion. In normal usage no one confuses these different functions of predicates. We would not expect anyone to ask us how it is possible for "numerous" or "manufactured" to be predicates. We simply do not look for a manufactured or a numerous property in the same way we might look for a green property. Yet all these predicates serve important functions. It is of some consequence to be told that an object is manufactured or that chocolates are packaged.

We ought now to inquire whether it is not possible that "exists" is analogous to those predicates we have just mentioned. It may very well be that we have not been asking a genuine question at all when we ask: Can "exists" be a predicate? We ought perhaps better to have asked: Can there be some category of predicates other than the basic one that includes "green," etc., to which "exists" can belong? We know that confusing a collective with a distributive term can cause various logical paradoxes. Can it be that the paradoxes of "exists" arise only because we have confused it with some other more familiar category of expressions?

Consider again the previously mentioned predicates, "Manufactured," "useful," "non-empty," and "packaged." Note how they function. To say an object is useful is to say its characteristics lend themselves to the satisfaction of some human need. To say an object is manufactured is to say that the characteristics of an object have been produced by human means. A non-empty box, like a filled one, is one whose properties are so combined that it can and does hold things. Packaged, or wrapped, chocolates are chocolates whose properties are being preserved in a certain specific way. In each instance the predicate is not a direct one in the way "green" is. Each predicate tells us something about other predicates; it is not directly attributable to an object. A thing is not "manufactured" in the same way that it is "green." "Being packaged" does not belong to a piece of chocolate in the same way that "being sweet" does. We distinguish between directly and indirectly attributable predicates.

Now let us ask whether "exists" is analogous to these indirectly attributable predicates and, if it is, whether this means we can employ it as a predicate without becoming involved in the usual logical difficulties. We shall begin with a recent attempt to analyze "exists" as an indirect predicate.

Imagine an example of the following sort: I am a lion hunter who distributes lions to various zoos. Now I might some day, out of curiosity or perhaps to find out whether lion catching might still be profitable, want to discover how many of these lions still survived. Then, after discovering that they were all alive after a number of years had passed I might say, "Extraordinary, they all exist." [19] My use of "exists" here would not serve to add anything to the property of lions. Rather it woud serve as a way of ruling out death in captivity, escape, or shipment back to Africa. "Exists" would here be a predicate but it would not involve any of the traditional difficulties. It would simply be a word that indicates, according to the context, the absence of some predicates which could or ought to be present. It is what has been called an "excluder" word [20] that serves to "rule out something without adding anything, and ambiguously rule out different things according to the context." [21]

Undoubtedly, this is a possible use of "exists." But even though this is perfectly good usage, it has nothing to do with the philosophical issue of "exists." To say "Lions exist" can under some circumstances mean "None of the lions have died, or escaped, or been shipped back to Africa." But in such cases we are using "exists" in the sense of being alive or some other easily substitutable predicate, and we have already argued that the sense of being alive is not the philosophically significant sense that has been attributed to "exists." In this analysis dead lions would not be existent lions. But the traditional problem supersedes the question of being alive or dead. If something called a lion exists then it is indeed alive. But this does not mean that its existing and its being alive are equivalent. We may want to reject the application of "lion" to an object if it is not alive. But it would still make sense to say that whatever the object is—alive or not—it does exist. Even corpses have an existence in this basic sense. And it is this sense of "exists," and not others, that has produced the major philosophical issues of the past. Thus even though "exists" does often operate as an excluder word, this is still not the "exists" that has been so troublesome.

Another possible way of treating "exists" as a predicate which deals with other predicates can be extracted from past philosophic thinking which sought to tie "exists" into the notion of guaranteed continuation. Predicates have one very important characteristic. We must be able to depend upon them in future undertakings. We sometimes would like the golf ball to move differently; a hole in one is a very fond dream. But even the occurrence of this hoped for event would be shocking if it resulted only after the ball sprouted wings and gracefully deposited itself in the cup. In fact, under such circumstances, no matter how much the hole in one may have been desired, the event would be rejected as an illusion. We would deny the existence of the ball. In other words, we question the existence of something when some rather unusual and unexpected incidents occur. A desert oasis is called a mirage, that is, its existence is questioned, because running towards it does not bring it any nearer and because it shimmers—something we do not expect of oases. What this suggests is that "exists" is simply a way of giving linguistic expression to the hope that properties which have been together will remain together. Thus to say "Dogs exist" is to say "a has the property of being a dog and will continue to have this property, or b has the property of being a dog and will continue to have this property . . . or n has the property of being a dog and will continue to have this property." What we are doing is revealing to others what we believe is assured in the future. "Exists" operates in our language like the warranty operates among mechanical objects. It assures us that anticipations about the future will be fulfilled.

This way of treating "exists," however, is also not satisfactory. First of all, there are standard objections to defining "exists" in terms of predicates alluding to future possibilities or anticipations. To begin with, it would make the whole notion of existence a strict psychological affair. Something exists because of my strong hope that it will continue to have the predicates that I attribute to it now. But let something disrupt this hope, let me suddenly despair about what I attribute to objects, then suddenly nothing at all exists. The solipsism of this position is obvious. But even more than this we become involved in an infinite regress in which nothing can ever be said to exist. For consider if I say that x exists only insofar as certain predicates are found to be applicable in the future. Let us assume that the future arrives and we must now check whether or not the predicate is applicable. But now to check whether an object actually has a predicate applicable to it, that is, whether "x is red," for example, is true I must go on to check some set of future predicates that will assure me that it is actually the case that x is red. In other words, for every future predication that becomes testable. I must posit another future predication and so on *ad infinitum*. Thus nothing exists, or more explicitly, no predication can ever be attributed to an object.

These attempts, therefore, to permit "exists" to remain a predicate but to give it a meaning which avoids paradox are not successful. Either they substitute meanings of which most philosophers have been aware and which have been recognized as irrelevant, or else they involve dilemmas that seem to lead to an infinite regress of perplexities. There are no doubt other ways of changing "exists" into a safe predicate although no successful procedure has yet appeared. But I should now like to turn to what, on the basis of remarks made in the preceding chapter, may give us a successful way of dealing with "exists."

"Exists" is problematic because it apparently states exactly what is stated by the existential quantifier. If I say "Socrates exists" I am saying no more than "There is something which is named 'Socrates.'" For similar reasons if I say "Some animals do not exist" I am making the contradictory statement "There exists at least one animal that does not exist," that is, the statement is contradictory if I treat "exists" as a predicate distinct from the existential quantifier. But we have claimed that there are times when it is sensible to say that certain things exist even if the quantifier is not available to express this and that it is also sensible to say that there is such-and-such even if it does not exist, e.g., Hamlet, Pegasus, etc. But we can make these references only if we can adequately distinguish the quantifier from "exists." And this is what we did endeavor to do in the preceding chapter. We argued that the existential quantifier ought to be taken as a locator quantifier indicating that something is locatable without necessarily being locatable in a space-time coordinate system. Thus if I say "There is something called 'Hamlet'" I am simply saying that I can locate Hamlet for anyone who asks. I can show anyone the situation which would enable him to understand what I mean by "Hamlet." No reference to Hamlet's having lived at a certain time and at a certain place would be necessary except insofar as such references are made in Shakespeare's plays. In brief, to identify Hamlet I would only need to go to Shakespeare's play and not to any space-time system of reference. But once we separate space and time from location, a function for "exists" distinct from the quantifier begins to appear. To use the quantifier means that we are claiming that every substituend for the variable is locatable. But to also add the predicate of existence is to say that every predicate that is locatable is also accompanied by space-time predicates. This is surely what we mean by "exists" in most of these discourses in which the word is philosophically significant. If someone tells me that unicorns exist, I ask him whether he can show one to me or make some operational test which can be used to prove that there are unicorns. Then once the evidence is shown to be missing I can only deduce that there are no unicorns and that it is simply false to say unicorns have a single horn or have any other property. Yet we do think it is proper to speak of large or small unicorns, or of suffering or jeweled unicorns.[22] But these paradoxes arise because we have not distinguished "exists" from the quantifier. Even though I do want to talk about unicorns, so long as "exists" is identified with the existential quantifier such talk cannot even commence. However, once location is distinguished from space and time, both the quantifier as well as "exists" as a predicate become perfectly compatible. I can say, without any contradiction, "There are unicorns, but they do not exist" because I mean that, just as in the case of Hamlet, I can show you, i.e., locate for you, the context in which "unicorns" appears, but this context does not place unicorns into a space-time continuum. In the discourses in which unicorns are discussed, being in space and time is not predicated of unicorns. Mythology books do not intend their readers to believe that unicorns actually existed at some place and at some time.

Thus it may seem rather pedestrian, but "exists" as a predicate says nothing more than that spatial and temporal considerations are applicable. Many things are locatable which are not in space or time, but when I say that they also must exist then I mean them to be capable of being placed into a space-time coordinate system. I think then that identifying existence with the quantifier creates a series of unnecessary philosophical problems. We can identify things and we can also find them at a given place and time. But something can be identified and located without existing or ever having existed.

14
Synonymity

THE IMPORTANCE of the notion of synonymity has been stressed by C. I. Lewis, Carnap, and Quine, who have pointed out that an understanding of the nature of analytic statements rests on what is meant by synonymity.[1] The analyticity of ordinary identity statements is easily determined on the basis of the logical rules in the language. Thus "all unmarried men are unmarried" is shown to be analytic by noting that it is a substitution instance of the tautological schema, "$(x)(Fx \supset Fx)$." But the genuinely significant sentences are not mere identities, but ones in which the subject and the predicate are not identical. Therefore, they do convey important information and yet they are apparently analytic, e.g., "all unmarried men are bachelors." The analyticity of this latter type of statement requires clarification. And such clarification is possible only if some kind of criterion can be specified to show that "bachelors" and "unmarried men" are synonymous.

Criteria have frequently been suggested in terms of similarity of meaning. But the phrase "similarity of meaning" is notoriously ambiguous and has, at least in the past, led to the introduction of many ontological questions. Thus, for example, if meaning refers to something extralinguistic, then similarity of meaning must refer to some common feature that is extralinguistic. This interpretation makes it a comparatively easy matter to bring in the whole notion of certain abstract entities called universals—precisely those entities anti-ontologists seek to avoid. Thus an important task for many contemporary philosophers has been to show that either the ontology implicit in definitions of synonymity is trivial or that the notion of synonymity is neutral in regard to any ontology. In this chapter I shall examine this claim.

Schlick once stated that the new kind of linguistic analyses fashionable in philosophical circles would finally reduce all metaphysical difficulties to linguistic ones. And Herbert Feigl reiterated this point when he stated that questions of ontology would finally be shown to be strictly "pseudo-problems . . . arising only out of linguistic confusion." [2] Metaphysics, he continued, will finally be eliminated by a "logical analysis of language." [3] Whether this will finally occur I do not know. But in this chapter I should like to examine several definitions of synonymity, either implicit or explicit, in the literature of linguistic analysis, and I shall try to show that these definitions do not produce ontological neutrality. The definitions to be considered are the following: *1*] A term *A* is synonymous with a term *B* when *B* is arbitrarily designated as a substituend for *A; 2*] A term *A* is to be considered synonymous with another term *B* when both refer to the same entity.   *3*] Two expressions are synonymous in a language, *L,* if and only if they may be interchanged in each sentence in *L* without altering the truth-value of that sentence;   *4*] a term is synonymous with another term when the means for verifying the meaning of one are the same as the means for verifying the meaning of the other.

If definition [*1*] is the legitimate view of synonymity, it would be the most ontologically neutral of all the definitions. What could be clearer and philosophically safer? A term *A* is a synonym if it has been arbitrarily stipulated by human beings that it should be a legitimate substitute for *B*. We need not examine the reasons which might account for this stipulation. Perhaps one expression is easier to utter or even to spell, or one sounds better, or some variety is lacking in the language, or various psychological explanations can be given by the psychiatrist. But whatever the reasons may be, in definition [*1*] the synonymy of terms would be no more than a man-made convention with no ontological import. However, even though some terms are synonymous in this way, such synonymity cannot be a criterion for many important instances appearing in the language. "Evening star" and "morning star," for example, are surely not made equivalent by any conventional means. Nor can it be that some arbitrary decision has made "Sir Walter Scott" equivalent (at least in extensional contexts) to "The author of Waverley." All kinds of stipulations can be made by anyone. But the fact remains that, except in some very restricted area, terms are taken to be synonyms on some other ground besides stipulation. This is especially true if we are dealing with a language that purports to be applicable to empirical data, for then we apparently say that the facts or experience or reality or some other extralinguistic element govern the statements we make and not some purely linguistic rule. But no sooner do we make this concession then we are indeed required to explicate some issues with all the traditional ontological earmarks. What exactly is being referred to? How do we go about discovering what is extralinguistic? Do we move from the commitments implicit in the language itself or do we "know," in some yet undetermined sense of "know," what is extralinguistic and then seek to use language to show what we know. If we accept the former alternative, we can be accused of dealing only with language, and it makes no sense to speak of something external to it. We become what might be called "linguistic solipsists"—philosophers who believe that only language is real. On the other hand, if we accept the latter alternative, then we must decide how it is possible to know what is extralinguistic without having the knowledge mediated by the very language we use. Can we speak of a language and its referent as two separate subject matters that, in some way, "correspond" to one another? This is highly dubious. As we have argued previously, the language is with us like a set of Kantian categories. Whatever is extralinguistic is understood by us only in terms of the way we formulate it in our particular linguistic forms. Thus if we pursue this first definition in all its ramifications, we will finally be led into the whole ontological inquiry of necessity in a language and how such necessity arises.

A distinction might be made between "safe" and "dangerous" ontologies. A safe ontology would require that what is extralinguistic contains only concrete entities. Only with the advent of abstract entities do we begin to move into a dangerous ontology, one that populates the world with objects not open to empirical or scientific scrutiny. Thus we might claim that by "extralinguistic" we are only committing ourselves to concrete entities and nothing more. Hence the synonymity of terms is to be held as referring to the same given entity. And this leads us to a consideration of definition [2], i.e. that a term A is to be considered synonymous with another term B when both refer to the same entity. Here the reference is only to a concrete entity and, therefore, whatever our ontology is, it is not too significant. At most it would require us to accept a nominalist position and this has usually been thought of as a very safe type of ontology. "Entity" might still be problematic, but it might be neutralized by taking it to be some slice of what is observed or simply some limited segment of interest. However, even if we could allay the fear about "entity" this definition would still lead us into ontological speculation.

Taken at its face value, definition [2] is much too broad for terms could obviously refer to the same entity and yet not be synonyms. "Tire" and "steering wheel" could be said to refer to the same entity but these terms are certainly not synonyms. This difficulty might be overcome by adding the further proviso that the terms being considered as synonyms must refer to the same entity *in the same respect*. Thus if we wished to explain why "tire" and "steering wheel" are not synonymous, we might state that even though they refer to the same entity they do not do so in the same respect. But now what of "same respect"? Does this phrase mean we must observe the entity from the same perspective or does it mean that we have to be observing the same property or characteristic in the object itself? If it is referring to perspectives, then only an identity of perspectives would make the meanings of the two terms synonymous. But since perspectives are always different—your view of an object at a given time is always necessarily different from mine —a notion of synonymity on this ground would be impossible. Furthermore, "perspective" itself is by no means a neutral term, especially when we consider the important role it played in the development of some traditional metaphysical systems.[4] Thus if "in the same respect" is to avoid immediate involvement in either psychologism or metaphysics we must give it a different definition. We might think of it as merely indicating distinctions in an object. An object consists of a multitude of properties and two expressions refer to an object in the same respect when they refer to the same property. But reference to the same property poses the same difficulty as reference to the same object. If color is considered a property, then two expressions can refer to the same property, color, but actually they are designating red and green. We might again try to remedy this defect by distinguishing determinables from determinates. Determinates would then be the specific instance of the determinable. Thus we could proceed to define synonymity by having terms refer to the same determinate of a given determinable. But in this connection an indefinite number of divisions can be made. Who can really tell how many hues and shades there are or can be in the color red? And thus we would gradually be led into an infinite regress since any property can be redefined as an infinite number of properties. Furthermore, once we are permitted to speak of the same property we are presumably maintaining that two objects or two events can have the same property. But if we formalize this, we obtain: $(\exists x)(\exists y)(\exists F)(Fx \cdot Fy)$ where quantification of the predicate term immediately commits us, if we follow Quine, to a belief in classes and other such abstract entities. Nor can we avoid predicate quantification here since it is the only way we can obtain the sense that the "F" of "Fx" and "Fy" is to be taken as the same predicate.

Finally, even without the problems of "the same respect" the standard objection to [2] is that if we assume oblique contexts and sentences to be perfectly good features in a language, then two terms cannot be held to be synonyms merely because they refer to the same entity. "Sir Walter Scott" and "The author of Waverley" refer to the same entity but this does not make them synonyms. Otherwise there would be no way of distinguishing between "George IV believed that Sir Walter Scott was the author of Waverley" and "George IV believed that Sir Walter Scott was Sir Walter Scott." Thus even Carnap has been forced to differentiate between reference to entities and reference to meanings. The simple concrete entity is assumed to be imbued with something strange and abstract called a "meaning" or an "intension" or a "connotation" or, if we follow Frege, a "sense." I need hardly add that the analyses of these terms again conjures up all the traditional questions about whether abstract entities are to have the same ontological status as concrete things. What are these "intensions" or "senses" which both

Carnap and Frege take to be as objective as any other entity? This question has still to be answered without an appeal to terminology containing reference to notions of ontology.

These criticisms of the "entity" type of definition with its inability to account for what occurs in oblique contexts are also applicable to definition [3] which is taken to be a more technical definition occurring in a formal language.

Definition [3] states: "Two expressions are synonymous in a language, L, if and only if they may be interchanged in each sentence in L without altering the truth value of that sentence." [5]

Now, of course, if the language also contains oblique and modal sentences, this definition could never be satisfied since it is always possible to present some oblique or modal sentence in which the substitution would not be legitimate. Thus "the number of planets," "9," and "3^2," are equivalent in all contexts except when they appear in such sentences as "It is necessary that the number of planets is equivalent to 9" and "Jones believes that 9 is equivalent to 3^2." The first sentence is, of course, false and the second sentence *can* be false. However, it is usually implicitly assumed that if belief sentences and modal operators could be converted in some way into ordinary declarative or other truth-functional sentences then definition [3] would be satisfactory. But it is a mistake to think that if it were not for these curious sentences of modality and belief, definition [3] would be satisfactory. For if the language were of a very restricted sort and contained a limited number of predicates, definition [3] would not be at all adequate. Thus consider a language in which only the following predicates are available: juicy, red, round, edible. In a language of such a narrow scope both "apple" and "pomegranate" as two terms introduced into the language could serve as substituends for x in the four sentences:

1] x is juicy.   *3]* x is round.
2] x is red.   *4]* x is edible.

If these were the only sentences in the language, then definition [3] would, indeed, make "apple" and "pomegranate" synonyms since the truth-values of the individual sentences would not be affected by an interchange of these terms. But this kind of synonymy would be clearly objectionable. We would, at least, want a test which would determine whether "apple" and "pomegranate" are

being interchanged in more than those sentences which deal with
only the most incidental predicates. Thus it might be argued that by
positing such a narrow language we have unfairly loaded the dice.
The language in which definition [3] must operate must be a fully
developed language which has a rich variety of synthetic sentences.
But an analysis of what is meant by a "fully developed language"
would be found to have a meaning that would introduce those very
metaphysical problems we are trying to avoid. For consider at what
point the language would be so developed that "apple" and "pomegranate" could no longer be substituted for one another. Only where
there are sufficient predicates could instances be given of unallow-
able interchangeability. But when do we have sufficient predicates?
The answer apparently is that there are sufficient predicates when
the language can do more than describe or otherwise indicate properties which are merely incidental to the object. In other words, we
must have in the language predicates referring to the more last-
ing or more essential properties of an object. And if we admit the
need for this dichotomy, then we are indeed claiming that there
must be contingent-indicating and essential-indicating predicates. I
need hardly point out the kind of ontological inquiry this dichotomy
would now require.

Furthermore, there is the entire matter of interchangeability of
terms. How are we to proceed in determining whether the replacement of one term by another does or does not change a truth-value
of a sentence? In a given language (without oblique sentences) with
which we are very familiar, we might never question that "Sir Walter
Scott" can replace "the author of Waverley" in all contexts. But we
accept the synonymity of these two terms for reasons other than
that they as a matter of fact are mutually replaceable one by the
other. If I am told that the truth-value of "Sir Walter Scott is
Scottish" will always be the same as the truth-value of "The author
of Waverley is Scottish" I can legitimately ask why this should be
so. It would not satisfy me to be told that in the language it so
happens that both sentences happen always to have the same truth-
value. Nor would it satisfy me to be told that in all contexts I can
always substitute "Sir Walter Scott" for "the author of Waverley"
for then I would want to know why this is so. There is nothing about
the two names that immediately tells me they are synonyms. It
seems to me we would finally have to say that two expressions are

synonymous because they refer or otherwise indicate some entity. In the case of "Sir Walter Scott" and "The author of Waverley" we would finally have to say that "Sir Walter Scott names or designates the same person as does the author of Waverley." Then after we have made this statement, we could go on to use these terms as synonyms in all other contexts. But as soon as we make this move we have jumped into the very frying pan we have been so assiduously avoiding, for we must now go on to explore what a "person" is and to ask why we continue to apply "Sir Walter Scott" and "the author of Waverley" to a continually changing entity. Is there a person who persists even though all his physical parts change? Furthermore, how is a person distinguished from other sorts of entities? I will not try to answer these questions. I should like simply to point out that in examining definition [3] we have moved very far from a strict syntactic inquiry. We have become involved in one of the thorniest issues of traditional metaphysics.

The last definition of synonymity that we have given—definition [4]—is the pragmatic one. "A term is synonymous with another term when the means for verifying the meaning of one are the same as the means for verifying the meaning of the other." But now this definition requires further explication for at least part of it is in what Carnap would call the material mode of language. "Means for verifying the meaning" ought better to be formulated in terms of sentences for we know what the means are only when we know the sentences that refer to them. Thus Lewis [6] and others have already shown us how "means" statements are formulated linguistically. They are described by counterfactual sentences such as "if X were done then Y would occur," etc. Definition [4], therefore, is more adequately stated in the following way: "A term A is synonymous with the term B if the counterfactuals that verify a sentence with A also verify the same sentence with B replacing A." But objections can be raised to definition [4] that are very similar to those raised against definition [3]. In what kind of language is definition [4] given? If only few counterfactuals can be formed, then the same counterfactuals can theoretically be used to verify "This is an apple" and "This is a pomegranate." Again the reply might be that we are assuming a language with sufficient predicates so that the distinction between these two sentences can be drawn. But again the question would arise concerning how many and what kind of predicates are needed in order to have sufficient predicates. Furthermore, so far counterfactual statements have not been proved to be ontologically neutral. Counterfactuals, unlike ordinary truth-functional molecular sentences, have their own particular truth-value regardless of the truth-value of the parts. But now how is this truth-value obtained? The answer has often been given that subjunctive conditionals describe certain special kind of properties called dispositional properties. Thus if one says "if X were placed in water then it would dissolve" we are describing a certain kind of property of X. Of course we could have spoken of the powers of X or the potencies of X. But dispositions are supposed to be a little less ontologically charged than powers and potencies. But how are we to deal with dispositions? The counterfactuals that describe them suggests some kind of connection between antecedent and consequent since even if the antecedent is false the particular consequent given is said to follow. Are we then to say that dispositions really reflect a lawlike relationship? But what are lawlike relationships and can they be made compatible with Hume's criticism of laws? I am not saying that these questions could not possibly be answered without any reference to ontological matters. But it might prove very difficult.

Other definitions of synonymity have been proposed besides the four that we have examined here. Most of these are variants of the four given and are open to similar objections. Thus a recent variant of definition [4] is the following: "Two statements are to be understood as synonymous for a person A at time T if his testing procedures are the same for the two statements." [7] But this definition is dependent upon the ability of testing procedures to distinguish important from unimportant characteristics. Otherwise the testing procedures for "This is an apple" would be the same as the testing procedures for "This is a pomegranate." Furthermore "testing procedures" is better stated in the formal mode of language since by "testing procedures" we are indicating the relationship between some set of behavior statements and a statement to be confirmed or disconfirmed. But are not these behavior statements the very counterfactual statements that have caused so much difficulty in the discussion of definition [4]? A statement concerning the testing of an object, as Hempel, Carnap and others have repeatedly told us, is either a counterfactual or a reductive statement. With either alternative we become concerned with those questions which have been part of the subject matters of the most important ontologies.

Lewis has also proposed a view of synonymity, namely, that two expressions are synonymous if they are logically equivalent.[8] But as Quine has pointed out,[9] this definition is really circular since an understanding of logical equivalence in important examples requires us to understand synonymity. Or to put it differently we can understand why A is logically equivalent to A by a strict appeal to the rules of logic. But how are we to tell when A is logically equivalent to B as in "Sir Walter Scott" and "the author of Waverley?" We can do this only by an appeal to synonymity.

Carnap has also proposed that two sentences are to be taken as synonymous when they are intensionally isomorphic,[10] that is, when the intensions of the expressions in one sentence correspond to the intensions of the parallel expressions in the other sentence. But as we have seen, intensions pose serious problems. Both Quine and White have found the whole notion of intensions to be vague and unintelligible.[11] Secondly, this criterion would seem to hold only for those trivial cases in which two sentences are exactly alike, that is, where exactly the same words are used in exactly the same position, for only identical expressions have the same intension. Thus we could never ask whether "Sir Walter Scott is Scottish" is synonymous with "The author of Waverley is Scottish." Since at least one of the expressions does not correspond in intension to the parallel expression in the other sentence, synonymy cannot be asserted. But then why be concerned with synonymy at all? The criterion could simply have stated that only identical statements are synonymous. But this kind of synonymity is obviously not the sort for which we are searching. What we want is a way of showing that two expressions which have different symbols are still to be taken as synonymous.

In conclusion I am aware that I have not given any explication of synonymity. My whole approach has been negative. But at least I have tried to indicate that even in the most significant linguistic inquiries—such as those dealing with synonymity—we are led into an ontological inquiry.

15
"Make"

IN THIS CHAPTER I should like to examine a specific dyadic term, namely, "make" or "is making" or "makes" as in such sentences as "John makes a table" or "John is making a table" where the sense of the verb is one of constructing or forming or building. There are many different uses of "make" as in "I am going to make that girl," or "I will make him talk," or "I can make my toe move." These, as well as other uses, could undoubtedly involve us in some interesting philosophical problems. "I can make my toe move," for example, entails many serious issues about our notions of causation and possibility. In fact, it has been argued that a sentence of this sort necessarily commits us to a belief in "immanent causes," "powers" or "forces"—whatever these curious entities may be.[1] But I shall not be concerned with "make" in any of these uses except in so far as they have some bearing on my examination of "make" in its sense of constructing or building.

My interest in this specific sort of "make" stems from the fact that scrutiny of sentences about the construction of objects has been strangely avoided by those who make linguistic analyses, and yet sentences of this sort are very critical in science, technology, and art. In fact, according to one commentator, a science is not possible without some use, either explicit or implicit, of statements referring to the making of things.[2] Furthermore, it is supposedly perfectly intelligible to say "John is making a table" and to expect that such a sentence ought to be statable in a formalized language. Except for those perennially troublesome sentences involving reference to infinite classes, dispositions, and psychological states, most sentences, after some minor changes, lend themselves to formalization processes. But curiously enough, the attempt to formalize the specific kind of "make" sentence we are here discussing seems to commit us to a set of beliefs formalists would prefer to reject.

Thus, to begin with, in any formalization we would undoubtedly take "make" to be a dyadic rather than a monadic predicate. We always make something. But most dyadic terms occur with names or variables that have or, at least have had, some range of denotable substituends. If I say "John walks to his home" the expressions "John" and "his home" are respectively a proper name and a denotable instance of a range of possible substituends.[3] John can walk to many places besides his own home, but in so far as he is walking to any place he is always walking somewhere. That is to say, there is always a place to which he goes even if it so happens that he never gets there. If "John walks to the house on 39th Street" is to be a utilizable sentence in some context, then "the house on 39th Street" must be what Geach calls "a referring phrase."[4] It must be the sort of expression about which it is legitimate to ask "To which house on 39th Street is John walking?" Similarly, if I say "Caesar crossed the Rubicon" the dyadic term "crossed" links two expressions both of which must be taken to have referring power if the sentence is to be meaningful. It might well turn out that there is no Rubicon River just as there no longer is any Caesar. But in making the assertion about Caesar and the Rubicon I am using these expressions as referring phrases. If someone asked me whether Caesar still lived or whether he ever had lived, he would not be asking because he did not understand my sentence. He would recognize that I am using "Caesar" and "Rubicon River" as referring phrases, but he would be questioning whether they actually did refer to anything. On the other hand, if he asked about which table I was referring to after I had asserted "John is making a table" he would not have understood my sentence. He would apparently be thinking that because dyadic predicates generally have referring terms on both sides of them that, therefore, the terms relating to "make" ought also to have referents. But, of course, this is wrong.

The point made above might be expressed more precisely if we symbolize some ordinary sentences containing ordinary dyadic predicates and then endeavor to make the same sort of symbolization with our "make" sentence. Thus if I say "John runs to the store" I can formulate this as "$(\exists x)(Sx \cdot Rjx)$," that is, "there is something which is a store and John runs to it." [5] Similarly, in "Caesar crossed the Rubicon" I can eliminate "Caesar" and "the Rubicon" in favor of two definite descriptions which, a lá Russell and Quine, we can then transcribe into an existentially quantified sentence using a time variable. Or, in a perhaps less complicated way, I can simply transcribe "Caesar crossed the Rubicon" using constants and, of course, the employment of constants would mean that we take them to be referential even if no ostensive devices for indicating the reference are available. But now let us make a similar attempt to symbolize "John is making a table." I think it should be quite apparent that we cannot symbolize this sentence as "$(\exists x)(Tx \cdot Mjx)$" for such a transcription commits us to an existential quantification of "table" and this is precisely what is not intended. There is no intention, it would seem to me, of making the same claim about "a table" as might be made about "the store" in "John runs to the store" or about "a dog" in "John sees a dog." In both of these latter sentences, it is clearly sensible to ask "Which store did John run to?" or "Which dog did John see?" But in "John is making a table" it is not at all intelligible to ask "Which table is John making?" We could quite legitimately ask, "Which table did John make?" But this would be a question that could be raised with the statement "John made a table" and not with "John is making a table."

It should be noted that "make" cannot be classified as one of the pseudo relations—whatever these may be—mentioned by Copi.[6] Nor does it belong to the group of intentional words discussed by Chisholm.[7] These categories primarily include psychological verbs such as desiring, hoping, planning, believing, wishing, etc. But it would seem to be quite clear that even though the word "table" in

"John is making a table" does not refer and is not meant to refer to any existent table, the sentence is not about anyone's psychological makeup. It may well be that further investigation of "make" will lead to some implicit psychological assumption. Perhaps such notions as "planning" or "having an idea" are required to gain an understanding of "make." We shall have to discuss whether the having of ideas or the making of plans are necessary prerequisites for the making of objects. But clearly on first inspection "make" is not the kind of verb normally classified as psychological.

Thus it would seem that "make" expressions—at least in the way they are being employed here—are very curious. If they were dyadic in the same way that psychological terms are dyadic then, of course, we could attribute all our difficulties to the fact that we have not yet been able to eliminate mentalistic in favor of behavioral terminology. We could then take the view of Carnap, Hempel, and others that perhaps in a more rigorous language all such expressions could be treated as theoretical constructs.[8] I am not saying that being able to call a phrase a "theoretical construct" solves the problem of psychological verbs. For the introduction of such constructs, as numerous critics have already pointed out, means that psychological expressions must always contain an element of meaning which is not reducible to overt behavior. But if we were able to transform "make" into a construct, then at least it would not be any more or less troublesome than many other similar words. "Make," however, defies this easy classification. To say that someone is making a table is not to say anything about what one believes or thinks. The making of something has a straightforward empirical character usually attributed to other sorts of activities, such as running, walking, or turning the pages of a book. I might never be able to observe anyone else's intentions or beliefs or concepts or ideas, but I certainly do observe men making objects. I could perhaps be convinced that I never see anyone else thinking or perceiving or willing, but it seems incredible that anyone could convince me that I never see anyone making a table or a chair or a toy or some other such object. Yet it does seem odd that a relative term can have this empirical quality and still have a component part which not only does not have a referent but also *cannot* have one.

There are other reasons why "makes" is a curious word. Something teleological seems to be present as well, for the making of something seems to be due to an end that is still in the future. At least on closer examination, the making of a table seems to be influenced by something which does not yet exist or by something which we call an "idea." And all of this clearly smacks of a commitment to a subsistent entity or some other form of teleology! But enough has been said to show that analysis of this expression is a worthwhile philosophical task, and I should like, therefore, to attempt the formalization of the sentence "John is making a table." For simplification purposes I shall henceforth call this sentence "S_1."

We have already seen that S_1 cannot be translated into:

1]　$(\exists x)(Tx \cdot Mjx)$,

for John has not built a table. Thus the question arises as to whether we can translate S_1 in such a way that the meaning is not lost and no commitment is made to the existence of a table.

One way that suggests itself is that we treat S_1 as a sentence whose form is not at all what it appears to be. Many sentences look as if they are interrogatives and yet they ought legitimately to be treated as commands or indicatives. If I say to my wife while she is dressing, "Do you know the play begins in ten minutes?" she would hardly take this to be a question. Similarly, sentences using the historical present are actually referring to past events as in "Caesar crosses the Rubicon and conquers Rome." Still other sentences look like ordinary indicatives and yet should properly be symbolized as conditionals. In "x is an actor," "is an actor" is not an ordinary predicate to be equated with such predicates as "is five foot ten inches tall" or "is round-shouldered." By calling someone an actor we do not mean that he is acting now or even that he is about to act. On the contrary we mean something such as "if x is placed in the appropriate conditions and he so desires, then he will act." Some sentences, like those very simple atomic ones usually given in the initial interpretation of a formal calculus, are quite easily formalizable. But this is not always the case and for this reason we ought to consider the possibility that S_1 is not an ordinary descriptive sentence.

Now the problem with "table" in S_1 seems to be that it refers to an object which is supposed to appear in the future. The table comes into existence *after* I have finished making it. Thus what may be needed is some translation which includes some token-reflexive

variable specifying the futurity of the object designated by "table."
Perhaps our problem here is like the example given by Quine.[9] We
cannot symbolize "We saw Stromboli and it was erupting" as a
simple conjunction; otherwise the essential temporal reference is
lost. The more adequate analysis is: "Some moment of our seeing
Stromboli was a moment of its erupting." Thus let us symbolize S_1
in such a way that if we are committed to the existence of a table,
at least its existence is correlated with some future time. Using the
symbolism of $T =$ table, $t > t_o$ as "a time later than the assertion of
this sentence," $m =$ makes, and $j =$ John, we obtain the following
symbolization of S_1:

2] $(\exists y)(\exists x)(ty \cdot ty > t_o \cdot Tx \cdot Mjxt)$.

There is, of course, a very obvious problem here—so obvious
that many contemporary philosophers have simply ignored it—concerning what it means to use time as a predicate, or to quantify over
time. Logicians have objected to using abstract terms as substituends of variables or to quantifying over predicates but few seem
to be concerned about the use of time as a substituend. Yet this is
precisely the point of the traditional arguments about time—what is
this entity that makes it suitable for inclusion in a formal language?
There must be criteria for allowing terms into a language, but what
are these criteria that permit "is a time" to be a perfectly legitimate
predicate? However, we need not press this kind of discussion for
even if time is an acceptable predicate there are major difficulties in
taking [2] as an analysis of S_1. [2] tells us that there is a table at
some future time that John will build, or, more precisely, John will
make a table at some future time. Now assuming we can speak
sensibly of something existing at a future time, we can accept [2] as
an adequate way of symbolizing a future tense verb. But what does
this have to do with S_1? It is one thing to say "John will make a
table at some future time" but something else again to say "John is
(now) making a table." [2] has simply catapulted the whole making of the table into the future. But this is not what S_1 is stating. S_1
is indicating that something is occurring now which will be completed in the future and what we need is a formula that will incorporate this fact. What this seems to mean then is that S_1 requires a
more drastic formulation than the mere addition of temporal predicates. We apparently need a conditional sentence that if such-and-
such occurs, then there will be a given resultant later. Can we give
this vague meaning a more precise formulation? The most obvious

beginning is to introduce a conditional sign for the "if . . . then," and thus it might be that S_1 is best expressed as "if John performs some given actions at this time then he will have made a table at some later time"; or, symbolically, using obvious symbols:

3] $(\exists x)(\exists y)(Ax \cdot ty \cdot Pjxt) \supset (\exists y)(\exists z)(ty \cdot ty > t_o \cdot Tz \cdot Mjzt)$.

Now if S_1 is the conditional exemplified in [3], what kind of conditional is present? It is clearly not a material conditional for then [3] would be false if the antecedent is true and the consequent false. But the truth of the antecedent and the falsity of the consequent seem to be precisely what we are asserting in S_1. We are saying that the making is occurring but the resultant product has not yet been made. Furthermore, if S_1 were a material conditional, it turns out to be true if it so happens that John is not making anything at all. And it would seem to be rather curious that one should be making a table even when he has not begun to make it.

Nor can [3] be taken as the expression of some entailment relationship. First to say that something at time, t_1, entails something at time, t_2, would be a flagrant violation of Hume's old but still undeniable views about necessary connections. Furthermore in an entailment relationship given the truth of the antecedent then the consequent must be true if the conditional is to be taken as true. But it should be clear that the sense of S_1 is that even if the table was begun but not completed, that is, even if the antecedent was true but the consequent false, S_1 could still be regarded as true. Frequently a person starts to build a table or some other object but he never completes it. Yet we would not be accused of lying or of being mistaken if we said "He is making a table." Yet oddly enough if the consequent were false in a *certain way*, then it would be correct to say that we had lied or that we had been mistaken. Thus if the falsity was due to the acknowledgement of the contrary of the consequent, then the assertion of S_1 would not have been legitimate. In other words, if it turned out that John had built a chair instead of a table, then I would have been wrong in asserting S_1. I might have *believed* that John was building a table, but I would still have been wrong in claiming he was building it. Thus S_1, like [3], does attempt to state a relationship between a present state-of-affairs and something in the future. But the relationship is not of the entailment kind. There is a presumption of necessity about the future, but the necessity is not expressible by the available entailment logics.

Is [3] then a subjunctive conditional? If we could show this, then we might indeed still be left with all the problems of the subjunctive, but at least we would not be burdened with new philosophical headaches. However, unfortunately, [3] is not a subjunctive conditional. For in the subjunctive conditional we assert what would happen if something else would be the case. But clearly in S_1 I am stating what John is doing and not what he would do. In fact, this points up the reason why it is difficult to consider S_1 as a conditional since it is not asserting what is or would be the case if something else should occur. It tells us what is occurring. A table is being made! It is not as if we said, "if John were performing in a certain way (although perhaps he isn't) then he would produce a table." We are saying that John *is* performing in a certain way and there is no question about whether he is not performing. A simple translation of S_1 into a conditional form, therefore, is not feasible although we shall shortly examine the possibility that a conditional in addition to some other data might produce the desired translation.

We might try a different approach to S_1. Sometimes a sentence becomes philosophically troublesome not because its logical form is different from the form in which it presents itself. But rather the difficulty lies in the unwitting introduction of expressions not warranted by the subject matter. Thus Russell, in his famous distinction between acquaintance and description, has argued that when I say, "I see a table" I am unwittingly using an expression that, in more precise language, could not be attached to the verb "see." [10] I never see a table. I only experience sense data of color or touch, which in conjunction with future possible sense data, make up what I mean by "table." In other words, my use of "table" in a sentence such as "I see a table" commits me to more than is actually given. And my being committed in this way by the language leads to my believing that the subject matter of my sentences is other than it is, e.g., that there are physical objects which are independent of any sense data. Similarly, we know that the description of some given phenomenon varies in accordance with the observer's linguistic capabilities. A biologist, for example, who describes data in accordance with the biological language he has inherited without making any careful study of his terminology could very easily be led to describe his data in terms of "essences," "aims," and "final ends." Yet, as Nagel has pointed out,[11] such terminology is archaic. It commits one to the acceptance of entities which are simply not present in the subject matter. According to Nagel, a teleological description "can always be translated, with respect to what it explicitly asserts, into an equivalent non-teleological one." [12]

Perhaps then what we ought to do is to re-examine the subject matter described by S_1 more carefully, trying as best we can, in Cartesian fashion, to commit ourselves as little as possible to anything which is not explicitly given. Can we then describe the subject matter of S_1 in such a way that the strange difficulties we have been encountering can be avoided?

Let us begin then by attempting to formulate what probably would not be challenged in a description of the subject matter of S_1. We shall, therefore, omit any reference to the existence of a table and also any suggestion of conditionality. Our new formulation is now taken to read: "John changes a given material at time t_1, which resultant material is then changed by John at t_2, which resultant material is then changed by John at t_3 . . . which resultant material is then changed by John at t_n, and this resultant material is not further changed by John." Symbolizing this sentence, we obtain:

4] $(\exists y)(\exists z)((ty \cdot Mz \cdot Cjzt_{1\rightarrow2}) \cdot (zt_2 = z_1) \cdot (Cjz_1t_{2\rightarrow3}) \cdot$
$(z_1t_3 = z_2) \cdot \quad . . . (Cjz_{n-1}t_{(1-n)\rightarrow n}) \cdot (z_{n-1}t_n = z_n)) \cdot$
$(z)(y) (z = z_n \cdot ty \supset \sim Cjzt).$

This is a rather complicated formula but the complication would be worthwhile if it really explicated S_1. But even with the omission of reference to a future existent table, some serious issues arise with [4]. The first and most obvious shortcoming is that we do not include the important fact that the last resultant change must be a table. However, this does not seem to be a major defect. We can simply give the last resultant change, "$(z_{n-1}t_n = z_n)$," the name "table." We have then the following:

5] $(\exists y)(\exists z)((ty \cdot Mz \cdot Cjzt_{1\rightarrow2}) \cdot (zt_2 = z_1) \cdot (Cjz_1t_{2\rightarrow3}) \cdot$
$(z_1t_3 = z_2 \cdot \quad . . . (Cjz_{n-1}t_{(1-n) \rightarrow n}) \cdot (z_{n-1}t_n = z_n) \cdot$
$(Des\ "T"z_nt_n)) \cdot (z)(y) (z = z_n \cdot ty \supset \sim Cjzt).$

The addition of "T" ("table") to the formula, however, does not solve the real problem. To begin with, is "change" a legitimate predicate? It would seem to be an incomplete expression to say "John changes M at t." Change requires, in the old Aristotelian sense, a change from something to something. We never simply change something; we also change it to something. If then we must

228   LANGUAGE AND ONTOLOGY

characterize change in this way we find that "change" has now
became a quadratic rather than a triadic predicate, Cjz_1z_2t. But now
note what is beginning to happen. Change does not take place at one
time; at least two times are required. Otherwise how are we to
account for a change of material, M_1, to some other material, M_2,
unless it takes place from one time to another. Thus our quadratic
predicate now becomes, $Cjz_1t_1z_2t_2$, i.e., John changes z_1 at t_1 to z_2 at
t_2. But there is more; t_2 is later than t_1. Thus we must now account
for "later than" since we presumably would not leave this expression as primitive. I shall not pursue this, for it would lead to further
questioning about what it means to have time as a variable. When
we quantify over time and say that time exists, is the existence of
time to be taken as acceptable in the same way as the existence of
objects? I think this is a profound question which has not been
adequately answered by those who calmly accept quantification over
temporal variables. But there are also other questions which must be
raised about the use of "change" as a predicate. Even if we were to
accept "change" as a proper quadratic term, we ought to ask whether
some telic element is present in the concept of change. For the use of
"resultant" means we are considering change to involve a beginning,
a middle, and an end, and this surely seems to involve an implicit
teleology. I am not sure that we can speak of change, as we do in
describing the construction of an object, without having to admit the
telic factor. But perhaps positing an end in the construction of an
object is at least less ontologically significant than positing an end in
a more universal context. It is possible to accept intentions and
purposes *in* the universe without accepting intentions and purposes
for the universe. Thus "change" can be taken as a legitimate—although not altogether ontologically neutral—predicate. However,
there are other, perhaps more serious, objections.

   If any conjunct of [5] is false then, of course, [5] is false. But
on this analysis if it should turn out that John does not complete the
making of the table, then it is false that John is making a table.
Again we have not made provision for an essential part of the
meaning of S_1, namely, that the table is being made even though it
has not yet been made. We want to say, "John makes a table" even
though John has not yet made it. Furthermore, [5] does not distinguish the accidental from the intentional changing of something. [5]
could very well be true—that is, every conjunct could be true—yet

the final resultant might have been an accident. We could imagine someone whimsically putting things together and, as an accidental result, producing a table. We would not then say "John is making a table," although we might say, at a given time, "John made a table." In the making of an object—as distinct from the mere occurrence of an object—we require some additional data that will account for the planning and guiding of material to the completion of the object.

[5], therefore, is also not satisfactory. But, like [4], it does grasp part of the meaning which we intuitively ascribe to S_1. What we might now try is a combination of [4] and [5]. In other words, S_1 might appear to be a simple descriptive sentence, but perhaps it ought to be regarded as a combination of both descriptive and hypothetical elements. The Russell example is interesting because it reveals more than the mere need to make more careful analysis of what a sentence purports to describe. It also suggests the possibility that a sentence may appear to be very simple and straightforward and yet conceal an entire argument. Thus "I see a table" is really a shorthand construction for "I see a specific color datum; this color datum is a member of a cluster of other data which may appear under specific conditions in the future; this entire cluster of data is called 'table.' " In traditional terminology much of our knowledge is mediated. Our sentences do not describe exactly what is seen.[13] Inferences permeate our observations; metonymy and synecdoche constantly intrude. And all of this is quite understandable since, as in other areas so also in the use of language, we seek ways of simplifying what otherwise might take more time and analysis. Thus I should like to suggest that S_1 is a kind of enthymeme expressing an argument whose structure has not been made explicit. To say of someone that he is making a table is to [1] state that he is engaged in certain activities, [2] infer that these activities have, with some probability, resulted in the production of a certain kind of object, and [3] predict, with some probability, that he will produce a certain kind of object. We arrive then at the following frightening formulation:

6] $(\exists y)(\exists z)(ty \cdot Mz \cdot Cjzt_{1 \to 2}) \cdot (zt_2 = z_1) \cdot (Cjz_1t_{2 \to 3}) \cdot$
    $(z_1t_3 = z_2)) \cdot (z)\ (y)\ (z = z_2 \cdot ty \supset \sim Cjzt) \cdot (x)(y)(z)$
    $[(Px \cdot ty \cdot Mz \cdot Cxzt_{1 \to 3}) \supset$ with Probability P
    $Cxzt_n \cdot Des\ "T"\ zt_n)] \supset$ (with Probability P
    $Cjzt_n \cdot Des\ "T"\ zt_n).$

In spite of its complexity, [6] does have certain advantages. Even if John does not complete the table, it does not at all follow that John is not making certain changes in material. What does follow is that the statement asserting that such changes result in the production of some future object is lawlike but not a law. In other words, all kinds of changes can be made in a material and yet it does not follow that an expected resultant will be produced. And this seems to catch the sense of S_1. We do not want to deny that John is making something even if what we, or even he, believed was to be made did not occur at all. Furthermore, the use of probabilities in the formulation of the lawlike statement connecting making with production also gives the sense of S_1 which ties present making with a future result without requiring the tie to be a necessary one.

However, a serious issue still remains concerning the aforementioned lawlike statement. For whereas a great deal of analysis has been expended on general statements of the pure sciences, little has been done on the general sentences appearing in technological and other fields involving the making of objects. Yet before a "make" sentence such as S_1 can be clearly explicated, these technological sentences must undergo some philosophical scrutiny. It is to an analysis of these sentences that I should now like to turn.

II [14]

EMPIRICIST philosophers have traditionally distinguished between two types of knowledge, knowledge about space-time entities and knowledge about mathematical and logical entities. There appear to be two main reasons for this distinction: 1] the rules for validating statements about space-time entities are different from the rules for validating logical statements; thus, for example, "if A then A" is clearly neither verifiable nor falsifiable in the same sense as the statement "an object starting from rest will fall 32 feet per second per second"; 2] whereas knowledge about space-time entities is found by observation of natural events, knowledge about logical entities is *made* by manipulation of conventional concepts or symbols.

Knowledge, therefore, is generally viewed as being compartmentalized into two main divisions. First there is that knowledge which results from observation of natural phenomena and their interrelationships, and second there is that which results from the construction of "games" in which arbitrary rules are devised for the movement of symbols. These two divisions make up what is called "scientific inquiry."

This dichotomy has entailed certain consequences concerning the aims of scientific investigation. The first consequence has been the acceptance of the belief that the natural sciences can only formulate *descriptive* laws of nature; they cannot formulate *prescriptive* laws. Prescription may be allowable in logic and mathematics, where the entities are either variables or terms empty of empirical signification, or where descriptive terms occur vacuously. But prescription is not allowable in any inquiry that alludes to an empirical subject matter.

A second consequence of the division of knowledge has been the belief that two and only two kinds of statements are scientifically meaningful—the analytic and the synthetic. Involved with this belief is the conviction that all and only necessary statements are analytic and that all synthetic statements are contingent. From time to time some philosophers raise questions about certain seemingly synthetic necessary statements in a way reminiscent of Kant.[15] But these statements have been regarded by most philosophers of science as analytic.

Quine and White have pointed out the difficulties in formulating an adequate criterion for differentiating the synthetic from the analytic.[16] But they do not question the distinction between statements of pure logic and mathematics and those of science. Their concern is with formulating a criterion of analyticity that would not only demonstrate this distinction, but would also account for such curiously unclassifiable statements as "All bachelors are unmarried men." But whatever this criterion may turn out to be, they do not deny that scientifically meaningful statements are either analytic or synthetic.[17] Analytic statements are those prescriptive but nonempirical concepts found in logic and mathematics. Synthetic statements are those descriptive but empirical concepts found in the sciences.

The consequence of accepting this dichotomy that one department of science aims at the formulation of descriptive laws and the other at prescriptive laws, and that one department deals with synthetic statements while the other deals with analytic ones—has been to reduce the number of metaphysical presuppositions which formerly permeated the philosopher's interpretation of scientific inquiry. Thus, for example, concepts involving essences, affinities, or teleological causation are no longer part of biological or physical theories because the prescriptive element in knowledge has been relegated to logic and mathematics. Nevertheless, the strictness of the analytic-synthetic dichotomy has tended to make philosophers overlook or minimize a kind of knowledge and consequently a kind of statement that is of primary importance in modern scientific pursuits.

Perhaps the most appropriate way of introducing the "kind of knowledge" and the "kind of statement" which has been neglected is to make several observations on the nature of all scientific investigations. Pragmatists and instrumentalists, especially those of the Dewey school, have frequently asserted that scientific knowledge is instrumental in that it serves to give us an element of control over natural and social phenomena. As C. I. Lewis points out, if a particular state of affairs signifies rain tomorrow, then one can plan his actions accordingly.[18] In this way the scientific enterprise is most vital for human affairs. However, such a view is only partially correct. Human beings require scientific data not only to be able to decide which choices will most probably not be frustrated by natural or social events, but such data also play a role in the construction of a nature that would allow choices which, in an unconstructed nature, would not be allowable. The knowledge that it will rain tomorrow makes us search for our raincoats today. But such knowledge also makes us search for tools that could control or prevent tomorrow's rain. What has been ignored in analyses of the scientific enterprise is the fact that knowledge is not to be acquired merely for the sake of understanding nature better so that better predictions can be made. Science also makes invention possible. We want to make new objects. In a very advanced science we want not only to describe nature but to create new objects in it.[19] New kinds of plants, for example, become the aim of modern botanists. In physics new elements are created. But in the advance of modern technology is seen the most vital and fruitful application of scientific knowledge.

The term "application" has had and to a large extent still has a pejorative connotation in philosophy. To discover how scientific laws can be formulated in a legitimate logical and empirical terminology has occupied the interest of most contemporary analytic philosophers. But an analysis of what is involved when a law is used to construct objects has rarely been forthcoming. Such neglect may be attributed to the fact that in the past invention was considered the art of geniuses and, therefore, an inexplicable activity.[20] But in the light of modern technology, in which invention is often a group concern and in which specific procedures and methods of attaining successful results have been explicated, such neglect is no longer justifiable. Investigation can now be directed to the relation of scientific statements to those statements introduced by creators or inventors of objects. A scientist constructs a system of knowledge, but his knowledge does not make him a creator of objects. What, then, does the creator of objects add to scientific knowledge? How does he "interpret" knowledge so that for him it suggests potential inventions? We have still to investigate the methods and techniques employed by those who seek to use nature rather than to describe it.

We cannot hope to deal with all of these questions here. But we should like to present and examine a kind of statement which we believe is *1*] central to technological inquiry, *2*] not reducible to the kind of statements discovered in the formal or empirical sciences, and *3*] indicative of a type of knowledge which has not been analyzed by contemporary philosophers.[21]

Consider the following statement:

X] For every x, if x is a properly constructed relay being operated under specified conditions, then x produces an output at o.

Is this an analytic statement? Clearly it is not analytic in the traditional Kantian sense that the predicate (consequent) is somehow deducible from or contained in the subject (antecedent). Although a relay may be contructed so as to produce a prescribed output at o, there is no logical contradiction if the relay fails to operate in the prescribed fashion. Nor is [X] analytic in the sense of being a stipulated definition. First of all, only certain kinds of properties can be stipulated for objects. We can stipulate that objects shall henceforth be considered "forms of currency." But we cannot stipulate that objects shall henceforth be "flexible" or "soluble in water." Legal or social properties can be given to objects, but natural ones cannot. Thus since "having an output at o" is neither a legal nor a social property in the sense of "being a form of currency," it is not stipulated. On the contrary, it is similar to a natural property—only in this case the object is endowed with the property by men rather than by nature.

Secondly, [X] is not stipulated as a classificatory statement might be stipulated in an empirical science. In an empirical investigation we might begin by arbitrarily defining what a given term will mean. For example, we might assert that anything having properties a, b, and c is to be called "metal." This assertion would then be considered analytic in the particular inquiry.[22] But if once having made this stipulation, we discover that a property d is also found with a, b, and c it would be false to assert that the following statement,

Y] For every x, if x is a metal, then x has the property d,

is also an analytic sentence. [Y] is a synthetic sentence. d is not stipulated; it is discovered. Similarly, [X] is analogous to [Y]. The kind of sentence that would be true by definition of a relay would be

Z] For every x, if x is a relay, then it is composed of a magnetic structure or framework, a winding, and a set of contacts mounted on springs.

But the fact that an object made up of such parts will produce an output at o is not deducible from [Z]. [X], therefore, unlike [Z], is not analytic in any stipulated sense. The operability of a relay has to be established by investigation and experiment.

If [X] is not analytic, is it then synthetic? If the analytic-synthetic division of meaningful sentences is accepted, then the fact that a statement is not analytic entails that it must be synthetic. But if [X] is synthetic, it is so in a very curious manner.

Consider the conditions that a sentence must satisfy if it is to be synthetic: 1] The predicate is not deducible from or contained in the subject. 2] The fact that the predicate is attached to the subject is discovered by empirical investigation. This condition does not restrict synthetic sentences to true ones, nor to statements which are about directly perceivable properties. The condition only requires that there be some logical tools by which empirical predicates can be reduced to immediately perceivable predicates. 3] A sentence is synthetic only if it is possible for some set of observations to verify or falsify it.

[1] We have already seen that [X] is synthetic in this sense. The predicate is not contained in the subject. To this extent [X] is synthetic.

With respect to [2] a fundamental difference appears between [X] and other synthetic sentences. Whereas normal synthetic sentences designate relationships found in the observation of natural phenomena, [X] designates a relationship created by men. The properties of relays are not observed in nature; they are invented by men and inserted into nature. The objects of nature are found and then described verbally; the relay is described verbally and then *made* into an object of nature. Consider some of the consequences if the term "synthetic" were taken to mean only those sentences which designated sets of relationships discovered in nature. First of all, the question would arise as to how sentences referring to technological phenomena could be possible. Since such phenomena are obviously not *discovered* in nature, there would be no way of accounting for them. And no one would want to consider such sentences as either "trivial" or "meaningless." Secondly, any argument that the definition of "synthetic" should be expanded to include reference to created objects would involve a serious problem. How could one accept the scientific axiom that all science is descriptive and at the same time accept [X]? [X] seems to be clearly a prescriptive statement. The predicate is not *found;* it is *prescribed.* The relay is constructed so as to have an output at o under certain conditions. Stipulations can be made about how a word is to be used. But how can there be stipulation of the existence of some state-of-affairs? Yet this is what does occur in the case of [X]. We have the curious paradox of a statement that is unquestionably scientifically meaningful and yet it *prescribes* the existence of an object with a specified property. It would be a serious mistake, therefore, to equate [X] with all other synthetic sentences.

[3] The rules of confirmation and disconfirmation do not apply equally to [X] and all other synthetic sentences. First of all, confirmation of a normal synthetic sentence consists in an indefinite number of empirical observations. There is never such a degree of confirmation that it is impossible for further observations to produce disconfirmation. Yet in [X] one successful instance is sufficient to produce almost complete confirmation. If a relay is set up under the appropriate conditions, is operated, and produces the intended output, then [X] is confirmed. Failure of any relay to produce an output on subsequent tests does not serve to disconfirm [X]. Future failures may be attributed to faulty construction or exceptional conditions of operation but they would not disconfirm

the statement. If one were to maintain that subsequent failures after *one* successful operation served to disconfirm [X], then he would also have to accept the falsification of the whole body of supporting electromagnetic theory. But this is clearly not a reasonable interpretation of the situation. Faulty operation of a humanly constructed device can hardly be taken as grounds for rejecting a law of physics.

Secondly, the disconfirmation of a scientific synthetic statement is ordinarily obtained by *one* contrary instance. On the other hand, a statement such as [X] is disconfirmed only after an indefinitely long series of attempts to get an output from the relay. Again, an engineer would be reluctant to discard [X] because of the destructive implications of such a step for the whole body of scientific theory which he, in his role, must take for granted. In summary, *a scientific statement is confirmed only in the long run, while statements like [X] are confirmed by one successful test; on the other hand, scientific synthetic statements are ordinarily disconfirmed by one falsifying fact, while statements about humanly constructed objects are disconfirmed only in the long run.*

We may make the same point in a different way. Let us assume that a scientific law can be formulated in the following form: U] Everything which is A is also C. Confirmation of [U] would then consist in the assertion of the antecedent, [A], and the occurrence of the consequent, [C]. If [C] turned out true then [U] would be true whereas [A] could be either true or false. If [C] turned out false then either [A] is false and [U] is true, or [U] is false and [A] is true. If [U] is the statement of a scientific law then the falsification of [C] would imply the second alternative, viz., [U] is false and [A] is true.

Now let us regard [U] not as a statement of a scientific law, but rather as an [X] statement. Then confirmation of [U] would proceed in the same way as confirmation of a scientific law. But whereas in a scientific law the occurrence of [C] increases the probability of [U], when [U] is regarded as an [X] statement then the occurrence of [C] makes [U] almost necessarily true. If [C] turned out false, then the first alternative is implied, viz., [U] is true and [A] is false. The antecedent, rather than [U], is denied.

An [X] statement, therefore, which we shall call a *tectonic* statement, is not easily categorized as analytic or synthetic. Obviously, all tectonic statements are related to scientific ones. If the laws of electromagnetism were false then [X] would be false. In fact, without scientific systems there could not be tectonic statements. However, scientific knowledge is a necessary but not a sufficient condition for the assertion of tectonic statements. Part of the justification of [X] is derived from the laws of electromagnetism. But another part of it is derived from technological design requirements which never form a part of scientific hypotheses. In fact, if tectonic statements were reducible to scientific ones, then any kind of invention would be trivial. It would be a mere instance of the deduction of a theorem from a scientific system. But obviously invention is not a simple case of deduction from scientific premises. A scientist does not necessarily make a good inventor. The design of a relay is not a jejune exercise in electromagnetic theory. A tectonic statement is grounded in scientific information as well as that kind of information which is obtained from operation with materials that are not specially prepared for laboratory use. Airplanes are built with a knowledge of the most advanced theories in physics, chemistry, and even biology. But the knowledge of how objects react under conditions encountered outside the laboratory is not derived from science. Such information, as Dewey has indeed consistently pointed out, comes from practice and from those generalizations based on what has actually occurred in practice.

III

A FULL ANALYSIS of the tectonic statement, therefore, is one of the crucial tasks which must be undertaken before the ordinary "make" sentence can be explicated. In formulating [6] in Section I of this chapter, we assume that it is legitimate to make generalizations involving the completion of an object at some future date. But tectonic statements of this sort are not to be equated with the universal statements of science, and until the differences are made precise [6] will remain inadequate.

However, the tectonic statement involved in [6] is not the sole problem. [6] still apparently lacks the intentional characteristic implicit in S_1. Can we have a statement involving the making of objects which does not require some reference to planning or desiring or intending? At first glance it would certainly seem that the statement that anyone making such-and-such changes in a material will produce a given object depends upon the changes being planned or organized in some specific fashion. I can change things haphazardly or in some carefree manner. But I should want to distinguish changes of this sort from changes in which the production of a specific object is being aimed at. Can the notion of direction in change be formalized?

One way, of course, is to show that all psychological expressions are reducible to some series of behavioristic descriptions. But this kind of extreme reductionism has been shown to be inadequate. Someone might intend to go to the theater and yet he might never exhibit behavior indicative of this fact. And, conversely, he might be behaving in a variety of ways and yet not have any intention of doing what the behavior seems to indicate. Similarly, I can be changing many objects, but only if I can note some plan or direction, can I say that the changes are in some way aimed at making a given object such as a table.

However, one other way of formalizing direction in change is to be willing to countenance a set of expressions such as "intentions," "aims," and "ends." But now even if we were willing to accept these terms, how do we go about admitting them into a formal language? How, for example, are we to symbolize an intention? Are we to make "intention" a substituend for an individual variable as in "John has the intention of making a table"? But then since individual variables can be quantified, are we to acknowledge the existence of particular things called "intentions"? It seems difficult to accept such an extreme ontology.

Are we then to regard "intention" as a polyadic predicate as in "John intends to build a table"? But both Copi and Chisholm have examined in some detail the oddity of having a relation between two terms—one of which refers to a nonexistent entity.[23] Furthermore what is the relation being put forth here? Is it "intends to" or "intends to build?" On either alternative it is difficult to determine the status of the relative terms. If I say "John runs to the store" then "runs to" relates "John" to the "store." But what am I relating with "intends to" or "intends to build"? Neither "building" nor "building a table" are on a par with "John" or "the store." We cannot use "building" or "building a table" as designative in the same way "John" or "the store" are designative.

It might be argued that there is a third way of treating "intends," namely, as signifying an oblique sentence connecting "intends" with a statement. Thus instead of "John intends to build a table" we have "John intends that he should build a table." But now what is this statement that follows "intends"? Are we relating "intends" to the *sentence* "John should build a table" or to the abstract entity, the *proposition,* which the sentence expresses? Israel Scheffler has argued that only the sentence is required here. On his analysis "John intends that p" indicates a relation between John and the inscription, p, the physical symbols themselves.[24] We talk not about propositions but about a particular set of linguistic marks. But this view is clearly not satisfactory. It is not to the linguistic marks that I wish to relate "intends." If I say "John intends 'he should build a table' " the statement is simply absurd. It would be as if I said "I am going to the theater with 'Jim' " where the quotation marks around "Jim" would make the sentence mean that I am going to the theater with the word "Jim"—whatever this might mean. Or it is as if I said "He sees the bird" which is not at all the same as saying "He sees 'the bird.' " We may recall that Church probably offered the definitive argument showing that indirect discourse cannot be translated into direct discourse.[25] In the following sentences the indirect statement and the direct quotation are both identical; yet one is a proposition and the other is a sentence:

A] Seneca said that all men are rational.
B] Seneca said, "All men are rational."

If [A] and [B] are completely identical, then their translation into a foreign language ought still to reveal their identity. But consider the following German translation:

C] Seneca gesagt das vernunft seinen alle manen.
D] Seneca gesagt, "All men are rational."

The identity is no longer present. Nor are we permitted to translate the quotation into German since [B] states what Seneca actually did say, i.e., what words he used, and [D] tries to tell someone who only understands German exactly what words Seneca used.

"Intends," therefore, may be translatable into an oblique statement. But the price is that we must acknowledge the existence of propositions. Again a strong ontological commitment would seem to be unavoidable.

However, the most important point to be noted is that just as the full meaning of "make" is not be found in the analysis of the tectonic statement, so also it is not to be found solely in the investigation of "intends." "John intends to make a table" is not identical to "John is making a table." The latter may imply—in some intensional sense of "imply"—the former, but the former does not imply the latter. John may intend to make a table, but not really make it at all. Thus something has still eluded us in the examination of "make." But we know now that a complete explanation depends at least upon a clarification of *1*] what a tectonic statement is and *2*] what one is committed to when an intention is being asserted. It is not clear whether the definition of the tectonic statement requires us to acknowledge that there are synthetic a priori sentences; but "intentions" would seem to lead us directly to the admission of certain curious abstract relations or entities.

16
"Can"

ONE OF the most philosophically troublesome sentences—one that has constantly seemed to involve something ontological—has been a certain kind of "can" sentence, such as "I can build a house," "He can do it," where the meaning in a general way, is "I am able to build a house," and "He is able to do it." [1] There are other uses of "can" as when a stern father dismisses his son with the curt remark "You can go," or as in the statement "I wonder what can be keeping her," or as in "I can now eat beets." But these uses, it seems to me, are not very troublesome since they are easily translatable into sentences that have the same respective meanings but do not involve any serious philosophical problems. Thus they can be changed into "You are permitted to go," "I wonder who (or what) is keeping her," and "I am now permitted to eat beets." These latter sentences contain troublesome words, e.g., "wonder," "permitted," and they also have puzzling grammatical constructions. For instance we are still unable to give a good logical analysis of oblique sentences beginning with "I wonder that . . . ," "I think that . . . ," "I

believe that . . ." and so forth.[2] But these issues are not the kind
that are especially related to "can" when this word is philosophically perplexing. I shall, therefore, be concerned with "can" in its
sense of "being able to" or "having the power to" or "having the
ability to" for "can" in these usages causes the most philosophical
difficulties.[3]

I should note here that explication concerning the usage of an
expression ought not to be confused with explication of meaning.
The fact that I am able to discern a number of different contexts in
which an expression is employed does not mean that I have therefore explained how the expression functions in any given context. In
his *Sense and Sensibilia* Austin stresses the fact that a word can
have various different meanings, and he rightly accuses Ayer of not
distinguishing the various ways in which "real" and also "see" are
used in the language.[4] But by pointing to the different usages of an
expression we are not resolving the difficulty presented by any
specific use of an expression. In "she is a real doll!" the word "real"
is very easily and clearly explicated. But it is not so clearly explicated in "What I am seeing now is not real." My knowledge that
"real" has many different usages helps me to avoid ambiguities. It
helps me to recognize that all attempts to find one specific meaning
for a term is doomed to failure. But this recognition does not help
me to explain the difficulties posed by any given usage. I know now
not to confuse "right" in its legal sense with "right" in its moral
sense. But I am still left with the question "What is it that gives
'right' moral instead of legal connotations?" Of course, it has been
argued that by distinguishing the various ways in which a word is
used, we will also be able to distinguish correct from incorrect usage.
Thus it would be very significant if it could be shown that "real" in
"She is a real doll" is, in some sense, a correct use while "real" in
"What I am now seeing is not real" is not. But it seems to me that
all attempts to make this distinction have been unsatisfactory.
Linguist philosophers, such as Ziff, have sought to differentiate deviant from nondeviant sentences.[5] Thus they are able to say that
"real" in "She is a real doll" is improperly used or that the sentence
itself is improper because it violates some standard way of constructing sentences. But even though we could speak of deviation in
this manner, it would seem that it has little application to such
sentences as "What I am seeing now is not real." Not only is this a

much used sentence in philosophical discourse, but it could also appear in ordinary discourse. After several martinis I could easily imagine someone rubbing his eyes and looking at some pink elephant and saying "I must be losing my mind. What I am seeing now is (simply) not real!" Similar examples can be cited for "There are things," "There are properties," and even "There are absolute truths." These sentences may not appear in discourse about food and living quarters, but they are quite easily elicited in discussions on theology, ethics, epistemology, and physics. Thus it may be very important to know that the "real" we wish to discuss is not the "real" of "This is real and that is unreal." But this does not mean that we are, therefore, now aware of the function of "real" in the context in which we are using it, or, for that matter, that we have in any way eliminated any sentence which uses "real" in a traditional philosophical way. Objecting to the use of an expression in context, C, merely because it has another use in context, C_1, is simply philosophically worthless. To quote part of Hempel's criticism of Scriven who had argued that "explain" has uses other than the ones in inductions and deductions: "This is like objecting to a definition of 'proof' constructed in metamathematical proof theory on the ground that it does not fit the use of the word 'proof' in 'the proof of the pudding is in the eating,' let alone in '90 proof gin.' " [6]

I shall, therefore, be concerned with "can" in a very specific use, namely, in the use of "having the power to." I hope to be able to propose a way of treating such "can" sentences so that most of the current controversies are avoided while all the meaning implicitly attributed to "can" is still retained.

In recent years several analyses of "can" have been presented, but all have involved major problems. Thus at one time it was maintained that "can" sentences do have referents like other sorts of sentences. But whereas other sorts of sentences refer to objects and to properties of objects, the "can" sentence refers to objects and dispositions of objects. It should be clear, however, that dispositions and abilities have the same objectionable characteristics traditionally attributed to potencies and powers. If some one were to say "X has the power to do Y" we criticize him for using a term that has no designatum or for formulating a sentence whose truth or falsity is not determinable by any set of observations. A similar criticism can be made against "X has the disposition to do Y." The fact that X

does or does not do Y is irrelevant to his having the disposition to do Y. Like Platonic essences dispositions are taken to exist even if they do not manifest themselves. But the introduction of such curious entities does for purposes of explanation what noumena did for Kant—nothing.[7]

Another kind of explication—one that has been very popular in contemporary philosophy—is to view the "can" sentence as one which for some reason or another is only partially formulated. It looks like an indicative sentence, but, as Austin and Nowell-Smith have informed us, it is really a conditional of some sort.[8] On their view an "if" clause is a required adjunct to the "can" sentence. But if the "can" sentence is an implicit conditional, it is not the kind with which we are at all familiar.

Clearly it is not a material implication for the truth-values of conditionals of this sort are determined by the truth-values of the antecedent and the consequent. But since "can" sentences are not true or false in the way that indicative sentences are—the truth-values of indicatives are determined by observations—the truth of this implication is not derived from the component truth-values. Furthermore, even if true or false were in some way applicable to "can" sentences, there are all sorts of "if" sentences, as Austin has pointed out,[9] whose attachment to a "can" sentence would produce inferences that would not be permissible in any ordinary truth-functional analysis. Thus if I say "If I run then I pant" I can infer "if I do not pant then I do not run" but I cannot infer that I pant regardless of whether I run or not. On the other hand, if I say "if I so choose then I can" it does not follow that "if I cannot, then I do not so choose." But I can infer that I can regardless of whether I choose or not. Similarly, in "There are biscuits on the sideboard if you want them" I can derive "There are biscuits on the sideboard whether you want them or not," but this is not inferable on any truth-functional analysis.

Nor is the conditional an entailment implication. Except for logically true or for such obvious and trivial analytic implications as "If x is an unmarried man then x is a bachelor" no antecedent entails a consequent. The formulation of the conditions stated in the antecedent does not necessitate the assertion of the consequent unless there is an unnoticed circularity. Thus no matter what training or knowledge a man may have it does not mean that he can perform a given task. In fact, we refer to the genius or ability of an individual because we recognize that describing what a man does do is often irrelevant to what he can do. Thus we say "if he has the training and he wants to do X and he has the *ability* to do X, then he can do it." But the use of such expressions in the antecedent makes the entire analysis of "can" circular. For clearly a genius or someone who has the ability to do something is one who *can* do something of a given sort under appropriate circumstances. For this reason, in our cautious moments, we do not assert a "can" sentence on the basis of a set of conditions that do not have reference to ability. We say, "if he has the training and he wants to do it, then he *might be able* to do it." We say that *perhaps* he can do it, but not that he simply can do it.

However, the argument has usually been that the "can" sentence is not a kind of emasculated statement requiring an "if" adjunct. On the contrary, "can" disguises the fact that the sentence really present is neither an indicative nor a conditional of the ordinary variety. What we have here is simply another way of asserting a subjunctive conditional. The very word itself is capable of being eliminated in favor of a subjunctive tense. But I do not think the "can" sentence is a subjunctive conditional and I shall try to show this in a moment. And, furthermore, even if it were, it does not seem to me to be much of a solution to a problem to introduce an explanation that is itself highly suspect. This is, indeed, jumping from the frying pan into the fire. For Nelson Goodman, who has probably done the most exhaustive studies of the counterfactual, has very frankly admitted that there is no satisfactory analysis of the subjunctive.[10] So that even if there were some logical device by which the "can" sentence could be translated into some form of subjunctive, I should deem it highly unsatisfactory. But, of course, the discussion is academic since the "can" sentence is not reducible to a subjunctive conditional—at least not any such conditional with which we are acquainted.

The problem of the counterfactual involves how it is possible to move from an antecedent without denotation to the statement that if it did have a denotation then a proposed consequent would also have one. Or, more specifically, we might think of a counterfactual as a statement which claims that even though the universe might be empty it still makes sense to say that there are two statements such

that one is not identical to nor a synonym of the other but if one has
a denotation then so also does the other. But, whereas in a subjunctive conditional the consequent—some actual occurrence—is taken
to be entailed by some (possible) set of antecedent conditions, as we
have seen, a "can" sentence is assertable even if there is no occurrence. This, it seems to me, is the reason why we must reject Chisholm's attempt to treat the "can" sentence as a "try" sentence.
Chisholm takes "M can do y" to be appropriately translated into
"There is a y such that if M tried to do y then he would do X." [11]
But this translation makes an action X necessary if M tries to do y.
But in our usual use of "can," we mean that it makes sense to say of
someone that even if he tries to do X and fails that he still can do it.
We do not identify trying and being able to. If I try to lift this rock
I might fail. But the failure could be due to many reasons, e.g., that
I had a bad sprain in my back; it does not follow that I cannot, that
I am unable to lift the rock. In brief, an athlete might, for various
reasons, try and fail to complete the hundred yard dash, but we
might still want to bet that he can do it. Secondly, even if it could be
shown in some way that a "can" sentence is statable in an "if . . .
then - - -" form, we would still not obtain a familiar subjunctive
sentence—and, again, for the simple reason that the "can" sentence
apparently never has a denotation. The possible translation of the
"can" sentence into a subjunctive conditional is not either of the
following two forms:

1]   If Z conditions were present, then X will make a Y.

2]   If Z conditions were present, then X would make a Y.

Both [1] and [2] commit X to the making of Y if Z conditions
were present. But the "can" sentence makes the claim that regardless of what conditions prevail, nothing is to be denotatively given in
the consequent. To say a man can do something is not to say he will
or would do something under certain conditions, but that he is able
to do something under those conditions whereas he would not have
been able to do it otherwise. For this reason if we are somehow
required to think of the "can" sentence as a conditional, it seems to
me that its meaning is better expressed in

3]   If Z conditions were present, then X could make a Y.

At least in [3] we are incorporating in the consequent the
non-denotative sense that is intended in the "can" sentence. But, of
course, the serious problem would now arise about what sort of

sentence a "could" sentence is. And I believe that in attempting to explain "could," we would require some further conditional which would again be a deviation from those so-called normal subjunctives. For example, "X could make a Y" might become "If Z conditions were present then X would be able to make a Y." I am not at all sure how we would deal with "X would be able to make a Y." But the important point here is that in attempting to define the "can" sentence as a subjunctive conditional, we seem to be led into an infinite regress of subjunctives all of which have some far more unusual characteristic than those we normally analyze.

I do not think, however, that we are necessarily led into a discussion of these strange conditionals, for it is simply not correct to claim that "can" sentences are constitutionally "iffy." I do not see why sentences are constitutionally anything else than what they are. It seems to me that the only justification for claiming that a sentence of a given form is really one of a different form is that by making this change we have found a substitute sentence which [1] functions in the same manner as the original and [2] eliminates some, if not all, the logical problems of the original. Thus we change "All A's are B's" into "For all x, if x is an A then x is a B" because the latter functions in the same way as the former and because it also lends itself more easily to the use of logical rules. In other words, "For all x, if x is an A then x is a B" is a logically formed sentence and can, therefore, be connected by standard logical rules to numerous other sentences such as "There is an x which is an A and a B" or "For all x if x is not a B then x is not an A"; and if in some particular inquiry there appears "For all x if x is a B then x is a C" we can obtain a new sentence "For all x if x is an A then x is a C." The form of the sentence gives us a means of drawing inferences that would not otherwise be possible.

Thus we can transform sentences if the new result keeps the same function and also if it produces fruitful consequences. But I do not see what fruitful consequences have come about by speaking of "cans" as "iffy." We are simply left with a conditional that is more problematic than any subjunctive that has yet been encountered. I cannot see any intrinsic reason for attaching an "if" clause to a "can" sentence.

Another reason for rejecting the "iffiness" of "can" is that there are some fairly standard sentences which do not at all seem to require an "if" clause nor is such a clause needed in the analysis of such sentences. For example, consider someone who insists, "I can do it! I know I can!" It would seem to me that one who makes these statements with this vehemence is *not* implicitly intending some conditional or causal "if" sentence as an antecedent. In fact, such sentences are usually prefaced with the remark, "I don't care what the conditions are! I can do it!" The following sentences also seem to me not to require an "if" addition:

4]   He can get it for you wholesale.

5]   He can do it, but he won't.

6]   No one can predict the future.

7]   He can outrun John.

All of these sentences use the sort of "can" with which we are here concerned and yet none of them have any obvious need for an "if" clause. They are not like such sentences as "he has stopped beating his wife" or "he is no longer a member of the Communist Party," both of which have an obviously implicit commitment respectively to "he has beat his wife" and "he was a member of the Communist Party." Nor are they like "Thank you for the gift" or "please open the door" where the sense of these sentences requires an implicit acknowledgment of some other sentences such as "you gave me a gift" and "the door is closed."

Of course, the indexical term "he" is used in [4], [5], and [7], and this commits us to a semantic context in which "he" is taken as an abbreviation for a proper name. Also some minimum amount of prior information is assumed, e.g., we must know what it means to get something wholesale. But no specific "if" clause is required to complete the meaning of the sentences.

It could be argued that "if" clauses can be supplied with [4] through [7]. [4], for example, could be read as "if he has the right connections then he can get it for you wholesale." [7] can become "if he is strong enough then he can outrun John." But it is one thing to argue that a "can" sentence can be supplied with an "if" clause and something else again to claim that it must be so supplied. If "can" sentences are "iffy" in some way other than the way ordinary indicative sentences are sometimes taken to be "iffy," then this has still to be shown. There is no logical necessity for positing an "if" clause and, clearly, in the ordinary use of language such clauses are rarely added. Therefore, if Austin and Nowell-Smith wish to assert the necessity of such "iffiness" in the case of "can" sentences, then they ought to inform us how such necessity came about, why there seems to be some urgency in making "can" sentences conditional while no such urgency is said to hold in the case of indicative sentences.

II

I SHOULD like now to suggest another way of thinking about the "can" sentence which will, I believe, explicate "can" without involving us in any of the dilemmas of "if." It will produce other sorts of philosophically perplexing difficulties, but none, I shall argue, which are incapable of resolution.

In his analysis of "can" Austin begins by examining the dictionary definition of "if." [12] This definition, one involving doubt and hesitation, leads him to develop all the different ways in which "if" can function with a "can" sentence. I should like to take a similar approach, but instead of dealing with "if," which it seems to me does not lead to very fruitful results, I will begin with the dictionary definition of the problem word itself, namely, "can."

Webster's *New International Dictionary Second Edition* gives us several definitions of "can," but there is one in particular which has been carefully avoided by those interested in the "can" sentence. Yet it is the one that performs two important tasks: [1] in most contexts it is a synonym for "can"; [2] it avoids all reference to "ifs" or any of the attendant problems involving the subjunctive conditional. Among other alternative meanings attributed to "can" we find the following:

> B Expressing a contingency that may be possible:
> May perhaps; as do you think he *can* yet be living?
> c Expressing possibility.

What this definition tells us is that there are at least some "can" sentences which we ought to be able to translate into ones that use the word "possible" (or "impossible") as a substitute for "can." And, indeed, there is little difficulty in making the translation for most ordinary sentences. For example, [4]–[7] become:

4] It is possible that he will get it for you wholesale.

5]   It is possible that he will do it, but he won't.
6]   It is impossible that anyone will predict the future.
7]   It is possible that he will outrun John.

Sometimes the translation is difficult, especially when the "can" sentence is incomplete. Thus in "Who can tell" we have to supply some context such as "She asked, 'Will they ever find happiness again?' The inspector shrugged his shoulders and said, 'Who can tell.' " This context would then be translated into "She asked, 'Will they ever find happiness again?' The inspector shrugged his shoulders and said, 'It is possible that they will.' " But even if such translations could not be done for some uses of "can," I think that it can be done for those uses of "can" that primarily concern us here, namely, uses in which "can" has the sense of "being able to" or "has the power to."

It would seem then that some of the important philosophical problems relating to the "can" sentence we are here considering are easily solved. We get rid of "can" by using "possible" and in this way supposedly avoid all commitments to powers, dispositions, and the complexities of the subjunctive conditional. "Can" and its attendant problems no longer exist.

However, few philosophers will be pleased with this solution. They can point to good reasons for not substituting "possible" for "can" and until these reasons are satisfactorily refuted the problem of "can" still exists. Thus it might be countered that after all our objections to dispositions and powers, we have suddenly committed ourselves to a whole new realm of entities. The vague concept of possibility with all its ties to intensions and subsistent entities begins to appear. How are possibilities to be discussed intelligently? How are we to distinguish between the actual box that was made and the possible one? Is there a universe of essences, similar to Santayana's realm of essences, which is simply waiting its turn to be enacted? I think that without accepting Santayana's extreme position, we might claim that if a language requires us to speak of what is possible then we may very well be committed to intensions, in Carnap's sense, or to a subsistent entity in Meinong's sense or simply to a psychological entity such as an idea or a concept. We may deplore the fact that a language refers to what is possible, but if we require this to be the case then a good argument can be made that there apparently must be designative terms designating entities that have a status uniquely different from those entities designated by terms in nonmodal contexts. However, in the case of "possible" there is another way out. Whereas other expressions might commit us to an ontology of abstract entities, I do not believe this must be the case with "possible."

Recent linguistic analysis has made it abundantly clear that numerous functions are performed by the symbols of a language. The symbols can operate as logical connectives, as designators, as exclamatory or hortatory devices, as signs indicating emotive contours, etc. According to Wittgenstein there are "countless different kinds of use of what we call 'symbols,' 'words,' 'sentences.' "[13] Among these functions is one involving the designation of other expressions rather than something extralinguistic. Thus, for example, in ordinary language words such as "misspelled" and "correct" are usually applicable only to other linguistic elements. A natural phenomenon is neither "misspelled" nor "correct"; only words or sentences are characterized in this way.

In purely formal calculi the use of these expressions are more clearly displayed. Sentential combinations are "well-formed" or "syntactically correct." They are also *"L-true"* or *"L-false"* or *"F-true"* or *"F-false."* In fact, the syntactical metalanguage of a language is concerned strictly with the expressions of the language and not with its designata. "Red" in the metalanguage refers to red in the object language; it does not refer to the designatum of red.

That there are such expressions in a language, or in the metalinguistic part of a formal language, is, on the one hand, not very significant. They are simply ways of indicating either that an expression is formed in accordance with the rules or is either an axiom or a theorem of the language system. A word is misspelled as a result of the conventions adopted for spelling it. A sentence is incorrect as a result of logical and/or grammatical rules that have been traditionally accepted. A formula in a calculus is *WF* simply because of the formation rules that have been stipulated for the system. In such instances we are not enlarging our knowledge by describing something that has not been known before or that indicates some natural phenomenon. We are simply pointing out where we are or are not violating some convention agreed upon previously.

However there is also a sense in which our knowledge of such terms in the language is extremely important. For our recognition of terms which appear to be descriptive and yet are purely syntactical in function has led to a closer examination of many expressions whose descriptive character has usually been taken for granted. Thus it is only in recent times that "true" and "false" have been shown to be ways of marking certain kinds of sentences and not designators of certain states-of-affairs.[14] And the consequence of this has been that the search for *the* Truth rather than sentential truth has become a search which is considered by many not to be very philosophically meaningful. In a somewhat similar fashion Austin has discerned that at least one function of the word "real" is to be what he calls an "adjuster-word," that is, a word "by the use of which other words are adjusted to meet the innumerable and unforeseeable demands of the world upon language." [15] I am not sure that I understand how one word "adjusts" another. But I think that Austin's point is that "real" in many of its contexts is not designative at all. It simply acts as a means of cautioning us about the use of some other word. Thus by saying, under certain problematic circumstances, "This is not a real pig" the word "real" is functioning as a way of indicating that there is some uncertainty about whether "pig" is the appropriate word, but it is the only word that seems to fit the occasion. Be cautious, "real" tells us. "Pig" may turn out to be an incorrect word in this context.

I should now like to argue that "possible" has no extralinguistic function and for this reason we need not avoid using the word for fear of involving ourselves in some strange ontology.[16] To say "An event X is possible," I should like to maintain, is not to speak of a subsistent event, X, but rather to say " 'There will be an event X' is possible" where "possible" plays a role similar to that played by "correct" and "well-formed" in the above examples. By saying something is possible or impossible, we are using words whose function is not to designate but rather to indicate some special characteristic or some special logical status of the sentence to which they are attached. But these remarks are much too general and we ought now to turn to the basic question, namely, what is the specific linguistic function that is performed by "possible" or "it is possible that" when it is attached to a sentence?

First of all, it should be quite clear that in the ordinary use of "possible," there is no intention of stating a commitment to a subsistent or to a science-fiction realm of mythical entities. If I say to a friend, "It is possible that it will rain," I am not making the kind of statement that would, in its most usual contexts, be construed as fictitious or as entailing a commitment to the present existence of some hypothetical state-of-affairs. Secondly, an important feature of a language is often mentioned but rarely examined: sentences usually do not appear alone. Only in a philosophy class might we suddenly say, out of a clear blue sky, "All men are mortal," although even here the sentence is usually stated in conjunction with other sentences which make its assertion relevant. Normally sentences appear in clusters which, in a vague way, we name "discourses" or "inquiries" or "contexts." There can be simple ceremonial phrases such as "Hello" or "Good morning" or "How do you do?" which frequently do occur alone. But where the intent is to communicate information or to clarify some problematic situation, sentences always appear in conjunction with other sentences. One can indeed talk to oneself but in this situation groups of sentences are also usually asserted.

Now let us consider for a moment how we might describe such clusters of sentences if we were trying to determine the various relations one sentence might have to another. It would seem to me that certain kinds of observations would clearly be forthcoming. *1*] Some sentences in this cluster are operating as premises or evidence. *2*] Others are taken as conclusions. *3*] Some sentences are taken to be true or false or doubtful. These would be the kinds of description we might give if we were asked to describe any given cluster of sentences. But sooner or later, if we wished to make our analysis precise, we would be required to compare a series of such clusters. If we wished to know the different connotations of a given expression we might have to inspect its use in numerous different contexts. Ziff, for example, has shown that in trying to determine the meaning of the word "good" he was required to consider more than one hundred discourses in which the word is employed.[17] If we wished to know whether a certain sound was playing a syntactic, designative, or some other role in the language we would have to inspect many contexts in order to determine such data. Quine seems to think that such information is easily come by. If we wished to discover the expression for negation, for example, we would look for that which "turns any short sentence to which one will assent into a sentence from which one will dissent, and vice-versa." [18] But such possible expressions cannot be discovered except on a comparative basis. In the following two sentences there is only one additional part which would cause anyone who would affirm one to deny the other:

8] Jean is a male.

9] Jean is a female.

Yet clearly we would not speak of "fe" as the expression for negation. Only as we observed the regular appearance of certain terms in contexts in which dissent was given would we be able to discriminate "not" from other expressions.

Now in comparing clusters of sentences, we would probably become aware that different clusters have many similar features. Sentences S_1 and S_2 of cluster C_1 are logically identical or synonymous with P_1 and P_2 of C_2.[19] Or, whereas, S_1 and S_2 of C_1 are taken to be indubitable, their counterparts P_1 and P_2 in C_2 are taken to be questionable. Or we might find that whereas, in C_1, S_1 and S_2 are taken as evidence for the assertion of some other sentence S_3, on the other hand, in C_2, P_1 and P_2 are taken as evidence for a sentence P_3 which is not at all identical or synonymous with S_3. Especially if we observed these clusters in a temporal sequence we might find that in one discourse a sentence S_3 is taken to be legitimately inferable from S_1 and S_2 while in some later discourse where identical or synonymous sentences for S_1 and S_2 are given, no such inference is allowed. In fact, in many instances we would find that during the same temporal span more than one sentence can be derived from the same set of data. For example, it is no surprise to find two different weather predictions based on the same set of evidence.

Nor should it be a surprise to find that those using a given language are themselves frequently conscious of the fact that the sentence inferred in one discourse from S_1 and S_2 is often not the same sentence inferred from analogous premises in some other discourse. Most of us are aware that the same data often produce diametrically opposed conclusions. And it would seem to me that when we might want to make an important decision or be very precise, we would have to acknowledge the fact that in other discussions a sentence S_1 inferred in ours was replaced by some other sentence P_1. It might be important to know not only what we take to be legitimate inferences, but also what others, under the same circumstances, take to be legitimate inferences. For by knowing what these other inferences are, we can take steps to counter them if it were to turn out that our inference was wrong and someone else's was right. What would be more plausible than to mark off in some way all those statements which we know have served as replacements for the sentence we have inferred. Thus, we might say on the basis of S_1 and S_2, S_3 is inferred, but S_4 . . . S_n have served to replace S_3 in other discourses. Or we might say, given S_1 and S_2, the following is a list of sentences that have been inferred from them in various discourses: S_3, S_4 . . . S_n. Now we could mark off the fact that such replacements have occurred in various ways. We might simply say: "S_3 is inferred. Its replacements have been S_4 and S_n." Or we might use other devices: "S_3 is inferred. But also consider S_4* and S_n*, where * marks sentences that have replaced S_3 in other inquiries." Or if we wished we could simply assert S_3 and italicize S_4 and S_n where the italics would signify other sentences that have been asserted under similar circumstances. And, finally, as another alternative, since in a language any sound can be used to serve any function, we might use some new verbal mechanism: "S_3 is inferred. But S_4 . . . S_n are possible." In this case "possible" is doing no more than marking certain kinds of sentences which have played important roles in similar inquiries. Just as in the previous example given by Austin "real" warned us about the use of some other word, so also "possible" is here supposed to warn us that other sentences have played roles similar to that being played by S_3. Or where S_3 is not explicitly asserted, "possible" warns us that a number of alternative sentences have been used in inquiries of the present sort. And actually is not this precisely the way we do use "possible"? Something is given and then we try to indicate that other things are possible or impossible and all we mean by these two terms is that the statements marked by them have either been inferred or considered and then rejected in other discourses using similar premises. Thus we ask, "Is it possible for him to win?" and we mean that our knowledge and information at the present is such that "he will lose" is the probable conclusion. But we are asking whether given the same sort of discourse revolving about similar objects and events, the inference drawn has been "he will win." In other words, "possible" calls our attention to other alternatives.

Now I have been using the expression "possible" in the sense of factually rather than logically possible. But it should be clear that the same sort of analysis is applicable to both kinds of possibility. Sometimes all I want to be told is that the assertion of a statement different from one drawn is at least not a violation of any logical rules in the language. Thus I might ask in the instance of someone dying from some incurable disease, "Is it possible for him to pull through?" We might simply be asking whether "he pulled through" has ever been inferred from a similar discourse. But probably we are simply looking for some assurance that "he has pulled through" is not out of the question by the very nature of the language we are using. We want the assurance that at least "he has pulled through" does not have the logical contradictoriness of "he is both large and not large."

Thus words like "possible" and "impossible" and, therefore, "can" and "cannot" have no ontological import. They are devices by which we mark sentences which we ought to keep in mind when we are involved in any discourse. They tell us: S_3 is what you infer here. But do you know that $S_4 \ldots S_n$ have been inferred elsewhere in very similar cases? They indicate kinds of sentences and not kinds of existences.

Thus we move from one discourse to another and in most of these discourses there are both syntactical and descriptive features. But some of our most serious problems in communication arise because we forget that linguistic expressions have many functions. I think we ought to take it as a rule that before we assign any expression a descriptive function we ought first to ask whether its function cannot be explained without reference to anything descriptive. This would be the linguistic application of Occam's rule.

17
Conclusion

I

I HAVE TRIED to show that some expressions that are vital in both ordinary and scientific discourse cannot be given a formal analysis without an implicit or explicit commitment to an abstract entity. Thus expressions such as "make," "is synonymous with" as well as the truth-functional connectives lead into precisely those inquiries that can be characterized as metaphysical. But some philosophically significant expressions would only *seem* to have ontological implications. In every instance only a detailed analysis can show whether an expression can be redefined without the intrusion of some necessary statement about what a universe must contain. If we need to posit some abstract entity or concept called an "intension" or an "intention" or a "universal" in order to explain important expressions in a language, then these entities must be admitted as members of the universe being described by that language.

I have also sought to show that formal languages themselves are not free of significant ontological positions. But in this concluding chapter I should like to summarize my views on the relation of a formal language to the issue of ontological inquiry.

I will begin by introducing certain formal considerations. The language I am using, with all its implicit and explicit grammatical rules, I shall call L_1. I shall also assume that there is a subgroup of expressions of L_1, which is called L_2, and which serves as a metalanguage for a purely formal calculus, C_1. C_2 is to be equated with the formal calculi constructed by Quine, Rosser, Carnap, and Church. However, one important modification is introduced. No mark in the calculus is characterized by a descriptive term of L_1 or L_2. Thus we can refer to the P-variables, F, G, and H, with or without subscripts and superscripts. But by a P-variable is not meant a predicate or functional variable, but rather a particular written inscription governed by specific rules in the metalanguage. The reason for this modification is that the use of such descriptive terms as "predicate" and "function" entails a commitment to a formalized language having monadic and polyadic predicate expressions as substituends for variables. In a pure calculus, however, there must be no such inclusion of a reference to a specific kind of interpretation.

Similarly, the calculus contains I-variables rather than individual ones since here also we seek to avoid any employment of expressions that explicitly predispose the calculus towards a specific interpretation. In interpreting the calculus we may require terms that designate individuals. But in the construction of a pure calculus no necessity of this sort is admissible.

In this same connection references to sentential or propositional variables are omitted although some alphabetical letters are listed as S-variables, but always with the understanding that in the pure calculus itself S-variables are distinguished from P and I variables only by virtue of the different rules governing their use. Furthermore, even though our prime concern will be with how variables rather than quantifiers are interpreted, it might be of interest to indicate that neither *existential* nor *universal* nor *is a member of the class of* are properly identifiable with the quantifiers, the epsilon, or the P-variable, for otherwise it might seem as if the very calculus itself is not constructible unless some of the marks of the calculus are taken to signify universals or classes or something existential. In the construction of pure formal calculi we need not and ought not to permit such predispositions. Finally, we might note that all vocabulary referring to truth-functional analyses are eliminated since this vocabulary would be required only if we were to make the decision to interpret the calculus as a truth-functional system.

Calculi, therefore, so far as interpretations are concerned, are strictly neutral. They are no more than marks governed by rules which specify their possible combinations. They need not be taken as marks characterized as individual or predicate variables, as existential or universal quantifiers, or as abbreviations for truth functions. All such descriptive terminology is external to the calculus itself.[1]

Having posited a calculus that is purified of any extrinsic features, we can now raise the question of what occurs when a calculus is interpreted. To begin with, interpretations ought to be distinguished from *exemplifications*. It is sometimes thought that an interpretation occurs whenever the marks of the calculus are replaced or made to stand for other marks. Thus, for example, "$p \supset q$" can be replaced by "$\diagdown \supset \diagup$," or else "$p$" and "$q$" can be labelled as menon variables taking the names of menons, meaningless entities, as substituends.[2] But exemplification of this sort ought not to be confused with interpretation. When we interpret a calculus we supply expressions which, even before their inclusion in a formal system, have some important function. Thus we can have mathematical, biological, or physical interpretations which consist of the insertion into a pure calculus of expressions that have, prior to inclusion in the calculus, served an important pragmatic or theoretical purpose. Or we might have a minimal interpretation in which certain marks of the calculus are taken to be syntactic and then are replaced by words such as "or," or "and" or "not," etc., which abbreviate certain truth-functional functions. But in both of these cases—the one involving a full-blown scientific interpretation or the mere minimal one—the expressions employed already have a prior use. "Or" may become part of the interpretation of C_1, but this does not minimize the fact that even before this employment "or" was already functioning in the languages L_1 and L_2.

L_2, then, can be taken as consisting of two types of expressions. There are those that are strictly *syntactical*, that is, they produce the framework of the language, the essential elements without which the language would not be possible. Thus when P and I variables are taken as predicate and individual variables, we are giving a syntactic interpretation. We are stating that if a designating term—one that refers to something other than itself—is to be a substituend for the P or I variable, then it must be respectively either a predicate term or an individual term which is usually a name. These are formal conditions, set down prior to any considerations of what specific predicate terms or individual expressions are included in the language. Similarly, if we specify S-variables as sentential variables and allow them to be characterized as true or false, then we are stating that if a linguistic segment is identifiable as a sentence to which true or false is applicable, then it can be admitted as an element in the interpretation of C_1. This is a formal consideration since we are not stating what specific sentences are to be introduced. Our interpretation tells us only what conditions must be satisfied if any subject matter is to become an interpretation of C_1. On the other hand, if we did specify which specific substituends are to be allowed for the various variables, then we would be adding a *semantic* interpretation to the syntactic one. Thus if we were dealing with physics we would have a specification stating that "atomic" or "molecular" are to be allowable predicates. In other words, in a semantic interpretation a dictionary of specific terms would be supplied as well as rules differentiating high-level expressions, that is, constructs, from zero-level expressions which stand for concrete objects or immediately observable phenomena.

What is worth reiterating here, then, is that calculi do *not* entail any interpretation, syntactic or semantic. Marks are by themselves neutral and a decision is required if they are to be interpreted. Variables are not inherently place-holders for predicates, names or descriptions. They are assigned meanings by a user of a language. Thus what we must now determine is what occurs when words are assigned to marks.

Perhaps the first point to note is that words do not function alone. In order for a sign to become a word it has to be employed as an element of a linguistic system. The sound "dog" is no more than a sound which can be equated with a sudden cough or any other noise until it becomes recognized as an English word operating in accordance with certain general patterns of linguistic organization found in the English language. Thus the expressions that will serve to interpret C_1 are derived from an already functioning language which, in this instance, turns out to be L_2. To be able to say " 'Atomic' is an allowable substituend for a P-variable," for example, means that "atomic" must be allowable as a linguistic expression in L_2.[3] Otherwise we would merely be substituting another mark for the P-variable and in this way we would obtain an exemplification of C_1 rather than an interpretation. Whatever words are used with C_1 they come with their own special restrictions and conditions.

But it is especially interesting to note that if we employ the terms of L_2, then at least certain rules of employment for those terms must also be introduced as part of the interpretation of C_1. In other words, if I use "atomic" as part of the interpretation of C_1, then I am also required to employ this term with those conditions that are at least necessary, if not sufficient, for the manipulation of "atomic" in L_2. Whatever else we shall attribute to the interpretation of C_1, if "atomic" or "or" or "and" are allowable, a differentiation must be made among different *kinds* of words. There must be an acknowledgment that "a" serves a different role from "John Smith" and "atomic" and "and." But even more important, we are obliged to recognize a sharp distinction between conventional and nonconventional elements of a language. "Atomic" may or may not be a part of L_2, but there must always be rules indicating the *kinds* of words that are permissible. Elementary organizational features are demanded of L_2, if it is to be a language, and are required of any interpretation of C_1. In a sense we are caught in a Kantian circularity in which the construction of a language always contains certain necessary characteristics of the metalanguage.

Not everything, then, is conventional in the interpretation of C_1. If we wish to interpret C_1 as a language of biology, then the designative expressions of biology would have to be admitted into L_2. In a language of physics or of a social science, the designative expressions of physics and the social science would have to be admitted into L_2. But none of these designative expressions are necessary. Even without the inclusion of "atomic" or "epithelium" a language could still function. We can always substitute one subject matter for another. But what is necessary and essential is the following: *If C_1 is to have an interpretation then P, I, and S variables are to be called respectively Predicate, Individual, and Sentential variables; and any designative expression that is introduced must be either a predicate term, an individual naming term, or a sentence.* In other words, in interpreting C_1 some expressions are conventional in the sense that a language is still possible even if they are not present or are eliminated. But the absence of other expressions would make it impossible to have a language. These latter expressions are those syntactic ones that we have labelled predicate, individual, and sentential variables. The labelling of variables in this way is not a conventional matter that can be eliminated in the same way we can eliminate any specific substituend.

A language, then, has this odd characteristic. The very least we ought to be able to find in it are predicate terms, individual terms, and sentences. And if this is the case, then we ought now to ask what it means to say that a language categorizes in these ways. I have argued in this book that it ought to mean that whatever we call a universe must have as its population those entities designated by the referential expressions of the language. Thus if the language must contain names or definite descriptions, then, if Carnap is right and all designative terms have both an extension and an intension, then there must be individuals and individual concepts since every language will contain at least one name or one definite description. And if the language must contain predicate terms then, again following Carnap, there must be properties and classes since every language will contain at least one predicate term. Finally, if there must be sentences, then there must be propositions and Fregean Truths since every language must contain at least one sentence. All these entities ought to be taken as part of the general population in the same sense that if I make up a game of baseball which requires baseball players if the game is to be played, then Carl Yastrzemski may not play at all but I am perfectly within my rights to say that if the game is to be played there must be at least one baseball player. The argument then is this: if a language must utilize a certain kind of designative term then insofar as the language is functioning there must be designata of that term. In brief, if we must have names, predicates, and sentences in the language then there must be individuals, individual concepts, classes, properties, propositions, and Truths (perhaps Falsehoods as well). However, as we have seen in preceding chapters this kind of wholesale commitment to the designata of all the designative terms in a language has been rejected by most nominalists and partial nominalists such as Quine.[4] In the remainder of this conclusion I shall examine some of the more important objections and show why I consider them to be unwarranted.

II

THE FIRST objection is that we have been taken in by the fact that a certain kind of calculus has been constructed. We can have a calculus whose interpretation utilizes the various features we have been attributing to it. But such a calculus is a mere convention. In the system constructed by both Schönfinkel and Curry no variables at all are admitted but rather a set of constants called combinators.[5] Thus without variables we can, at least theoretically, construct a language that is not committed to the use of sentences, predicate terms, or expressions referring to individuals. But as Quine points out, "The entities presupposed by statements which use combinators turn out . . . to be just the entities that must be reckoned as arguments or values of functions in order that the statements in question be true."[6] In other words, even in a combinatorial language we are committed precisely to those same entities indicated by predicates, names, and sentences.

Quine himself has also suggested a method of eliminating variables by incorporating them into predicates.[7] Thus "*x* bites something" becomes "*x* bitessomething" (where "bitessomething" is a monadic predicate) or, using Quine's symbols, "(*Der B*)*x*." And since "*x*" can itself be treated as the pronoun "something" we can change "*x* bitessomething" into "Something bitessomething," or "(*Der Der B*)," where both variables and quantifiers are no longer needed.[8] The difficulty with this conversion, however, is that it requires us to make wholesale revisions in our understanding of what a semantic interpretation is. Predicate terms are said to have extensions and intensions. But how, on Quine's analysis, are we to analyze the monadic predicate "bitessomething"? Since "something" is no longer operating as a variable, we cannot interpret "bitessomething" in terms of the extensions and intensions of variables.[9] But how then are we to proceed to determine when "bitessomething" is applicable? Presumably, unless some major changes of meaning are introduced, this odd predicate would still retain the one essential characteristic usually attributed to the existential quantifier, namely, that it is applicable if any one of a series of disjuncts become applicable. In other words something has the predicate "bitessomething" if it also has the predicate "bites*a*" or "bites*b*" or "bites*c*," etc. But since a disjunctive series in a language with an infinite domain cannot be conclusively falsified "bitessomething" has the peculiar status of never being rejectible. Once we predicate it of something, the predication can never be wrong. But even more important is the fact that if we follow Quine it no longer makes sense to speak of a predicate since there is nothing left of which predicates can be predicated. Rightfully, we ought to change "predicate terms" into "designator terms" and then define a sentence as a series of designator terms, no one of which can be said to be a subject or to allude to "something" having properties indicated by the remaining terms. But Quine's obvious attempt here to reinstate the Hume-Russell argument for eliminating things and names of things founders on a traditional objection that has never been adequately answered. How is a distinction to be drawn between a combination of designator terms that "belong to the same individual" and a combination that is merely accidental or unrelated? I can list a series of adjectival terms, but some of these series would be said to have a single owner while the others would not. How is this distinction to be made if we are no longer able to speak of predicates being predicated of something? In the extensional kind of logic with which Quine is dealing, predicates are independent of one another. But how then are we to formulate the sense of ownership of predicates without permitting a reference to an owner?

Quine, then, may indeed present us with a language system that is free of both variables and quantifiers. But the resultant language would seem to have more the status of an exemplification than an interpretation.

Thus various sorts of calculi are constructible, but it is their interpretation that matters. We can eliminate the tilde in a calculus but this does not mean that we can then go on to construct a negationless language. Similarly, we can play all kinds of games with a series of marks, but it is what we need when we interpret these marks that determines how free we are from a commitment to abstract entities.

Another objection to the wholesale commitment to entities referred to by designator terms is that names can be and, indeed, have been removed from certain formal language systems. Thus, following Russell and Quine, we can change all proper names into descriptions and in this way we can have a namefree language. But this conversion of names into descriptions introduces a certain mystic quality into a language. The whole notion of a variable becomes strangely puzzling. What is this *"x"* that is normally taken to be replaceable by names but which we are now told can no longer take names as replacements? What is the function of *"x"* in *"($\exists x)Fx$"* if *"x"* is no longer permitted to be instantiated into *"FavFbvFc . . . ."* where *"a . . b . . c . ."* are names or at least those special definite descriptions introduced in Chapter 12? Church tells us that "involved in the meaning of a variable . . . are the kinds of meaning which belong to a proper name of the range." [10] And Quine also feels no compunction in speaking of the "things in place of whose names variables stand" [11] or of telling us that "the variable stands in *place* of *names* . . . ." [12] But if individual-naming expressions are no longer permitted then what can the meaning of an individual variable be? Peculiar difficulties arise when we attempt to define a proper name, but even more peculiar difficulties arise when we attempt to explicate a variable that is no longer permitted to function as a variable. Furthermore, as Strawson asks,[13] can predicate terms be understood without counterposing them to names or to some expressions with which predicates are allowable? Predicates predicate something of something else. They are designators of properties or of classes. But can "property" be understood as other than "property of something" and, even though there are null classes, can "class" be defined without demarcating it from entities which are members of classes? It might be argued that predicating a property of something means predicating it of something *or other*. No specific entity is intended. But even though it is probably false that there is a property which is predicated of every specific object, it is clearly not false that for every specific object there is a property that predicates it. In other words, in any given instance a property is predicated of a specific entity which is denotable and, therefore, nameable, or else not denotable and, therefore, unnameable or mystical. Thus perhaps individual-naming-terms can be eliminated from a language, but the price would seem to be a mystical commitment to substance or to Locke's "something-I-know-not-what."

Although names have often been denied admission into a language the commitment to predicates and sentences has seldom been questioned. Even Quine's variableless language must include a reference to predicates and sentences. (Strictly speaking, however, Quine's "sentence" is by no means of the usual sort. It is an extrapolation from a monadic, that is, a "one-place" predicate to a "no-place" predicate. Sentences are really predicates which, unlike other kinds of predicates, do not require other terms in order to function. "F," as a monadic predicate operating in the usual formal language, would require the accompaniment of a variable or a specific name as in "Fx." But "F" as a sentence requires no variables or names at all.) [14] But the force of this commitment has been taken to be minimized by the neutralization of what these terms designate. Thus Quine permits both predicate and sentential letters into his NF and ML languages but he denies that they entail any introduction of either classes or propositions. Only insofar as these letters are used as bound variables subject to quantifiers, do we then introduce propositions and classes. But if we refuse to permit such quantification then both sentential and predicate letters are merely "schematic," standing for possible predicates or sentences. As Quine tells us, "The schematic letters 'p,' 'q,' etc., stand in schemata to take the place of component statements, just as the schematic letters 'F,' 'G,' etc., stand in schemata to take the place of predicates; and there is nothing in the logic of truth functions or quantification to cause us to view these schematic letters as variables taking any such entities as values. It is only the bound variable that demands values." [15] However, there are two points to be noted here.

First of all, at least in the case of predicates, Quine, with some hesitation, admits that some quantification must occur in order to define the ancestor relation as well as the class of natural numbers. But presumably such quantification can be carefully restricted by accepting an appropriately modified theory of types in which all classes are such that "membership in any of them is equivalent to some condition expressible in L_o (the language of concrete objects)." [16] In this way classes become conceived as "conceptual in nature and created by man." [17] I am not sure what this last phrase really means but in any event Quine does acknowledge that some classes must be admitted as entities for the predicate term.

But, secondly, we ought to examine Quine's main contention, namely, that only insofar as we are committed to quantification over a given term, that is, when the term begins to operate as a bound variable, do we have to speak of the referents of that term. Let us consider what the status is of "F" in "$(\exists x)Fx$." Since quantification has occurred over the individual variable, we are acknowledging that the population of the universe must at least contain individuals. But since quantification has not occurred over "F," are we to claim that there are no properties of individuals or that even though an individual may have the property F it does not belong to the class of F individuals? Ordinarily, if we state "There is a brown cat on the mat," then it must also be true to say "There is a class of brown things of which the cat is a member or the sole member," for it would surely be strange to affirm the truth of the former without affirming the truth of the latter. If something is brown, we can either say, "It has brown as a property," or, "It is an element of the class of brown elements." Or, in more idiomatic terms, if object A exists and has a property P then surely there must be this property that A has. Thus it is not at all clear how we can claim to populate the universe with individuals and at the same time deny that the properties attributed to such individuals are not really properties at all or do not entail any commitment to classes. Quine has sometimes sought to eliminate the referring characteristic of predicate terms by taking them to be "true of" each concrete entity rather than names of any property or class.[18] But, first of all, we ought not to confuse the use of an entity or an expression with the entity or expression itself. "F" may be true of "x," but this does not tell me what "F" is. We may claim that "fish" is true of each concrete fish, but this does not answer the question of what it is that is true of each concrete fish. I may be told that paint is what I apply to houses, but this does not tell me what paint is. An expression has a use, but this is not identical to its reference.

Secondly, Quine would seem to be saying that, for example, "The house is brown" means the same as " 'Brown' is applicable to the house." But clearly these two are not identical since a German who understands the translation of the former sentence, namely,

$1]$ "Das Haus ist braun"

would not necessarily understand the translation of the latter sentence, namely,

$2]$ " 'Brown' ist anwendbar auf das Haus"

even if he understood each German word. Thus the referents of predicate terms cannot be eliminated in favor of the terms themselves.

However, not only is it my contention that the referents of

predicate terms—be they properties, classes, or both—must be admitted as the entities required by a language, I should now like to argue that the quantification of predicates is not restricted, as Quine seems to think it is, solely to the definition of certain special concepts. Predicate quantification necessarily arises at the very first introduction of two or more individual variables. Consider the following unquantified schema:

3] $Fx \cdot Gx$.

Without quantification over the individual variable it does not at all follow that we are saying that something has the property F and the property G. The "x" of Fx need not be the same "x" as that of Gx. [3] says ambiguously "it is F and it is G" but "it" need not be the same or have the same reference. We accomplish the sameness of "it" by quantifying over the individual variable. When [3] becomes:

4] $(\exists x)(Fx \cdot Gx)$

then and only then can we say that something has both the property F and the property G. But now consider the following unquantified schema:

5] $Fx \cdot Fy$.

Like [3], [5] says ambiguously that something—perhaps the same thing—has a property. But it also has another ambiguity, namely, that the property "F" of Fx may or may not be the same property as the "F" of Fy. Just as in [3] the guarantee that the substituends of "x" will be the same is obtained by the use of [4], so also the guarantee that the substituends of "F" will be the same comes only with the quantification of the predicate. In other words if [5] is to be used to formulate an unambiguous sentence then we must quantify both individual and predicate variables:

6] $(\exists x)(\exists y)(\exists F)(Fx \cdot Fy)$.

Thus predicate quantification arises at the very earliest attempt to employ the same predicate variable with different individual ones.

Finally, in dealing with propositions, Quine uses Tarski's technique of showing that $(\exists P) \ldots P \ldots$ dissolves into $s_1 \ldots v \ldots s_2 \ldots v \ldots s_3$, etc., where s_1, s_2, s_3, etc., are sentences.[19] But if this is a way of eliminating a commitment to an abstract entity then why did Quine not employ this with classes and properties as well? If $(\exists P)$ becomes changed into sentences, then why should not $(\exists F)$ become changed into predicate terms or class terms and in this way dispel in one quick movement every commitment to an abstract entity? In fact, on this analysis, we need not even be concerned with whether there are individuals in the universe since $(\exists x)$ can presumably lead to the disjunction . . . a . . . v . . . b . . . v . . . c . . . etc., where a, b, and c, etc., are names or other individual terms. I think the answer is that in the instantiation of predicate and individual variables, we are still left with the question of determining what are the referents of predicate terms and individual-naming terms. We have the Wittgensteinian issue of what it is that an atomic sentence purports to designate. Similarly, Quine may indeed eliminate quantification over propositions by reducing them to sentences. But even Carnap is required to admit propositions as the intensions of sentences. At one time Quine took propositional variables to be sentential variables which were, oddly enough, "symbols of nothing" or indicative of "ambiguous sentences." [20] But this kind of terminology would seem to produce more problems than it solves.

In concluding I should like to make clear that it has not been my intention in this book to defend a metaphysical thesis. Abstract entities do have an unsettling effect on the nerves, and in an age concerned with the population explosion, it is extremely presumptuous if not dangerous to add more members to the population, even if they are abstract and take up no room. But it would seem to me that formalism, despite its precision, has not yet succeeded in dispelling a serious commitment to an ontology of abstract entities.

NOTES

SELECTED BIBLIOGRAPHY

INDEX

Notes

1. Language and Ontology

[1] For a more detailed discussion of the logical terminology used in the construction of a formal system see A. Church, *Introduction to Mathematical Logic* (rev. ed.; Princeton, N. J., 1956), Introduction and Chap. I; also R. Carnap, *Logical Syntax of Language* (London, 1937). There are alternative kinds of symbolism, e.g., the Polish notation of Lukasiewicz. But, unless otherwise specified, we shall employ the symbolism of A. N. Whitehead and B. Russell's *Principia Mathematica* (2d ed.; Cambridge, England, 1925–27) and W. V. O. Quine's *Mathematical Logic* (rev. ed.; Cambridge, Mass., 1961).

[2] For different kinds of interpretations of constructed systems see E. W. Beth, "Carnap's Views on the Advantages of Constructed Systems over Natural Languages in the Philosophy of Science," *The Philosophy of Rudolph Carnap*, ed. P. A. Schilpp (Chicago, 1963), pp. 469–518; also Church, *Introduction to Mathematical Logic*, pp. 116 ff.

[3] The proof of the equivalence is easily forthcoming. From $\sim(p\sim q)\cdot\sim(\sim p\sim q)$ we obtain $\sim pvq\cdot pvq$. Then by cross distribution we derive $\sim pq$ v qp v q which then can be shown to be equivalent to q.

[4] W. V. O. Quine, *Set Theory and Its Logic* (Cambridge, Mass., 1963), pp. 9 ff.

[5] *Tractatus Logico-Philosophicus*, trans. D. F. Pears and B. F. McGuinness (London, 1961), p. 51, 4.12–4.122. But this would not mean the syntax of ordinary language, as some philosophers have maintained. See Paul Marhenke,

"The Criterion of Significance" in *Semantics and the Philosophy of Language,* ed. L. Linsky (Urbana, Ill., 1952), p. 142.

[6] Carnap, *The Logical Syntax of Language,* p. 53.

[7] The metaphor is mentioned by W. V. O. Quine, *From a Logical Point of View* (Cambridge, Mass., 1953), p. 79.

[8] A system of getting rid of variables altogether by means of certain constants called combinators was proposed by H. B. Curry and Moses Schönfinkel. But the values presupposed by their system turn out to be the same values presupposed in ordinary logics containing variables. See Curry, "A Simplification of the Theory of Combinators," *Synthese,* VII (1948–49), 391–99; Schönfinkel, "Ueber die Bausteine der Mathematischen Logik," *Mathematische Annalen,* XCII (1924), 305–16; also Quine, *From a Logical Point of View,* pp. 104 ff.; also H. B. Curry, R. Feys, and W. Craig, *Combinatory Logic,* I (Amsterdam, 1958). Quine has also proposed a way of eliminating variables, but even in his system some linguistic segments must be interpreted as sentences and others as predicates which we must presume are predicated of something. See W. V. O. Quine, "Variables Explained Away," *Journal of Symbolic Logic,* XIX (1954); also reprinted in Quine's *Selected Logic Papers* (New York, 1966), Chap. XXII.

[9] I wish to thank *Philosophy and Phenomenological Research* for allowing me to reprint in this chapter several parts of my article on "Ontology and Language" which appeared in December, 1962, Vol. XXII.

[10] But this ought not to be taken to mean that the inclusion of quantification does not posit its own serious issues. For a discussion of the paradoxes that arise in confirming or disconfirming quantified sentences see the (by now) classic paper by Carl Hempel, "Problems and Changes in the Empiricist Criterion of Meaning," *Revue Internationale de Philosophie,* XI (1950), 41–63; also Arthur Pap, *The Philosophy of Science* (New York, 1962), Chap. II; and Israel Scheffler, *The Anatomy of Inquiry* (New York, 1963), Part III.

[11] A. N. Prior, *Formal Logic* (Oxford, England, 1955), p. 13.

[12] C. S. Peirce, *Collected Papers,* eds. Charles Hartshorne and Paul Weiss (Cambridge, Mass., 1933), IV, 13–18, 215–16; H. M. Sheffer, in *Transactions of the American Mathematical Society,* XIV (1913), 481–88; J. G. P. Nicod, in *Proceedings of the Cambridge Philosophical Society,* XIX (1917–20), 32–41.

[13] C. S. Peirce, in *American Journal of Mathematics,* VII (1885), 189–90. See also Church, *Introduction to Mathematical Logic,* p. 151.

[14] Church, *Introduction to Mathematical Logic,* p. 151.

[15] *Ibid.*

[16] *Tractatus,* p. 99, 5.512. However, the intuitionist in mathematics has claimed that the rule of double negation is not valid.

[17] Max Black, *A Companion to Wittgenstein's 'Tractatus'* (Ithaca, N. Y., 1964), pp. 224 ff.

[18] For an elaborate analysis of Wittgenstein's discussion of negation in the *Tractatus* see also G. E. M. Anscombe, *An Introduction to Wittgenstein's Tractatus* (2d ed., rev.; London, 1963), Chaps. III and IV.

[19] See I. Kant, *Critique of Pure Reason,* trans. N. Kemp-Smith (New York, 1934), pp. 108, 490, 574.

[20] H. Bergson, *Creative Evolution*, pp. 287 ff.

[21] Franz Brentano, *Wahrheit und Evidenz* (Leipzig, 1930), pp. 94, 124.

[22] W. H. Sheldon, "The Concept of the Negative," *Philosophical Review*, XI(1902), 485–96.

[23] C. J. Ducasse, "Propositions, Opinions, Sentences, and Facts," *Journal of Philosophy*, XXXVII (1940), 701–11.

[24] Richard Taylor, "Negative Things," *Journal of Philosophy*, XLIX (1952), 448.

[25] Black, *A Companion to Wittgenstein's 'Tractatus,'* p. 221.

[26] *Ibid.*

[27] *Ibid.*

[28] For a full exposition of the view that an ontological commitment begins to arise when we begin to employ quantification see the essays by Quine in *From a Logical Point of View* (2d ed., rev.; Cambridge, Mass., 1961).

[29] P. F. Strawson, *Individuals* (London, 1959).

[30] W. V. O. Quine, *Methods of Logic* (rev. ed.; New York, 1959), p. 89.

[31] A first-order scientific generalization is a generalization whose domain is every entity without qualification, i.e., "All bodies exert on each other a force that is directly proportional to the product of their masses and inversely proportional to their distance."

[32] This problem also plagued the early logical atomists. See J. O. Urmson, *Philosophical Analysis* (Oxford, 1956), pp. 62 ff.; see also Russell's argument that generalizations cannot be "purely extensional."—*An Inquiry into Meaning and Truth* (New York, 1940), pp. 254–55.

[33] C. S. Peirce, *Collected Papers*, eds. Hartshorne and Weiss (Cambridge, Mass., 1935), VI, 204.

For further discussion of the nonapplicability of Hegel's system see Jack Kaminsky, *Hegel on Art* (New York, 1962), Chap. IX. However, there are many dissenting views. See, for example, C. J. Friedrich, "Hegel's Dialectic and Totalitarian Ideology," in *A Hegel Symposium*, ed. D. C. Travis (Austin, Texas, 1962), pp. 13 ff, and J. Loewenberg, *Hegel's Phenomenology* (Chicago, 1965), pp. 354 ff.

[34] G. E. Moore asked whether it might not be the case that along with existential quantification we might not still require the word "exists." We would want to be able to say that even though something exists it might not have existed; and this cannot be expressed by simple existential quantification. See "Is Existence a Predicate?" *Proceedings of the Aristotelian Society*, Supplementary Vol. XV, 1936.

[35] Technically, of course, this allusion to Kant is not altogether correct since Kant did believe that at least one state-of-affairs—that which is described in Newtonian physics—was a necessary characteristic of all experience, i.e., was necessarily described either implicitly or explicitly in all languages. But it is fairly well taken for granted that Kant's main thesis concerning the categories and the forms of space and time is still arguable in spite of his Newtonian bias. See S. Körner, *Kant* (London, 1955), pp. 50 ff.

2. The Ontology of Karl Popper

[1] See, for example, Mark Pontifex, "The Question of Evil," in *Prospect for Metaphysics,* ed. Ian Ramsey (New York, 1961), Chap. VIII.

[2] For Popper's criticism of Carnap and the thesis that a formal language can eliminate the need for metaphysical inquiry see Popper's main position in *The Logic of Scientific Discovery* (3d rev. ed.; New York, 1965); also *The Philosophy of Rudolph Carnap,* ed. P. A. Schilpp (Chicago, 1963), pp. 183–226. For Carnap's affirmation of the physicalistic thesis with its explicit rejection of any metaphysical implications see his replies to Popper and Feigl in *The Philosophy of Rudolph Carnap,* pp. 877 ff.

[3] In his reply to Popper, Carnap points out that some sentences are formulable in a physicalistic language and yet look like metaphysical sentences, e.g., those of astrology and magic and myth. But sentences of this sort are simply false. The sentences that cannot be given an appropriate formulation are those such as Heidegger's "The Nothing Nothingeth" or "The cardinal number five is blue."—*The Philosophy of Rudolph Carnap,* p. 878.

[4] *The Logic of Scientific Discovery,* pp. 196 ff.

[5] C. G. Hempel, *Fundamentals of Concept Formation in Empirical Science,* International Encyclopedia of Unified Science, XI (1952), No. 7, p. 30. See also Hempel's criticism of operationism in *Philosophy of Natural Science* (Englewood Cliffs, N. J., 1966), pp. 89 ff.; *Aspects of Scientific Explanation* (New York, 1965), pp. 123 ff.

[6] See F. P. Ramsey, *The Foundations of Mathematics* (London, 1931), pp. 212 ff.; R. B. Braithwaite, *Scientific Explanation* (Cambridge, England, 1953), pp. 50 ff.

[7] For a full discussion of the shortcomings of Carnap's reduction sentences see Hempel, *Fundamentals of Concept Formation in Empirical Science,* pp. 23 ff.

[8] *The Philosophy of Rudolph Carnap,* p. 211.

[9] *Ibid.*

[10] *Ibid.,* p. 187.

[11] For some suggested ways of solving the dispositional problem see C. G. Hempel, *Fundamentals of Concept Formation in Empirical Science,* pp. 23–29; A. Kaplan, "Definition and Specification of Meaning," *Journal of Philosophy,* XLIII (1946), 281–88; Arthur Pap, *The Philosophy of Science,* Chap. XV.

[12] For a full discussion of reduction sentences and dispositional terms, with all the attendant successes, failures, and suggested remedies, see Israel Scheffler, *The Anatomy of Inquiry* (New York, 1963), pp. 162 ff.

[13] For Carnap's most recent analysis of theoretical terms and how they are to be distinguished from metaphysical ones see *Philosophical Foundations of Physics* (New York, 1966), Part V.

[14] Popper's decision to introduce "thinks" as a predicate is not arbitrary. The recommendation for its inclusion in a formal system already appears in

Carnap. See "Testability and Meaning," Sec. 18, in *Classics of Analytic Philosophy*, ed. R. R. Ammerman (Madison, Wis., 1965), p. 169.

[15] Other sorts of predicates defined by Popper are: "*a* knows that *b* is in position *c*"; "*a* knows that *b* can put *c* into the position *d*"; "*a* knows that *b* thinks *c*"; "*a* is unfathomable"; "*a* knows the fact *b*." These are defined by bilateral reduction sentences.—*Philosophy of Rudolph Carnap*, p. 208.

[16] *Ibid.*, pp. 208–9.

[17] See especially *Tractatus Logico-Philosophicus*, trans. D. F. Pears and B. F. McGuinness, 6.53, p. 151.

[18] *Philosophy of Rudolph Carnap*, p. 189.

[19] See Carnap's replies in *The Philosophy of Rudolph Carnap*, pp. 878 ff.

[20] *Ibid.*

[21] *Ibid.*, p. 875.

[22] W. D. Ross, *Aristotle* (London, 1923), p. 180.

[23] F. C. Copleston, *Aquinas* (London, 1955), p. 109.

[24] It ought to be noted, however, that even Plotinus did not completely divorce his mystic insight from the ordinary facts of experience. As Stephen C. Pepper points out, mystics such as Plotinus never quite escape the problem of tying experience to their mystic intuitions. "These men assume the absolute credibility of (their) experience. But they have a cognitive curiosity to know how this indubitable experience is connected with the ordinary 'facts' of the world."—*World Hypotheses* (Berkeley, Calif., 1948), p. 131.

[25] R. Carnap, *Introduction to Semantics* (Cambridge, Mass., 1948), p. 104; also Richard Martin, "On Carnap's Conception of Semantics," in *The Philosophy of Rudolph Carnap*, p. 369.

[26] *Philosophy of Rudolph Carnap*, p. 209.

[27] R. Carnap, "Testability and Meaning," in *Classics of Analytic Philosophy*, ed. R. R. Ammerman, pp. 35 ff; also C. I. Lewis, *An Analysis of Knowledge and Valuation* (Chicago, 1946), p. 180.

[28] A. Tarski, "The Semantic Conception of Truth," in *Readings in Philosophical Analysis*, eds. H. Feigl and W. Sellars (New York, 1949), pp. 52 ff.; in the same volume see R. Carnap, "Truth and Confirmation," pp. 119 ff. The significance of Tarski's remarks in the early part of his paper have completely overshadowed some of his important points in the later part, where he argues that the function of "true" and "false" is to show us whether a given theory has a contradiction within it. Once we make "certain assumptions regarding the truth of empirical sentences" we can devise a method of testing whether a given theory contains false sentences.—Tarski, "The Semantic Conception of Truth," p. 77.

[29] However, there might be an instance in which a disjunct of an existential sentence is highly confirmed, but we might still discount it and take it to be false if we wished to test what inferences could be drawn if the sentence were false. For example, a statement about the corpuscular theory of light might, for logical purposes in a scientific language, be labelled "true." But we might also want to test what could be inferred from it in conjunction with other scientific statements if we labelled it "false."

[30] *Philosophy of Rudolph Carnap,* pp. 209–10, *n.* 57*a.*

[31] R. Carnap, *Logical Foundations of Probability* (2d ed.; Chicago, 1962), p. 349.

3. The Ontology of P. F. Strawson

[1] *Individuals, An Essay in Descriptive Metaphysics* (London, 1959), p. xiv.

[2] *Ibid.,* pp. xiv–xv.

[3] *Ibid.,* p. 2.

[4] *Ibid.,* pp. 28–29.

[5] *Ibid.,* p. 29.

[6] *Ibid.,* pp. 51 ff.

[7] *Ibid.,* p. 61.

[8] W. V. O. Quine, *Word and Object* (New York, 1960), p. 238 *n.*

[9] Strawson, *Individuals,* p. 112.

[10] *Ibid.*

[11] *Ibid.,* p. 113.

[12] *Treatise of Human Nature* (London, 1911), II, Appendix, 318–19.

[13] For a discussion of the difficulties in Hume's analysis of the self see A. H. Basson, *David Hume* (London, 1958), pp. 126 ff.; for a modern defense of the view that the "I" is dissolvable into a series of basic observational predicates see Bertrand Russell, *An Inquiry Into Meaning and Truth* (New York, 1940), Chap. VII.

[14] Strawson, *Individuals,* p. 101.

[15] See *Philosophical Investigations* (New York, 1953), Secs. 43, 117, 120. See also George Pitcher, *The Philosophy of Wittgenstein* (Englewood Cliffs, N. J., 1964), Chaps. X, XI, and XII.

[16] Strawson, *Individuals,* p. 102.

[17] *Ibid.,* pp. 104–5.

[18] Chapter XI.

[19] See especially Kant's *First Analogy* where he tries to show that cognition requires permanence—or the category of substance—to be present amidst phenomena. *Critique of Pure Reason,* trans. F. Max Muller (2d ed. rev.; New York, 1896), pp. 149 ff. It has sometimes been argued that perhaps Kant also wishes to speak of substance among the realm of noumena. But, first of all, as Paton points out, the categories cannot apply to noumena since one can never know what does or does not apply to noumena.—H. J. Paton, *Kant's Metaphysic of Experience* (New York, 1936), II, 175–76. Secondly, both Fichte and Hegel eliminated noumena altogether and made *object* a strict category of consciousness.

[20] C. D. Broad, *Examination of McTaggart's Philosophy* (Cambridge, England, 1938), II, Part I, 75.

[21] *Dialogues,* II, p. 276 in *Berkeley,* ed. M. W. Calkins (New York, 1929).

[22] Broad, *Examination of McTaggart's Philosophy,* I, 418.

[23] I am of course doing little justice to the full detailed development of McTaggart's ingenious argument. His two important principles of infinite divisibility and determining correspondence are crucial to an analytical understanding of his proof for the existence of another self. See Broad, *Examination of McTaggart's Philosophy*, I, Chaps. XIX, XX, and XXI.

[24] F. H. Bradley, *Appearance and Reality* (New York, 1902), p. 89.

[25] For a critical discussion of the significance of ordinary language assumptions on Strawson's analysis see G. Bergmann, "Strawson's Ontology," *The Journal of Philosophy*, LVII (1960), 601–22.

[26] See Wittgenstein, *Notebooks 1914–1916* (Oxford, England, 1961), 24.5.15; also George Pitcher, *The Philosophy of Wittgenstein* (Englewood Cliffs, N. J., 1964), pp. 130 ff.

[27] For a discussion of Wittgenstein's analysis of complex and simple objects and its relation to the views of classical philosophers see Max Black, *A Companion to Wittgenstein's Tractatus* (Ithaca, N. Y., 1964), pp. 58 ff.

[28] Thus D. Pears, in his review of *Individuals*, was able to say of Strawson's omissions of some of these central problems that "it is difficult not to feel uneasy at the completeness of his isolation of ordinary thought from technical thought."—"Critical Study," *Philosophical Quarterly*, XI (1961), 172.

[29] Strawson, *Individuals*, p. 24.

[30] See *Philosophical Investigations* (New York, 1953), Sec. 258. For a detailed criticism of Wittgenstein's view that there cannot be a private language, see A. J. Ayer, *The Concept of a Person* (New York, 1963), pp. 36 ff.

[31] *Philosophical Investigations*, Secs. 154, 155, 179, 180, 210–14.

[32] *Ibid.*, Sec. 153.

[33] Ayer, *The Concept of a Person*, pp. 44 ff.

[34] That there are external objects, however, is not a view held by Ayer. He goes on to maintain that the Crusoe on the island could construct a purely phenomenalistic language. However, he questions whether such a language could be taught to anyone else.—Ayer, *The Concept of a Person*, pp. 48, 78.

[35] Strawson, *Individuals*, pp. 97 ff.

[36] For a full discussion of some of the difficulties that arise when this dichotomy is unequivocally accepted see Chapter 7.

[37] Carnap, *The Logical Syntax of Language*, pp. 284 ff.

[38] Nelson Goodman, *The Structure of Appearance* (2d ed.; New York, 1966); see also Goodman's defense of phenomenalism against physicalism in "The Significance of *Der Logische Aufbau Der Welt*," in *The Philosophy of Rudolph Carnap*, ed. P. A. Schilpp (Chicago, 1963), pp. 545 ff.

[39] For a somewhat similar attempt to show how Kant's views on the categories are translatable into terms relating to contemporary investigations of logical and linguistic form see L. W. Beck, "On the Meta-Semantics of the Problem of the Synthetic a Priori," *Mind*, LXVI (1957), 228–32; reprinted in L. W. Beck, *Studies in the Philosophy of Kant* (New York, 1965), pp. 92 ff.

4. Quine on Ontological Commitment

[1] Strawson points out that philosophers have used other verbs, accordingly as a subject or a predicate was being discussed. Thus subjects referred to, named, indicated, designated, or mentioned while predicates described, characterized, ascribed, predicated, or said something about. *Individuals, an Essay in Descriptive Metaphysics* (London, 1959), p. 138. But the language used, at least from the traditional viewpoint, is not as important as the fact that the terms were applied to different kinds of entities. It is easy to imagine a language using "referred to" in the case of both subjects and predicates. The distinction would consist in what they were taken to refer to.

[2] R. Carnap, *Introduction to Semantics* (Cambridge, Mass., 1942), pp. 16–17.

[3] John Dewey, *Logic, The Theory of Inquiry* (New York, 1938), p. 124.

[4] See also Gilbert Ryle's discussion of descriptive expressions in "Systematically Misleading Expressions," in *Logic and Language,* ed. A. Flew (New York, 1965), pp. 25 ff.

[5] Quine's most important discussions dealing with the implications of formal systems for ontology and philosophical issues in general appear in *From a Logical Point of View* (2d ed. rev.; Cambridge, Mass., 1961); *Word and Object* (New York, 1960); *Selected Logic Papers* (New York, 1966), Chap. XIII; *The Ways of Paradox* (New York, 1966); "Notes on Existence and Necessity," *The Journal of Philosophy,* XL (1943), reprinted in *Semantics and the Philosophy of Language,* ed. L. Linsky (Urbana, Ill., 1952); "Designation and Existence," *The Journal of Philosophy,* XXXVI (1939); reprinted also in H. Feigl and W. Sellars (eds.), *Readings in Philosophical Analysis* (New York, 1949).

[6] But there would still remain a further puzzle about how to distinguish a predicate such as "blue" from one such as "a man." Something can be a man but it cannot be a blue.

[7] "Notes on Existence and Necessity," *The Journal of Philosophy,* XL (1943), 116 ff.

[8] *Ibid.,* p. 117.

[9] See *The Philosophy of Rudolph Carnap,* ed. P. A. Schilpp (Chicago, 1963), pp. 897 ff.

[10] Feigl and Sellars, "Designation and Existence," p. 49.

[11] Quine, "On Carnap's Views on Ontology," *Philosophical Studies,* II (1951), 67; reprinted in *The Ways of Paradox.*

[12] In his "New Foundations of Mathematical Logic" Quine rejects the theory of types except in the one case of the theorem that causes Russell's paradox. In this theorem, $(\exists x)(y)(y \epsilon x) \equiv \underline{\phi})$, ϕ must be stratified, that is, it must have a connotation of type and must not contain "x". In his "Logic and the Reification of Universals" a type theory very comparable to Russell's ramified theory of types is reintroduced. The only difference is that classes are

treated as "constructions" which are in some sense not genuinely real. See *From a Logical Point of View,* Chaps. V and VI.

[13] The reference to Carnap here is from his *The Logical Structure of the World,* trans. R. A. George (Berkeley, Calif., 1967), p. 107. For a full discussion of this early system of Carnap's see Nelson Goodman, *The Structure of Appearance,* Chap. V. Goodman abbreviates Carnap's basic entities to "erlebs."

[14] Ryle, "Systematically Misleading Expressions," p. 23.

[15] Quine, *From a Logical Point of View,* p. 121.

[16] Quine, *Methods of Logic* (rev. ed.; New York, 1950), p. 90. For Quine there are also unquantified variables but formulae that contain them are of interest "only as potential parts of *closed* (quantified) *sentences.*"

[17] *Ibid.,* p. 89.

[18] However, Quine ought not to be regarded as a nominalist. At an earlier stage in his career, especially in his paper with Nelson Goodman, Quine did accept a nominalist position. But this later became modified to "conceptualism." See W. V. O. Quine, "Steps Towards a Constructive Nominalism," *Journal of Symbolic Logic,* XII (1947), 105–22; *From a Logical Point of View,* p. 127; and *Word and Object,* p. 243 *n.*

[19] *From a Logical Point of View,* p. 109.

[20] *Ibid.,* p. 103.

[21] *Ibid.,* pp. 109 ff.

[22] Instead of quantifying predicates directly, as in $(F)Fx$, Quine adopts a new notation using ϵ to stand for "is a member of" and the variables $a, \beta, y \ldots$ for classes. See *Methods of Logic,* p. 225.

[23] *Ibid.,* p. 227.

[24] *Ibid.,* p. 228.

[25] *Ibid.* For a nominalistic attempt to deal with the ancestor relationship see Nelson Goodman, *The Structure of Appearance,* pp. 44–45.

[26] *Ibid.,* pp. 229 ff.

[27] Following Church's system we would merely have to change the fifth formation rule to read "any variable" instead of "individual variable."—*Introduction to Mathematical Logic* (Princeton, N. J., 1956), pp. 295 ff.

[28] Even in his more recent work where he posits a theory of "virtual classes" which carry no presumption of existence, Quine must still admit real classes.—*Set Theory and its Logic* (Cambridge, Mass., 1963), p. 38.

[29] See *Translations from the Philosophical Writings of Gottlob Frege,* eds. P. Geach and M. Black (Oxford, England, 1960), pp. 63 ff.

[30] Nicholas Rescher, "Definitions of 'Existence,' " *Philosophical Studies,* VIII (1957), 66.

[31] For a discussion of Santayana's unenacted essences and their limitations see the articles on Santayana in *The Journal of Philosophy,* LI(1954), 29–64.

[32] *From a Logical Point of View,* pp. 89 ff.

[33] *Ibid.,* p. 123.

[34] *Ibid.,* p. 124.

[35] *Ibid.*

[36] The paradoxes as well as most of the difficulties in Russell's theory of

types are avoided if Quine's *ML* system is employed. See *ibid.*, pp. 91 ff. For the relation of the *NF* system to the *ML* system presented in *Mathematical Logic* see Quine's *Set Theory*, pp. 302 ff.

[37] *From a Logical Point of View*, p. 125.

[38] *Ibid.*, p. 127.

[39] *Ibid.*, p. 128.

[40] *Ibid.*, p. 122.

[41] Quine himself shows the consequences of Cantor's proof in "On Cantor's Theorem," *Journal of Symbolic Logic*, II (1937), 120–24.

[42] Henry S. Leonard has made the charge against Quine and other logicians that they have tended to overlook modal logic and its implications for ontological issues and difficulties in the philosophy of science. See Leonard's paper, "The Logic of Existence," *Philosophical Studies*, VII (1956), 49–64.

5. Carnap on Ontological Commitment—Thing and Property

[1] *Logical Syntax of Language* (London, 1937), pp. 248 ff. Carnap also refers to sentences of (2) as those in the *formal mode of speech* while those of (3) are in the *material mode of speech*.

[2] For a discussion of some of the problems in drawing such inferences see I. Scheffler, *The Anatomy of Inquiry* (New York, 1963), pp. 31 ff.

[3] That there are such fictions constantly employed in all fields of inquiry is of course well known. Probably one of the most definitive studies of such fictions—even though it is a bit dated—is in Hans Vaihinger's *The Philosophy of 'As If,'* trans. C. K. Ogden (New York, 1924).

[4] Thus in his reply to Nelson Goodman, Carnap agrees that both physicalistic and phenomenalistic systems are possible. But "the intersubjective character of the physicalistic basic concepts (different observers will in general agree about the observable properties of things in their environments although their subjective experiences might differ) makes the physicalistic system more practical."—*The Philosophy of Rudolph Carnap*, ed. P. A. Schilpp (Chicago, 1963), p. 945.

[5] "Meaning Postulates," *Philosophical Studies*, III (1952), 65–73; also reprinted in *Meaning and Necessity* (enlarged ed.; Chicago, 1956), pp. 222 ff.

[6] See Friedrich Waismann, "Language Strata," in *Logic and Language*, ed. A. Flew (New York, 1965), pp. 226 ff.

[7] *Introduction to Symbolic Logic*, trans. W. H. Meyer and J. Wilkinson (New York, 1958), p. 36. But see also pp. 213 ff. where Carnap does accept "is a thing" as a predicate in biology.

[8] *Logical Syntax of Language*, p. 285.

[9] *Ibid.*

[10] *Ibid.*, p. 303.

[11] *Ibid.*, pp. 304–5.

[12] *Ibid.*, p. 304.

[13] *Ibid.*, p. 304. The reference to synthetic predication does not appear in Carnap's definition, but it is of course implicit when he refers to analytic predicates.

[14] *Ibid.*

[15] Errol E. Harris accuses Carnap of employing a "sophistical argument" in showing how the doctrine of internal and external properties leads to contradiction. Harris claims that in the example used by Carnap if we knew that *c* were both the father of Charles as well as the owner of this piece of land no contradiction would arise. Both being related to Charles and being a landowner would be essential. *Nature, Mind, and Modern Science* (New York, 1954), p. 24. But Carnap's point is that so long as we are dealing with properties and not their descriptions then if property p of an object o entails property q, while property r of the same object does not entail q, then we are apparently committed to the paradoxical view of calling q a property that is essential to o, but not always. Thus the property of being the father of Charles does not entail the property of being a landowner, nor does the converse hold. Thus given any set of properties we could always show that a property entailed by one is not entailed by the others. Ergo at least one property is both essential and inessential. On the other hand if we are dealing solely with descriptions, then we can speak of descriptions contradicting one another without also thinking that the object contains contradictions.

[16] Carnap, *Logical Syntax of Language*, p. 304.

[17] *Meaning and Necessity*, p. 22.

[18] See, for example, Henry Margenau, *The Nature of Physical Reality* (New York, 1950), p. 70.

[19] Milic Capek, *The Philosophical Impact of Contemporary Physics* (Princeton, N. J., 1961), p. 379.

[20] David Bohm, for example, deduces that the scientific understanding of "things," (which includes properties, qualities, levels, etc.) leads to the belief that "no feature of anything has as yet been found which does not undergo necessary and characteristic motions."—*Causality and Chance in Modern Physics* (Princeton, N. J., 1957), p. 148.

[21] At one point in his analysis of names Russell makes the same error of thinking that he can define names by means of position in a formal system. Russell states that "We may define a 'name' as any word that can occur in *any* species of atomic sentences, i.e., in a subject-predicate sentence, a dyadic-relation sentence, a triadic-relation sentence, and so on."—*An Inquiry into Meaning and Truth* (New York, 1940), p. 118. This is an unusual extension of "name" but the primary difficulty still remains. How are we to tell when a word can occur in any species of atomic sentence? Obviously not all words can occur in this way. But what distinguishes those which can from those which cannot?

[22] *Tractatus-Logico-Philosophicus*, trans. D. F. Pears and B. F. McGuinness (London, 1960), p. 57, 4.1272.

[23] See, for example, Hughes Leblanc, *Deductive Logic* (New York, 1955), p. 61; I. Copi, *Symbolic Logic* (3d ed.; New York, 1968), p. 72.

[24] *Meaning and Necessity*, p. 205 ff.

[25] *Philosophical Investigations*, pp. 31 ff. The same point is reiterated by J. L. Austin. See his *Philosophical Papers* (Oxford, England, 1961), pp. 6, 23 ff.; also *Sense and Sensibilia* (Oxford, England, 1962), pp. 62 ff.

[26] See Copi, *Symbolic Logic*, pp. 345 ff.; also Quine, *From A Logical Point of View*, pp. 91 ff.

6. Carnap on Ontological Commitment—Intensions

[1] These matters are discussed by Carnap in *Meaning and Necessity*. See also Carnap's comments in *The Philosophy of Rudolph Carnap*, pp. 915 ff.

[2] See "On Sense and Nominatum," by Gottlob Frege, trans. H. Feigl, in *Readings in Philosophical Analysis*, eds. H. Feigl and W. Sellars (New York, 1949); also reprinted in *Meaning and Knowledge*, eds. E. Nagel and R. B. Brandt (New York, 1965). See also "On Sense and Reference," in *Translations from the Philosophical Writings of Gottlob Frege*, eds. Peter Geach and Max Black (2d ed.; Oxford, England, 1960). For a full commentary, see J. D. B. Walker, *A Study of Frege* (Ithaca, N. Y., 1965).

[3] See John Stuart Mill, *A System of Logic* (10th ed.; London, 1879), Book I, Chaps. I and II. The book was first published in 1843.

[4] "On Sense and Nominatum" in *Meaning and Knowledge*, eds. E. Nagel and R. B. Brandt, p. 73.

[5] *Ibid.*

[6] A. Church, *Introduction to Mathematical Logic* (Princeton, N. J., 1956), p. 25, *n* 66.

[7] *Meaning and Necessity*, p. 94.

[8] *Ibid.*

[9] *Ibid.*, pp. 27 ff.

[10] C. I. Lewis, *An Analysis of Knowledge and Valuation* (Chicago, Ill., 1946), p. 52.

[11] *Meaning and Necessity*, p. 94.

[12] *Ibid.*, p. 10.

[13] But see Carnap's remark: "I would not assert that the use of concepts like intension . . . are necessary, but their use seems to me convenient and natural . . . ,"—*The Philosophy of Rudolph Carnap*, p. 915.

[14] For a more complete discussion of this point see Donald Davidson, "The Method of Extension and Intension," in *The Philosophy of Rudolph Carnap*, pp. 311 ff.

[15] *Meaning and Necessity*, pp. 130 ff.

[16] A. Church, "A Review of Quine," *Journal of Symbolic Logic*, VIII (1943), 46.

[17] *Meaning and Necessity*, p. 23.

[18] *Ibid.*, p. 23.

[19] *Ibid.*, p. 27.

[20] See Quine, *From a Logical Point of View* (2d ed. rev.; Cambridge, Mass.,

1961), Chaps. II, III, and VI; also Morton White, "The Analytic and the Synthetic: An Untenable Dualism," in *John Dewey*, ed. Sidney Hook (New York, 1950).

²¹ Carnap maintains that even if intensional terminology were eliminated in favor of an extensional terminology, such reductionism could never be complete "since in an extensional language there can be no designator *L*-equivalent to '*N*.' "—*The Philosophy of Rudolph Carnap*, p. 894.

²² *Meaning and Necessity*, p. 236.

²³ *Ibid.*, p. 238.

²⁴ *Ibid.*

²⁵ Thus J. N. Findlay points out: "Intensional accounts cover what *could* be the case . . . whereas extensional treatments confine themselves to what actually is the case."—*Language, Mind, and Value* (London, 1963), p. 157.

²⁶ *Theaetetus*, 183 b.

²⁷ *Meaning and Necessity*, p. 238.

²⁸ For a recent defense of the ontological argument, however, see Norman Malcolm, "Anselm's Ontological Arguments," *The Philosophical Review*, LXIX (1960); also reprinted in Norman Malcolm, *Knowledge and Certainty* (Englewood Cliffs, N. J., 1963), pp. 141–62.

²⁹ However, in Chapter 16 I suggest another way of treating "possible."

³⁰ *Meaning and Necessity*, p. 243.

³¹ It should be pointed out, however, that in his analysis of dispositional predicates Carnap introduces reduction sentences for the prime purpose of tying dispositions to some series of physicalistic test procedures. Even though he does not reduce dispositional predicates to purely physicalistic terms, he does attempt to make it meaningless to speak of dispositions that have no actual instances. See "Testability and Meaning," in *Classics of Analytic Philosophy*, ed. Robert R. Ammerman (New York, 1965), pp. 130 ff.

³² *Meaning and Necessity*, p. 154.

³³ *Ibid.*, pp. 155 ff.

³⁴ *Ibid.*, p. 154.

³⁵ *Ibid.*, p. 234.

³⁶ *From a Logical Point of View* (Cambridge, Mass., 1953), p. 157. Quine remarks here that "Admission of attributes and propositions . . . rules out individuals and classes." But in the second edition revised, 1961, this remark does not appear.

7. The Function of Language—Language and the Extralinguistic

¹ *Science and Sanity* (3d ed.; Lakeville, Conn., 1948), p. 11. See also S. Zollette, *Basic Principles of General Semantics* (Philadelphia, 1955), p. 28.

² S. Hayakawa, *Language and Thought in Action* (New York, 1949), pp. 31–32.

³ See Nelson Goodman's most recent statement, "The Significance of *Der*

Logische Aufbau der Welt," in *The Philosophy of Rudolph Carnap,* ed. P. A. Schilpp (Chicago, 1963), pp. 545 ff.

[4] R. Carnap, *Logical Foundation of Probability* (2d ed.; Chicago, 1962), Introduction.

[5] B. Croce, *Aesthetic,* trans. Douglas Ainslie (rev. ed.; London, 1953), Chap. I.

[6] For a full discussion dealing with the differences between a map and a language see E. Daitz, "The Picture Theory of Meaning," in *Essays in Conceptual Analysis,* ed. A. Flew (New York, 1956). For further comments see H. N. Lee, "A Fitting Theory of Truth," in *Tulane Studies in Philosophy,* XIV (1965), 105 ff.

[7] See especially Lanier's prose work, *The Science of English Verse,* where he argues that the most effective expressions of poetic feelings and moods occur when the language almost attains the sound of music. But there are, of course, major criticisms of this position made by such diverse critics as Croce, I. A. Richards, and T. S. Eliot. In this connection see Marshall Cohen, "Aesthetic Essence," in *Philosophy in America,* ed. Max Black (Ithaca, New York, 1965), pp. 15 ff.

[8] For an analysis of the differences between a physical and a linguistic response to pain or some other emotion see W. P. Alston, "Expressing" in *Philosophy in America,* pp. 15 ff.

[9] On this point see Carnap's reply to Strawson in *The Philosophy of Rudolph Carnap,* pp. 933 ff.

[10] Paul Edwards, "Bertrand Russell's Doubts about Induction," in *Logic and Language,* ed. A. Flew (New York, 1965), pp. 59 ff; J. N. Findlay, *Language, Mind and Value* (London, 1963), pp. 39 ff.

[11] Austin, *Philosophical Papers* (Oxford, England, 1961), Chap. VII.

[12] Austin, *How to Do Things with Words* (Cambridge, Mass., 1962).

[13] *The Philosophy of Rudolph Carnap,* pp. 933 ff.

[14] Wittgenstein's Platonism is discussed by both Pitcher and Black. See G. Pitcher, *The Philosophy of Wittgenstein,* pp. 41 ff; M. Black, *Philosophy in America,* pp. 11 ff.

[15] *Philosophical Investigations,* pp. 40, 117.

[16] For the classic formulation of this view of truth see A. Tarski, "The Concept of Truth in Formalized Languages," in *Logic, Semantics, Metamathematics,* trans. J. H. Woodger (Oxford, England, 1956); "The Semantic Conception of Truth," *Philosophy and Phenomenological Research,* IV (1944); and also reprinted in H. Feigl and W. Sellars (eds.), *Readings in Philosophical Analysis* (New York, 1949), and L. Linsky (ed.), *Semantics and the Philosophy of Language* (Urbana, Ill., 1952).

[17] Wittgenstein, *Tractatus,* 7.

[18] Peter Caws, *The Philosophy of Science* (Princeton, N. J., 1965), p. 33.

[19] D. F. Pears, "Universals" in *Logic and Language,* ed. A. Flew, p. 271.

[20] See G. H. Mead, *Mind, Self, and Society* (Chicago, 1934), pp. 111 ff; John Dewey, *Logic, the Theory of Inquiry* (New York, 1938), Chap. VIII, and *Experience and Nature* (New York, 1936), p. 180; John Dewey and A. F.

Bentley, *Knowing and the Known* (Boston, 1949), p. 56; A. F. Bentley, *Inquiry into Inquiries* (Boston, 1954), p. 352; N. H. Bronko and J. W. Bowles, Jr., *Empirical Foundations of Psychology* (New York, 1951), p. 229; B. F. Skinner, *Science and Human Behavior* (New York, 1953), pp. 266 ff.

[21] For a discussion of the Ames experiments and other pertinent information see the papers on psychology and scientific research by H. Cantril, A. Ames Jr., A. H. Hastorf, and W. H. Ittelson, *Science*, CX (1949).

[22] J. Z. Young, *Doubt and Certainty in Science* (Oxford, England, 1951), p. 62. For further analysis of what is involved in "seeing," see M. Polanyi, *Personal Knowledge* (Chicago, Ill., 1958), pp. 96–97.

[23] B. L. Whorf, *Language, Thought, and Reality* (New York, 1956), p. 221; also see pp. 213–14.

[24] N. Goodman, "The Significance of *Der Logische Aufbau der Welt*" in *The Philosophy of Rudolph Carnap*, p. 548.

[25] Findlay, *Language, Mind and Value*, p. 18.

[26] W. J. Entwistle, *Aspects of Language* (New York, 1953), p. 162.

[27] Whorf, *Language, Thought and Reality*, pp. 98–99.

[28] M. Schlauch, *The Gift of Tongues* (New York, 1945), pp. 150 ff.

[29] Laws, II, 656–57.

[30] For a history of the changes in the English language see A. C. Baugh, *A History of the English Language* (New York, 1935).

8. The Function of Language—Inference

[1] For a major attempt to show the rules governing the derivation of probabilities within the framework of a functional calculus see R. Carnap, *Logical Foundations of Probability* (2d ed.; Chicago, 1962).

[2] Emile Meyerson summarizes and dramatizes the whole instrumentalist viewpoint when he says, "Surrounded by hostile nature, [an organism of the human kingdom] must act, it must foresee, if it wishes to live. 'All life, all action,' says Fouillée, 'is a conscious or unconscious divining. Divine or you will be devoured.'"—*Identity and Reality*, trans. K. Loewenberg (London, 1930), p. 22.

[3] Heffner, *General Phonetics* (Madison, Wis., 1950), p. 23.

[4] Probably, as Wittgenstein has pointed out, the study of primitive languages could be very revealing about the primary aims and functions of a language. "It disperses the fog to study the phenomena of a language in primitive kinds of application in which one can command a clear view of the aim and functioning of the words."—*Philosophical Investigations*, trans. G. E. M. Anscombe (New York, 1953), p. 4e.

[5] In his *Gulliver's Travels* Swift tells us of a linguist who proposed that men eliminate language altogether by carrying "about them such things as were necessary to express the particular business they are to discourse on."—"A Voyage to Laputa," Chap. V. Obviously this would eliminate psychiatrists and Platonist philosophers!

⁶ D. S. Lee argues that scientific language is constructed in order to "provide anticipation of future experience."—"Truth in Empirical Science," in *Tulane Studies in Philosophy*, XIV (1965), p. 58. But even ordinary languages have such anticipation as their function.

⁷ C. I. Lewis, *An Analysis of Knowledge and Valuation* (Chicago, 1946), p. 19.

⁸ J. L. Austin, *How to do Things with Words* (Cambridge, Mass., 1962), Lecture I.

⁹ *Ibid.*, p. 5.

¹⁰ W. P. Alston, *Philosophy of Language* (Englewood Cliffs, N. J., 1964), Chap. II.

¹¹ For an analysis and criticism of some of the major attempts to define synonymy see Chapter 14 and also Benson Mates, "Synonymity," in *Semantics and the Philosophy of Language,* ed. L. Linsky (Urbana, Ill., 1952).

¹² Alston, *Philosophy of Language*, p. 37.

¹³ *Ibid.*, p. 36.

¹⁴ *Ibid.*

¹⁵ "Possible" and "impossible" ought also to be applicable. But we shall assume that the same sort of analysis made here for "true" and "false" are also applicable to "possible" and "impossible."

¹⁶ That "true" and "false" can be regarded as performatives is the point made by Austin, *How to do Things with Words* (Cambridge, Mass., 1962), pp. 139 ff. But Austin tries to show that "true" and "false" are performative and therefore not truth-functional. I am maintaining that they can also be performative even in their truth-functional context.

¹⁷ *The Concept of Mind*, pp. 130 ff.

¹⁸ See Schlauch, *The Gift of Tongues* (New York, 1945), p. 126.

¹⁹ Although I must confess that an aesthetician might prefer the latter to the former sentence.

²⁰ See Chapter 11.

9. Logic and Ontology

¹ G. H. Von Wright, *Logical Studies* (London, 1957), p. 8.

² Quine, *Word and Object,* p. 59. See also Quine's "Carnap and Logical Truth," in *The Philosophy of Rudolph Carnap,* ed. P. A. Schilpp (Chicago, 1963), p. 387.

³ See John B. Noss, *Man's Religions* (New York, 1949), pp. 142 ff. See also R. T. Blackwood, "Comments on the Jaina Logic of Syadvada," *Memorias del XIII Congreso Internacional de Filosofia* (Mexico City, 1964), V, 33–43.

⁴ Aristotle, *Metaphysics*, Book IV, Chap. IV.

⁵ See especially *Science of Logic*, trans. Johnston and Struthers (New York, 1929), I, 94. See also Findlay's remarks in *Language, Mind and Value* (London, 1963), p. 114.

[6] A. Korzybski, *Science and Sanity* (3d ed.; Lakeville, Conn., 1946), pp. 201 ff.

[7] In fact, the formalist mathematician believes he can do without any logical laws. But S. Körner remarks: *"Prima facie the formalist does not rely on logical principles but merely on perceptual statements such as 'a given construction of perceptual objects with perceptual characteristics C ipso facto possesses characteristics D.'* To this the qualification has to be added that the construction has to be correct. The proposition, however, that a construction is correct, i.e., that it conforms to an adopted rule, is no longer perceptual but involves a logical implication or an inference the validity of which depends on logical principles. These principles must be adopted before we can decide the correctness of a construction."—*The Philosophy of Mathematics* (New York, 1960), p. 118.

[8] A. Church, "Review of Carnap's *Formalization of Logic,*" *The Philosophical Review,* LII (1944), 494. See also Max Black's discussion of Church's "non-standard" interpretation in *A Companion to Wittgenstein's 'Tractatus'* (Ithaca, N. Y., 1964), pp. 335 ff.

[9] Alston, *Philosophy of Language,* p. 96.

[10] *Ibid.,* p. 86.

[11] F. Waismann, "Verifiability," in *Logic and Language,* ed. A. Flew (Oxford, England, 1965), pp. 122 ff. In the same volume Waismann also argues for the existence of one or more ordinary language logics that determine the operation of expressions of the same sort, e.g., psychological, physiological and other similar strata of expressions. But, unfortunately, Waismann does not show us the structure of the logics, how they vary from or compare with the formal ones with which we are acquainted. See "Language Strata," *ibid.,* pp. 226 ff.

[12] Thus Wittgenstein believed that the vagueness of ordinary propositions "can be justified."—*Wittgenstein Notebooks 1914–1916,* eds. G. H. Von Wright and G. E. M. Anscombe (Oxford, England, 1961), p. 70; see also *Philosophical Investigations,* trans. G. E. M. Anscombe (New York, 1953), p. 34.

[13] S. Körner, *The Philosophy of Mathematics,* p. 150.

[14] For an introduction to intuitionist theory see A. Heyting, *Intuitionism— An Introduction* (Amsterdam, 1956). For detailed discussion and criticism of the intuitionist position see Körner, *The Philosophy of Mathematics,* Chap. VI; S. F. Barker, *Philosophy of Mathematics* (Englewood Cliffs, N. J., 1964), pp. 76 ff; S. C. Kleene, *Introduction to Metamathematics* (Princeton, N. J., 1952), pp. 46 ff; A. N. Prior, *Formal Logic* (Oxford, England, 1955), pp. 250 ff.

[15] For a full discussion of the theorem, see H. S. Vandiver, "Fermat's Last Theorem: Its History and the Nature of the Known Results Concerning It," *American Mathematical Monthly,* LII (1946), 555–78.

[16] Max Black, *The Nature of Mathematics* (London, 1933), p. 10. Black also maintains that the intuitionists do not really deny the law of excluded middle. The law is applicable to all meaningful statements. But statements that cannot be constructed are meaningless. Therefore, the law simply does not apply.

[17] Körner, *The Philosophy of Mathematics,* p. 138.

[18] *Ibid.*

[19] For discussions of the Axiom of Choice see A. Fraenkel, *Einleitung in die Mengenlehre* (3d ed.; Berlin, 1928); and also J. Jorgensen, *A Treatise of Formal Logic* (Copenhagen and London, 1931).

[20] C. G. Hempel, "On the Nature of Mathematical Truth," in *Readings in Philosophical Analysis,* eds. H. Feigl and W. Sellars (New York, 1949), p. 229.

[21] For some possible alternatives to Zermelo's axiom see A. Church, "Alternatives to Zermelo's axiom," *Transactions of the American Mathematical Society,* XXIX (1927), 178–208.

[22] Kleene, *Introduction to Metamathematics,* pp. 42 ff.

[23] Barker, *Philosophy of Mathematics,* p. 77.

[24] See C. I. Lewis and C. H. Langford, *Symbolic Logic* (2d ed.; New York, 1959), p. 222; also A. N. Prior, *Formal Logic,* p. 249.

[25] Thus Russell requires that verifiable sentences be a sub-class of true sentences before the law of excluded middle can be employed.—*An Inquiry into Meaning and Truth* (New York, 1940), p. 368.

[26] *Notes on Logic,* p. 93; Appendix in *Notebooks 1914–1916,* eds. G. H. Von Wright and G. E. M. Anscombe (Oxford, England, 1961). See also Black's remarks about this point in *A Companion to Wittgenstein's 'Tractatus,'* Introduction.

[27] H. Veatch, *Intentional Logic* (New Haven, Conn., 1952), p. 57.

[28] M. Dufrenne, *Language and Philosophy,* trans. H. B. Veatch (Bloomington, Ind., 1963), p. 100.

[29] See Whitehead and Russell, *Principia Mathematica* (2d ed.; Cambridge, 1925–1927), I, 93; also Russell says elsewhere that "logic is concerned with the real world just as truly as zoology, though with its more abstract and general features."—*Introduction to Mathematical Philosophy* (London, 1919), p. 169.

[30] Thus A. J. Ayer admits "I do not think that [Mill's] solution of the empiricist's difficulty with regard to the propositions of logic and mathematics is acceptable."—*Language, Truth, and Logic* (2d ed.; London, 1946), p. 74.

[31] For Carnap the truth or falsity of such logical forms would be established "on the basis of the semantical rules of the [language] system alone, without any reference to (extralinguistic) facts."—*Meaning and Necessity* (enlarged ed.; Chicago, 1956), p. 10.

[32] *Tractatus,* 6.12–6.13.

[33] See Black, *The Nature of Mathematics,* pp. 7, 190.

[34] Barker, *The Philosophy of Mathematics,* p. 6.

[35] E. Nagel, "Logic without Ontology," in *Naturalism and the Human Spirit,* ed. Y. H. Krikorian (New York, 1944), p. 230.

10. The Truth-Functional Analysis of Logic

[1] See Ayer, *Language, Truth and Logic* (2d ed.; London, 1946), Chap. IV.

[2] See L. Wittgenstein, *Tractatus Logico-Philosophicus,* trans. D. F. Pears

and B. F. McGuinness (London, 1961); Bertrand Russell, *The Principles of Mathematics* (2d ed.; New York, 1938), new Introduction; R. Carnap, *Logical Syntax of Language* (London, 1937), Part V; Ernest Nagel, "Logic Without Ontology," in *Naturalism and the Human Spirit*, ed. Y. H. Krikorian (New York, 1944), pp. 210 ff.; W. V. O. Quine, *From a Logical Point of View* (Cambridge, Mass., 1953). It ought to be noted that Russell's views about the relation of metaphysics to logic have undergone considerable changes. In the original first edition of *The Principles of Mathematics* (Cambridge, England, 1903), he espoused the position that a realist metaphysics was entailed by the notions of logic. But he denied this in the introduction of the second edition. In *An Inquiry into Meaning and Truth* (New York, 1940), he apparently reverted to the earlier position since he claimed that "Logic, and the whole conception of words and sentences as opposed to verbal and sentential utterances, is thus incurably Platonic" (p. 70) and "complete metaphysical agnosticism is not compatible with the maintenance of linguistic propositions" (p. 437). For a discussion of Russell's metaphysics see James Feibleman, "A Reply to Bertrand Russell's Introduction to the second edition of *The Principles of Mathematics*," in *The Philosophy of Bertrand Russell*, ed. P. A. Schilpp (Evanston, Ill., 1946), pp. 157 ff. In his reply to Feibleman Russell claims "I will not describe myself as either a nominalist or a realist" (p. 686). But he does admit that there are universals.

Wittgenstein himself believed that even though there were no logical objects and that logical propositions have no subject matter, logic does have a "connection" with the world (*Tractatus*, 6.124c) and does "show something about the world" (*Tractatus*, 6.124d). However, Black's remarks are here appropriate: "It is fair to say that according to him [Wittgenstein] certain kinds of inference . . . from logic to ontology are possible—though it is very hard to see what such inferences would be."—Max Black, *A Companion to Wittgenstein's 'Tractatus,'* 1964, p. 330.

[3] *Tractatus*, 4.46 ff.

[4] Although the seminal idea of using truth tables to account for logical truths must be attributed to Wittgenstein, the analysis presented here is to be taken as more of an elaboration rather than an interpretation of his views.

[5] Church, *Introduction to Mathematical Logic*, I, p. 117.

[6] I am assuming that $\sim$ is interpreted as the sign of negation.

[7] Leibniz, *The Monadology and Other Philosophical Writings*, trans. R. Latta (1st ed.; Oxford, 1898), pp. 340 ff.

[8] G. H. Von Wright, *Form and Content in Logic* (Cambridge, England, 1949), p. 20.

[9] To see how the truth-functions for three or more variables could be constructed see I. Copi, *Symbolic Logic* (3d ed. New York, 1968), pp. 217 ff.

[10] Alonzo Church, "A Note on the Entscheidungsproblem," *Journal of Symbolic Logic*, I (1936), 40–41, 101–2; see also Kleene, *Introduction to Metamathematics* (Princeton, N. J., 1952), pp. 432 ff. and David Hilbert and P. Bernays, *Grundlagen der Mathematik* (Ann Arbor, Michigan, 1944), II, 416–21.

[11] Quine, *Methods of Logic*, pp. 190 ff.; D. Hilbert and W. Ackerman,

Mathematical Logic (New York, 1950), pp. 119–23. There are also decision procedures for other groups of quantified formulae. See Church, *Introduction to Mathematical Logic* (Princeton, N. J., 1956), I, 246 ff.

[12] Church, *Introduction to Mathematical Logic,* pp. 270 ff.

[13] The example is taken from Richard B. Angell, *Reasoning and Logic* (New York, 1964), p. 230.

[14] G. E. Moore, "Wittgenstein's Lectures in 1930–1933," in *Classics of Analytic Philosophy,* ed. R. Ammerman (New York, 1965), pp. 265–66.

[15] See Max Black's formulation of this criticism in *A Companion to Wittgenstein's 'Tractatus,'* p. 15.

[16] We might note how difficult it is to read the truth table without bringing in one of the logical particles. It would have been quite "natural" to say "p is to the left of q *and* directly below p is *T and then* below *T* is another *T,* etc."

[17] Aristotle, *Metaphysics,* Book IV, Chaps. III ff.

[18] Black, *A Companion to Wittgenstein's 'Tractatus,'* p. 17.

[19] B. Russell, "The Philosophical Importance of Mathematical Logic," *The Monist,* XXIII (1913), 492.

[20] H. H. Price, *Thinking and Experience* (Cambridge, Mass., 1953), p. 124.

[21] *Ibid.,* pp. 124 ff. The same point is made by John Dewey. Dewey, very much like Price, insisted that there is a logic of signs and symbols as distinct from a purely formal logic. The expressions of the former, including the conditional and alternation signs, were derived directly from an existential subject matter. The latter dealt strictly with the manipulation of uninterpreted marks. Dewey, of course, considered interest in such manipulations of marks as trivial. See *Logic* (New York, 1938), pp. 51 ff.

[22] Mikel Dufrenne, *Language and Philosophy,* trans. H. B. Veatch (Bloomington, Indiana, 1963), p. 31. See also Margaret Gorman, *General Semantics* (Lincoln, Nebraska, 1962), who summarizes the semanticist's views as "The world is in process, meanings are in process, and language must reflect this changing nature of both the world and the meanings. Language must represent the relational structure of the world" (pp. 37–38). Gorman is here referring to Korzybski, but these would obviously not be the views of Carnap and others of his school.

[23] Hume, *Dialogues Concerning Natural Religion,* Part IX.

[24] Wittgenstein apparently believed that no set of rules or directions could ever be so complete that error or misinterpretation would be impossible.—*Philosophical Investigations,* trans. G. E. M. Anscombe (New York, 1953), Secs. 197 ff., pp. 80 ff. But the important problem for us here is not whether directions or rules could ever be complete but whether they would finally require the introduction of logical connectives.

[25] *Philosophical Investigations,* Secs. 2 ff., pp. 3 ff.

[26] *Ibid.*

11. Subject and Predicate

[1] Edward Sapir, *Language* (New York, 1921), p. 93.

[2] N. Chomsky, "Current Issues in Linguistic Theory," in *The Structure of Language*, eds. J. A. Fodor and J. J. Katz (Englewood Cliffs, N. J., 1964), p. 61.

[3] "Systematically Misleading Expressions," in *Logic and Language,* ed. A. Flew (New York, 1965), pp. 37–38.

[4] Sapir, *Language,* p. 38. See also C. F. Voegelin, "Casual and Noncasual Utterances," in *Style in Language,* ed. T. A. Sebeok (New York, 1960), p. 65.

[5] P. G. Perrin, *Writer's Guide and Index to English* (3d ed.; Chicago, 1959), p. 725.

[6] R. M. Gorrell and C. Laird, *Modern English Handbook* (2d ed.; Englewood Cliffs, N. J., 1956), p. 197.

[7] Paul Ziff, *Semantic Analysis* (Ithaca, N. Y., 1960), pp. 32 ff.

[8] P. T. Geach, *Reference and Generality* (Ithaca, N. Y., 1962), p. 26. However, Geach believes that even though the use of such questions may show us which expressions are designators, they do not show us which are subjects. To know whether a part of a sentence is functioning as a subject, such an expression must always be able to be used "outside the context of a sentence simply to name something—to acknowledge the presence of the thing named."—*Ibid.*

[9] Linguists also admit that a pure syntactical analysis is not sufficient to define the nature of a subject expression. See N. Chomsky, "Current Issues in Linguistic Theory," p. 55.

[10] Max Black, "Language and Reality," *Proceedings and Addresses of the American Philosophical Association,* 1958–59, pp. 12 ff.

[11] *Ibid.,* p. 13.

[12] Carnap, *Logical Foundations of Probability* (2d ed.; Chicago, 1962), pp. 8 ff.

[13] S. Toulmin, *The Philosophy of Science* (London, 1953), p. 35.

[14] H. Poincaré, *The Foundations of Science,* trans. G. B. Halsted (London, 1921), pp. 326–28.

[15] For a detailed discussion of these matters see Church, *Introduction to Mathematical Logic,* p. 70.

[16] In a similar vein, R. B. Braithwaite has shown that if there is to be a science and it is to proceed in accordance with some axiomatic scheme, then some of the axioms must contain descriptive and not purely logical or mathematical terms. See *Scientific Explanation* (Cambridge, England, 1953), Chap. II. See also the discussion by Peter Caws, *The Philosophy of Science* (Princeton, N. J., 1965), Chap. XVIII.

[17] For a full discussion of the distinctions Frege makes between object and concept see G. Frege, *Die Grundlagen der Arithmetik* (Breslau, 1884), Secs. 51, 56; also *Translations from the Philosophical Writings of Gottlob Frege,* eds. P. Geach and M. Black (Oxford, England, 1960), pp. 21–55. See also J. D. B. Walker, *A Study of Frege* (Ithaca, N. Y., 1965).

[18] Geach and Black, *Translations from the Philosophical Writings of Gottlob Frege*, p. 43.

[19] *Ibid.*, pp. 47–48.

[20] *Ibid.*, p. 42.

[21] *Ibid.*

[22] *Ibid.*

[23] *Ibid.*, p. 43.

[24] *Ibid.*, p. 45.

[25] On the proper analysis of this connection rests the entire issue of how analytic sentences are to be distinguished from synthetic ones. This issue becomes fundamental with Kant. For a more recent discussion see W. V. O. Quine, "Two Dogmas of Empiricism," *From a Logical Point of View* (2d ed. rev.; Cambridge, Mass., 1961), pp. 20 ff.

[26] *Parmenides*, 131.

[27] Geach and Black, *Translations from the Philosophical Writings of Gottlob Frege*, p. 54.

[28] Frege's final view was that some words can appear outside of sentences. In *The Foundations of Arithmetic*, trans. J. L. Austin (Oxford, 1950), Secs. 60, and 62, he reiterates that "only in the context of a proposition do words mean something." But in his essay "Sense and Reference" in Geach and Black, *Translations from the Philosophical Writings of Gottlob Frege*, he acknowledges that certain designators can have reference exclusive of sentential formulation.

[29] F. P. Ramsey, *The Foundations of Mathematics* (London, 1931), p. 121.

[30] Geach and Black, *Translations from the Philosophical Writings of Gottlob Frege*, p. 62; see also G. Frege, "The Thought: A Logical Inquiry," *Mind*, LXV (1956), 289–311.

[31] Geach, *Reference and Generality*, p. 22.

[32] *Ibid.*, p. 23.

[33] P. F. Strawson, *Individuals* (London, 1959), p. 143. Strawson is commenting on an earlier article of Geach, "Subject and Object," *Mind*, LIX (1950) in which Geach has a similar definition.

[34] See C. S. Peirce, *Collected Papers*, eds. C. Hartshorne and P. Weiss (Cambridge, Mass., 1932), II, Par. 228.

[35] Geach, *Reference and Generality*, p. 26.

[36] Thus Wittgenstein says: "Only propositions have sense; only in the nexus of a proposition does a name have meaning."—*Tractatus*, Trans. D. F. Pears and B. F. McGuinness, p. 25.

[37] Geach, *Reference and Generality*, p. 26.

[38] It should be noted that even the most independent use requires some linguistic framework that is left unsaid. "Fire!" surely means "There is a fire here in the vicinity!" One would not yell "Fire!" if the fire were several hundred miles away. Similarly, one would cry "Wolf!" insofar as he believed that everyone would supply the rest of the framework, namely, that there is a wolf in the neighborhood.

[39] Russell, *Introduction to Mathematical Philosophy* (London, 1920), p. 142.

[40] Geach, *Reference and Generality*, p. 26.

[41] Russell, *Introduction to Mathematical Philosophy*, p. 142.

[42] Geach, *Reference and Generality*, p. 31.

[43] Quine, *Word and Object*, p. 179.

[44] Strawson, *Individuals*, p. 153.

[45] *Ibid.*

[46] Strawson, *Individuals*, p. 191.

[47] *Ibid.*, p. 218.

[48] See Russell, *Introduction to Mathematical Philosophy*, Chap. XVI. For one of the major attempts to show the inadequacies of Russell's view see P. F. Strawson, "On Referring," *Mind*, LIX (1950). Both Russell's chapter on descriptions and Strawson's criticism appear in R. R. Ammerman (ed.), *Classics of Analytical Philosophy* (New York, 1965); for further discussion see G. E. Moore, "Russell's 'Theory of Descriptions,'" in *The Philosophy of Bertrand Russell*, ed. P. A. Schilpp (Evanston, Ill., 1946). See also Quine's attempt to eliminate individual variables altogether in favor of predicate variables, *Selected Logic Papers* (New York, 1966), Chap. XXII.

[49] See W. V. O. Quine, "Designation and Existence," *Journal of Philosophy*, XXXVI (1939); also reprinted in H. Feigl and W. Sellars, *Readings in Philosophical Analysis* (New York, 1949). Also see Quine, *Word and Object*, pp. 176 ff.

[50] For further discussion of the distinction between the syntactic and the semantic aspects of a language see R. Carnap, "Foundations of Logic and Mathematics," *International Encyclopedia of Unified Science*, I, No. 3 (1939), 7; R. M. Martin, *Truth and Denotation* (Chicago, 1959), p. 13; J. H. Woodger, *The Axiomatic Method in Biology* (Cambridge, England, 1937), p. ix.

[51] See H. J. Paton, *Kant's Metaphysic of Experience* (London, 1936), II, 270–71.

[52] Ramsey, *The Foundations of Mathematics*, p. 117.

[53] Russell, *An Inquiry into Meaning and Truth*, pp. 119 ff.

[54] Y. Bar-Hillel, "Indexical Expressions," *Mind*, LXIII (1954), 368.

12. Descriptive Sentences

[1] See especially Quine's "Two Dogmas of Empiricism," *Philosophical Review*, LX (1951), pp. 20–43; reprinted also in *From a Logical Point of View*. Also see M. White, "The Analytic and the Synthetic: An Untenable Dualism," in *John Dewey: Philosopher of Science and Freedom*, ed. Sidney Hook (New York, 1950).

[2] J. L. Austin, *How to do Things with Words* (Cambridge, Mass., 1962). See also his criticism of this dichotomy in "The Meaning of a Word," in *Philosophical Papers*, eds. J. O. Urmson and G. J. Warnock (Oxford, England, 1961).

[3] R. Carnap, *The Logical Syntax of Language* (London, 1937), pp. 40 ff. In fairness to Carnap, however, it must be pointed out that he does go on to make more positive statements about synthetic sentences.

[4] Quine, "Two Dogmas of Empiricism," pp. 20 ff. See also the discussion by Arthur Pap, *Philosophy of Science* (New York, 1962), pp. 95 ff.

[5] Quine, *Ibid.;* see also Chap. 14.

[6] Quine, *Ibid.*

[7] Carnap, *The Logical Syntax of Language,* p. 41.

[8] P. T. Geach, *Reference and Generality* (Ithaca, N. Y., 1962), Chap. I.

[9] I speak of the series as consisting of "possible descriptive sentences" in the sense that these sentences may not turn out to be descriptive at all.

[10] For a full discussion of the formal logic involved see W. V. O. Quine, *Methods of Logic* (rev. ed.; New York, 1961), pp. 88 ff.

[11] In this connection see Wittgenstein's discussion, *Philosophical Investigations,* pp. 56, 74, 83.

[12] Of course, if the v sign is interpreted exclusively then it tells us that the truth of Fa would also be incompatible with the truth of Ga.

[13] *Foundations of Logic and Mathematics,* International Encyclopedia of Unified Sciences, I (1939), 7.

[14] The example is Carnap's. See *Introduction to Symbolic Logic* (New York, 1958), pp. 41 ff.

[15] Chapter 16.

[16] Carnap, *Meaning and Necessity* (enlarged ed.; Chicago, 1956), p. 41.

[17] For criticism of intensional logic see Quine, *From a Logical Point of View,* Chaps. II, III, and VII; Morton White, "The Analytic and the Synthetic: An Untenable Dualism," in *John Dewey,* ed. Sidney Hook (New York, 1950). In response to criticism from both Church and Carnap, Quine later admitted that quantification could occur over variables taking intensions as values. However, he believed that the values would then refer to "individual concepts" and these were difficult to explicate. But Carnap has no difficulty using individuals as extensions and individual concepts as intensions. Intensions are determined by using the same behavioral techniques employed in psychology to explicate "ideas," "hopes," "dreams," etc. But even Carnap admits that there always seems to be an *intensional vagueness* in such explications. See Alonzo Church, "Review of Quine's 'Notes on Existence and Necessity,'" *Journal of Symbolic Logic,* VIII (1943), 45–47; also Carnap, *Meaning and Necessity,* pp. 193 ff. For some recent analyses and criticisms of intensions see the articles by John Myhill and Donald Davidson in *The Philosophy of Rudolph Carnap,* ed. P. A. Schilpp (Chicago, 1963).

[18] For a full discussion of some of the complications in obtaining descriptive sentences in an intensional logic see the article by Donald Davidson in *The Philosophy of Rudolph Carnap.*

[19] Russell, *An Inquiry into Meaning and Truth* (New York, 1940), p. 117.

[20] Technically "the dog barked" ought to be symbolized with a time variable. But this more formal symbolization is not necessary here.

[21] Church also lists singular descriptions as proper names. But then it seems

to me difficult to determine what can be substituted for the individual variables in a singular description. See Church, *Introduction to Mathematical Logic*, p. 3.

²² Russell's rejection of proper names appears in "On Denoting," *Mind*, XIV (1905), 479–93; in the Introduction to the first volume of *Principia Mathematica*; and in *An Inquiry into Meaning and Truth*, Chap. VI. See also Quine, *From a Logical Point of View* (Cambridge, Mass., 1953), pp. 5 ff.

²³ Church, *Introduction to Mathematical Logic*, p. 5; P. F. Strawson, "Singular Terms, Ontology, and Identity," *Mind*, LXV (1956), pp. 446 ff.; *Individuals* (London, 1959); Carnap, *Meaning and Necessity*, pp. 74 ff.

²⁴ Nor is it a general predicate. Russell, *Inquiry*, p. 137.

²⁵ *Ibid.*

²⁶ *Ibid.*, p. 132.

²⁷ Black, *A Companion to Wittgenstein's Tractatus* (Ithaca, N. Y., 1964), p. 11.

²⁸ Max Black remarks that "The language of which Wittgenstein speaks with the confidence of a priori insight is a never-never language in which essence is adequately manifested."—*ibid.*, pp. 11–12.

²⁹ R. M. Martin, *Truth and Denotation* (Chicago, 1958), p. 3.

³⁰ Quine, *Word and Object*, p. 192 *n*. But elsewhere Quine has distinguished *values* from *substituends*. Names are the substituends for the variable. Values are what are named by names. It would seem, then, that values arise only with the introduction of names. There could not be values which are unnameable. See Quine, "Designation and Existence," in *Readings in Philosophical Analysis*, eds. H. Feigl and W. Sellars (New York, 1949), p. 50.

³¹ I. Copi, *Symbolic Logic* (3d ed. New York, 1968), p. 72.

13. "Exists"

¹ For a discussion of some further uses see F. B. Fitch, "Actuality, Possibility and Being," *Review of Metaphysics*, III (1950), 367–84; also Alan R. Anderson, "What Do Symbols Symbolize?: Platonism," in *Philosophy of Science*, ed. B. Baumrin (New York, 1963), I, 143 ff.

² Quine, *Word and Object*, p. 176.

³ See Church's article "Ontological Commitment," *Journal of Philosophy*, LV (1958), 1008–14.

⁴ W. C. Kneale, "Is Existence a Predicate?" in *Readings in Philosophical Analysis*, eds. H. Feigl and W. Sellars (New York, 1949).

⁵ Quine, *Word and Object*, p. 178.

⁶ For a detailed discussion of how the use of appearance sentences has not helped resolve the traditional issues relating to experience and reality see R. M. Chisholm, *Perceiving* (Ithaca, New York, 1957), pp. 189 ff.

⁷ C. G. Hempel, "Problems and Changes in the Empiricist Criterion of Meaning," *Revue Internationale de Philosophie*, IV (1950), 47.

⁸ Hempel, "Problems and Changes in the Empiricist Criterion of Meaning," p. 51.

[9] R. Carnap, *Meaning and Necessity* (2d ed.; Chicago, 1955), p. 27.

[10] It has been objected, however, that the logical particles cannot be defined by mere reference to truth tables. See N. L. Wilson, *The Concept of Language* (Toronto, Canada, 1959), pp. 14 ff. See also Chapter 10.

[11] For criticisms of the argument that it is redundant to say "There is something which exists" see M. Kiteley, "Is Existence a Predicate?" *Mind*, LXXIII(1964), 369.

[12] *The Critique of Pure Reason*, trans. Norman Kemp Smith (London, 1929), p. 505.

[13] G. E. Moore, "Is Existence a Predicate?" *Aristotelian Society Supplement*, 1936.

[14] Kneale, "Is Existence a Predicate?"

[15] N. Malcolm, "Anselm's Ontological Arguments," *Philosophical Review*, LXIX(1960), 42–44.

[16] Criticisms have also been made by Ayer, Wisdom, and Broad. Their arguments are summarized in G. Nakhnikian and W. C. Salmon, " 'Exists' as a Predicate," *Philosophical Review*, LXVI(1957), 535.

[17] I am here assuming the use of the theory of types. But even where this is rejected or modified, as in *NF* or *ML* of Quine, some restrictions of predicates are required. Quine's systems must still distinguish stratified from unstratified formulas. See Quine, *From a Logical Point of View* (Cambridge, Mass., 1953), pp. 90 ff.

[18] The examples employing "non-empty" and "packaged" are taken from Kiteley, "Is Existence a Predicate?" p. 364.

[19] This example also, with some modifications, has been taken from Kiteley, "Is Existence a Predicate?" p. 369.

[20] See Roland Hall, "Excluders," *Analysis*, XX(1959).

[21] *Ibid.*, p. 1.

[22] The allusions appear in Iris Murdoch's *The Unicorn* (New York, 1963), p. 106; also in T. S. Eliot's "Ash Wednesday."

14. Synonymity

[1] Some portions of this chapter appeared in *Philosophy and Phenomenological Research*, XIV(1953). See also C. I. Lewis, "The Modes of Meaning," *Philosophy and Phenomenological Research*, IV(1943–44), 245; Carnap, *Meaning and Necessity*, pp. 59 ff.; Quine, "Two Dogmas of Empiricism," *The Philosophical Review*, LX(1951), 20–43.

[2] *Readings in Philosophical Analysis*, eds. H. Feigl and W. Sellars (New York, 1949), p. 5.

[3] *Ibid.*, p. 6.

[4] See, for example, S. Alexander, *Space, Time and Deity* (New York, 1920), I, Chap. II.

[5] Benson Mates, "Synonymity," *University of California Publications*,

XXV(1950), 201; also in *Semantics and the Philosophy of Language,* ed. L. Linsky (Urbana, Ill., 1952), Chap. VII. However, Mates later rejected this definition and concluded that "one is justified in saying that there are 'intuitive' notions of analyticity and synonymy."—"Analytic Sentences," *Philosophical Review,* LX(1951), 532. Mates also criticizes both Quine and Morton White for finally relying upon pragmatist means for defining synonymy. But after rejecting the pragmatic criterion he asks, oddly enough, for a pragmatic justification for pragmatism. "Where is a proof—even a pragmatic one—to show that there is anything useful or fruitful about pragmatism?"—*ibid.,* p. 534. Compare also Nelson Goodman's rejection of the substitution criterion on the grounds that in at least one sentence—"*p* and *q* are the same"—the synonymity of *p* and *q* must be determined by other means.—*The Structure of Appearance* (2d ed.; New York, 1966), p. 8.

⁶ C. I. Lewis, *An Analysis of Knowledge and Valuation* (Chicago, 1946), p. 176.

⁷ Moreland Perkins and Irving Singer, "Analyticity," *Journal of Philosophy,* XLVIII(1951), 485–97.

⁸ Lewis, *An Analysis of Knowledge and Valuation,* p. 86.

⁹ Quine, "Two Dogmas of Empiricism," pp. 20 ff.

¹⁰ R. Carnap, *Meaning and Necessity* (enlarged ed.; Chicago, 1956), pp. 56 ff.

¹¹ See Quine, *From a Logical Point of View* (Cambridge, Mass., 1953), Chaps. II, III, and VII; also Morton White, "The Analytic and the Synthetic: An Untenable Dualism," in *John Dewey,* ed. S. Hook (New York, 1950). Reprinted in Linsky, *Semantics and the Philosophy of Language.*

15. "Make"

¹ See Richard Taylor, "I can," *The Philosophical Review,* LXIX(1960) 78–89. Also R. Chisholm, "Freedom and Action," in *Freedom and Determinism,* ed. K. Lehrer (New York, 1966), p. 21.

² See Leonard K. Nash, *The Nature of the Natural Sciences* (Boston, 1963), pp. 68, 107.

³ Technically, "his home" is not a simple denotative term, but rather one which requires transformation into "the home of him (John)." But in either case the expression is taken to have reference. See Quine, *Word and Object,* p. 107.

⁴ P. T. Geach, *Reference and Generality* (Ithaca, N. Y., 1962), Chap. III. See also Strawson's discussion of expressions that refer but do not assert.—"On Referring," *Mind,* LIX(1950); reprinted in *Classics of Analytic Philosophy,* ed. R. R. Ammermann (New York, 1965).

⁵ Or, if I am referring to a specific store my transcription would become $(\exists x)(Sx \cdot (y)(Sy \supset y = x) \cdot Rjx)$. In any case the existential quantification of "store" would still remain.

[6] Copi, *Symbolic Logic* (New York, 1954), p. 129.

[7] Chisholm, *Perceiving*, p. 170.

[8] Carnap, *Meaning and Necessity* (Chicago, 1956), p. 230; also C. G. Hempel, "Fundamentals of Concept Formation in Empirical Science," *Encyclopedia of Unified Science*, II(1952). See also "The General Discussion of Theoretical Terms" in Carnap's *Philosophical Foundations of Physics* (New York, 1966), Part V, and Hempel's *Philosophy of Natural Science* (Englewood Cliffs, N. J.), 1966.

[9] Quine, *Methods of Logic*, p. 44.

[10] *The Problems of Philosophy*, Chap. V.

[11] Ernest Nagel, *The Structure of Science* (New York, 1961), pp. 398 ff.

[12] Nagel, *The Structure of Science*, p. 421. Colin Murray Turbayne has also shown that the implicit commitment to metaphorical terms has been responsible for our constantly attributing various occult entities and forces to nature.—*The Myth of Metaphor* (New Haven, Conn., 1962), Chap. III.

[13] In fact, it may well be that it makes no sense to speak of a "pure" observation. The point is discussed in Chapter 7.

[14] Except for minor revisions the material of this section—section II—is a copy of the article written by myself and Professor Raymond J. Nelson of Case Institute of Technology and which appeared under the title "Scientific Statements and Statements about Humanly Created Objects," in *Journal of Philosophy* (July 1958), 641–48. I am grateful to Professor Nelson and *The Journal of Philosophy* for permitting me to use the article here.

[15] See, for example, C. H. Langford, "A Proof that Synthetic *A Priori* Propositions Exist," *Journal of Philosophy*, XLVI(1949), 20–24; I. M. Copi, "Modern Logic and the Synthetic *A Priori*," *Journal of Philosophy*, XLVI(1949), 243–45.

[16] Quine, "Two Dogmas of Empiricism," *The Philosophical Review*, LX (1951), reprinted in *From a Logical Point of View* (Cambridge, Mass., 1953); Morton White, "The Analytic and the Synthetic: An Untenable Dualism," in *John Dewey: Philosopher of Science and Freedom*, ed. Sidney Hook (New York, 1950).

[17] Quine suggests that perhaps there are no inherently analytic or synthetic statements. They may be one or the other in accordance with the context. But it is difficult to see how some context could be formulated in which a pure mathematical statement could be synthetic.

[18] Lewis, *An Analysis of Knowledge and Valuation*, p. 4.

[19] In fact, one of the important implications of Hume's analysis of causality is that there is no logical or empirical contradiction in a science that seeks to change laws of nature. No given constant conjunction is inherently unchangeable.

[20] See, for example, Santayana's statement: ". . . Creation or invention is automatic. The ideas come of themselves, being new and unthought-of figments, similar, no doubt, to old perceptions and compacted of familiar materials, but reproduced in a novel fashion and dropping in their sudden form from the blue."
—*Reason in Art* (New York, 1942), p. 7.

²¹ It should be noted, however, that Waismann tried to argue for the possibility of a new kind of logic that might exist in mechanics and other scientific areas. See his "Verifiability" in *Meaning and Knowledge,* eds. E. Nagel and R. B. Brandt (New York, 1965), p. 45.

²² Although, of course, it would not necessarily be analytic in every inquiry.

²³ Copi, *Symbolic Logic,* p. 129; R. M. Chisholm, "Intentionality and the Theory of Signs," *Philosophical Studies,* III(1952). Reprinted in *Meaning and Knowledge.*

²⁴ I. Scheffler, *The Anatomy of Inquiry* (New York, 1963), pp. 88 ff.

²⁵ A. Church, "On Carnap's Analysis of Statements of Assertion and Belief," *Analysis,* X(1950), 97–99. See also Carnap's reply to Church in *Meaning and Necessity* (enlarged ed.; Chicago, 1955), pp. 230 ff.

16. "Can"

¹ It was this notion of "can" that Wittgenstein found so fascinating in the *Philosophical Investigations.* And even though he rejects the possibility that there is some odd experience relating to "can," he goes on to warn against thinking that a "can" sentence can be reduced to some set of physicalistic or phenomenalistic sentences. Similar objections relate to sentences whose main verbs are "could." See *Philosophical Investigations,* pp. 72, 74.

² For some analyses of these constructions see Quine, *From a Logical Point of View,* Chap. VIII; A. Church, *Introduction to Mathematical Logic,* (rev. ed.; Princeton, N. J., 1956), p. 8.

³ For some relevant discussions of "can" see J. L. Austin, *Philosophical Papers* (Oxford, England, 1961), Chap. VII; P. H. Nowell-Smith, "Ifs and Cans," *Theoria,* XXVI(1960); Richard Taylor, "I can," *The Philosophical Review,* LXIX(1960), 78–89.

⁴ J. L. Austin, *Sense and Sensibilia* (Oxford, England, 1962), pp. 20 ff.

⁵ Paul Ziff, *Semantic Analysis* (Ithaca, N. Y., 1960), Chap. II.

⁶ C. G. Hempel, "Explanation and Prediction," in *Philosophy of Science,* ed. B. Baumrin (New York, 1963), p. 127. Roderick Chisholm makes the same criticism against those who believe that showing the different uses of "know" will in some way eliminate the problems of "know" when this word appears in a philosophical context. See R. Chisholm, *The Theory of Knowledge* (Englewood Cliffs, N. J., 1966), pp. 15 ff.

⁷ More correctly I ought to say that, according to the critics of Kant, noumena had no explanatory purpose. But, of course, they presumably did have such a purpose for Kant.

⁸ Austin, *ibid.;* Nowell-Smith, *ibid.*

⁹ Austin, *Sense and Sensibilia,* pp. 158 ff.

¹⁰ See Goodman's detailed analysis in *Fact, Fiction and Forecast* (Cambridge, Mass., 1955).

¹¹ R. M. Chisholm, "J. L. Austin's Philosophical Papers," *Mind,*

LXXIII(1964), 20–25; for further criticism of Chisholm's position see Arthur Danto, "Freedom and Forbearance," in *Freedom and Determinism*, ed. K. Lehrer (New York, 1966), pp. 55 ff.

[12] Austin, *Sense and Sensibilia*, p. 159.

[13] Wittgenstein, *Philosophical Investigations*, p. 11.

[14] The classic formulation of this view appears in A. Tarski, "The Semantic Conception of Truth and the Foundations of Semantics," *Philosophy and Phenomenological Research*, IV(1944), 341–76; reprinted in H. Feigl and W. Sellars, *Readings in Philosophical Analysis* (New York, 1949). A similar approach is found in Carnap, *Meaning and Necessity* (Chicago, 1956).

[15] Austin, *Sense and Sensibilia*, p. 73.

[16] Quine, especially, has fostered the view that "possible" leads to some strange ontology. He has maintained that if we admit the notion of a possible object then we cannot distinguish between possible object, *A*, and possible object, *B*.—*From a Logical Point of View*, Chap. I. Anderson has sought to counter this by claiming that all adjectival uses of "possible" can be converted into operators.—A. R. Anderson, "What do Symbols Symbolize?: Platonism" in *Philosophy of Science*, ed. B. Baumrin, p. 158. But Quine has countered this by showing that this use of "possible" is applicable only with intensions and the problems of intensions are well known.

[17] Ziff, *Semantic Analysis*, Chap. VI.

[18] Quine, *Word and Object*, p. 57.

[19] We assume here logical identity and synonymity can be given appropriate definitions.

17. Conclusion

[1] The same point is made by Jørgen Jørgensen, "Languages, Calculuses, and Logic," in *Logic and Language*, eds. B. H. Kazemier and D. Vuysje (Dorrecht, Holland, 1962), p. 28.

[2] For a detailed discussion of normal and nonnormal interpretations of calculi see E. W. Beth, "Carnap on Constructed Systems," in *The Philosophy of Rudolph Carnap*, ed. P. A. Schilpp (Chicago, 1963), pp. 488 ff.

[3] Compare the remark of Nelson Goodman: "The terms employed [in an interpreted system] are ordinarily selected according to their usage, and the correctness of the interpreted definition is legitimately testable by examination of that usage."—*The Structure of Appearance* (2d ed.; New York, 1966), p. 4.

[4] Quine's "partial" nominalism appears in his statements: "I have indeed inveighed against making and imputing platonistic assumptions gratuitously, but equally against obscuring them. Where I have speculated on what can be got from a nominalistic basis, I have stressed the difficulties and limitations."— *Word and Object* (Cambridge, Mass., and New York, 1960), p. 243 *n.*

[5] H. B. Curry, "A Simplification of the Theory of Combinators," *Synthese*, VII(1948–49), 391–99; M. Schönfinkel, "Ueber die Bausteine der Mathema-

tischen Logik," *Mathematische Annalen*, XCII(1924), 305–16; see also H. B. Curry, R. Feys, and W. Craig, *Combinatory Logic* (Amsterdam, 1958), I.

[6] *From a Logical Point of View*, p. 104.

[7] See Quine, *Selected Logic Papers* (New York, 1966), Chap. XXII, "Variables Explained Away."

[8] *Ibid.*, p. 230.

[9] As Carnap attempts to do in *Meaning and Necessity*, pp. 42 ff.

[10] Church, *Introduction to Mathematical Logic*, p. 9.

[11] *From a Logical Point of View*, p. 108.

[12] *Ibid.*, p. 110. Compare the statement by Bertrand Russell: "The variable 'x' here is to be allowed to take all values for which the sentence 'x is a man' is significant, i.e., in this case, all values that are proper names."—*An Inquiry Into Meaning and Truth* (New York, 1940), p. 246.

[13] Strawson, *Individuals*, p. 201.

[14] *Selected Logic Papers*, p. 230.

[15] *From a Logical Point of View*, p. 109.

[16] *Ibid.*, p. 123.

[17] *Ibid.*

[18] See *Methods of Logic* (rev. ed.; New York, 1959), p. 65; also see *The Ways of Paradox* (New York, 1966), p. 127.

[19] *From a Logical Point of View*, p. 118.

[20] *The Ways of Paradox*, p. 60.

Selected Bibliography

Alexander, S. *Space, Time, and Deity.* New York: Macmillan, 1920.

Alston, W. P. *Philosophy of Language.* Englewood Cliffs, New Jersey: Prentice-Hall, 1964.

Ammerman, R. R. (ed.). *Classics of Analytic Philosophy.* Madison: University of Wisconsin Press, 1965.

Angell, Richard B. *Reasoning and Logic.* New York: Appleton-Century-Crofts, 1964.

Anscombe, G. E. M. *An Introduction to Wittgenstein's Tractatus.* 2d rev. ed., London: Hutchinson, 1963.

Aristotle, *Basic Works,* Ed. R. Mckeon. New York: Random House, 1941.

Austin, J. L. *How to Do Things With Words.* Cambridge: Harvard University Press, 1962.

———. *Philosophical Papers.* Oxford: Oxford University Press, 1961.

———. *Sense and Sensibilia.* Oxford: Oxford University Press, 1962.

Ayer, A. J. *The Concept of a Person.* New York: St. Martin's Press, 1963.

———. *Language, Truth and Logic.* London: Gollancz, 1936, 1946.

Bar-Hillel, Y. "Indexical Expressions," *Mind,* LXIII(1954), 359–79.

Barker, S. F. *Philosophy of Mathematics.* Englewood Cliffs, New Jersey: Prentice-Hall, 1964.

Basson, A. H. *David Hume.* London: Penguin Books, 1958.

Baugh, A. C. *A History of the English Language.* New York: Appleton-Century-Crofts, 1935.

Baumrin, B. (ed.). *Philosophy of Science.* 2 vols. New York: Wiley, 1963.

306

Beck, L. W. *Studies in the Philosophy of Kant.* New York: Bobbs-Merrill, 1965.
Bergmann, G. "Strawson's Ontology," *Journal of Philosophy,* LVII(1960), 601–22.
Bergson, H. *Creative Evolution.* Trans. A. Mitchell, New York: Henry Holt, 1913.
Berkeley, G. *Selections,* ed. M. W. Calkins. New York: Scribner's, 1929.
Black, M. *A Companion to Wittgenstein's 'Tractatus.'* Ithaca: Cornell University Press, 1964.
———. "Language and Reality," *Proceedings and Addresses of the American Philosophical Association* (1958–59), 5–17.
———. *The Nature of Mathematics.* London: Routledge and Kegan Paul, 1933.
———, (ed.). *Philosophy in America.* Ithaca: Cornell University Press, 1965.
Blackwood, R. T. "Comments on the Jaina Logic of Syadvada," *Memorias del XIII Congreso Internacional de Filosofía,* Mexico City, 1964, Vol. V, 33–43.
Bohm, D. *Causality and Change in Modern Physics.* Princeton: D. Van Nostrand, 1957.
Bradley, F. H. *Appearance and Reality.* New York: Macmillan, 1902.
Braithwaite, R. B. *Scientific Explanation.* Cambridge, England: Cambridge University Press, 1953.
Brentano, F. *Wahrheit und Evidenz.* Leipzig: F. Meiner, 1930.
Broad, C. D. *Examination of McTaggart's Philosophy.* 3 vols. Cambridge, England: Cambridge University Press, 1938.
Bronko, N. H. and Bowles, Jr., J. W. *Empirical Foundations of Psychology.* New York: Rinehart, 1951.
Cantril, H., Ames, A. J., Hastorf, A. H., and Ittelson, W. H. Papers on Psychology and Scientific Research. *Science,* CX(1949).
Capek, M. *The Philosophical Impact of Contemporary Physics.* Princeton: D. Van Nostrand, 1961.
Carnap, R. *Foundations of Logic and Mathematics.* Chicago: University of Chicago Press (International Encyclopedia of Unified Science), 1939.
———. *Introduction to Semantics.* Cambridge: Harvard University Press, 1948.
———. *Introduction to Symbolic Logic.* Trans. W. H. Meyer and J. Wilkinson. New York: Dover Publications, 1958.
———. *Logical Foundations of Probability.* 2d ed. Chicago: University of Chicago Press, 1962.
———. *The Logical Structure of the World.* Trans. R. A. George. Berkeley: University of California Press, 1967.
———. *Logical Syntax of Language.* London: Routledge & Kegan Paul, 1937.
———. *Meaning and Necessity.* enlarged ed. Chicago: University of Chicago Press, 1956.
———. *Philosophical Foundations of Physics.* New York: Basic Books, 1966.
Caws, Peter. *The Philosophy of Science.* Princeton: D. Van Nostrand, 1965.
Chisholm, R. M. "J. L. Austin's Philosophical Papers," *Mind,* LXXIII(1964), 20–25.
———. *Perceiving.* Ithaca: Cornell University Press, 1957.

————. *The Theory of Knowledge.* Englewood Cliffs, New Jersey: Prentice-Hall, 1966.

Church, A. "A Note on the Entscheidungsproblem," *Journal of Symbolic Logic,* I(1936), 40–41, 101–2.

————. "Alternatives to Zermelo's Axiom," *Transactions of the American Mathematical Society,* XXIX(1927), 178–208.

————. "A Review of Quine's 'Notes on existence and necessity,'" *Journal of Symbolic Logic,* VIII(1943), 45–47.

————. *Introduction to Mathematical Logic.* Princeton: Princeton University Press, 1956.

————. "On Carnap's Analysis of Statements of Assertion and Belief," *Analysis,* X(1950), 97–99.

————. "Ontological Commitment," *Journal of Philosophy,* LV(1958), 1008–14.

————. "Review of Carnap's *Formalization of Logic,*" *Philosophical Review,* LII(1944), 494.

Copi, I. "Modern Logic and the Synthetic *a Priori,*" *Journal of Philosophy,* XLVI(1949), 243–45.

————. *Symbolic Logic.* New York: Macmillan, 1954, 1965, 1968.

Copleston, F. C. *Aquinas.* London: Penguin Books, 1955.

Croce, B. *Aesthetic.* Trans. D. Ainslie. rev. ed. London: Vision Press and Peter Owen, 1953.

Curry, H. B. and Feys, R. and Craig, W. *Combinatory Logic.* Amsterdam: North Holland Publishing Co., 1958.

————. "A Simplification of the Theory of Combinators," *Synthese,* VII(1948–49), 391–99.

Dewey, J. *Experience and Nature.* New York: Macmillan, 1936.

————, and Bentley, A. F. *Knowing and the Known.* Boston: Beacon Press, 1949.

————. *Logic, The Theory of Inquiry.* New York: Henry Holt, 1938.

Ducasse, C. J. "Propositions, Opinions, Sentences, and Facts," *Journal of Philosophy,* XXXVII(1940), 701–11.

Dufrenne, M. *Language and Philosophy.* Trans. H. B. Veatch. Bloomington: University of Indiana Press, 1963.

Entwistle, W. J. *Aspects of Language.* New York: Macmillan, 1953.

Feigl, H. and Sellars, W. (eds.). *Readings in Philosophical Analysis.* New York: Appleton-Century-Crofts, 1949.

Findlay, J. N. *Language, Mind, and Value.* London: Allen and Unwin, 1963.

Fitch, F. B. "Actuality, Possibility and Being," *Review of Metaphysics,* III(1950), 367–84.

Flew, A. (ed.). *Essays in Conceptual Analysis.* New York: Macmillan, 1956.

————, (ed.). *Logic and Language.* New York: Anchor Edition, 1965.

Fodor, J. A. and Katz, J. J. *The Structure of Language.* Englewood Cliffs, New Jersey: Prentice-Hall, 1964.

Fraenkel, A. *Einleitung in die Mengenlehre.* 3d ed. Berlin: Springer, 1928.

Frege, G. *The Foundations of Arithmetic.* Trans. J. L. Austin. Oxford: Blackwell, 1950.

————. "The Thought: A Logical Inquiry," *Mind,* LXV(1956), 289–311.

Frege, G. *Philosophical Writings*, eds. Peter Geach and Max Black. Oxford: Blackwell, 1952.

Geach, P. T. *Reference and Generality*. Ithaca: Cornell University Press, 1962.

Goodman, N. *Fact, Fiction, and Forecast*. Cambridge: Harvard University Press, 1955.

–––, and W. V. O. Quine. "Steps towards a Constructive Nominalism," *Journal of Symbolic Logic*, XII(1947), 105–22.

–––. *The Structure of Appearance*. 2d ed. New York: Bobbs-Merrill, 1966.

Gorman, M. *General Semantics*. Lincoln: University of Nebraska Press, 1962.

Gorrell, R. M. and Laird, C. *Modern English Handbook*. 2d ed. Englewood Cliffs, New Jersey: Prentice-Hall, 1956.

Hall, Roland, "Excluders," *Analysis*, XX(1959), 1–7.

Harris, E. *Nature, Mind, and Modern Science*. New York: Macmillan, 1954.

Heffner, R. M. S. *General Phonetics*. Madison: University of Wisconsin Press, 1950.

Hegel, G. W. F. *Science of Logic*. Trans. W. H. Johnston and L. G. Struthers. London: Allen and Unwin, 1929.

Hempel, C. G. *Aspects of Scientific Explanation*. New York: Glencoe Free Press, 1965.

–––. "Problems and Changes in the Empiricist Criterion of Meaning," *Revue Internationale de Philosophie*, XI(1950), 41–63.

–––. *Philosophy of Natural Science*. Englewood Cliffs, New Jersey: Prentice-Hall, 1966.

–––. *Fundamentals of Concept Formation*. Chicago: University of Chicago Press (International Encyclopedia of Unified Science), 1952.

Heyting, A. *Intuitionism—An Introduction*. Amsterdam: North Holland Publishing Co., 1956.

Hilbert, D. and Ackerman, W. *Mathematical Logic*. New York: Chelsea Publishing Co., 1950.

–––, and Bernays, P. *Grundlagen der Mathematik*. Berlin: Springer, 1934.

Hook, Sidney (ed.). *John Dewey*. New York: Dial Press, 1950.

Hume, David. *Treatise of Human Nature*. London: J. M. Dent, 1911.

Jørgensen, J. *A Treatise of Formal Logic*. Copenhagen: Levin and Munksgaard, 1931.

Kaminsky, J. *Hegel on Art*. New York: State University of New York Press, 1962.

–––. "Metaphysics and the Problem of Synonymity," *Philosophy and Phenomenological Research*, XIV(1953), 49–61.

–––. "Ontology and Language," *Philosophy and Phenomenological Research*, XXII(1962), 176–91.

–––, and Raymond J. Nelson, "Scientific Statements and Statements about Humanly Created Objects," *Journal of Philosophy*, LV(1958), 641–48.

Kant, I. *Critique of Pure Reason*. Trans. N. Kemp-Smith. New York: Macmillan, 1934.

–––. *Critique of Pure Reason*. Trans. F. Max Muller. 2d ed. rev. New York: Macmillan, 1896.

Kaplan, A. "Definition and Specification of Meaning," *Journal of Philosophy* XLIII(1946), 281–88.

Kazemier, B. H. and Vuysje, D. *Logic and Language*. Dorrecht, Holland: D. Reidel, 1962.

Kiteley, M. "Is Existence a Predicate?" *Mind*, LXXIII(1964), 364–73.

Kleene, S. C. *Introduction to Metamathematics*. Princeton: D. Van Nostrand, 1952.

Körner, S. *Kant*. London: Penguin Books, 1955.

———. *The Philosophy of Mathematics*. New York: Harper and Bros., 1960.

Korzybski, A. *Science and Sanity*. Lakeville, Conn.: International Non-Aristotelian Library Publishing Co., 1948.

Krikorian, Y. H. (ed.). *Naturalism and the Human Spirit*. New York: Columbia University Press, 1944.

Langford, C. H. "A Proof that Synthetic *a Priori* Propositions Exist," *Journal of Philosophy*, XLVI(1949), 20–24.

Leblanc, H. *Deductive Logic*. New York: Wiley, 1955.

Lehrer, K. (ed.). *Freedom and Determinism*. New York: Random House, 1966.

Leibniz, G. W. *The Monadology*. Trans. R. Latta. 1st ed. Oxford: Oxford University Press, 1898.

Leonard, H. S. "The Logic of Existence," *Philosophical Studies*, VII(1956), 49–64.

Lewis, C. I. *An Analysis of Knowledge and Valuation*. Chicago: Open Court, 1946.

———, and Langford, C. H. *Symbolic Logic*. 2d ed. New York: Dover Publications, 1959.

———. "The Modes of Meaning." *Philosophy and Phenomenological Research*, IV(1943–44), 236–50.

Linsky, L. (ed.). *Semantics and the Philosophy of Language*. Urbana: University of Illinois, 1952.

Loewenberg, J. *Hegel's Phenomenology*. Chicago: Open Court, 1965.

Malcolm, N. *Knowledge and Certainty*. Englewood Cliffs, New Jersey: Prentice-Hall, 1963.

Margenau, H. *The Nature of Physical Reality*. New York: McGraw-Hill, 1950.

Martin, R. M. *Truth and Denotation*. Chicago: University of Chicago Press, 1959.

Mates, B. "Analytic Sentences," *Philosophical Review*, LX(1951), 523–34.

Mead, G. H. *Mind, Self, and Society*. Chicago: University of Chicago Press, 1934.

Meyerson, E. *Identity and Reality*. Trans. K. Loewenberg. London: Allen and Unwin, 1930.

Mill, J. S. *A System of Logic*. 10th ed. London: Longmans, Green, 1879.

Moore, G. E. "Is Existence a Predicate?" *Proceedings of the Aristotelian Society*, Suppl. Vol. XV(1936).

Nagel, E. and Brandt, R. B. (eds.). *Meaning and Knowledge*. New York: Harcourt, Brace, 1965.

———. *The Structure of Science*. New York: Harcourt, Brace, 1961.

Nash, L. K. *The Nature of the Natural Sciences*. Boston: Little, Brown and Company, 1963.

Nicod, J. G. P. "A Reduction in the Number of the Primitive Propositions of Logic," *Proceedings of the Cambridge Philosophical Society*, XIX(1916), 32–41.

Noss, J. B. *Man's Religions*. New York: Macmillan, 1949.

Nowell-Smith, P. H. "Ifs and Cans," *Theoria*, XXVI(1960), 85–101.

Pap, A. *The Philosophy of Science*. New York: Glencoe Free Press, 1962.

Paton, H. J. *Kant's Metaphysic of Experience*. New York: Macmillan, 1936.

Pears, D. "Critical Study," *Philosophical Quarterly*, XI(1961), 172.

Peirce, C. S. *Collected Papers*, eds. C. Hartshorne and P. Weiss. Cambridge: Harvard University Press, 1933.

———. "On the Algebra of Logic: A Contribution to the Philosophy of Notation," *American Journal of Mathematics*, VII(1885), 180–202.

Pepper, S. C. *World Hypotheses*. Berkeley: University of California, 1948.

Perkins, M. and Singer, I. "Analyticity," *Journal of Philosophy*, XLVIII (1951), 485–97.

Perrin, P. G. *Writer's Guide and Index to English*. 3d ed. Chicago: Foresman, 1959.

Pitcher, G. *The Philosophy of Wittgenstein*. Englewood Cliffs, New Jersey: Prentice-Hall, 1964.

Poincaré, H. *The Foundations of Science*. Trans. G. B. Halsted. London: Constable, 1921.

Polanyi, M. *Personal Knowledge*. Chicago: University of Chicago Press, 1958.

Popper, K. *The Logic of Scientific Discovery*. 3d rev. ed. New York: Harper and Row, 1965.

Price, H. H. *Thinking and Experience*. Cambridge: Harvard University Press, 1953.

Prior, A. N. *Formal Logic*. Oxford: Clarendon Press, 1955.

Quine, W. V. O. *From a Logical Point of View*. Cambridge: Harvard University Press, 1953.

———. *Mathematical Logic*. rev. ed. Cambridge: Harvard University Press, 1961.

———. *Methods of Logic*. rev. ed. New York: Henry Holt, 1959.

———. *Selected Logic Papers*. New York: Random House, 1966.

———. "On Cantor's Theorem," *Journal of Symbolic Logic*, II(1937), 120–24.

———. *Set Theory and Its Logic*. Cambridge: Harvard University Press, 1963.

———. *The Ways of Paradox*. New York: Random House, 1966.

———. *Word and Object*. New York: Wiley, 1960.

Ramsey, F. P. *The Foundations of Mathematics*. London: Kegan Paul, 1931.

Ramsey, I. *Prospect for Metaphysics*. New York: Philosophical Library, 1961.

Rescher, N. "Definitions of 'Existence,'" *Philosophical Studies*, VIII (1957), 66.

Ross, W. D. *Aristotle*. London: Methuen, 1923.

Russell, B. *An Inquiry into Meaning and Truth*. New York: W. W. Norton, 1940.

— — —. *Introduction to Mathematical Philosophy*. London: Allen and Unwin, 1919.

— — —. "The Philosophical Importance of Mathematical Logic," *The Monist*, XXIII(1913), 481–93.

— — —. *The Principles of Mathematics*. 2d ed. New York: W. W. Norton, 1938.

— — —. *The Problems of Philosophy*. London: Oxford University Press, 1912.

Ryle, G. *The Concept of Mind*. London: Hutchinson, 1949.

Salmon, W. C. " 'Exists' as a Predicate," *Philosophical Review*, LXVI(1957), 535–42.

Santayana, G. commemorative articles in *Journal of Philosophy*, LI(1954), 29–64.

— — —. *Reason in Art*. New York: Scribner's, 1942.

Sapir, E. *Language*. New York: Harcourt, Brace, 1921.

Scheffler, I. *The Anatomy of Inquiry*. New York: Alfred A. Knopf, 1963.

Schilpp, P. A. (ed.). *The Philosophy of Bertrand Russell*. Chicago: Open Court, 1946.

— — —, (ed.) *The Philosophy of Rudolph Carnap*. Chicago: Open Court, 1963.

Schlauch, M. *The Gift of Tongues*. New York: Viking, 1945.

Schönfinkel, M. "Ueber die Bausteine der Mathematischen Logik," *Mathematische Annalen*, XCII(1924), 305–16.

Sebeok, T. A. (ed.). *Style in Language*. New York: Wiley, 1960.

Sheffer, H. M. "A Set of Five Independent Postulates for Boolean Algebras," *American Mathematical Society*, XIV(1913), 481–88.

Sheldon, W. H. "The Concept of the Negative," *Philosophical Review*, XI(1902), 485–96.

Skinner, B. F. *Science and Human Behavior*. New York: Macmillan, 1953.

Strawson, P. F. *Individuals*. London: Methuen, 1959.

— — —. "Singular Terms, Ontology, and Identity," *Mind*, LXV(1956), 433–54.

Tarski, A. *Logic, Semantics, and Metamathematics*. Trans. J. H. Woodger. Oxford: Oxford University Press, 1956.

Taylor, R. "I can," *Philosophical Review*, LXIX(1969), 78–89.

— — —. "Negative Things," *Journal of Philosophy*, XLIX(1952), 433–49.

Toulmin, S. *The Philosophy of Science*. London: Hutchinson, 1953.

Travis, D. C. (ed.). *A Hegel Symposium*. Austin: University of Texas, 1962.

Tulane Studies in Philosophy, XIV(1965).

Turbayne, C. M. *Myth of Metaphor*. New Haven: Yale University Press, 1962.

Urmson, J. O. *Philosophical Analysis*. Oxford: Clarendon, 1956.

Vaihinger, H. *The Philosophy of 'As If'*. Trans. C. K. Ogden. New York: Harcourt, Brace, 1924.

Vandiver, H. S. "Fermat's Last Theorem," *American Mathematical Monthly*, LII(1946), 555–78.

Veatch, H. *Intentional Logic*. New Haven: Yale University Press, 1952.

Walker, J. D. B. *A Study of Frege*. Ithaca: Cornell University Press, 1965.

Whitehead, A. N. and Russell, B. *Principia Mathematica*. rev. ed. Cambridge, England: Cambridge University Press, 1925–27.

Whorf, B. L. *Language, Thought, and Reality*. New York: Wiley, 1956.

Wilson, N. L. *The Concept of Language*. Toronto: University of Toronto, 1959.

Wittgenstein, L. *Notebooks 1914–16*. Oxford: Blackwell, 1961.

――. *Philosophical Investigations*. Trans. G. E. M. Anscombe. New York: Macmillan Co., 1953.

――. *Tractatus Logico-Philosophicus*. Trans. D. F. Pears and B. F. McGuinness. London: Routledge and Kegan, 1961.

Woodger, J. H. *The Axiomatic Method in Biology*. Cambridge, England: Cambridge University Press, 1937.

Wright, G. H. von. *Form and Content in Logic*. Cambridge, England: Cambridge University Press, 1949.

Young, J. Z. *Doubt and Certainty in Science*. Oxford: Oxford University Press, 1951.

Ziff, P. *Semantic Analysis*. Ithaca: Cornell University Press, 1960.

Zollette, S. *Basic Principles of General Semantics*. Philadelphia: Drexel Institute of Technology, 1955.

Index

Abstract entities, 13, 14, 49, 51, 55, 59, 60, 73, 86, 157, 211, 212, 269
"Adjuster-words," 252
Alston, W. P., 110, 111 ff., 124, 126, 286
Ames experiments, 100, 287
Analytic sentences, 172, 173, 174, 231 ff.
Ancestor relation, 59
Anderson, A., 297, 302
Anscombe, G. E. M., 274
Aquinas, Thomas, 23
Arch-Metaphysical Assertion, 22, 23, 25, 26, 29
Aristotle, 16, 23, 114, 123, 131, 143, 163, 227
Atomic objects, 38, 121
Atomic sentences, 121, 141, 168, 180, 185, 194, 223
Attributes, 14, 285
Austin, J. L.: 109, 284, 295; on uses of a language, 91; on non-truth-functional sentences, 97; on performatives, 109, 110, 173; word has many uses, 242, 255; iffiness in "can" sentences, 244, 249, 301; on adjuster-words, 252. *See also* Performatives
Axiom of Choice, 129, 290
Ayer, A. J., 42, 242, 279, 290

Bar-Hillel, Y., 168
Barker, S. F., 130, 133
Basson, A. H., 278
Baugh, A. C., 287
Beck, L. W., 279
Beowulf, 156
Bergmann, G., 279
Bergson, H., 11
Beth, E. W., 273, 302
Black, M.: 286, 290, 292, 297; language can be negation free, 11, 12; Wittgenstein's view of "showing" is confusing, 132; Wittgenstein's notion of logical truth unsatisfactory, 143, 147; subject-predicate distinction unnecessary, 153 ff., 157, 167; Wittgenstein's elementary propositions never discoverable, 185, 297; institutionists do not really deny law of excluded middle, 289; Wittgenstein's inference from logic to ontology untenable, 291
Blackwood, R. T., 288
Bohm, D., 283
Bradley, F. H., 37, 38
Braithwaite, R. B., 18, 293
Brentano, F., 11
"Bridge" rules, 21
Broad, C. D., 279
Brouwer, L. E. J., 127, 128

Calculus, i ff., 5, 7, 14, 258 ff.
"Can," x, Chap. 16
Cantor, G., 63, 186, 282
Carnap, R.: 47, 114, 135, 258, 280, 284, 286, 287, 295, 300, 301, 303; committed to an ontology, xi, xii, 91; language strictly conventional, 6; on physicalism, 18; on reduction sentences, 19, 20, 177, 217; on Popper's metaphysics, 23, 24, 276; basic sentences not open to disconfirmation or confirmation, 27; on existential sentences, 28, 29, 30; material object sentences not ontological, 45; distinction between subjects and predicates, 48; extension and intention, 52, 60, 213, 218, 250, 262, 285; "elementary experiences," 55; observation terms to be replaced by mathematical ones, 92, 154, 183; no ordinary language logic, 97; on logical truth, 132, 134, 178, 290; thing and property, 166; on analytic-synthetic distinction, 173, 174, 209, 296; propositions designate, 200, 269; material mode of language,